ALTERNATIVE FILM CULTURE IN INTER-WAR BRITAIN

In the first book-length study to concentrate specifically on Britain, Jamie Sexton examines the rise of avant-garde and experimental filmmaking between the wars. The book provides a detailed view of how modernist and anti-mainstream currents emerged in the film industry.

It traces the growth of new approaches to film through exhibition and writing on cinema, and looks at how this cultural formation shaped filmmaking. As such, it takes an interdisciplinary approach in which a study of independent filmmaking in this era is firmly placed within a cultural context, linking the ways in which films were presented, received and produced.

Sexton combines history with analysis of the films themselves, and looks at the operations of a key contemporary institution, the original Film Society.

Jamie Sexton is Lecturer in Film Studies in the University of Wales, Aberystwyth. His other books include *Cult Cinema: An Introduction* (with Ernest Mathijs, forthcoming 2009); *Experimental British Television* (edited with Laura Mulvey, 2007); *Music, Sound and Multimedia* (edited, 2007).

Exeter Studies in Film History

Published by University of Exeter Press in association with the Bill Douglas Centre for the History of Cinema and Popular Culture

Series Editors: **Richard Maltby,** Professor of Screen Studies, Flinders University, South Australia and **Steve Neale,** Professor of Film Studies and Academic Director of the Bill Douglas Centre for the History of Cinema and Popular Culture, University of Exeter.

Parallel Tracks: The Railroad and Silent Cinema
Lynne Kirby (1997)

The World According to Hollywood, 1918–1939
Ruth Vasey (1997)

'Film Europe' and 'Film America': Cinema, Commerce and Cultural Exchange 1920–1939
edited by Andrew Higson and Richard Maltby (1999)

A Paul Rotha Reader
edited by Duncan Petrie and Robert Kruger (1999)

A Chorus of Raspberries: British Film Comedy 1929–1939
David Sutton (2000)

The Great Art of Light and Shadow: Archaeology of the Cinema
Laurent Mannoni, translated by Richard Crangle (2000)

Popular Filmgoing in 1930s Britain: A Choice of Pleasures
John Sedgwick (2000)

Alternative Empires: European Modernist Cinemas and Cultures of Imperialism
Martin Stollery (2000)

Hollywood, Westerns and the 1930s: The Lost Trail
Peter Stanfield (2001)

Young and Innocent? The Cinema in Britain 1896–1930
edited by Andrew Higson (2002)

Legitimate Cinema: Theatre Stars in Silent British Films 1908–1918
Jon Burrows (2003)

The Big Show: British Cinema Culture in the Great War (1914–1918)
Michael Hammond (2006)

Multimedia Histories: From the Magic Lantern to the Internet
edited by James Lyons and John Plunkett (2007)

Going to the Movies: Hollywood and the Social Experience of Cinema
edited by Richard Maltby, Melvyn Stokes and Robert C. Allen (2007)

University of Exeter Press also publishes the celebrated five-volume series looking at the early years of English cinema, *The Beginnings of the Cinema in England*, by John Barnes.

Alternative Film Culture
in Inter-War Britain

Jamie Sexton

UNIVERSITY
of
EXETER
PRESS

First published in 2008 by
University of Exeter Press
Reed Hall, Streatham Drive
Exeter EX4 4QR
UK
www.exeterpress.co.uk

British Library Cataloguing in Publication Data
A catalogue record for this book is available
from the British Library.

ISBN 978 0 85989 810 2

Typeset in Adobe Caslon
by JCS Publishing Services Ltd

Printed in Great Britain by Cromwell Press, Trowbridge

Contents

Illustrations

Acknowledgements

This book has its roots in a PhD that I undertook at the University of East Anglia. I would like to thank Charles Barr for encouraging me to undertake this study, and the Department of Film Studies at the University of East Anglia for awarding me a scholarship. I would also like to thank Andrew Higson for supervising the thesis and Michael O'Pray who, along with Charles Barr, provided constructive comments as a referee.

A number of other people have helped in various ways with the research, or have provided help away from it. They include: Thomas Austin, Zoe Breen, Jon Burrows, Phil Butcher, Glen Creeber, David Curtis, Kay Dickinson, Kate Egan, Malte Hagener, Laura Mulvey, Mark Pilkington, Anna Shepherd, Mark Smith, Alistair Strachan, Steven Uzzell and Haidee Wasson. Thanks also to the staff at the BFI library, staff at the John Grierson Archive, University of Stirling, and staff at the Beinecke Rare Book and Manuscript Library, Yale University, for providing helpful access to materials. Also, thanks to Erich Sargeant and David Sin at BFI Video for granting me permission to use stills from the BFI DVD release of *Borderline* (2007).

Finally, and most importantly, thanks to my parents for all the support over the years.

Introduction

From Avant-Garde Film to Alternative Film Culture

In earlier, more canonical accounts of avant-garde film practice in the inter-war period, a number of 'artist' filmmakers, as well as predominant artistic 'movements', were privileged, and these mainly stemmed from France, Germany and the Soviet Union, with a few isolated examples existing outside such countries.[1] In France and Germany, films such as *Ballet Mécanique* (Léger and Murphy, France, 1924), *Entr'acte* (Clair, France, 1924) and *Ghosts Before Breakfast* (Richter, Germany, 1928) were connected with already recognized artists who had worked in other media and who were associated with avant-garde movements such as Cubism and Dada. In the Soviet Union the situation was slightly different, in that many of the films celebrated were narrative features, yet there were also links with pre-existing avant-garde traditions (e.g. Eisenstein's involvement with the Moscow Proletkult). More importantly, however, these films were emerging from fierce theoretical debates about the nature and purpose of cinema. A few narrative films from outside the Soviet Union, often made within commercial frameworks, have also been canonized within histories and accounts of avant-garde film of the 1920s and 1930s, such as Weine's *The Cabinet of Dr. Caligari* (Germany, 1919) and Gance's *La Roue* (France, 1922).

With the exception of the work produced by Len Lye in the 1930s, Britain has largely been absent from such 'canonical' accounts. My book attempts to chart a significant form of alternative film culture and associated productions in Britain during the inter-war period. Such an account necessarily has to move away from more traditional conceptions of a filmic 'avant-garde', beset as it is by a number of problems.

1

The Avant-Garde and Problems of Definition

The term 'avant-garde' is certainly not straightforward, but is, as Ian Christie has argued, 'an essentially contested concept, always open to dispute or redefinition'.[2] In the 1970s, when a new historical focus on avant-garde filmmaking emerged, it tended to be distinguished from mainstream cinema by a 'radical otherness'.[3] Attention was paid to avant-garde filmmaking representing an alternative tradition of cinema, often focused upon the work of small-scale, independent productions by individual (or small groups of) artists. Thus, there was a distinction between commercialism and a serious, less compromised, exploration of the medium. Connected to such a view was the feeling that the avant-garde should in some way question mainstream cinema and the role it plays within everyday life. As A.L. Rees argues, in a more recent survey: 'The avant-garde rejects and critiques both the mainstream entertainment cinema and the audience responses which flow from it. It has sought "ways of seeing" outside the conventions of cinema's dominant tradition in the drama film and its industrial mode of production.'[4]

Another feature that was striking in 1970s avant-garde film theory, practice and history was the notion of self-reflexivity: many artists were concerned to explore the 'essential properties' of film. This was a tactic that was allied to avant-garde work in other media; for example, certain forms of abstract painting that rejected 'illusionist' forms of representation and instead experimented with the materials of the medium, so that subject matter became reflective (or form became content). This is a form of avant-garde practice that is in line with the influential art critic Clement Greenberg's argument that avant-garde art is 'absolute art', in which the artist turns away from 'subject matter of common experience' and towards a focus 'upon the medium of his own craft'.[5] Such a turn has been criticized for being mere art for art's sake, yet has also been defended in more ideological terms, particularly so in the 1970s. For example, in the 'structural' or 'structural-materialist' films of Malcolm Le Grice and Peter Gidal, both of whom would construct historical traditions of avant-garde filmmaking, the exploration of film as film was a challenge to dominant modes of perception that were reinforced by the 'illusionist' dominant cinema. Through exposing the actual properties of film, the viewer could become engaged in a critical construction of the film experience, rather than absorbed in the realist film world. Such arguments have been criticized for the manner by which they assume modes of viewer response, assumptions that have been put in serious doubt through a number of reception and audience studies. Nevertheless, the aim of producing a film that differs from mainstream features through aesthetics and ideological import has remained central to avant-garde filmmaking and theory.

It should also be noted that, throughout many of the histories constructed in the 1970s, and in more modern reflections on avant-garde film, the artisanal nature of production has been stressed as important: these are films made outside the industry, by small groups or individuals at low cost, often funded through private patronage or arts grants, and distributed and exhibited in locations such as film societies or museums.[6] Yet, while the avant-garde is often portrayed in such a way, to align it completely with the 'artist's' film would be to overlook the centrality that many industrially produced films have played within avant-garde traditions (most notably the films of Eisenstein).

To return to Christie's comment on the 'contested' nature of the avant-garde, we have to take into consideration the different ways in which avant-garde filmmaking is defined, and that there may be more than a single avant-garde. According to A.L. Rees:

> the avant-garde has traded under many other names: experimental, absolute, pure, non-narrative, underground, expanded, abstract; none of them satisfactory or generally accepted. This lack of agreement points to inherent differences and even conflicts within the avant-garde, just as it implies a search for unity across broad terrain. Because avant-gardes tend to spark off each other, this search is always open.[7]

This 'search' has been problematized to some extent by the emergence, at least since the mid-1980s, of revisionist histories of avant-garde cinema in the inter-war period, as well as the rise of postmodernism. Thus it is now common in overviews of avant-garde filmmaking for the actual concept to be scrutinized and examined, but not to be defined in any straightforward manner.[8] A key revisionist history is Richard Abel's account of the French avant-garde, which occupies a large proportion of his comprehensive study of French cinema between 1915 and 1929.[9] Abel focused here on a narrative avant-garde, but he placed this body of films firmly in the context of an alternative cinema network. Through focusing on this 'alternative network', Abel looked at how specialist film journals received films, and he analysed the types of films that were shown within this cultural milieu. Those films that have been canonized as 'avant-garde' were not straightforwardly differentiated from a number of other films at the time; rather, various critics perceived a number of films as progressive and innovative. These could include 'artisanal' films, but they could also include commercial feature films or sponsored documentary films. There was not, at the time, a straightforward demarcation between such modes of cinema; even though they would be distinguished through classification, they would not automatically be differentiated ideologically.

During the inter-war period fixed conceptual divisions between types of film production did not exist; these are demarcations that have subsequently led to firm (if not always neat) distinctions between commercial mainstream cinema, art cinema and avant-garde/underground cinema. Instead, these types of films could all be seen and praised within the alternative cinema networks, alongside educational films, documentaries and early comedy shorts (to give a few examples). Such a network meant that there was a broad and hazy definition of the avant-garde in use at the time, as can be summed up in the following quotation from Jean Tedesco in 1923: 'The actual exhibition market of the film industry [...] is almost completely closed to one category of films. We have called them avant-garde films only for the purpose of better distinguishing them from the current production and not because of any preconceived idea of a chapel or school.'[10]

In this mode of classification, avant-garde films are those that slip through the net of 'official' culture only to be reinvigorated by a select group of film 'connoisseurs' (or, occasionally, they are films that are both popular and representative of cinematic art). At the time, because alternatives to mainstream film culture were scarce, specialist sub-distinctions were not as prevalent as they subsequently became. In this sense, avant-garde film referred to a broader array of films than it would in later years. In actual fact, unlike the later ciné clubs that emerged in the 1960s and which privileged independently produced films, film critics in the 1920s generally tended to locate the vanguard of film art as existing within industrially produced, narrative feature films.[11]

There was, however, not only less use of the term 'avant-garde' in relation to film at this time, but also deep disagreement over its applications when it was employed. Many surrealist filmmakers who would fit neatly into canons of avant-garde filmmaking written over subsequent decades rejected the term 'avant-garde' because they thought of it as bourgeois.[12] It is because the term is so problematic that I tend to avoid using it frequently within this particular study. While I do think that many of the films that I survey can be called avant-garde, the remit of this work is broader in scope than such a term would imply. As I look at the emergence of a cultural network that aimed to provide an alternative to commercial cinema, in terms of critical writings about film and exhibition sites, which—it was hoped—would feed into film production, I prefer to conceptualize my terrain of study as 'alternative film culture'. The films that I study are thus related to this broader alternative network in some way, not privileging artists' films, but engaging with and celebrating filmmaking considered artistically excellent and/or capable of opening up new pathways for the progression of film as art.

Such a conception, broad as it may be, needs to be qualified, for there are a number of ways in which film can be considered as art. While there were many differences between the ways that film art was defined within alternative film cultures across different nations as well as within particular nations, there were also a number of recurring tropes that seemed to bind these cultural networks together. (Such similarities undoubtedly facilitated the establishment of national and international networks in the first place.) These tropes are themselves reflective of an aesthetic outlook that is broadly modernist. They include: an insistence upon film as an art in its own right, which excluded the (conscious) mimicking of other art forms and an exploration of essentially filmic properties; a hostility towards 'middle-brow' artistic forms and a celebration of both the 'popular' and 'high art' (but with a preference for the latter); and a strong belief in the international nature of art, with a concomitant rejection of jingoistic, nationalist discourses.

In one sense, this brings us back to properties that have been associated with avant-gardism. Nevertheless, there are certain accounts of the avant-garde that are more rigidly constructed than this and which do not allow for the full inclusion of cultural activities that I intend to focus on. These include theories of the avant-garde that tend follow in the footsteps of Peter Bürger's influential account of avant-garde art (which does not, it should be noted, investigate the medium of film).[13] Here, the avant-garde is portrayed as an intensely political project, the aim of which is to counter the increasing commodification of art and to question the role of art within society. Andreas Huyssen's study on the avant-garde can be seen as following this line, as can the work of Paul Willemen, who looks at film.[14] Unlike Bürger and Huyssen, who saw the avant-garde as a failed historical project, Willemen perceives it as a more dynamic, continuing force. If avant-gardism is seen in such a political manner, the range of international alternative film cultures in the inter-war period is more identifiably modernist (even if they do contain avant-garde elements).

We should also be alert to the fact that 'avant-garde' as a term was only infrequently (and inconsistently) applied during this period. More often, a number of other terms would be used in order to distinguish film art as a distinctive force: 'progressive' and 'artistic', for example, would be used to class any type of film into the vanguard of cinematic achievement, while classifications such as 'abstract', 'absolute' and 'experimental' would be used in preference to the phrase 'avant-garde'. Crucially, however, terms were often bandied about without attempts at conceptual clarification, which is what distinguishes many writings of this period from later, academic studies of film art. Thus, even though much of this serious, intellectual criticism and reflection on cinema fed into later theoretical work, it tended to be more impressionistic and speculative than the more rigorous conventions to which academic work generally has to conform.

Alternative Networks

Before focusing on British alternative film culture, it is necessary to provide a picture of similar activities occurring within other countries, for many such elements influenced, or intertwined with, British film culture. While the focus of my study is national, this was, as I have mentioned, a cultural formation that was international in outlook and in practice: that is, many cinéphiles involved in alternative forms of film culture believed that cinema was an international art; furthermore, this led to the formation of networks across national boundaries; various alternative formations exchanged information with each other, and there were also informal distribution exchanges.

While alternative film cultures arose within a number of different countries in the inter-war period, it was in France that isolated instances of such a culture first emerged, which would come to form the most widespread alternative cinema network in a single nation during the period. As Richard Abel has outlined in detail, the roots of such a culture began to materialize in the late 1910s and early 1920s, through the writings of a number of cinéphiles—including Louis Delluc, Léon Moussinac and the Italian Ricciotto Canudo—whose articles on film appeared in publications such as *Le Film* (first published in 1916) and *Ciné-pour-tous* (first published in 1919) and, perhaps most influential of all, *Cinéa* (the last two merged in 1923 to become *Cinéa-Ciné-pour-tous*).[15] As Abel notes, these and other cinéphiles began to establish the film as a modern, unique art form and to map out the potential of this new art through attempts 'to isolate its specific features in order to analyze and evaluate specific works'.[16] In *Cinéa* the much scrutinized and ambiguous concept of *photogénie* was developed, in which musical and poetic metaphors were employed to sketch out an aesthetic avenue for film art, based upon 'rhetorical and rhythmic patterning'.[17]

This writing led to the creation of a number of ciné clubs and, eventually, to specialist cinemas devoted to the cinema as an art form. For example, the first major ciné club to emerge was CASA (Club des amis du Septième), established in 1921 and run by Ricciotto Canudo. Members took part in a series of lectures on the cinema as well as attending special film screenings. The Vieux Colombier, meanwhile, programmed by Jean Tedesco, was the first major cinema to form in 1924.[18] These were followed by a number of other similar organizations, leading to a vibrant alternative film culture in France during the 1920s, which inspired a number of avant-garde filmmakers and also provided venues for their work to be shown and discussed.

Abel's groundbreaking research has led to a number of studies of alternative cultural networks in other countries, and while these may not have been as extensive as those established in France, subsequent research has shown that there did exist similar networks of writing about the cinema, showing films and delivering other related events (such as lectures and the organization of exhibitions). In the USA, for example, alternative exhibition was underway by 1925, when Symon Gould established the Screen Guild in New York, which arranged occasional programmes of experimental shorts and art films.[19] Gould began the first continuous 'art film programme' the following year at the Cameo Theatre, and by the end of the 1920s there were a number of film guilds and small cinemas dedicated to the film as art in various regions across the country.[20] In line with such developments, informal distribution exchanges were set up (such as the Amateur Cinema League's lending library and Gould's own, apparently not very reliable, distribution services), alongside the emergence of writings on the art of the cinema in journals such as *Experimental Cinema* (1931–34).[21]

Likewise, networks of exhibition, distribution and writing on cinema occurred in many other parts of Europe, providing a crucial cultural setting in which film was valued and promoted, thus encouraging 'artisanal' productions that could then be shown at small cinemas, alongside a range of other films.[22] These include the Gesellschaft Neuer Film (GNF, the Society New Film) and the Volksfilmverband für Filmkunst (VFV, People's Film Association for Film Art), which arose in Germany in 1928, alongside a number of intellectual discussions about the possibilities of cinematic art;[23] in the Netherlands the Filmliga was formed in 1927 and supported its programmes with a journal, *Film Liga*.[24] Ciné clubs, specialized theatres and dedicated writings about the cinema as a new art also occurred in Belgium, Spain, Poland and, outside Europe, in Japan and Canada.[25] Film culture in the Soviet Union was, of course, different, yet fierce theoretical debates about the aesthetics of the medium have been charted during the inter-war period.[26]

The British Context

This study outlines the context of an 'alternative' film culture within Britain, from which emerged a number of experimental films that were made outside the commercial industry. Such films cannot really be grouped together in any straightforward manner: although a number of films shared certain thematic preoccupations, others did not; some evidence similarities in formal construction, others conform to completely separate formal templates; some were made by a few individuals on a shoestring budget, others were made more expensively for industrial sponsors. In this sense, the investigation of an alternative culture and an examination of how a number of independent productions fitted into this cultural milieu is a more convenient and useful framework within which to undertake this study, as opposed to the employment of an avant-garde model.

As I have explained, many of the canonical avant-garde films have enjoyed privileged relations to other renowned artists or movements, in particular those connected to the fine arts. There were, of course, a number of modernist activities in the fine arts in inter-war Britain. Roger Fry's two Post-Impressionist exhibitions (in 1910 and 1912) are often seen as important landmarks in the arrival of 'modern art' to the country, and these gave rise to a number of artistic 'movements' (or at least groupings) in Britain. The Bloomsbury Group was perhaps the best known, although in reality it comprised a number of diverse artists and intellectuals, and was also connected with the London Group, an exhibiting collection formed in 1913 that encompassed a broad range of modern British artists (including the Camden Town Group and the Vorticists).[27] Influenced very much by French modern artists such as Cézanne and Gauguin, Bloomsbury critics Roger Fry and Clive Bell stressed the importance of form and railed against naturalist representation.

After the First World War, however, despite the appearance of other groupings—such as Wyndham Lewis's Group X and the Seven and Five Society—British modern art was marked more by, in Spalding's terms, 'a pursuit of the personal and idiosyncratic' than by group effort.[28] It was also marked by a retreat from the radical, abstract work that appeared before the war, as artists returned to traditional modes of representation, even if these were inflected by formal concerns (evident in the re-emergence of landscape painting). In this sense, there is difficulty in linking filmmaking directly with any movements because of this lack of coherence. And while the 1930s saw more identifiable trends emerging, such as the influence of Surrealism and Constructivism on artists associated with Unit One,[29] as well as more realist movements (the Euston Road School, the growth of socialist realism), it is still difficult to link films directly with the fine arts. It is certainly true that there were many links between film and other arts, but these links tended to be sporadic. While film certainly was infused by broader artistic influences (both national and international), these links were often multiple and opaque. In short, such influences are often difficult to pin down in a direct fashion.

Ironically, the filmmaking activities associated with alternative film culture seem to share with modernist fine art in 1920s Britain a 'pursuit of the personal and idiosyncratic', which makes it difficult to categorize them in any neat and tidy manner. Paralleling the more identifiable trends in the art world of the 1930s, a modern film movement also emerged in that decade: the documentary film movement. Yet this movement's aesthetic legacy is predicated on a small number of films, and these films themselves are often shot through with diverse stylistic and thematic currents.

Despite this diversity, a number of themes and alliances did exist and these have, to some extent, influenced some of the chapter and section headings of this book. Overall, though, what brings these films together is that they can all, to some extent, be linked to the emergence of an alternative film culture, reflecting the concerns of the cinéphiles who wrote passionately about the cinema as a modern art form, often influenced by the films that were playing in film societies and repertory cinemas, and ultimately (except on rare occasions) being screened in such venues.

My study, then, attempts to map an alternative network of British film culture, and to look at a number of independently produced films that emerged from this culture. It is certainly true that some of the elements that I discuss have gained previous academic attention: a few, such as selected areas of the documentary film movement and Len Lye, have been the subject of attention for quite some time; others, such as the Film Society and the journal *Close Up*, have more recently undergone evaluation; other elements have still barely been touched upon. Yet no full-length study has thus far accounted for all these as interconnected areas of a British alternative film culture, which is where the significance of this book lies.[30]

Within this study, then, I am keen to demonstrate that a number of independently produced films, some of which can be classed as avant-garde, were produced in Britain during the 1920s and 1930s, and to analyse these films in detail. I also want to stress the cultural context out of which these films emerged and which, in my view, significantly shaped them. This study is not merely a focus on film texts but also encompasses the exhibition of, and writing about, film. These foci demonstrate the practical struggles in constructing an alternative film culture, as well as the broad frameworks of thinking that helped to shape this culture. They also help illuminate the reception contexts within which such films circulated, at least in Britain.

My focus on a number of 'alternative' film productions during this period therefore contributes to a tradition and history of alternative British filmmaking, an essential component of any healthy film culture. The analysis of exhibition and writing, however, demonstrates the importance of a wider film culture in supporting such productions. Nevertheless, as I go on to show, there were sometimes tensions between the types of films that were produced and the broader cultural climate within which such films circulated (at least in Britain). While some of the films that I look at were championed, a number were ignored, and this undoubtedly fed into subsequent negative perceptions of 'avant-garde' filmmaking during the period. What follows is an attempt to delve beneath such negative perceptions in order to explore the dynamics and intricacies of an important period of 'alternative' British film culture.

I

The Network of Alternative Film Culture

The production of a number of small-scale, 'alternative' British films in the inter-war period was reliant upon a broader network of exhibition, distribution and criticism, elements that constituted an alternative 'network'. This network was both national and international, and while my focus on Britain leads me to concentrate on the former, the latter should not be ignored, for it shaped the British cultural situation in many ways.

In this chapter, then, I will outline some of the main themes that can be discerned within alternative film culture, in terms of exhibition programming and cultural approaches to the art of film; I will also spend some time analysing film writing in order to probe the main features of alternative film discourses. It is important to recognize the major components of alternative film culture, as it is only by doing so that one can fully get to grips with some of the chief influences upon the films that will be analysed. In addition, it is crucial to consider the discursive frameworks that existed, as these would have not only—to varying degrees—informed the attitudes of some filmmakers, but would also feed into the reception of the films themselves.

The whole production–distribution–exhibition–reception process can be seen as a loop in which each segment is constitutive of, and also influenced by, other segments in the chain. For example, without any form of distribution, there would be no films to exhibit, but likewise without an exhibition structure there would be no need for distribution. In terms of production, certain exhibited films viewed by filmmakers may seep into the production process (via direct or covert influence), while critical reception also constitutes a broad framework to which films should adhere if they are to be celebrated within cultural circles; otherwise, they risk the possibility of sinking without trace. (It may be the case that subsequent discursive frameworks find previously neglected films appealing for some reason, but if a film is neglected its chances of surviving posterity will decrease.) Such frameworks are never homogeneous or static, but I do believe that at particular moments in time there are detectable certain ways of approaching film, specific aesthetic elements that are privileged over others, and it is these that I wish to tease out in the subsequent text relating to discourse.

I will focus on exhibition primarily through the (London) Film Society, which will serve as a case study of exhibition (and, less centrally, distribution). This focus on one institution is limited to the extent that it marginalizes other societies that emerged in the inter-war period. Nevertheless, I believe that this was the most important society: it was the first of its kind to spring up, and it influenced (indeed supported) many of the societies that emerged subsequently. In addition, the wealth of archival material concerning the Film Society, in relation to other societies, allows us to construct a much more detailed portrait of an exhibition outlet.

In terms of attitudes to film, these will mostly be sketched through the work published in specialist film journals, the main ones being *Close Up* (1927–33), *Cinema Quarterly* (1932–36) and *Film/Film Art* (1933–37). I will also look at some writing that appeared in book-length form, as well as other writing that appeared in newspaper articles, reports (in the case of John Grierson) and exhibition programme notes (in the case of the Film Society). I will investigate the emerging network and the surrounding discourses up to 1930, as the rise of sound marks a distinct break in attitudes towards film, which will be the focus of a later chapter. There will, however, be occasional references to the post-1930s situation in this chapter as it is not always possible to cut off a time period in so neat a fashion.

The Film Society and the Emergence of an Alternative Film Culture

Origins

Against the background of the continuing domination of British screens by American films, many of which were made along highly standardized lines, there arose an alternative movement of people who opposed the excessive commercialism of the film industry. They were drawn to cinema as a new and modern art form, rather than as a straightforward, industrial entertainment. While film was beginning to be discussed as an art in the 1910s, this was often done in relation to other, more established media, such as literature and theatre. This inevitably had an effect on the films made in Britain, with the film industry often relying on the stage or the novel for its source material.[1] Literature and theatre provided respectable material with which to work, and an added incentive was that they also provided plots and characters already in cultural circulation. These adaptations were often perceived by intellectuals as too dependent upon their source material, a perception that endured until relatively recently.[2]

It is not my contention that such a view is correct; the growing research into early British cinema suggests that it is not.[3] Nevertheless, it was a perception that shaped the manner by which a certain group of intellectuals created an alternative vision of cinematic art. These cinéphiles disputed the idea that film should merely act as a filter for 'respectable' media. While they did not totally reject theatrical or literary influences at this point, they did think that film should incorporate other elements according to its own particular strengths. They therefore wanted to establish the medium itself as something that was respectable, as the most modern and 'progressive' of art forms, with the potential to become superior to literature and theatre.

The domination of the commercial imperative was reflected in trade papers that mainly focused on film from a commercial angle. In newspapers, coverage of film was extremely limited and was overwhelmed by space devoted to other arts.[4] While this was slowly beginning to change in the late 1910s and early 1920s, coverage was still not substantial. In the trade press cinema was still often treated as a business. 'Artistic' issues were sometimes addressed, but cinéphiles were often unhappy about the restrictions these papers imposed: Ivor Montagu, for example, complained about the demands of emphasizing 'commercial possibilities' when writing for the trade press.[5] These cinéphiles played an important role in writing seriously about film in the press.

Sporadic articles looking at the art of film began to appear in the trade press, newspapers and other publications in the early 1920s, gradually becoming more regular. Iris Barry, for example, began to write a film column for the literary journal the *Spectator* in 1923; she also started a regular film column for the popular newspaper the *Daily Mail* in 1925.[6] Caroline Lejeune had begun to write serious film criticism for the *Manchester Guardian* in 1922 and from 1928 wrote a regular, substantial film column for the *Observer*.[7] Ivor Montagu, after writing for the Cambridge magazine *Granta* in 1924, also contributed on film for the *Observer* and the *New Statesman* in the mid-1920s, and later for the *Sunday Times*.[8] Walter Mycroft wrote on film for both the *Evening Standard* and the *Illustrated Sunday Herald* in the mid-1920s,[9] while Robert Herring wrote for the literary journal *The London Mercury* from 1926. It should be noted that Lejeune—unlike the other writers mentioned—was not a member of the

Film Society, but she did hold many of the same assumptions about film art as the Society's members and was generally regarded as an important film critic.

It should be noted that there was no wholesale rejection of commercial, capitalist filmmaking. Many mainstream American films were liked but they were often seen as lacking in 'quality'. This was usually attributed to the fact that the financial imperative was seen to dominate the filmmaking process to a disproportionate degree. In an article written in 1925 for the *Evening Standard*, Film Society co-founder Hugh Miller wrote: 'The maker of pictures in America reduces the public's intelligence to the least common denominator. The whole business rests on a foundation of spurious values. Most of the genuine talent goes unrecognised. It is a business first and an art a very long time afterwards.'[10]

Some intellectuals were clearly dissatisfied with the way that commercial values held sway in the production, distribution and exhibition of films. Many believed that the rule of quantity overrode an interest in quality and they called for a more harmonious blending between financial and artistic imperatives. Miller asserted in the aforementioned article that:

> many do not know that there is a small and constant supply of films which are vital. Unfortunately, there is no place to show these pictures. [...] What we in London want is an independent film theatre, as advocated by your correspondent—a place where the vital film can get a fair show.[11]

The Film Society arose out of such wishes, and was set up by Miller, an actor, and Ivor Montagu. Montagu was a trained zoologist, the son of a peer, who was working for *The Times* in 1924. During an assignment that involved touring the Berlin Film Studios, he met Miller, who was working on an Anglo-German production. On their way back to England they came up with the idea of starting a film society. At a party given by Iris Barry, Montagu and Miller shared their ideas with director Adrian Brunel, journalist Walter Mycroft, exhibitor Sidney Bernstein and sculptor Frank Dobson.[12] All of these people became council members of the Film Society, organizing its activities, getting hold of films and putting together programmes.

Montagu, who became the first chairman of the Society, stated that the idea for a film society came from the London Stage Society, which was founded in 1899 and showed theatre productions that lay outside the usual West End fare, introducing the likes of Cocteau and Strindberg into the country.[13] There were also other national precedents: Adrian Brunel had attempted to form a Cinemagoers League in 1920 in order to articulate the demands of 'a new and more discriminating public';[14] the Cinema Art Group of the Faculty of Arts had been formed in 1923 'to give practical support for films of outstanding merit' and 'to influence the public to appreciate the cinema as an art medium'.[15] At this time a number of university film clubs also sprang up.[16] A few commercial cinemas such as the New Gallery and the Marble Arch Pavilion began to show a few foreign features in the early 1920s, though this was not on a regular basis.[17]

Aims, Membership Details, Finance and Contacts

The primary function of the Film Society was to offer a range of films that were not being shown in commercial cinemas, although it also attempted to influence film practice. In its constitution and rules, the Film Society listed its objectives as:

(1) To exhibit cinematograph films privately to the members of the Society and their guests, and to introduce films of artistic, technical and educational interest, and to encourage the study of cinematography, and to assist such experiments as may help the technical advance of film production.

(2) To arrange lectures and discussions on the art and technique of film.[18]

In this sense it was also a kind of film school, in which the art of film was not only appreciated, but also studied. Its attempt to influence commercial production was reflected in its offer of cut-price membership to people employed in the film industry. This shows that the Society was not an alternative space that attempted to negate the commercial cinema: rather, such a space was created in order to feed into the industry, as well as to encourage practices that did not adhere to the requirements of commercial cinema.

The Film Society was a non-profit, membership-only organization: people paid an annual subscription that enabled them to go to every performance for a whole season. A season lasted for a year, and usually consisted of eight performances,[19] held at 2.30 p.m. on Sundays, in commercial cinemas rented for the occasion. The first performance was at the New Gallery Kinema in Regent Street. In addition to this theatre, subsequent performances were held at the Tivoli, the Astoria and the New

Victoria, venues that the Society usually obtained free of charge.[20] For the first season (1925–26), there were three different subscription rates: 3 guineas, 2 guineas and 1 guinea.[21] The next season the subscription rates were 3 guineas, 2 guineas and £1, 5 shillings. The fees shifted from season to season, but generally remained reasonably consistent in line with inflation. The subscription would have been beyond the means of the average working person, indicating that the Society saw itself as catering for the middle to upper classes. These expensive fees enabled the Society to show films in high-quality surroundings, with a full orchestral accompaniment. In addition, as a non-commercial, members-only institution, the Society could show films that had not been passed for public exhibition, and thus elude censorship restrictions on many occasions.

In order to make the Film Society appear a 'respectable' enterprise, support was canvassed from Lord Ashfield, Lord David Cecil and Dame Ellen Terry, as well as from H.G. Wells and George Bernard Shaw. This respectable connection did not merely highlight the rather middle- to upper-class character of the Film Society; it was also a deliberate ploy to ensure that influential people would support it. For instance, the connection with Lord Ashfield enabled the Film Society to have its first performance at the New Gallery Kinema free of charge (Ashfield had connections with the owners of the cinema). Other founder members of the Film Society included the biologist Julian Huxley, film critic G.A. Atkinson, film director Anthony Asquith (at the time a student), theatre director John Strachey, film producer Michael Balcon, film director George Pearson and actors Ivor Novello and John Gielgud. The secretary of the Film Society was Miss J.M. Harvey, who took care of the day-to-day running of the organization, handling all of the membership subscriptions and most of the enquiries that were received. Artist E. McKnight Kauffer, who also became a member, designed the Film Society monogram.[22]

Although a non-profit organization, the Film Society still needed income to cover its considerable running costs; this was chiefly gained through membership subscription. Its expenses mainly consisted of payment for theatre rental, payment for staff and lighting at each performance, hiring of the orchestra, titling of films, customs duties and entertainment tax. Adrian Brunel and Ivor Montagu undertook titling of films, as well as occasional editing, for their editing firm Brunel and Montagu Ltd, which they ran with Frank Wells.[23] As most commercial cinemas did, the Society generally hired an orchestra to provide musical accompaniment at its screenings (it often employed the services of respected composer Edmund Meisel, who wrote the score for *Battleship Potemkin* (Eisenstein,

USSR, 1925)); the only exceptions were when it engaged in the occasional 'experiment', such as when it showed *Greed* (Von Stroheim, USA, 1925) totally silent.

The Film Society obtained films on an ad hoc basis, through contacts that its members had built up; each council member would travel abroad whenever possible to visit companies or directors. Because of the absence of any independent central distribution unit at that time it was necessary, in many ways, for international cinéphiles to establish a network of informal connections, which would have contributed to similarities between them. In addition, Brunel and Montagu could obtain a number of films via work undertaken for their editing company, since they undertook duties for a number of other companies as well as their work for the Film Society.[24]

The Film Society did not, as a policy, pay for the rental of films. A complex process of negotiations was therefore entered into in order to obtain films free of charge, in which it had to make a number of agreements and stipulations. For instance, the Society had to agree to pay for the importation costs of the films it rented, as well as charges for insurance and the safe return of the film. The only films that it did pay for were small-scale, independent productions, in which a low fee of £10 was paid; these films included Cavalcanti's *Rien que les Heures* (France, 1926), Man Ray's *Emak Bakia* (France, 1926) and Webber's *The Fall of the House of Usher* (USA, 1929).[25]

The Society thus played a major role in international minority film culture. It had particularly close links with the New York Film Arts Guild, with whom it discussed the establishment of an international chain of small, independent film theatres and the possibility of arranging international conferences of small theatre groups. It was also engaged in an attempt to encourage the social circumstances in which minority film culture could flourish. By forging these international connections it was hoping to place independent film culture on a more systematic footing, so that marginal films could be distributed and exhibited with more ease and regularity. Such international cooperation led to the well-documented ten-day congress of international independent cinema at the Château de La Sarraz, Switzerland, in September 1929, followed by a second congress in Brussels the following year. Conferences such as these offered space for a variety of like-minded international cinéphiles to network and discuss ideas. They led to the creation of the International League of Independent Cinema, which was established to aid distribution between the member clubs and societies, which included the Film Society, the Ciné Club of France, the Ciné Club of Geneva, the National Board of Review of the

USA, ciné clubs in Rome and Madrid, and delegates from Germany, Austria and Japan.

Programmes

The Film Society screened a broad range of films in its fourteen-year span and although there were certain changes in programming policy, there were also continuities. I will chart the major trends up until 1930; although sound film was introduced earlier than this, it was at this point that its impact began to be genuinely felt within British alternative culture.

The first performance reveals the diversity of programming, the typical structures that programmes would subsequently take and the aesthetic preferences of Film Society council members. The screening times for the performance on 25 October 1925, were as follows:

- 2.30 p.m., *Opus 2, 3,* and *4* (1923–25), abstract shorts by German Walter Ruttman, a former engraver and lithographer, now firmly embedded within the avant-garde 'canon'. The programme notes described these as 'studies in pattern, with drum accompaniment';[26] the films were part of the Film Society's 'absolute films' series.
- 2.50 p.m., *How Broncho Billy Left Bear Country* (1912), an old two-reel American Western produced by the Essanay company and starring G.M. Anderson. This was part of the Film Society 'resurrection' series.[27]
- 3.00 p.m., *Typical Budget* (1925), a British burlesque film directed by Film Society council member Adrian Brunel and produced by Gainsborough Pictures. This film was part of a series and was exclusive in that it had yet to be trade shown or released.
- 3.15 p.m., *Waxworks* (1924), the main feature. This German film— now regarded as a classic 'Expressionist' text—was directed by Paul Leni, produced by Wilking Film, and starred Emil Jannings and Conradt Veidt. It had not at that time been purchased in Britain for film exhibition.
- 4.35 p.m., *Champion Charlie* (1916), an early Chaplin short.[28]

This programme is interesting in many ways. It is a basic skeleton of most future Film Society programmes. With a few exceptions—notably 'themed' programmes or single-feature programmes—subsequent programmes would offer a main narrative feature with a few other short films covering an eclectic variety of categories and representing different countries. The first programme showed films from Great Britain, Germany and America. Categories spanned burlesque, slapstick, abstract film, an early genre picture and an 'Expressionist' feature; recent productions were screened alongside 'archive' presentations. Although the main feature here was shown as the penultimate film, as it would be on a few other occasions, the typical programme would screen the main feature last.

Many countries were represented in the Film Society performances over the years, including Germany, France, Great Britain, America, the Soviet Union, Holland, Italy, Austria, Japan, China, Portugal, Poland, Czechoslovakia, Sweden, Belgium, Switzerland, Hungary, South Africa, Spain and Mexico. In terms of feature-length films, Germany dominated the first three seasons; thereafter the Soviet Union was heavily represented, while there were also a number of French feature films. Although international in scope, the Society thus drew most of its material from five core countries: Germany, the Soviet Union, France, Britain and America. There was therefore a definite European bias, which may to some extent be related to taste, though other factors such as the availability of films must be taken into account.

Besides the feature film, the main categories within which the Film Society programmed its films were as follows:

- the 'resurrection' series, which were old short films;
- the 'absolute' series of experimental, abstract films;
- the 'bionomics' series, which were films of scientific interest that illustrated biological phenomena, such as the Percy Smith's 'Secrets of Nature' films;
- sport films, such as those made by John Betts;
- comedies, including burlesque or slapstick films;
- technical films, for example, illustrations of technical innovations in cinematography;
- animation, like Lotte Reiniger's silhouette films or Walt Disney's 'Silly Symphonies'; and
- documentary films, such as publicity films, or personal and biographical documentaries.

The Film Society also occasionally showed extracts from films, such as the single-reel extracts from *The Lodger* (Hitchcock, UK, 1927) and *The Skin Game* (Hitchcock, UK, 1931), which were shown in performance 45 (8 February 1931). As these extracts were shown divorced from commercial or narrative context as self-sufficient objects of study, they could also be seen as a separate type of category within the Film Society programmes.

In its first three seasons the Film Society was marked by a clear preference for German narrative features, showing films such as *Waxworks*,

Raskolnikov (Wiene, 1923), *Nju* (Czinner, 1924) and *The Cabinet of Dr. Caligari*. The majority of these films are associated with 'Expressionism', a type of filmmaking that the Society favoured in its first few years of operation. Scholars such as Barry Salt have contested the validity of Expressionism as a generic cinematic concept. Salt argues that only a few films conform to the Expressionist style and that one should not apply this term to films that merely use looming shadows and extreme angles.[29] However, many of the films were promoted in this way at the time, and the term was used in some of the contemporary reviews of films such as *The Cabinet of Dr. Caligari* and *Waxworks*.[30] Thomas Elsaesser contends that the label has become an indelible part of some of the films' identities. However, he also argues that we should understand the generic label not in an art-historical sense, but in an economic-industrial sense. Expressionism, for Elsaesser, connotes a 'tool-box' of stylistic features—borrowed from painting, theatre, interior design and fashion—appropriated by the cinematic medium in order to imbue it with respectability.[31]

The Film Society tended to favour German films that utilized exaggerated acting styles, peculiar lighting techniques and elaborate sets, aspects that they referred to within their programme notes.[32] Yet while this seemed to be the prime interest of the Film Society, its members were also interested in other German films that have been less commonly associated with Expressionism. For example, they showed films by Paul Czinner and Lupu Pick, figures more associated with the *Kammerspiel*, or 'chamber-play' film, as well as—in particular—the films of G.W. Pabst, often connected to the 'New Objectivity' movement.

The focus on German Expressionist features would initially have to be explained as a turning away from American films. Since the Film Society were looking for an alternative to commercial cinema, they were likely to look outside Hollywood to locate a cinema that could serve as a paradigm of artistic excellence. In order to have film taken seriously as an art, they needed to promote a type of filmmaking that was easily distinguished from the 'typical' mainstream product. A serious industrial alternative to Hollywood was constructed in Weimar Germany, where a large body of films (which still, however, only constituted a fraction of the native output) were made on large budgets as international, 'prestige' products and promoted as art films.

Sabine Hake writes that these films were made with an explicit goal: 'to create a quality product and attract middle-class audiences to the cinema'.[33] Because they were made with an intellectual marketplace in mind (as well as more populist locations), they borrowed from established conventions, such as theatre and literature. The traditions they followed, however, had an anti-bourgeois, anti-authoritarian aura, and were perceived as containing 'progressive' attributes. Film companies took inspiration from other arts to instil cultural value into their products but also often displayed properties that overtly flaunted the specificity of the medium, such as special effects and fluid camera work. Such films therefore merged medium specificity and cultural respectability, traditional and progressive values, highbrow and populist idioms.[34] Therefore, while *Caligari* was celebrated within the international circuit as validating the medium, it also proved that this was a medium that was breaking away from the traditions of other arts through its visual rhythms and movements.[35] The Film Society promoted these films as expressions of a new, dynamic and modern medium that was nevertheless distinguished from the vulgarities of blunt commercialism.

Yet, while the Society distanced itself from commercial standardization, it did display a preference for films that were made within a commercial environment. It promoted and recommended many short films, but also privileged feature films, especially those displaying qualities associated with 'good production values'. Good production values were not enough in themselves, however. In the early years of the Film Society's existence, alternative culture turned towards films that were expressive of cinema as both an artistic and an intelligent medium. In this sense, German Expressionist films were indicative of film not as a technological reproduction of reality, but as an artistic manipulation and transformation of reality. They were thus, in Hake's words, an 'encounter between technology and imagination, with the former realizing the ambitions of the latter'.[36] They were also, with their emphasis on low-key lighting and intense acting, expressive of psychological subjectivity, illustrating that cinema could objectively visualize the soul of humanity. This relation to inwardness and darkness, in which psychological secrets are revealed, linked the cinema to the intellect in new, visual ways. Even many of the German 'chamber dramas' shown at the Film Society were linked to psychology; as Thompson and Bordwell argue, these films were typified by a concentration on a few characters in which their psychology was explored.[37] As a final comment, it should also be noted that Expressionist films were popular within the international network of intellectual film culture, especially in France.[38] Such prestige would have aided, albeit not guaranteed, a favourable reception for the films in Britain.

Towards the end of the 1920s this preference for German features began to give way to Soviet films. Although there were two Russian films shown in the first two seasons—*Father Sergius* (Protazanov and Volkoff, 1917), shown in performance 13 (13 February 1927), and *Polikushka* (Sanin, 1923), produced by Mezhrabpom and shown in performance 15 (10 April 1927)— Russian films were not regularly screened until the fourth season. In that season (1928–29), three Soviet features were shown, and this increased into the 1930s as the films became easier for the Society to obtain. The three most frequently screened Soviet directors were Eisenstein, Pudovkin and Vertov. The rise of the Soviet feature did not mean that German films were immediately rejected; traces of earlier inclinations still continued to shape programming to some extent, but were now subordinated to a new aesthetic preference: that of a more social or 'objective' conception of filmmaking. With the emphasis on montage (the interdependent structure of individual shots) overtaking that of elaborate *mise-en-scène* (the inherent quality of the individual shot), artistry could now be located in a more 'realistic' or 'objective' scene.

The reason for the dominant preference changing from German to Soviet features was perhaps a combination of a shift in British intellectual interests, an increase in the production and availability of the films from the Soviet Union, and the level of theoretical discussion that was taking place in the Soviet Union at this time. At its inception the Film Society had immediately taken an interest in Russia: Montagu had made a trip to Moscow and had also written an article on Russian film in *Kinematograph Weekly* in 1925. In it he expressed enthusiasm for the conditions in Russia, believing that they were capable of providing good cinematic material. However, although he found their productions interesting, he did not think that they were of a remarkable quality: 'Only the productions of Mezhrabpom persistently maintain a level high enough to bear comparison in this respect with the average technique of American films.'[39] The Film Society also expressed a wish to show more Russian films in their second annual report (1926–27), but stated that there were difficulties in securing permission from Russian authorities. A further difficulty was the constant change of the staff in Russian film companies with whom the Society negotiated.[40]

Interest in Russian films was not new, then, but I do not think that the shift in emphasis was solely due to availability problems in the early period. Montagu stated that the quality of the films available was not particularly good, despite his interest in them. What the Film Society thought was good art was a combination of stylistic innovation and technical competence. In this sense, what they desired of film art was a mixture of techniques associated with both the European avant-garde (experimentation, innovation, independent vision) and Hollywood (high technical standards): what later became known as the 'art film'. It was the Soviet films of the latter half of the 1920s that were perceived as most successful in blending these elements. The fact that many Soviet directors were analysing and theorizing about films also imbued their work with extra importance.

The move towards left-wing concerns by many British intellectuals would also have influenced the shift towards Soviet films during this period. This is not to say that all British intellectuals suddenly became political, but within those circles there was an increased interest in leftist politics. This was influenced by the revolutionary events in Russia, and towards the end of the 1920s the economic recession put doubts on the validity of capitalism itself, which saw many intellectuals turn to Marxism.[41] This made its mark on many film aesthetes: while artistry and technique were still highly valued, there was an increasing belief that film should have a more purposeful function, rather than existing in a self-enclosed realm ('art for art's sake').

The preference for certain features of German and Soviet films represented the Society's dominant patterns of interest in the 1920s, as well as the eclectic range of films according to the categories outlined above. It showed several films that have since become canonized within the realm of avant-garde film or art cinema. Most of the experimental films shown were from France and include *Entr'acte* (Clair, 1924), *Ballet Mécanique* (Léger and Murphy, 1924) and *Emak Bakia*. This would undoubtedly have been helped by the fact that France had such an extensive independent cinema culture, with a large network of ciné clubs, film journals and alternative cinemas, which encouraged the making of short experimental films. In fact, this network also enabled more financial aid to be given to independent filmmakers, since specialized cinemas such as the Ursulines, L'Oeil du Paris and Studio 28 were involved in sponsoring short films.[42] There were also several experimental films from Germany, by artists such as Hans Richter and Oskar Fischinger, as well as from America. The films shown that have become respected as art films or as part of a narrative avant-garde include *L'Inhumaine* (Le Herbier, France, 1924), *Greed* and *The Passion of Joan of Arc* (Dreyer, France, 1928).

It is interesting to note that although many intellectuals at the time were hostile to American films dominating the market, the Film Society did actually devote a significant portion of its programming space to American products. These fell into four main types:

- shorts by figures considered to have carved out unique individual oeuvres within film history (for example, early films by Griffith or starring Chaplin);
- shorts that were seen to be of historical or technical interest (in that they prefigured a popular genre, for example);
- animated shorts (in particular the work of Walt Disney); and
- feature-length films considered to be of particular artistic excellence. In its third annual report, the Society claimed that it showed 'certain American films of exceptional merit which have been abbreviated in this country'.[43] This therefore indicated that the Film Society could often show uncut films, though—as I will demonstrate below—not without a struggle.

It should therefore be noted that there was no wholesale rejection of American films. British alternative culture's rejection of American cinema has, I think, been overstated, at least for the period until the late 1920s.[44] It is true that American films were attacked, but not in a simplistic, automatic manner; intellectuals liked many American films, and the Film Society itself showed several. What actually characterized their opinions was a dismissal of the majority of products, which was perhaps inevitable, given a formative aesthetic taste privileging the artistic as the exceptional. It was the workings of the American film industry that were disliked, because they were perceived as producing a mass of 'inferior' films and also as ensuring that their films dominated British (as well as many other countries') screens. The Society valued individual American films themselves, as long as they deemed them to be of sufficient artistic quality. Germany was certainly seen as incorporating art into its commercial cinema on a more consistent basis and Russia was also perceived to be producing a more consistent output of industrially produced, 'quality' films.[45] However, with German and Russian productions set apart, it does not appear that America was denigrated more than any other country.

In addition to showing films, the Society organized a number of 'special events' that, along with its programme notes, constituted an attempt to create a cultural appreciation of film as an art, a cinéphilia that would stimulate both commercial and non-commercial filmmaking. At its first performance the Society had planned to exhibit a number of Paul Leni's set designs alongside the screening of *Waxworks*, which Leni directed. Although this exhibition did not take place, the Film Society did, during its fourteen-year existence, arrange a number of similar events. The majority of these took place in 1929.

At the end of its fourth season (1928–29) the Society programmed a lecture by Vsevolod Pudovkin, while in its fifth season (1929–30) it held a series of lectures by Sergei Eisenstein, a course on camerawork, overseen by Edouard Tissé and a practical course on abstract film production led by Hans Richter. These events were organized in order to encourage experimental and progressive attitudes towards filmmaking among the Society's members, many of whom were involved in film production. People like Hitchcock and Grierson were exposed to such theories; both admitted to having been influenced by Soviet films.[46] In addition, these lectures gained widespread press coverage that created more general notice and led to English translations of books by Eisenstein and Pudovkin.[47] These publications in turn meant that such theories reached people outside the Film Society. The course by Richter, meanwhile, led to the production of a film, *The Daily Round* (1929, later retitled *Everyday*), which will be discussed in Chapter 6. The Society also partly financed Len Lye's first film, *Tusalava* (1928), which was shown at its thirty-fourth performance (1 December 1929).

Legal Issues and Reactions to the Film Society

In its first five seasons, 50 per cent of the films shown by the Film Society had not been publicly exhibited and the British Board of Film Censors (BBFC) had not certified many of these.[48] This situation, along with the Society's screening of films on a Sunday (which was not at the time legal for commercial cinemas), meant that it needed to obtain permission from the London County Council (LCC) for its performances. As a result of a lapse in organizational proceedings, this had not been attained for the first performance, but the LCC gave the Film Society permission to go ahead with this performance by granting it an emergency sanction. Following this, the LCC held a vote on whether to grant the Film Society a permanent sanction. They eventually voted in favour of a seasonal sanction after lobbying by Society members helped to sway a close vote. This meant that the Film Society had to renew its permission each season to show unlicensed films at a commercial cinema on Sundays. The sanction was granted on the grounds that shows remained private and were for a restricted audience.[49]

Although the Film Society managed to retain permission from the LCC up until 1939, it often ran into legal problems. For its very first performance the BBFC objected to a character in *Waxworks* being called Jack the Ripper. Eventually this objection was overcome, and the character name remained unaltered. However, for performance 6 (14 March 1926) the BBFC again objected to disturbing subject matter, this time as portrayed in *The Cabinet of Dr. Caligari*, which led to some scenes being cut from the film.[50]

After the first season, the LCC had a special meeting in order to decide whether to renew the sanction. The BBFC was concerned that the Film Society was showing uncensored films and in turn put pressure on the LCC to demand that the Film Society account for its practices. In a 1927 memorandum to the LCC, the Film Society put forward a detailed defence of its programming policy: 'The Society maintains that certain pictures and parts of pictures may possibly be unsuited to indiscriminate public exhibition (being, if passed, liable to uncontrolled salacious or political advertisement), and yet not unsuited to sober consideration by an unimpassioned sober audience.'[51]

They went on to add that some scenes 'unsuitable for public show, may, by virtue of beautiful photography or ingenious lighting, be proper food for study by those more concerned with technique than with subject'.[52] The Film Society thus used its intellectual and respectable status as a cultural weapon, drawing a qualitative difference between its members and the audience that attended commercial cinemas. Its own audience was sober, reasonable, unimpassioned, in contrast to the general public, who were unreasonable and impressionable. This proved to be a skilful move, as such binary demarcations were already in cultural circulation and so seemed credible.

There was an intensification of hostilities between the LCC and the Film Society when the latter began to show Soviet propaganda films. The LCC's approach would undoubtedly have been influenced by hostile press reactions to these screenings. The LCC warned the Film Society that it should not show anything 'likely to be injurious to morality or to encourage or incite to crime'.[53]

A further source of conflict between the two organizations related to the 1909 Cinematograph Films Act, which empowered local authorities to safeguard theatres from the fire risks involved in projecting 35mm nitrate films. The LCC was concerned about the Film Society screening uncensored films to press representatives, which it deemed illegal. While the Act was not originally concerned with censorship, the LCC was using it to try and block the screening of uncensored films. Montagu argued that although there was nothing said about censorship in the bill, there was also nothing *not* said about censorship, which meant that local authorities were entitled to include censorship in the terms of their licence grants.[54]

Many letters of accusation were sent to the Film Society, who replied with staunch defences of their actions. The conflict was never resolved as such; it dissipated when the furore over Soviet propaganda died down, highlighting how the LCC was acting on outside pressure. It was as a result of such conflicts that Ivor Montagu became actively involved in protesting against some of the stringent censorship rules, and published a pamphlet, *The Political Censorship of Films* (1929), that explained his views. In this pamphlet, Montagu argued that the BBFC could only be replaced by legislative revision, and was thus 'unofficially' being controlled by government demands. He noted that neither the 1909 Films Act nor the 1927 Quota Act 'discussed nor expressly approved' censorship regulations 'at the time of their passage' and called for an overhaul of the censorship system, so that the censors were more open and 'official' about their operations.[55]

Through the defence of its own objectives in the face of hostility, and through its determination to enable more favourable conditions for the flourishing of a specialized film culture, the Film Society became involved in a number of legal appeals. In its fourth season (1928–29) it was responsible for bringing to the attention of the Board of Trade a possible consequence of the Quota Act by which the exhibition of specialist films in England might have been prevented, and thus it attempted to change this aspect of the Act to safeguard such exhibition.[56] By the end of the fifth season the Film Society had been represented on a deputation to the home secretary in connection with a parliamentary committee on censorship, and was promised a formal inquiry into censorship problems. It was through this that the Film Society was invited to give its views on a proposed international convention for the remission of custom duties on educational films. The late 1930s saw the Film Society, in conjunction with other film societies and repertory cinemas, involved in trying to limit the proposed increase in import duty on foreign films. The rise in import duty eventually went through in 1939, and although there was a reduction for specialist films, the duty was still raised from 1d to 2d (per foot of film).

There was also much discussion in the press about the films the Society showed, but it was not the censorship issue that first brought the Society to the attention of the press. Newspapers took a great interest in the Film Society from its very inception, which demonstrates that it possessed significant cultural capital. The trade press were largely dismissive of the Film Society: in the *Bioscope*, the Society was criticized for its reliance upon the marginal, the writer arguing that a ' "critical tradition" can hardly be established by an intensive study of the film producer's failures, however brilliant those failures, in some cases, may be'.[57] This point provoked a response from Iris Barry, who argued that quality could not be equated with quantity (while also defending some commercial works as art).[58] In many senses, Barry was right: it is these 'critical failures', more than popular commercial films, that constituted a critical tradition, which points to the importance of the Film Society's role in contributing to a shifting, yet historically established, 'canon' of excellent films.

Many films that the Society showed were dismissed as either boring or freakish, although in a harmless, eccentric manner. Thus, when it screened *Battleship Potemkin* many papers, while remarking on the distasteful politics of the film, thought that the Film Society should be allowed to see it because, unlike members of the public, they would not be so influenced by the propagandist message. Its intellectual, 'respectable', marginal reputation at first protected the Society: the papers defending it in the same terms as they defended themselves from censorship stipulations. In contrast, the LCC decided to ban the London Workers' Film Society from showing *Potemkin*, an act that was condemned by Bertrand Russell, who challenged the preferential treatment of one organization over another.[59]

The fact that the Society continually showed Soviet propaganda films, in line with the growing interest in left-wing politics and the increase in workers' film organizations, in the end made many people nervous. The Society was accused of being a communist organization and the initiator of the wave of interest in propaganda films. While it remained 'other', its image was transformed from a harmless freak show into a sinister, undercover operation. A typical view of the Society as being made up of undercover propagandists came from G.A. Atkinson, a former member of the Society, who wrote:

> Its membership is drawn chiefly from influential and well to do people whose interests are best described by the word 'cultural', and from university lecturers, school teachers, educational publicists, and others connected with the instruction of youth, the result being that its performances have a propaganda value far beyond that which would be attached to ordinary film exhibitions.[60]

Many other similar accusations followed. Even *The Times*, which was often supportive of the Society, became less so once questions of propaganda were raised. In addition, the question of Soviet films being shown was brought to the House of Commons, although it did not receive much serious attention and no laws were passed in relation to the topic.[61] The

Conservative Party did, however, issue a memorandum on Soviet Film Propaganda. In it, every aspect of the Film Society's functioning was interpreted as a veiled attempt to encourage Soviet invasion and subversion. The Film Society denied any such accusations, stating that it was merely an organization dedicated to the study of film art, and that it was interested in Soviet films because of their mastery of film technique.[62]

Another assault upon the Film Society came from a completely different angle, from working-class organizations. Instead of attacking the promotion of Bolshevik propaganda, working-class organizations criticized the Film Society on the grounds that it was blunting the political dimension of these films in order to focus upon aesthetic and formal qualities. In an article in the *Plebs*, in which Huntley Carter dealt with the issue of a working-class cinema, he attacked the Film Society, saying that: 'Their obvious game was the subordination of revolutionary and social content to the technique of aesthetic [sic], to fix the attention of the workers not on Eisenstein's or Pudovkin's Marxian message, but on their "montage".'[63] This was a strange accusation, considering that 'workers' would not have been in regular attendance at the Society's screenings. Nevertheless, the challenge to appreciating artistic excellence for its own sake, as against art being used in the service of a broader political objective, is a tension that has characterized theoretical and critical work on film at various times throughout history.

The Film Society members were thus criticized for being radical subversives on the one hand and apolitical aesthetes on the other. For many patriotic conservatives it was a leftist, radical organization; for many communist activists it was socially apathetic, a stuffy and elitist establishment perpetuating the status quo. In a sense, both of these perceptions were correct. The Film Society was primarily involved in formal and technical study: it did not aim to change the structure of society but was trying to encourage a climate in which artistic filmmaking could thrive. At the same time, this aim did entail certain activities—such as the screening of Communist films, and challenges to the way that films were received and perceived—that went against the grain of conventional opinion and were thus labelled radical. Some members of the Communist Party were also members of the Film Society, but this did not make it a centre for the promotion of Bolshevik propaganda. After all, Soviet films of this nature only accounted for a small, albeit significant, proportion of its overall programming.

The Establishment of a Network

As I have mentioned, the Film Society was not the first British group of its kind, but those elements that preceded it were often small and piecemeal, and did not grow into substantial cultural nodes. The Society was, for a minority cultural outlet, a significant party that systematically established an alternative film culture in Britain. It not only forged links with many other like-minded societies elsewhere in the world—thus creating an unofficial international network that aided distribution and the exchange of information—but also helped stimulate a number of other cultural organizations. Some film production and film writing that bore its influence will be discussed separately, but it is worth mentioning the exhibition outlets that arose in Britain in the wake of the Film Society.

By the beginning of the 1930s there were a number of film societies in operation, including those in Aberdeen, Birmingham, Cambridge, Dundee, Edinburgh, Ipswich, Glasgow, Leicester, Liverpool, Manchester, Oxford and Southampton. I am not trying to claim that the Film Society was some kind of origin from which these non-commercial locations for cinéphiles emerged. It was, however, important and influential to the extent that it demonstrated that such an institution could operate, and also because it actively encouraged the setting up of new societies and provided them with support. For example, the Society assisted with the construction of programmes in Birmingham, Cambridge, Dundee, Edinburgh, Glasgow and Oxford.[64] It therefore was key in establishing an informal national network of key metropolitan sites, which aided distribution and pooled information useful to setting up and running a society. It was a network that also reaped the benefits of substantial international connections.

The Film Society not only encouraged the emergence of non-commercial exhibition outlets, it also succeeded in influencing similar patterns of film screenings. The Edinburgh Film Guild, for example, which began in 1929, programmed regular screenings that were similar to the Film Society's, particularly in their reliance on certain German and Soviet features, many of which had been shown at the Society. The Edinburgh programme also featured lectures, debates, film production courses, as well as a few exhibitions.[65] A similar pattern was followed by several other societies. The Film Society was also influential in setting up the Federation of Film Societies in 1932, whose intention was to 'pool together information for the common interests of its members, to organise collective representation, and to explore the possibilities of co-operative booking'.[66] This was not a great success, and in 1936 a further attempt was made following a meeting in Leicester but did not fully take off until after the Second World War.[67] The independent Scottish Films Council, formed in 1934, was more successful in coordinating the interests of Scottish film societies.[68] Initially formed out of the Glasgow Film Society, the Edinburgh Film Guild and the Aberdeen Film Society, the Federation eventually launched its own journal at the end of the decade, entitled *Film Forum*.[69]

In addition to helping directly with the organization and programming of like-minded film societies that belonged to the Federation, the Film Society can also be linked to the emergence of other types of film groups, such as specialist commercial cinemas, or commercial cinemas that were more likely to show the occasional Continental production. Examples include the Shaftesbury Avenue Pavilion, which opened in 1927, and the Regent Street Polytechnic, which opened in 1929. More specialist cinemas opened in the 1930s, including Studio One, the Paris and the Canon. The most famous was the Academy in Oxford Street (set up by former Film Society member Elsie Cohen), which showed a number of (non-British) European films. Repertories were also opened in Leeds and Liverpool by the end of the 1920s, and the Cosmo Cinema opened in Glasgow in 1939.[70] The Film Society was the first institution to demonstrate that there was a regular, if only minority, demand for films that differed from the standard fare of commercial cinemas.

Despite the hostility from many involved in workers' film organizations towards the Film Society's aesthetically oriented programmes, the workers' movement was certainly influenced by the Society in certain ways. Not only were some of the people involved with the Film Society actively involved in workers' film groups, but the movement itself was an alternative take upon the 'aesthetic' film societies. The workers' societies inflected the movement in a more political direction, but the way in which they operated and even many of the films that they showed were very similar to the more 'aesthetic' societies. This line of development greatly influenced the whole area of alternative film culture, and led to a growing rejection of excessive formalism. However, this was not a completely clear-cut demarcation, and there were overlaps. For example, in Chapter 4, I will look at some of the films made with a primarily political purpose that nevertheless incorporated some aspects of formalist experimentation. In some respects, the attacks on the Film Society were excessive: while the Society was primarily a space in which aesthetic aspects of film were appreciated, it did not oppose the more political aspects of film culture that arose, and in turn became influenced by such developments.

The Film Society also had links with the British Film Institute (BFI), which was founded in 1933, with aims and objectives very similar to those of the Film Society. It was established as: 'a means of furthering effective co-operation between those who make, distribute and exhibit films on the one hand, and all who are interested in the artistic, educational and cultural possibilities of using film on the other'.[71] The BFI was formed out of a proposal put forward by the Commission on Educational and Cultural Films in its 1932 report *The Film in National Life*. It became feasible in 1932 when the government, through the Sunday Entertainment Act, established a Cinematograph Fund to be used for the development of film as a means of entertainment and instruction. The BFI constitutional agreement was reached between representatives of the film trade and representatives of the educational and cultural interests of the country, who included members of the Film Society.[72] Importantly, a large stock of films that the Film Society had accrued through its operations formed the core of the National Film Archive at the outbreak of the Second World War.[73]

Writing on Film

In addition to the emergence of an alternative exhibition structure, and informal distribution networks, there was a rise in serious writing about cinema in the 1920s. The Film Society itself propagated some of this via their programme notes, but attitudes towards film from British cinéphiles can also be found in a number of other sources: in occasional newspaper articles, in specialist journals, and in full-length books about cinema. During the 1920s, the most influential and sustained body of writing was published in the journal *Close Up*, which will be the main focus of this section on pre-sound discourse. I will also look at other views on film in the Film Society programme notes and in books written on the art of cinema.

Iris Barry and the Film Society Programme Notes

Before *Close Up*, 'serious' writing that treated cinema as an important new art appeared sporadically in literary journals, newspapers and, more regularly, in the Film Society programme notes. A founding member of the Film Society, Iris Barry was one of the most important writers to establish a regular film column before the establishment of the Film Society, writing in the literary journal the *Spectator*, as well as in the popular newspaper the *Daily Mail*, which was the highest circulation newspaper in Britain in

1925.[74] As Haidee Wasson notes, while Barry's discursive style would have been influenced by different editorial and readership concerns, as well as advertising revenue, her views remained quite coherent across separate publications, and were also propounded in her 1926 book *Let's Go to the Movies*.

Barry was concerned with creative expression in movies and her writing was firmly aimed at establishing cinema as an art. Thus, she both frequently referred to the strengths of the medium in an ontological sense, but also to some of the main directors who could harness such strengths into an artistic totality. Artistic strengths of the medium included camera movement and editing, in particular to create a visual rhythm or dramatic suspense. Like many writers connected to alternative film culture, at least up until the 1930s, she stressed the importance of innovating within a dramatic framework, and argued that 'artistic' films could be popular.

Barry also expressed a number of other beliefs central to alternative film discourse: a distaste for excessive sentimentality; a belief in cinematic progress and experimentation (favoured when developed within a narrative framework); an emphasis on coherence, so that each part of a film should contribute to its totality; a belief that artists should have more control in commercial filmmaking so that it is easier for them to express themselves; and a conception of cinema as a living thing, so that films are viewed as organic wholes, with cinematic progress defined in evolutionary terms. Last, but not least, she emphasized national trends in reductive terms, which involved a rather negative view of British cinema as opposed to other styles. Nevertheless, she did often address the 'problem' of British cinema, and began to sketch out what she thought British cinema should attempt to achieve. The tendency to nationalize cinematic trends and styles can, of course, lead to a negative dismissal of national filmmaking, as well as a more positive attempt to prescribe nationally specific ways in which cinematic art should develop. Barry vacillated between the two, but was much more optimistic than many of the writers associated with *Close Up*, which I address in the next section. She argued that, rather than slavishly copying Hollywood or relying upon provincial conceptions of the nation, British films should incorporate a host of international advances in a way that was still recognizably British.[75]

The Film Society programme notes were written by Ivor Montagu until 1929, when he resigned as chairman of the Film Society to devote more time to workers' film societies. Subsequent writers of the notes include Thorold Dickinson, Sidney Cole and Jack Isaacs.[76] They provided a framework or template by which films could be approached intellectually, often placing films within some kind of historical context. This could be the history of the production of the film, the history of a 'movement' out of which the film emerged, or the history of a film's 'artist'. As time passed, the Society began to place more emphasis upon the particular styles of directors whom it thought to be of particular note, rather than the actual 'personal history' of the artist. While historical or contextual concerns did not disappear, they were displaced by a greater emphasis upon formal concerns. The wider context of production sometimes came to be regarded only in so far as it hindered the artistic expression of an individual 'genius'. For example, notes accompanying the special screening of *October* (Eisenstein, USSR, 1928; performance 70, 11 March 1934) explained that the film had been criticized for being incoherent and episodic, but that this was due to shoddy post-production work. All the 'faults' of the film were thus attributed to the extra-biographical determinants and a picture was painted of an artistic genius battling against the forces of industrial restrictions.

The identification of a unique style became one of the major aesthetic interests of the Film Society. Interest in *The Marriage Circle* (USA, 1924; performance 4, 17 January 1926) centred upon the way that the director Ernst Lubitsch had developed an individual cinematic language, similar to Chaplin's, but 'smoothly expanded'. The absence of flashbacks, fade-outs and close-ups is noted, as well as the unfolding of the narrative entirely in images (the 'drastic reduction of continuity sub-titles').[77] Although Lubitsch was not credited with the innovation of such techniques, he was credited with their development, and therefore imbued with a progressive quality. In the notes to *Kaleidoscope* (UK, 1935; performance 88, 26 April 1936), Len Lye was credited with having 'developed an entirely new method of using colour movement in synchronisation with music'.[78] Dziga Vertov's approach to filmmaking was also seen as unique through his attempts 'at a cinematic language uninfluenced by literature or theatre'.[79]

The predilection for stylistic innovation of a coherent nature can partly be linked to the way that the programme notes cited the theoretical perspectives of directors, either through reference or direct quotation. For example, they referred to Ruttman's attempts to concern himself objectively with the filmstrip, or to Eisenstein's theory of ideological montage, or to Pudovkin's contrapuntal conception of sound. Accompanying the screening of Vertov's *Enthusiasm* (USSR, 1931; performance 49, 6 December 1931) there was even an additional supplement: a two-page explanation of the film, plus theoretical notes by Vertov, in which he updated his kino-eye theory in relation to sound.

The Film Society was drawn to such theoretical ideas, for they helped relate the film text to the coherent world-view of an individual artist. In addition, theoretical discussions were important to the Film Society for they bestowed intellectual validity upon cinema, boosting its status as a modern art. The absorption of Soviet film theory certainly appears to have influenced the programme notes. After the screenings of Soviet films became regular, the notes began to take on a more acutely theoretical edge themselves. A deeper, formal structure began to be discussed within the notes more regularly, which was distinguished from mere surface content. Great cinematic art was soon coded as containing interest on both levels. The analysis of what lay beyond manifest content countered those who dismissed film as mere entertainment. Such formal analysis recognized in the medium of film a capacity to deal with complex structural configurations, which validated film as high art.

Closely related to the search for a unique cinematic style was an interest in aesthetic experimentation. This freedom of the artist to play around with film style was often foregrounded, especially in relation to some of the avant-garde shorts that were shown. Experimentation and a unique individual style were admired for being progressive interventions in the film medium. A 'style' was privileged both because it was associated with a coherent artistic personality and because it was seen as a fully developed harnessing of innovative traits. Experimentation, on the other hand, represented a less coherent indicator of progressiveness: a hint at artistic avenues that could be developed, but which remained open. Experimentation was thus 'laboratory work' that had not quite been moulded into a symbol of individual creativity. In this sense, the Film Society was promoting coherence, of both identity and the employment of cinematic techniques.

Experimentation may have been encouraged, but the Society deemed more subtle diversions from cinematic norms as more 'progressive' than radical disruptions of those standards. Radical disruptions were not frowned upon, but they seemed to constitute something slightly too chaotic to be comfortably classed as art. After all, this was a culture attempting to promote the cinema as a significant art form, which involved the imposition of aesthetic customs. Chaotic disruptions in this sense were difficult to appropriate. In order to progress, cinematic art had to exist in a state of becoming, moving towards ever-higher modes of perfection. For this to happen, some kind of coherence and balance needed to be established. For the Film Society, this was evident in its promotion of a unique style. This involved the encouragement of an artistic vision, presupposing a coherent identity that was traceable throughout a filmmaker's body of work, but which could modify and change style so that it did not stagnate.

Such an aesthetic was not the only identifiable way by which the Film Society heralded certain films. As I have mentioned, it did see experimentation as a positive attribute, and endorsed films that were outside the norms of commercial cinematic practice, as well as films that were seen to represent the technical and educational possibilities of the cinematic medium. Slapstick comedy, for example, was a mode of filmmaking that was looked upon favourably, despite the fact that it was a genre that did not strictly fit into the aesthetic framework. In line with Gilbert Seldes, who wrote of the artistic qualities of slapstick comedy in his 1924 book *The Seven Lively Arts*, many cinéphiles thought this genre of filmmaking—through its pace and photographic tricks—was a uniquely cinematic form.[80] Overall, though, the notes favoured coherence: what were considered 'great' works of cinematic art coordinated all of its constituent parts into an 'organic' whole.

This reliance on a model of organic coherence and privileging of experimentation within narrative frameworks meant that, while British cinéphiles were eager to distinguish the cinema from the theatre and literature, they were reliant upon critical models that stemmed from such artistic media. This type of speculation into the art of cinema was also evident in criticism in countries such as France and Germany.[81] For example, in France Daimant-Berger and others thought that the exclusivity of cinema should be worked out within a dramatic, often narrative, framework. Daimant-Berger argued that the uniqueness of cinema lay in *découpage*, or cinematic editing.[82] Such groping towards what the cinema could be, encased within a narrative or dramatic framework, was the route the Film Society took, along with many other critics and theorists, in order to locate the artistic properties of film.[83]

The Film Society's conception of cinematic aesthetics should, then, be linked to ideas circulating in other countries. Such a framework was certainly very broad and could encapsulate films as different as *Battleship Potemkin* and *The Cabinet of Dr. Caligari*. The very broadness of the framework, however, meant that it was enduring and could persist when arguments about cinematic essence were in transition. Such an aesthetic notion was rather traditional and literary, harking back as it did to Hellenistic thought and, in Britain, to critics such as Matthew Arnold, who stressed the harmony of culture. It is interesting that Arnold thought that the work of literary genius was involved in 'synthesis and exposition' rather than analysis and discovery—which was seen as the preserve of scientists and philosophers.[84] This is similar to the manner in which the Society privileged an innovative style over mere experiment.

Close Up

Many of the discursive features detectable in the Film Society programme notes can also be found among various writings in *Close Up*. This journal represented the most extensive attempt to analyse film as art in Britain before the mid-1930s, and has been described by David Bordwell as perhaps 'the most internationally important journal' of the inter-war years.[85] While the Film Society programme notes only had a limited space in which to broach concepts, *Close Up* was able to discuss these ideas more thoroughly and passionately. Whereas the Film Society was established in order to showcase films that represented an alternative to the mainstream cinema, and often embodied the idea of the cinema as a modern, unique art form, *Close Up* was eager to corroborate and propagate such attitudes in an almost belligerent manner.

First published in July 1927, *Close Up* ran until December 1933. It was initially published as a monthly journal, but from March 1931 it became a quarterly. The journal was published by the POOL enterprise, which was initially a collaboration between Kenneth Macpherson, Bryher (whose real name was Annie Winifred Ellerman) and H.D. (whose real name was Hilda Doolittle).[86] In addition to *Close Up*, POOL published several books, covering literature, film criticism and memoirs, and made four films, which are discussed in Chapter 7. The trio of collaborators were all from literary backgrounds: H.D., of course, was a poet; assistant editor Bryher was a writer of novels and verse; editor Kenneth Macpherson was interested in many arts, including photography and literature, and his first novel, *Poolreflection*, was published by POOL in the spring of 1927.[87]

As Bryher received constant financial support from her family fortune, the POOL enterprise had a great deal of financial freedom.[88] This meant that *Close Up* was able to exist without having to advertise, and did not have to compromise itself for the sake of commercial survival. Macpherson and Bryher were married and lived in Territet, Switzerland, from where most of the magazine was edited. This Continental base allowed them to watch a whole range of international films that would not have been accessible in Britain. According to Roland Cosandey, this was because Switzerland had no protectionist measures in place before the arrival of sound, and was therefore an eclectic centre for the screening of international film.[89] Macpherson wrote in *Close Up* of their location: 'We see films as soon as they are released. Heavy advanced booking is not made. And we read six months after we have seen them of films reaching London and New York.'[90]

Although the journal was edited mostly from Switzerland and was fiercely international, it was still a British journal. It placed itself primarily within a British context and attempted to transform British film culture. Its European base, however, clearly influenced its desire to transform Britain into a more eclectic centre for film culture. It was first published in France because of the favourable exchange rate. Five hundred copies of the early editions were printed and were sent to bookshops in Paris, Berlin, London, Geneva, New York and Los Angeles. Twelve months later, publication was transferred to Mercury Press in London, and London offices for the journal were announced on the back cover of the August 1928 edition. *Close Up* was small and independent, and managed to become a very influential cultural force. It must therefore be aligned with the many other small-scale, literary magazines that emerged in the 1920s, such as T.S. Eliot's *The Criterion* and Wyndham Lewis's *The Tyro*.

While *Close Up* covered a broad range of subjects and featured contributions from many writers, diversity was, to an extent, circumscribed by editorial concerns and judgement. The editors may have disagreed with some of the articles that they included, but they still found them of interest. The editorial board thus gave the journal a coherence amid its diversity. This chimes with the general trend of the small magazines of the period, according to John Lucas, who sees them as being marked by a fragmentary structure and a coherent editorial policy.[91]

In its first few issues *Close Up* was concerned with establishing cinema as a modern art form. Traditional aesthetic notions were employed in order to defend the medium, but these were mixed with an emphasis upon the mechanical nature of the medium, which hinted at its radical modernity. This uneasy fusing between the aesthetic and the mechanical led to some rather contradictory attitudes: the popular nature of the medium was occasionally thought of positively; at other times it was considered an embarrassment. The journal often expressed a contemptuous attitude towards what it perceived as the glut of 'formulaic' films being churned out and the mass public that was happy to consume them. On the other hand, the journal could utilize the cinema's mass appeal as one of its attractions: an indication of the medium's universal appeal and its extreme power. Bryher argued that, while the majority of Hollywood films were not very good, the whole industry was responsible for technical accomplishments that were necessary for the overall progression of the medium.[92] The mass nature of the cinema, then, fed into the technical advances that appealed to many of the journal's writers.

For this reason, *Close Up* believed that an advance guard could operate within the confines of the commercial industry. So, along similar lines to the Film Society, it encouraged independent and amateur film activities, but privileged commercial films that incorporated innovative and 'uniquely cinematic' elements. The journal desired more amateur and independent experiments and more artistic freedom within the commercial sector. It believed that both the commercial and independent spheres could be improved and could positively influence each other. Thus Macpherson argued that: 'The real plant will have taken nourishment from an improving commercial standard, and spread its roots there. And finally there will be co-ordination. A treaty perhaps, or a more subtle agreement—a growing together. And by that time the power of film will be immense beyond prediction.'[93]

So, following the established line of alternative discourse, *Close Up* believed experimentation should be incorporated within narrative-centred, dramatic frameworks, often relying upon the superior technical resources of the commercial film industry. This led the journal to take a harsh view of 'avant-garde' film when it became cloistered and 'inward looking'. Though it championed many abstract and experimental shorts, the journal was sceptical when these attempted to sever all relations with the commercial film world.[94]

In a similar vein to the Film Society, *Close Up* admired 'artistic' features from Germany and the Soviet Union. Many German films were admitted for qualities such as movement, visual patterns, technical sophistication and stylized acting. They were also respected because they had a much more intellectual appeal than most Hollywood fare because of their seriousness and emphasis on psychology. It was this latter aspect that most attracted *Close Up*: its core writers were interested in cinema that appealed to the psychology of the spectator and dealt with psychological issues. While this element was also apparent in previous alternative discourse, it became more marked in the writings in *Close Up* and proved more enduring, not least because of Bryher, H.D. and Macpherson's interest in psychoanalysis. *Close Up* tended to evaluate films with frequent reference to psychological notions. For example, Bryher wrote of G.W. Pabst, who was one of the editorial board's favourite directors: 'He sees psychologically and because of this, because in a flash he knows the sub-conscious impulse or hunger that prompted an apparently trivial action, his intense realism becomes its truth, poetry.'[95]

In addition to aesthetic evaluation related to psychology, the journal often printed articles on the experience of cinema going, most notably through the regular contributions from Dorothy M. Richardson.[96] Such work foreshadowed later theorists such as Christian Metz, who speculated upon the subjective, psychological aspects of cinema viewing.

Like the Film Society, *Close Up* eventually began to lose interest in German films. Even though it continued to favour a few German directors, especially Pabst, it became far more interested in Soviet montage productions. Macpherson was impressed by the dynamic tempo of these films, and argued that Russian films had initiated a 'new technique' and contributed to the 'regeneration, or rather the revolution of the film' by finding a new adaptation of and use for the medium.[97] As with the Film Society, Eisenstein and Pudovkin became, once again, the most celebrated directors; praise was also given to Room, Starbovoj and Preobrashenskaja.

Many of the political aspects of Soviet films, though, were downplayed. The reactions to these films were certainly not homogeneous, but they did tend to share one thing in common: they interpreted the political content of these films in a metaphorical, 'universal' way. Macpherson interpreted them in a humanist and psychological manner. For him, the films represented an intellectual, spiritual and complex use of the medium. H.D. felt that the films could be seen in biblical terms, as religious parables.[98] Robert Herring, meanwhile, interpreted the work of Eisenstein in purely aesthetic terms. He argued that Eisenstein's art worked on two levels: visually, through repetition of design, which reached the viewer's subconscious, and dramatically, through composition, in which objects became charged with symbolic value.[99]

The reaction to Soviet films, as well as film theory emanating from Eisenstein, Pudovkin and others, shifted the emphasis of what was important within a film: montage and location shooting now became important aspects of film aesthetics. Nevertheless, these films could still fit into prevailing frameworks that *Close Up* valued: cinematic progression, dramatic structure and psychological concerns. In the psychological sense, the films themselves may not have attempted to probe the character's minds, but they were seen to create complex psychological relations between the artist and the audience.

Close Up did actually publish a number of influential articles by Soviet theorists. Many of these were related to sound and I will return to them at a later stage. For the purposes of looking at how Soviet ideas were modified within *Close Up*, however, it is worth referring to Eisenstein's 'The Fourth Dimension of the Kino'.[100] In this article, Eisenstein discussed his theory of overtonal montage, in which each shot is said to contain a 'dominant' meaning and a host of 'overtonal' meanings. Overtonal montage was a process of editing according to 'a-dominant' principles: the editing of all rhythmic and sensual nuances of combined pieces according to the 'psycho-physiological' (as opposed to narrative) vibrations of each piece. The qualities of this editing could not therefore be traced in a static frame, only within the dynamics of the cinematic process.

In his introduction to the article, Macpherson ignored the dialectic aspects of Eisenstein's theories. Rather, he emphasized the organic nature of this process, which would lead to the natural replacement of ignorance by education, culture and discipline. Macpherson also painted a picture of Eisenstein as an artistic genius who was aiding the progression of film form through expressing his artistic vision within the confines of a 'grammatically imposed' context.[101] Macpherson also replaced Eisenstein's emphasis on the physiological with an emphasis on the psychic, thus substituting a behavioural mode of psychology with a more psychoanalytical mode. For Macpherson, overtonal montage was ultimately editing according to the principles of the unconscious.

Many Soviet films were seen as merging industrial and artistic concerns in a progressive manner. The fact that these films were widely seen reinforced the idea that a populist-progressive cinema was feasible. There is no doubt that many people did watch some of the more experimental Soviet films: *Battleship Potemkin*, for example, was seen by a huge number of people worldwide and appealed to both popular and intellectual audiences.[102] However, even if some of these films were popular, *Close Up* did tend to overplay their popularity and any integral connection between a progressive form of cinema and the psychology of popular audiences. Denise J. Youngblood has argued that there was a sharp division between mass and elite opinion in Soviet Russia, and that native critics often exaggerated the popularity of 'montage' films.[103]

The first two or three years of *Close Up* were, then, marked by the establishment of the cinema as an art along particular lines that continued pre-existing cultural interests. Beside the issues that I have already broached it is also significant that *Close Up* was fiercely committed to cinema as an international art, an idea that it frequently referred to. The very notion of internationalism was ingrained in the journal's identity. Not only was it written by British people writing in exile, and published in Paris and then London, it also had an international network of contributors, with correspondents in Paris, London, Hollywood, New York, Berlin and Geneva. These correspondents—often centrally involved in alternative culture in their own countries—subtended the editorial team's contributions, adding more specific, local information to the editors' more general observations.[104]

Although the journal drew on pre-existing cultural values and critical perspectives, it also differed from established aspects of alternative culture in two main ways. First, it extended the hostility towards British cinema so that it became, for a while at least, an almost hysterical prejudice (discussed further in the next section). Second, while alternative culture was marked by a psychological interest, *Close Up* tended to emphasize a more psychoanalytical mode than was common in alternative culture; while, at the end of the 1920s, many people involved in alternative culture were moving away from interiority, *Close Up* always stressed the importance of subjective psychology.

Close Up: Production and British Cinema

One of the actual aims of the Film Society was an attempt to influence British filmmaking through exposing production personnel to a wide array of international filmmaking, but most particularly European modernist influences. Such a desire expressed covert dissatisfaction with British cinema, dissatisfaction more clearly expressed in the criticism of Society council member Iris Barry, in which British cinema is portrayed as either lacking the skill and continuity of American pictures, or the intelligence and artistic sophistication of German films. This antipathy towards British films was more marked in *Close Up*, which attempted to encourage new forms of British production to emerge so that improvement could take place.

Prior to the consolidation of sound cinema, *Close Up* believed that a transformation of commercial British film culture should take place from the bottom up; it was hoped that a healthy amateur movement would provide the breeding ground for new auteurs who might infiltrate the industry and thus change its foundations. Macpherson believed that there were 'geniuses' waiting to be found, who could construct 'new facts of film'.[105] As I will demonstrate, however, the journal's attempts to encourage an alternative British film movement in the production area were seriously undermined by two factors: the aesthetic preferences of the journal and its more general views about the compatibility of the terms 'British' and 'good filmmaking'.

The main way in which *Close Up* attempted to foster a healthy amateur movement was by giving technical tips on how films could be made on a small-scale budget, often by amateur filmmakers themselves.[106] The journal gave coverage to the films made by film societies, but while it wanted to foster a healthy independent movement, its own coverage worked against this. *Close Up* was more interested in artistic commercial films, and its interest in small-scale independent films was secondary to this. It therefore only gave marginal coverage to 'independent' or 'amateur' films within Britain. Nearly all of the extended textual analyses, or summaries of crucial 'movements', were about films that could be described, in today's terms, as 'art' cinema, or films that had 'cross-over' potential. Films made on extremely low budgets were hardly ever given aesthetic consideration; instead they languished in the 'Comment and Review' section, where they received only passing reference. There were very few exceptions to this; for instance, MacPherson cited Robert Florey and Slavko Vorkapich's *The Life and Death of 9413* (USA, 1928) as an example of how a good film could be made on a low budget, along with films by Joris Ivens, Man Ray and Walter Ruttman.[107] Another of the very few low-budget films to be truly admired as great was Alberto Cavalcanti's *Rien que les Heures* (France, 1926). Significantly, none of these films was British.

In a letter to *Close Up* in 1927, J.A. Hardy touched on some major points in relation to the journal's aesthetics. He suggested that cinema was not an artistic but a commercial medium, which therefore made it extremely difficult for amateurs to take part; even if they did get involved in film production, the quality of their films would be negatively influenced by their small budgets.[108] Though Macpherson argued that £100 will 'make a film as noble as anything you can wish to see', this was in fact a disingenuous comment, for the aesthetic preferences evident in the journal's criticism did not conform to such a belief. There was therefore a chasm between its advocacy of a cheap, amateur, independent film movement developing from the grassroots, and the general artistic line it promoted. Its aesthetic preferences stemmed from a desire to establish cinema as a unique medium that could produce great artistic works, or 'classics'. It therefore perceived 'quality' to be a sophisticated property, which might be extracted from the viewing of films made on a reasonably large scale. Amateur films were of a different order, and would have to be judged by different standards to commercial films. Yet, although the journal did take into consideration the different circumstances under which these films were made, they always placed them on a lower hierarchical plane than those films that conformed to their aesthetic ideals. The value of amateur and independent films mostly lay in what they could contribute to large-scale film production, so that they once again constituted a kind of 'laboratory work'.

So, while *Close Up* did genuinely desire independent film activity, it could not bring itself to champion such filmmaking in the same manner as it supported films by, say, Eisenstein or Pabst. There were a few exceptions, as I have shown. Yet even films by Ivens and Man Ray, although admired, did not feature in the journal's top-rank canon that often appeared in its back pages. Thus the amateur film movement was relegated to a marginal aesthetic position in the journal. As this was one of the few outlets where such films would have gained media space in the late 1920s, this must also be seen as a major cause of the fact that many British amateur films of this period have 'disappeared' and thus elude the possibility of historical revaluation. Whether or not they would have been more favourably evaluated under more recent aesthetic frameworks cannot be determined.

An additional factor that worked against the promotion of an independent and amateur British film movement in the latter half of the 1920s was the journal's intense hostility to British film production itself, which permeated the journal at almost every level for at least its first two years. Even though it did abate somewhat, such prejudice still informed subsequent commentary. Thus, even when some favourable reviews were given to British films, they were still couched in language that viewed the British as unable to compete at the level of German or Russian films. For instance, Hugh Castle argued in 1929 that some British productions were getting better, but they were not quite great. Productions such as Walter Summers' *The Lost Patrol* (UK, 1929) were seen as good films, but still lacking in originality: 'It may still be imitation American, but it is better imitation than it once was.'[109] This type of attitude, on one level, may be seen as a reflection upon the state of British filmmaking, but it also influenced the way in which future British productions were viewed, to the extent that they were forever relegated to a place in the shadows of other filmmaking nations. Such aesthetic views reveal that much international thinking was still informed by a nationally inflected language, in which films reflected innate, and enduring, characteristics of an entire nation. 'Britishness', for *Close Up*, was connected to a nostalgic and patriotic ideology and was thus seen in negative terms. So, if British films were recognizably British they were criticized; if they were seen to adopt traits connected to other nationalities, they were labelled imitative.

As *Close Up* was, for most of its existence, informed by this extreme anti-British prejudice, the attempt to foster an amateur and independent production movement was doomed. Ultimately, the journal's beliefs meant that a transformation in British film culture would have to take place primarily in the exhibition arena. The main priority was to get good films (mostly foreign films) shown in Britain in order to show the anti-cinema brigade that 'film' and 'art' were compatible. It is noteworthy that when Bryher made her suggestions about starting a film club she did not think that there were any English films worthy of being shown in such a programme.[110] Although I do not suggest that this is the only reason why such films have not been documented or acclaimed in any manner, I do feel that it is a significant factor, since *Close Up*, with its emphasis on promoting alternative culture, was the only British journal at the time where such films could have gained extensive promotion. Other factors include the lack of amateur cooperation within the country, leading to a paucity of resources. Orlton West, who expressed a concern that amateur filmmakers in London lacked organization, discussed the possibilities of collaboration within *Close Up*, encouraging amalgamation in order to make it possible to work with greater resources and achieve better results.[111] Eventually the Amateur Film League of Great Britain and Ireland was formed, but it was not a great success.[112]

In order for attention to be focused upon British cinema in a less negative manner, notions of 'British specificity'—perceived to be different from the more fiercely patriotic and conservative notions—had to be constructed. By the end of the 1920s a softening towards the notion of British cinema had begun, though many older prejudices often underlay prevailing attitudes. Ralph Bond, for example, in arguing against an uninspired and formulaic imitation of Soviet methods (which he saw as prevalent within amateur productions), proposed a cinema that drew upon the modern realities of Britain. He argued that the working classes and problems of social poverty and injustice should be addressed in British films. This is unsurprising, given that Bond played a central role in the development of the workers' film societies and was thus developing a political notion of British filmmaking based on subject matter. When it came to the actual formal modes of representing this subject matter, Bond refrained from laying down any prescriptive methods. Given his criticism of filmmakers who adopted experimental methods connected with other countries, it would seem that he proposed an uncomplicated presentation of events in either narrative or documentary form.

This type of 'realist' aesthetics was much favoured by the workers' film movements emerging at the time. The editorial team of *Close Up* did not take up such a position, though it did influence their openness to the notion of 'British' cinema.[113] Thus, in October 1929, two British films were very well received by the journal: these were *Blackmail* (Hitchcock) and *Drifters* (John Grierson, which will be discussed later in more detail). In the same issue praise was heaped upon a British amateur production: J.H. Ahern and G.H. Sewell's *The Gaiety of Nations* (1929), which was 350 feet, produced on 16mm film stock, made with models and portrayed the life of a city. It was said to be 'a remarkably good essay on creative imagination', with 'excellent' cutting and editing.[114] It is important to note, however, that serious attention to British films only came towards the end of the 1920s. It is no surprise, then, that there are more 'alternative' and non-commercial British films still extant from the 1930s than from the 1920s.

Books on Cinema

There were also more full-length books on cinema arriving in Britain in the late 1920s and early 1930s, which despite their differences also contained a number of similarities. In addition to Barry's *Let's Go to the Movies*, there was Ernest Betts's *Heraclitus, or the Future of Films* (1928), Eric Elliott's *Anatomy of Motion Picture Art* (1928), Robert Herring's *Films of the Year, 1927–28* (1928), Bryher's *Film Problems of Soviet Russia* (1929), Paul Rotha's *The Film Till Now* (1930) and Caroline Lejeune's *Cinema* (1931). We might add to this list Oswell Blakeston's *Through a Yellow Glass* (1928), which though a novel, does address the film industry. Space restrictions prevent me from going into detail on all of these books, so the focus will mainly be on Roth's *The Film Till Now* because it was so influential. Although it was published in 1930 and briefly addresses sound issues, it is mostly a book that belongs to the pre-sound era. Before a detailed examination of Roth's work, we will briefly look at perhaps the two most theoretically oriented of the other books: *Heraclitus, or the Future of Films* and *Anatomy of Motion Picture Art*.

Betts's book looked at film as an art in biological and evolutionary terms. If film remained purely commercial, claimed Betts, there would be no development. Change and progress were necessary if the full artistic potential of the medium was to be realized and the mechanical basis of the medium was to be built upon, as summed up in the phrase 'who will wrest the art from these machines?'[115] Betts acknowledged the mechanical underpinning and the technical brilliance of the cinema and saw them as crucial to the modernity and distinctiveness of the medium. At the same time, he felt that there needed to be more creative input into the artistic side of filmmaking, so that all of the disparate creative segments could be moulded into a unity. For this to happen, an 'autocratic' director must control all of the filmmaking segments and mould them into a whole that expressed his or her vision. Again, then, Betts emphasized individual creativity, organic coherence and progress within the framework of industrial, narrative filmmaking. He believed that a truly artistic film movement could emerge by simplifying the existing cinematic stages, in order to develop a film language 'with a tradition and blood of its own'.[116] This language was defined as essentially visual and as containing fluidity of movement, rhythm and poeticism.

Elliott's *Anatomy of Motion Picture Art* was a more systematic attempt to get to grips with the specificity of the medium. Elliott conceived of cinema as a merging between art and science: he thought theory would have to mix analysis and impression, while a film itself, heavily dependent upon technical considerations, also had to be thought of creatively. Elliott took the familiar line of distinguishing cinema from theatre while still relying on a vision of the cinema as a dramatic medium. He then devoted much space to analysing what he considered as the most artistically important and cinematic techniques, identified as the close-up, the flashback, fluid parallel cuts and various camera tricks. As was common, he stressed that these elements were raw materials that had to be used in a creative manner by film artists.[117]

Paul Rotha had studied design at the Slade School of Art, and worked briefly in the art department at British International Pictures (BIP). Since 1927, he had contributed articles on film to several journals, including *Close Up* and *Film Weekly*, and it was an article written for the latter—criticizing art production for British films—that led to his dismissal from BIP.[118] He wrote *The Film Till Now* during a period in which he was unable to secure regular work within the film industry.

The Film Till Now was ambitious in scope, aiming to provide a world survey of film practice, a theory of the cinema, and offered a series of views typical of alternative cinéphiles. It engaged in a categorization of films that resembled classifications sketched in the Film Society programme notes, and it also surveyed the cinema in a manner that tended to look at films as essentially tied to national character. Thus mass production, 'efficiency' and a general lack of intelligence typified America, but nevertheless Hollywood was responsible for a firm grip on cinematic language, and many of its films had rhythm, pace and spaciousness. Rotha expressed ambivalence towards Hollywood: on the one hand, its efficiency and organization led to sophisticated technical developments; on the other hand, this had resulted in a crushing of individuality and a concomitant lack of sincerity. The few individual innovators who had managed, against the odds, to imprint their personality upon the film represented exceptions to this rule: Griffith and Chaplin were the most privileged in such a hierarchy.

Rotha cited Germany and the Soviet Union as the countries that had produced the most significant cinematic developments in film history, while Britain was attacked for producing too many films that were artificial and imitative. Perhaps the most telling criticism that Rotha made of British cinema was that it had not at this time produced a coherent movement; this meant that Britain was marked by isolated fragments of inspiration that did not cohere into anything substantial. Asquith and Hitchcock produced flashes of brilliance but were ultimately too inconsistent and lacked sincerity.

Like other aesthetes of the cinema, Rotha depended not only on the notion of the cinematic text as an 'organic' and 'coherent' work, in which every part reflected the whole; he also saw nationalities as independent (but interconnected) wholes with their own themes and motifs, which should be expressed in a meaningful way through the cinema. Britain was unable to do this. It had no movement in which independent artists expressed creative visions and exploited themes or formal devices that were representative of national spirit. Rotha seemed unaware of a paradox in his argument here. He continually stressed sincerity of purpose and the independent vision of the artist as paramount, but if such vision did not cohere into something that could be identified through an employment of what critics considered representative of national spirit, they failed to constitute anything substantial. Rotha was therefore, implicitly, relegating the artist as a servant of predisposed national themes. He could thus argue that the British film 'has never been self-sufficient, in that it has never achieved its independence [. . .]. It has no other aim than that of the imitation of the cinema of other countries.'[119]

There were isolated trends that Rotha did identify as significant aspects of British filmmaking, but they were not substantial enough to represent a strong national 'movement'. Nevertheless, they did offer hints of what British filmmaking could achieve and thus served as reference points to be drawn on by future British filmmakers. The trends Rotha identified were: 'reconstructions' of war events made for BIF and New Era, such as *Armageddon* (Woolfe, 1923) and *The Somme* (Wetherell, 1927); the comedies made by Ivor Montagu and H.G. Wells; and the 'Secrets of Nature' series. Rotha also praised Asquith and Hitchcock, but his greatest approval of a British film was given to *Drifters*, which he proclaimed as 'the only film produced in this country that reveals any real evidence of construction, montage of material, or sense of cinema as understood within these pages'.[120]

In the second section of his book, Rotha discussed the aesthetics of the medium in a more abstract and theoretical manner. He developed some familiar notions of cinematic art, based around the individual artist expressing her or himself in a coherent and unified manner. He singled out movement, editing and pictorial composition as extremely important artistic devices and engaged in a lengthy discussion of the ways in which they could be deployed. He placed special emphasis on the role of psychology in the cinema, and in this sense he was somewhat aligned to the editorial team of *Close Up*. He stressed the importance of psychology in three senses: the psychology of characters within a film, the psychology of the artistic force behind a film and the psychology of the spectator watching the film. Within a film, the psychology or 'inner reality' of the characters could be expressed through outward phenomena: 'The camera itself is unable to penetrate the world before it, but the creative mind of the director can reveal in his *selection* of the visual images this intrinsic essence of life by using the basic resources of the cinema, viz., editing, angle, pictorial composition, suggestion, symbolism, etc.'[121]

In the process of organizing a system of representation that tapped into the mind of the characters, the director could also express her or his psychology by constructively organizing the material in a distinctive manner. Rotha then argued that when a viewer watched a film in an 'informed' manner, he or she could become aware of the presence of the director. In this sense, the spectator and director fused psychologically, in a kind of spiritual unity. In contrast, an appreciation of film on a purely entertainment basis was more of a collective, technical experience. Rotha here used the binary distinctions mass/individual and surface/depth to distinguish between the technical and the psychological film.

Although *The Film Till Now* remained firmly locked within the discursive framework of British film writing of the 1920s, it did represent a very slight change from the earlier writings, and thus foreshadowed some of the larger shifts that occurred in the 1930s. For example, Rotha was certainly influenced by the aesthetic attention paid to both objects of modernity (such as machines) and the exterior world of locations as opposed to studios. The first of these is a significant development not clearly evident in many earlier alternative writings, but which would become more influential in the 1930s. The influence of the 'machine complex' is explicitly mentioned by Rotha at one stage, when he notes that many German films in the mid-1920s incorporated 'composite shots of trains, factories, and all types of machinery'; the exposure of wheels in motion was seen as a particularly common trope.[122] The emphasis on exterior, location shooting was influenced by more general trends, and came to be prescribed by many documentary filmmakers in the 1930s. This is something that was already being written about by John Grierson, and such aesthetic discourses will be examined further in Chapter 3.

The writings of Grierson will be discussed separately as not only was much of it written outside the context of Britain (in US publications), but it also marks a gradual shift in alternative discourse, from a distinctly anti-British stance towards a more active promotion of a certain type of 'artistic' and broadly modernist filmmaking. This will be considered specifically in relation to Grierson's first film, *Drifters*, as this was generally seen as a British film that answered such calls.

Conclusion

This chapter has demonstrated the major currents of alternative film culture in the 1920s, currents that very much fed into the types of films produced in the latter half of the 1920s, which I will investigate within the next two chapters. This network was reliant on national precedents (in sporadic, piecemeal form) as well as international ones, which acted not just as inspiration, but as important facilitating coordinates. Yet, it was not until the establishment of the Film Society—which was followed by a number of other, like-minded, specialist exhibition outlets—that this network was established on a systematic basis. In tandem with this arose an increasingly prevalent range of published writings that acted as a voice for this cultural formation. *Close Up* was the most regular, and vociferous, example of such written work.

Within the programming and writing connected to alternative film culture, there existed a number of trends, reflecting cultural tastes and attitudes. In particular, the favoured films exhibited, and written about, display an evident preference for films made on a large scale and within narrative frameworks. Thus, in the 1920s alternative film culture in Britain was attempting to locate the vanguard of cinematic art within the commercial film industry. In this sense, independent production was encouraged in order to feed into, and improve, the quality of commercial productions. This was evident within such discursive ambivalence towards the commercial industry, in which the dominant trends of commercialism were denigrated, but selected elements were championed (including the technical tools of the professional trade—such as cameras and film stock—that led to the visual 'sophistication' of many Hollywood films in particular). Concurrently, the aesthetic frameworks that were developed to appreciate film and celebrate it as a new and significant art form tended to combine traditional aesthetic appreciation (dramatic frameworks, the emphasis on organic unity and a romantic vision of the artistic director) with newer, modernist currents (the celebration of cinema's mechanical nature, for instance).

These features fed into the reception of, and the eventual prescriptions for, British filmmaking. Significantly, they sat alongside a very nationally inflected form of internationalism, in which 'Britishness' was negatively encoded as imitative and backward. During the 1930s a shift occurred in alternative film culture, in which an 'artistic' vein of British production was encouraged, and where enthusiasm for the commercial film industry soured. This change will be covered in subsequent chapters. The next chapter, however, focuses on film production that very much accompanied the views that I have charted, marked as they were by anti-British cinéphobia, as well as international cinéphilia.

Deconstruction, Burlesque and Parody

While many aspects of alternative film culture in Britain have been critically appraised in piecemeal form, a number of parody films made in this milieu have been largely overlooked. I would argue that these films have been ignored because they do not represent obvious 'progressive' interventions in British filmmaking; they were too busily engaged in a process of generating laughter to be accepted as 'serious'. Alternative and modernist filmmaking is often seen as a serious business and histories have generally been concerned with identifying films that are considered to have initiated new cinematic developments. This was also the type of discursive framework within which alternative film culture operated, which led to the relative marginalization of these films.

I will argue that many burlesque and parody films made in the mid- to late 1920s constituted the earliest examples of filmmaking that were connected to alternative film cultural institutions and discourses. Not only were many of the personnel playing a part in making these films—Oswell Blakeston, Adrian Brunel and Ivor Montagu, for instance—involved in the operations of alternative institutions, but the films themselves also relate to many of the issues discussed in alternative discourses. It is my argument that these films constituted a playful attack on aspects of film culture that they found distasteful, attempting to expose what were thought to be rigid and formulaic conventions or attitudes.

Adrian Brunel and his 'Ultra-Cheap Experiments in Cinematography'

In 1924 Adrian Brunel made *Crossing the Great Sagrada*, a spoof of expedition-travel films, which were a popular staple of British filmmaking in the early 1920s. This film pre-dates the establishment of the Film Society, but it can be linked to the attitudes developing among intellectual cinéphiles at the time. Brunel was a cosmopolitan figure with a wide knowledge of film and, although he worked in the commercial film industry, he was also involved in many side projects concerning non-commercial, artistic activities. He was a founding member of the Film Society when it was formed in 1925, despite the fact that his employers, Gainsborough, put pressure on him to leave. Even after leaving the Society he continued to carry out technical preparation of films for Film Society performances for Brunel and Montagu Ltd. And, as noted in the previous chapter, Brunel was involved in an early attempt to construct an alternative, more highbrow and artistic cinematic sphere when he tried to set up a Cinemagoers League in 1920.

Brunel had a great knowledge of film, gained from extensive practical experience. In 1920 he co-founded Minerva Films with actor Leslie Howard and writer A.A. Milne, a playwright, poet and novelist now best known for his Winnie-the-Pooh stories.[1] In 1920 they made four comedies: *The Bump*, *£5 Reward*, *Bookworms* and *Twice Two*, followed by *A Temporary Lady* in 1921. He made his first commercial feature, *The Man Without Desire*, in 1923 for Atlas-Biocraft—a company that he had formed with actor Miles Mander in 1922—for £5,000.[2] He thus had experience of working in different areas of film production and of the financial dealings involved in funding and maintaining a production company.

Much of Brunel's film work was commercially oriented and thus involved a controlled degree of calculation. In *Crossing the Great Sagrada*, however, he was free from commercial restrictions, which enabled him to adopt a more anarchic style that cocked a snook at numerous aspects of film culture. It is this film, and the burlesques that he made later, which are most pertinent in relation to alternative film culture. These films can be connected to some of the currents that I have identified in alternative discourse, namely an anti-patriotic stance, a suspicion of any set formula, and a scathing attitude towards different aspects of the British film industry. Such an approach reveals the frustrations involved in making British movies at the time, and it is in Brunel's burlesque films that these frustrations surface in mordantly comic fashion.

Crossing the Great Sagrada was made in 1924, during a lull in Brunel's commercial filmmaking activities. After his first feature, *The Man Without Desire* (1923), he was unable to get any further work directing feature films until 1927, when he made *Blighty* for Gainsborough Pictures. He therefore decided to make a personal comic experiment with limited financial resources. According to Brunel, the film cost only £80 to make. One-third of it was composed of titles, a third of footage from old travel pictures, and a third of footage in which he dressed up in various costumes.[3] Though Brunel had limited finances, he was still able to experiment a great deal, creating a hotchpotch collage of text and image.

Crossing the Great Sagrada takes its name from *Crossing the Great Sahara*, an expedition film made by Angus Buchanan in 1924. The expedition film was a type of travel film, a popular cinematic genre at this time. *Crossing the Great Sahara* was one of several films that exploited the appeal of the genre by arranging trips in order to document a constructed expedition.[4] The film was, like many others, an imperialist adventure in exotic territory and reflected the gung-ho patriotic attitudes connected with the conservative aristocracy. There was a strong vein of romanticism running through such films, which employed formulaic elements that harked back to the 'Victorian quest' literature of writers such as Rider Haggard and Rudyard Kipling,[5] as well as *Boy's Own* paper, with their stories of patriotic, religious and conservative masculinity.[6] The films continued the mythic exaggeration of the romantic group questing into unknown lands for the sake of national expediency.

It would not have been nationalism per se that Brunel and like-minded intellectuals found distasteful, rather a stereotypical nationalism that was based on imperial myths. Brunel was involved in the propaganda efforts of the First World War and was firmly behind the national effort.[7] What he disliked was a certain type of aristocratic, jingoist nationalism that glorified war. Brunel was part of a younger generation who understood the horrors of war and would have felt aggrieved at its promotion as a glorious affair.[8] The post-war continuation of stories glorifying war and other national affairs within 'Boy's Own' frameworks would have appeared ludicrous in their denial of history.[9]

Such attitudes underlined some of the attempts to create specifically British films, and it is no surprise to find that *Crossing the Great Sahara* was shown in the first of the British national film weeks, which began on 3 February 1924.[10] Considering that Brunel's burlesque took the name of a film shown during one of the national film weeks, it would be fair to assume that it was made partly in response to those showings. The film weeks were a defence of the British industry in a time of crisis, and were cast in a particularly imperialist mode of discourse.

British responses to American domination had, understandably, often been cast in nationalist terms: in 1921 the British National Film League was formed to encourage the production and exhibition of British-made films, and to raise the standard and quality of the films.[11] Within such a climate, when artistry was referred to, it was done so mainly in two ways:

either through encouraging British filmmaking to rely on the prestige of other British artistic traditions or emphasizing the need for British filmmakers to adopt the more populist strategies of Hollywood practices.[12] Modern cinéphiles did not at this stage adopt the type of aggressive anti-nationalism later found in *Close Up*. As mentioned in the previous chapter, Iris Barry may have criticized the state of British cinema, but she also thought about ways in which new forms of British cinema could emerge. Like her, many others did not automatically reject the notion of a British cinema, but disagreed with the type of nationalist films being promoted.

Crossing the Great Sagrada mocks both values pervading British society and the film techniques and formulae of the film industry. Brunel—ciné-literate and knowledgeable about many aspects of filmmaking—criticizes the ways that cinematic codes could become falsely equated with authenticity. The film uses titles, parodic imitations and incongruous juxtapositions in order to undertake such iconoclastic operations. It opens with punning titles, which constantly recur within the film.

Immediately the film plays upon words in order to signal its intentions. Its silly names show that it is not a serious picture through parodying one of the conventions of film: credits. These titles also evoke aspects of 'official', traditional British culture held to be sacred by some of the more nationalist British citizens, including references to Anglo-German tensions and to (Sherlock) Holmes and literary tradition. The film even indulges in self-mockery by ridiculing the paltry budget on which it is made.

The excessive use of titles in the film was a convenient way to exploit a low budget and to critique what was generally seen as a fault of many

1. The opening, punning titles of *Crossing the Great Sagrada* (frame grab)

British films: a literary intrusion on the visual nature of the medium. The way that the images are constantly interrupted by titles exaggerates this failing and almost frustrates any desire to become absorbed within the images. Not only this, but when the titles appear, they are littered with words that mock national self-congratulation, or just poke fun: for example, 'An All British Production', 'An Indolent Film', 'A Thirst National Production'.

The film begins with a comic prologue in which Brunel and his assistant are seen financing and making the film, and it proceeds to deconstruct this genre of filmmaking thoroughly. Overall, it critiques the manner by which many imperialist travel films were seen as authentic representations of actual events. In reality, this was open to question. There had already been widespread controversy over Richard Kearn's 1924 expedition film *Toto's Wife* when it was discovered that he reconstructed episodes of travellers in the sand wastes of the Sahara (i.e. he faked footage).[13] In the light of such a revelation, Brunel's film can be seen as a warning against the way in which such films were accepted as truth.

For example, Brunel flaunts the 'inauthenticity' of the picture, by dressing in ridiculous costumes and filming on locations that are obviously not what the titles indicate they are. The film even announces that the desert scenes were shot on Blackpool beach; conversely, when the titles indicate that a scene is set in Wapping, we see a small village of mud huts and are thus alerted to the incongruity between what is being stated and what is seen. Similar points are made both through the blurring between filmic realities and by continually playing around with cinematic codes. For example, the film shows the three heroes riding through 'exotic' foreign terrain on their horses (in a long, silhouetted shot); a little later they are riding on camels, shown through an animated silhouette. This illogical jump and the contrast between photographed reality and animation highlight the manner by which constructed and absurd fiction is presented as factual travelogue.

Brunel's next burlesque was *The Pathetic Gazette*, which parodied the Pathé newsreels of the period. This film was made independently in the same year as *Crossing the Great Sagrada*, it cost a similar amount of money and was distributed by the same renting company. Both films were shown at the Tivoli Theatre in London and reviewed in the trade press. Michael Balcon and C.M. Woolf then invited Brunel to make a further five burlesques for Gainsborough, to be distributed by Woolf's company W&F.[14] These films, which cost £150 each and were made in 1925, were: *A Typical Budget*, another newsreel satire; *Cut it Out*, which covered the topic of censorship; *Battling Bruisers*, a burlesque of boxing pictures; *The Blunderland of Big Game*, a satire on wildlife films; and *So This is Jolly Good*, in which British filmmaking came under attack. Only *The Blunderland of Big Game*, which took its name from the 1923 picture *Wonderland of Big Game*, and *The Pathetic Gazette* are apparently lost.

A Typical Budget, which took its name from the newsreel *Topical Budget*, mostly lampoons the newsreels and their claims to 'objectivity'. In fact, their selection of what constituted objective news was regarded as subjective and trivial in many intellectual quarters and, as I shall later demonstrate, was rejected by both the documentary movement and workers' film organizations. Brunel's film mainly parodies the means through which the newsreels claimed to be authoritative, official, reliable and 'true'. It is, for example, subtitled 'The Only Unreliable Film Review', while titles such as 'We guarantee that everything in this film is absolutely fictitious and totally inaccurate' appear regularly in order to debunk the claims being made. The film adopts the formula of the *Topical Budget* and experiments with film form in order to mock the 'trivial' nature of newsreels. For example, there is a sketch in which the titles remind viewers to put their clocks back, but warns not to do it too early: a shot of busy London in reverse is then shown as a consequence of what might happen.

The film satirizes both the content and the form of newsreels. Luke McKernan has written that the *Topical Budget* series did not often put much thought into the structural organization of their items, and that they often reflected a conservative, non-controversial viewpoint. Many of their items were of 'soft' news—such as sporting events and the appearances of celebrities—rather than 'hard' news, which was not easily translatable into simple text and visuals.[15] *A Typical Budget*'s continual bombardment of titles and short clips is self-referentially mentioned when the titles read: 'Sorry to keep on opening and closing the picture like this, but they do it in all the best topicals'. As well as commenting on the selection of safe and uncontroversial items presented in an unproblematic manner, the film is also a critique of the unimaginative and formulaic manner in which newsreels were presented.

Cut it Out has many similarities with Brunel's other burlesques but differs from them in one aspect: it is not solely a parody of a formulaic cycle or genre of films, but a fictional portrayal of the film censor at work. It does retain the familiar manic pace and is again concerned with attacking—in comic form—an aspect of the filmmaking industry regarded as stringent and restrictively conservative. It portrays the making of a film that is continually interrupted by a censor. It is supposedly a reflection of a

2. The censor interrupts a scene because of violent undertones in *Cut it Out*
(frame grab)

'typical' British film being made, but one that is being made with a censor actually present, who is stated as being affiliated to a society for 'detecting evil in others'. This refers to the manner by which the British Board of Film Censorship was often in thrall to moral groups. Though an independent body, it had to pay a great deal of attention to the views of local authorities, which had the power to overturn its decisions.[16] The censorship decisions were swayed by a number of diverse external pressures, including licensing authorities, social purity and social reform movements, the film trade and the Home Office.[17]

Cut it Out portrays the belief that British cinema was an antiquarian version of Hollywood. The film being made within the film borrows elements such as the last-minute rescue, supposedly an attempt to inject American pace and formula into a British production. However, attempts to add more modern American spice to the film, or add any controversial content, are restricted by the morality that underpinned censorship regulation. British filmmaking is seen as rooted in the past, while its potential for progression is further stymied by the censorship regulations.

The failings of commercial British cinema are also addressed in *So This is Jolly Good*, which focuses upon the widely held view that British films were engaged in a ridiculous attempt at aping Hollywood. The first shot, following a title announcing an aerial view of *Jolly Good*, is a pan across an industrial British landscape. This reveals the disparities between the locations of the different countries, and can also be read as a sign of the repressed: the industrial landscape is a pointer to what the British film industry is overlooking and escaping from. Likewise, we get to see the home of a typical British star, a terraced house in a rather run-down area. The film seems to be arguing that it is ridiculous to indulge in Hollywood imitation when, first, the industry lacks the cash, stars and locations to match this industry and, second, when there is a great section of British life that has been overlooked by British filmmakers. The rest of the film, portraying the preparation and shooting of a British commercial movie, satirically suggests that British filmmaking is incompetently engaged in regurgitating Hollywood formulae.

Made in 1924 and 1925, Brunel's burlesques pre-date many currents that would subsequently characterize alternative criticism. As I have shown, the British film industry and its supposedly lamentable films were attacked on a number of fronts: for reflecting a mediocre, nationally confined and patriotic outlook; for badly imitating some of the worst aspects of formulaic American cinema; for being driven by commercial concerns to the exclusion of artistic potentialities; for lacking professional personnel and adequate studio facilities. As a ciné-literate commercial filmmaker who was continually involved in the encouragement of more artistic films, Brunel's foregrounding of what he thought were the shortcomings of British filmmaking constitute an exposure of what he saw as aesthetic dead ends.

A Form of Deconstruction?

The ways in which Brunel's burlesques undermined some of the dominant aspects of British film culture and film production, and the styles that they adopted in so doing, could be seen as an early instance of deconstructionist filmmaking. *Crossing the Great Sagrada* and the newsreel parodies, especially, play with images and their relation to truth. These films teased out different meanings from existing footage, highlighting the way that the signification of images can vary according to contextual placement. Brunel also plays with 'multiple selves' in these films by acting in many different roles, thus mocking the artificiality of characters within film.

Brunel was not undertaking a systematic philosophical investigation of the cinematic apparatus, and he did not intervene in the textual criticism of film to any great extent. His immersion in alternative film culture, though, should be seen as a turn towards a greater self-consciousness about film as an aesthetic medium with its own set of conventions. His deconstructive tactics could partly be seen, then, as a foregrounding of the creative permutation of text and image, which further draws attention to the mediated (and creative) nature of film construction. Such tactics also reveal the dangers in confusing cinematic images with reality in any simplistic manner. British alternative discourse—and also Brunel's burlesques—involved a creative rejection of cinema as an imitation of reality combined with an ideological rejection of the 'real' that was being constructed in many films. Both of these points would feed into the shift towards an experimental, self-consciously artistic cinema that nevertheless attempted to reflect the 'real', rather than a 'fake', world.

While most of Brunel's burlesque targets were elements of mainstream British film culture, *Battling Bruisers* extends this canvas. This parody of boxing films involves the character Battling Buttler, who fights in London, Spain and then Russia. The locations of these fights are parodically represented by visual clichés: London is represented by tourist images such as Trafalgar Square and Big Ben; Spain is represented by a boxing fight in which a boxer apes a matador by waving a rag in front of his opponent (intercut with an actual bull fight). The arrival in Moscow is heralded by titles flashing up 'Moscow' three times at high speed, followed by a rapid montage sequence of train tracks, trains in motion and moving landscape seen from the train. Then 'Petrograd' flashes on the screen, followed by a rapid montage of political marches and political speakers, shown through canted and upside down camera angles. When a fight takes place, there is a dramatic montage of faces in close-up, reacting to the fight.

The satire here is different to Brunel's other burlesques: these rapid montage sequences apparently exaggerate certain tendencies within Soviet montage cinema. This is not, however, something that can be proved in any definitive manner; in fact, the evidence available leads one to doubt that these sequences were truly parodies. While experimental films using montage techniques were released in 1924 and early 1925 in Soviet Russia— such as Vertov's *Kino-Eye* (1924), Eisenstein's *Strike* (1925) and Kuleshov's *The Death Ray* (1925)—these were not shown in Britain in the same year.[18] Ivor Montagu took a trip to Soviet Russia in April 1925, when these films would have been released; yet, though he may have had a chance to see them, he was unable to bring any of them back into Britain.[19]

Three possibilities present themselves: Montagu could have reported some of the formal tendencies of experimental montage to Brunel, who then incorporated them into his satire; Brunel could have added these scenes to an updated edition of the film for a later showing; or the scenes are entirely coincidental. I think that the second possibility is the most credible, since it was not until the release of *Battleship Potemkin* that experimental montage became a regularly discussed tendency for alternative aesthetes. It is notable that there is a scene in *Battling*

Bruisers—close-ups of shocked faces rapidly intercut with the events in the ring—that seems to parody some of the reaction shots in the Odessa Steps sequence of the film. While I have no direct evidence to back up this point, and therefore must leave it as conjecture, Brunel did actually make subsequent additions to *Cut it Out* when it was shown at the Film Society.[20] Therefore, it would not have been anomalous if he cut in extra footage for a later presentation of *Battling Bruisers*. The film was not shown at the Film Society but it was shown at the Nottingham and District Workers' Film Society on 29 November 1931. This indicates that it was being shown after 'Soviet techniques' had become recognizable and could have been re-edited.[21]

If it is accepted that the Russian episodes of *Battling Bruisers* are parodying Soviet montage, it can be seen as demonstrating that Brunel was not just deconstructing those elements of film culture that he disliked, although this would certainly have been his main aim. Many Soviet montage films were, after all, much admired within alternative circles, and Brunel was himself an enthusiast. Parody, in this case, can be seen as a form of homage. This shows that the art of deconstructing negative tendencies could also lead to a deconstruction of all styles that were seen as overly standardized. This ability to homogenize certain tendencies was itself indicative of some of the criticism within alternative circles. As I have argued, there was a tendency to sum up particularly identifiable styles under the banner of a national style: the Russian sequence in *Battling Bruisers* seems to exemplify this (despite parodying it). Brunel was still promoting the same outlook in 1936, when he wrote that one should not imitate American or Soviet editing techniques unless there is a 'legitimate reason and a definite call for the application of such methods in the story'.[22] This further indicates that, if this was additional footage cut in at a later date, it may have been incorporated in order to mock British films produced in the late 1920s that were perceived as mimicking Soviet techniques in an uninspired fashion. Such views show that, despite attacking nationalist rhetoric and the reductive ways in which other countries were represented, alternative discourse did not altogether escape nationalist trappings.

This sensitivity to formula would have been borne out by the self-reflective character of alternative film culture. The viewing of so many different films and the critical eye that linked such films to the nature of the medium as a whole would have encouraged this. Brunel's diverse experience in different areas of film culture would also have made him sensitive to different formulae. For example, he worked on propaganda films for the Ministry of Information in the First World War; he made light-hearted comedies for Minerva films; he made some shadowgraphs, such as *The Shimmy Sheik* (1923); he made a travel film entitled *Moors and Minarets* (1923); he wrote scripts for cartoons such as the 'Bonzo the Dog' series, which began in 1924; and he had experience of editing other people's films, as well as having to deal with the financial side of the film business.[23]

While many filmmaking activities and supporting discourses were promoting selective areas of interest as new and innovative, Brunel's burlesques lampooned such pretensions. How should we understand such practices in terms of debates about modernism and avant-garde film culture? Rosalind Krauss has argued that the one thing that holds constant in modernist-vanguardist discourses is the theme of originality, of the artist constructing something new, free from tradition. She claims that this theme of originality is a fiction because it bases itself upon the assumption that there is 'an indisputable zero-ground beyond which there is no further model, or referent, or text'. By contrast, Krauss asserts that the only thing that modernist works succeed in doing is 'locating the signifier of another, prior system of grids, which have beyond them, yet another, even earlier system'.[24] She further argues that while modernist artists employed techniques of reproduction and uniqueness, they tended to repress the reproductive signifiers in order to promote uniqueness.

Krauss's argument certainly does identify major shifts within the modernist and postmodernist divide, though she tends to generalize about vast areas of artistic practice. For instance, there were elements of self-reflexive critique within modernist culture in the 1920s. The most obvious example would be the Dadaists, who questioned many of the basic tenets underlying artistic practice and discourse. In film, for example, René Clair's *Entr'acte* (France, 1924) mocks aspects of the commercial feature film and the conventions of the newsreel by employing elements of slapstick.[25]

With respect to Brunel's burlesques, there has not been any critical analysis of the films that would even situate them within a modernist framework. Perhaps it is the playful and deconstructive elements of these films that has led to their neglect, since the burlesque, by definition, does not aim for originality, the high-point of modernist acclaim, so much as it critiques something that has already been produced. Further, those aspects of canonical modernist filmmaking that contained deconstructive tendencies have tended to be associated with figures already established in avant-garde circles. *Entr'acte*, for example, featured Francis Picabia and had a soundtrack by Eric Satie; it was also part of a larger, avant-garde 'event', in that it was an interlude within Picabia's ballet *Relâche*.[26] No such privilege is attached to Brunel's films, bar his association with the Film Society (a privilege that nevertheless inspires his inclusion in this study). Their modernist-deconstructive aesthetic, however, should be placed in the same vein as canonized Dada films of the 1920s.

Meta-critical sensitivity pervaded even the most serious corners of alternative film culture: there was suspicion about any style that was adopted in a formulaic manner. Even *Close Up*, which was often convinced of the originality of its own discourse, displayed scepticism towards many modernist codes and conventions. For example, Kenneth Macpherson excoriated much of the French avant-garde (both practice and criticism) for being caught up in fashionable intellectual trends in which most people were considered guilty of 'mental kow-towing'.[27]

Even literary intellectuals from Bloomsbury made parodic films in the late 1920s. Bernard Penrose made home-movie spoofs with assistance from Dora Carrington and John Strachey at Ham Spray House in Wiltshire. *Dr. Turner's Mental Hospital* (1929) is a fast-paced farce about a doctor experimenting on the inmates of his mental home, while *Topical Budget Ham Spray September 1929* is, as its name suggests, another spoof on newsreels. Less focused than Brunel's satires on specific targets, it does often show long shots of a woman on horseback, as if imitating the inanity of newsreel content and its focus on the mundane movements of celebrities. This mode of film practice does not appear to relate to the famous Bloomsburian Virginia Woolf's appeal for a new form of cinema, with its aspirations for a secret language that can visibly display the processes of thought.[28] Earlier than this, Evelyn Waugh wrote and Terence Greenbridge directed a home-movie spoof entitled *The Scarlet Woman: An Ecclesiastical Adventure* (1925), which starred Elsa Lanchester.[29] It is clear that a parodic strain—often violently attacking filmmaking practices—was rife among different factions of intellectual film enthusiasts.

Oswell Blakeston also parodied some of the excesses of Parisian film culture, even though he admired much of it. In 1927, for instance, he made a film, *I Do Like to Be Beside the Seaside*, which parodied several avant-garde film styles. Unfortunately the film has been lost but there remain stills from, and comments about, the film. The *Architectural Review*, for instance, described the film in the following terms: 'Held together by an airy thread of a story, it expresses, by a constant reduction to absurdity, more clearly than learned disquisition or exact analysis, the merits, the defects, the potentialities and the dangers, of the methods they [certain filmmakers] employ.'[30]

The film, which featured Macpherson and H.D., is described as parodying familiar techniques of filmmakers such as Germaine Dulac, Paul Leni, Man Ray, Carl Dreyer and Sergei Eisenstein. Blakeston is said to have used some of the more 'obvious' techniques of these filmmakers (such as distorted shots, symbolic shots and shadowy shots) in a deliberately absurd manner.[31] In so doing, he was thus being at once reverent and irreverent. He was (and this can be gauged from his writings) mimicking the techniques of those directors that he admired and paying homage to their individual, expressive techniques. At the same time he was refusing to take them too seriously and parodied the ways in which certain 'techniques' can easily become standardized.

This deconstructive aspect of alternative British film culture should not be seen as a total repudiation of the modernist project, however. It is clear that *Close Up* and the Film Society were not undertaking an extensive critique of modernist claims to originality. They were, on the whole, operating from within an identifiably modernist context in which the innovative, serious and creative aspects of artistry were celebrated. There was a tendency, however, to deflate the claims and stances of other movements (whether filmmaking or criticism). This tendency led Brunel occasionally to engage in self-critique; *Close Up*, however, remained resolutely committed to the originality of its own stance. This deconstructive strain largely arose out of the attacks on British film culture, but also spread towards aspects of international film culture that were seen as readily identifiable and thus subject to formulaic adoption. Ultimately, both anti-British and deconstructive strains combined in some circles of alternative culture, resulting in anti-British prejudice. Most commonly, the adoption of familiar, international styles within British films was seen as uninspired imitation.

A Continuation of British Traditions?

I have thus far argued that Brunel's burlesque films were a form of deconstructive cinema in which elements of 'official' British film culture were attacked. These films can also be seen as a continuation of forms that had characterized British and American cinema in earlier times, and other aspects of British culture. Within British society there has existed a long tradition of satire, burlesque and parodic art, which can be found not only in literature, but also in graphic art, theatre and cinema.[32] John Hawkridge has argued that parody films in the late 1900s and early 1910s were prominent because they could be made cheaply and proved very popular, and almost developed into a genre in their own right.[33]

These films pre-date the themes of Brunel's burlesques; Pimple (Fred Evans), whose films were extremely popular with British audiences, had even parodied a newsreel in 1921 with his *Topical Gazette*.[34] The main question here is whether this tradition of parody films negates the claims that Brunel was undermining aspects of mainstream film culture, as opposed to perpetuating them. A closer look at the lineage in which he can be placed, and how he employed these tactics within a specific context, will shed more light upon such a question.

Brunel's earlier Minerva comedies, made in the early 1920s with A.A. Milne, also contained moments of subversion. *The Bump*, according to Christine Gledhill, employs self-conscious narration, 'ironic and parodic juxtapositions and reversals in order to bring down the pretensions of generational, class, gendered and imperial authority by mixing the dignified and the low'.[35] These comedies were, however, rather refined. While they did make use of slapstick elements and contained mildly subversive moments, a refined framework tamed such tactics. In a sense, they were involved in a process of 'upgrading' the comedic form, moving it away from a cruder, more physical mode of filmmaking.[36]

In the burlesques such themes were continued, but in a more ruthless, less refined manner. I believe there are two reasons for this: the more independent nature of the burlesque films and the development of an alternative film culture during the ensuing years. Regarding the first point, the Milne collaborations were not only compromised affairs in terms of the people involved, they were also made as commercial propositions. The first two burlesque films, on the other hand, were independently made as cheap experiments, not as commercial artefacts. Though the later five were made for Gainsborough, Brunel was allowed to work along the same lines as he had with his first two burlesques. The productions with Milne were also affected by Milne himself: Brunel, at least in his comedic guise, tended to look at established culture with a very critical lens and was also a proponent of film art; Milne, by contrast, was a more conservative, literary figure who supported 'refined' notions of comedy.[37]

The Minerva films were also made at a time when an established alternative film culture did not exist. Some attempts had been made to construct a 'film art' sphere, but these did not actually contain any of the 'specifically cinematic' hallmarks that would come to characterize alternative film culture. When *Crossing the Great Sagrada* was made, an alternative culture was beginning to establish itself and Brunel was mixing with people who were to become involved in the founding of the Film Society. Also at this point, reaction against the dominant, patriotic discussion of cinema, as reliant upon other established forms, was more widely propounded.

If these burlesques are placed in context, then it is clear that they were firmly attacking elements of established culture rather than merely perpetuating them. This is not to deny their reliance upon generic forms that were already popular. These burlesques mixed high and low without attempting to extinguish the raw physicality of slapstick. In a sense, this was completely in line with the broader project of alternative culture, which attacked established culture, as well as some of the 'less intelligent' forms of popular culture. The films can thus be seen as degrading 'official' culture and upgrading 'degraded' culture. Their use of slapstick and subversion could appeal on two main levels: they could be appreciated for their simple, slapstick visual comedy, and on another plane as sophisticated deconstructions of the static, even backward, elements that were perceived as detrimental to film art.

The Montagu–Wells Collaborations

The spirit of Brunel's burlesques was continued in more coherent and modified form in the films that Ivor Montagu made in conjunction with the novelist H.G. Wells and his son Frank. H.G. Wells, of course, was a well-known novelist, writing both satirical and, more famously, science-fiction novels. He was also a prominent political writer and member of the Fabian Society. Montagu and Frank Wells directed the films; H.G. Wells wrote the stories upon which they were based. Montagu wrote that the films were financed by an American on the condition that H.G. Wells would write original stories for them; Wells agreed as long as Elsa Lanchester starred in them.[38] The films, *Bluebottles*, *Daydreams* and *The Tonic*, were all made in 1928 at the Gainsborough Studios in Islington, but were not released until 1929.[39] Unfortunately *The Tonic*—which concerns a money-hungry family sending their servant to kill their wealthy great-aunt—does not survive, but the other two do. The films were produced by Angle Pictures, an independent company run by Montagu (who was managing director), Frank Wells, Arthur Levy and Simon Rowson.[40] While the films do share some of the spirit of the Brunel burlesques, their more coherent and less anarchic feel is explained by the fact that they were seen as small commercial ventures: they cost around £4,600 each, much more than Brunel's small films.[41] These three films are approximately twenty minutes in length and were made as companion pieces, to be shown at the same time. Lanchester was the personality who linked them, and she plays a lowly maid servant, who is actually named Elsa Lanchester in all three films. Charles Laughton is also in all three and plays a villain in each piece, though it is a different character each time. The films were also linked by the tone of the stories and the form by which they were told.

Bluebottles is a light-hearted comic romp concerning the story of a clumsy working-class girl (Lanchester) who accidentally foils some thieves after blowing a police whistle that she finds on the street. The film blends slapstick and satire (mockery of the police is a constant) with some occasional moments of self-conscious stylization. For example, when Lanchester blows the police whistle, there is a cut to a policeman, who in turn blows a whistle himself; this is followed by five more similar, continuous close-ups of different policemen, each shot held for a short duration. This is succeeded by a stylized collage-type shot of a policeman blowing a whistle, his face splintered into multiple images, seemingly refracted through a special lens. This collage shot may convey story information, but it does so in a way that draws attention to itself as an insert that is fascinating to gaze at in a purely abstract manner. The hysterical reaction of the police is reinforced as several policemen in different areas frantically rush towards the source of the sound. The response of the many different policemen is parodied by inserts of an army, fighter planes, a warship and a tank. Non-diegetic material is thus used to create a series of images that mock not only the police in the story, but also symbols of official authority in its most bellicose guise.

Daydreams is similar to *Bluebottles* in tone but, instead of attacking the established authority of the police, it undermines the world of glamour and the cult of stardom, a theme constantly broached by many interested in cinema as a modern art. In this film Lanchester is visited by a friend who spots a picture in her room of a glamorous actress (which is actually a picture of Lanchester after she has been 'made-up'), which cues the story of the actress: a poor girl from Paris who falls in love with an aristocrat, and whose career is boosted after he is killed.

Again, small moments of self-conscious stylization punctuate the light-hearted satire. There is, for example, an abstract spiralling pattern employed to denote the passage into Lanchester's daydream. A particularly striking use of trick effects, meanwhile, occurs when the couple in the framed story visit the man's parents in order to sanction their union. The parents are disgusted at accepting a woman from such a poor background; this is shown by a slightly low-angled close-up in which we see them glowering in their resplendent jewellery and sparkly clothing. There follows a shot in which we see the parents towering over the couple, who are placed next to them in extreme miniature, symbolically dwarfed by the status of parental consent. This balance of power shifts, however, as the husband-to-be asserts himself and remonstrates with his family. He then begins to grow in size as the family cower; cut to him in close-up, facing the camera (and thus subjecting the audience to his angry outburst) and waving his finger; cut back to the family, who now shrink in size. This sequence flaunts trick shots and uses them to construct a symbolic visual summation of narrative detail in an expressive manner. The next shot shows the couple married.

Montagu's burlesque films are similar to Brunel's 'ultra-cheap experiments in cinematography' in that they mock authority, and in the manner by which they critique filmic illusionism. *Daydreams*, for example, dramatizes the emptiness of stardom, and by the end of the film the poor Lanchester character has been warned off the attractions of riches. *Daydreams* is also similar to some of the Brunel burlesques in that it contains two characters being played by the same person, a technique that not only foregrounds the artificiality of film reality but also hints at the fluidity of identity.

There are, however, certain differences between the Montagu–Wells films and Brunel's burlesques, despite the fact that both rework slapstick traditions from rather similar ideological positions. Montagu's films are mostly studio acted and original, whereas Brunel's films—at least his early ones—rely on found footage and footage shot in his garden. Montagu's films are longer (more than twice as long), more coherent and contain much more narrative continuity and character development than most of Brunel's burlesques. With the possible exception of *Cut it Out*, Brunel's films rely on situational comedy without much recourse to character development or narrative continuity. The slapstick traditions running through the Montagu films mean that there is no sophisticated characterization, but there are rudimentary sketches, enough to base a narrative around the trajectory of identifiable characters. This difference between the two sets of films is one of the reasons why their use of experimentation is different.

The experimentation in Brunel's films largely disrupts or fragments narrative. Narrative is not the point to the films; rather these experiments comment on the events taking place. The Montagu films, however, create a much tighter diegetic world in which continuity is not disrupted in any overt manner. They do contain experiments that, by their very saliency, draw attention to themselves, but they do not disrupt the narrative flow of events to any great extent. Rather, they can be seen as expressive uses of experimentation that reveal new dimensions within the story on a symbolic level. They may momentarily halt the forward motion of the narrative, but they do so only to take a lateral look at it from a different perspective. The narrative is therefore still easy to follow and the need for excessive titles is obviated. The experimentation within the Montagu films is an employment of what were considered essentially cinematic visual motifs, a chance to experiment with the way in which narrative and theme can be developed via purely visual imagery.

These differences, I would argue, demonstrate that the Montagu films are an extension of the Brunel films. Whereas the Brunel productions are mainly engaged in a thorough deconstruction of negative cultural elements, the Montagu ones, while certainly following this line, also employ aesthetic strategies in a more 'expressive' manner. This is indicative of a move towards constructing an alternative form of British cinema, while at the same time being immersed in the generic approach of deconstruction. Some of the differences, of course, should be attributed to the respective budgets of the films. Montagu's budget enabled him to construct a more coherent world-view than could Brunel, who had to improvise with a range of incompatible materials. Brunel thus used elements of negativity—for example, the excessive use of titles—as ironic weapons. The climate of cultural change should also be taken into account: Brunel's first burlesque was made in 1924, while the Montagu films were made in 1928, by which time the growing international influences promoted by the alternative movement were beginning to take effect. Montagu was able to construct a more visual language for his deconstructive parodies. Such a manoeuvre can be seen as contributing to the emergence of a 'serious', artistic British cinema.

It should also be kept in mind that the Montagu burlesques were commercial films. They may have been small-scale, 'independent' ventures, but they were part of a commercial package. This would undoubtedly have influenced the coherence of the films, as well as their controlled experimentation. However, they did not make a profit and this eventually led to the bankruptcy of Angle Pictures.[42] Montagu blamed the failure of the films on the fact that they had been held up by the distributor's programme for a year and that when they came out sound equipment had been installed in many exhibition outlets.[43] This was echoed in a *Daily Mail* article that noted the lack of bookings for the films. The reporter thought that this was a shame because they were 'interesting and funny first pictures by one of the most vivid young personalities in British films'.[44] The films were generally well received in the press, with special praise being reserved for the performances of Elsa Lanchester. There did seem to be some confusion in the trade press, however, concerning the films' mix of slapstick, parody, 'pictorial humour' and experimentation. The *Bioscope*, for example, while generally positive about the films, thought that this 'inconsistent' treatment detracted from the film's overall coherency. Discussing *Daydreams*, the reviewer noted that: 'On the whole it is well done and contains many funny moments, but the director should avoid an evident predilection for freak photographic effects and other "advanced" embellishments in treating subjects which are not at all assisted by such methods.'[45]

So, although these films were coherent compared to Brunel's films, this reviewer actually felt that the experimentation in the films detracted from their overall consistency. I have argued that this experimentation is encompassed within the expressive system of narrative coherence, so why did the reviewer feel that they disrupted the film? I would suggest it is because *Daydreams* was stranded between two different forms of recognizable genres: the parodic comedy and the European 'art film' (in particular the French Impressionist films). This made the reviewer feel that the use of expressive visual experimentation was not particularly merited in a film that was light-hearted and otherwise narrated in a more regular, simplistic manner. The fact that the *Bioscope* tended to dislike 'experimental' films was, of course, another factor that led to such hostility, yet the paper favourably reviewed some European art films if they were considered aesthetically consistent.

Interestingly, Brunel's more fragmented and incoherent burlesques were not met with such confusion.[46] Maybe this was because they were single-minded deconstructions, firmly locked within the slapstick tradition. They were therefore not read as narrative comedies because they were seen as part of a tradition of 'situation' comedies. Montagu's comedies were seemingly read as belonging more to the refined, pictorial comedy tradition that incorporated slapstick elements.

This confusion about how to locate such filmmaking is reflected by my own inclusion of the films in this survey. In a sense, these films were not attempts to create a new form of artistic British cinema. Despite his use of expressive visual tricks, Montagu himself seemed unsure of whether these films constituted a form of experimental or independent cinema. In a letter written regarding the International Congress of Independent Cinema held at La Sarraz in 1929, at which he was a British representative, Montagu expressed the opinion that independent filmmaking in Britain was practically nonexistent. He thought that Len Lye and Alex Stewart (better known as a society photographer under the alias Sasha) were the only people engaged in the making of experimental films, and added that he knew 'of no others, save amateur productions on small-sized stock, or satirical comedies like those of Adrian Brunel and myself'.[47] So while Montagu placed his and Brunel's burlesques in the independent category, he did so as an afterthought, as though they were not entirely engaged in instituting an independent film movement in Britain.

This was because they were not really doing so in a whole-hearted manner; their work might be better seen as attempts to clear the way for independent or artistic British filmmaking. It is therefore difficult to place these films firmly in a modernist category, even if they belong to an alternative cultural formation and articulate some of the concerns that were germane to that movement. It must be noted, however, that the comic burlesque is a genre of early film that has been seen as exerting a great influence over the avant-garde. A.L. Rees, for example, notes that a large number of avant-garde filmmakers from different periods—including the Surrealists, the Futurists and even Maya Deren—have admired this genre of film as 'uniquely cinematic'.[48] Rees notes two main reasons why early comic films had an influence on the avant-garde: first, they were seen as 'unchaining' film drama from narrative logic and 'realism', opening the way to an 'irrational-comic' style; second, they revelled in tricks and other film devices that were largely overlooked within mainstream cinema and thus offered 'alternative' paths.[49]

British cinéphiles were also attracted to the genre because of their photographic tricks and because they self-reflectively commented upon conventions. Yet, it was more probable that they perceived the form less as 'irrational', than as developing its own, alternative logic. This would have been in line with Gilbert Seldes's views on slapstick: that the logic and plot of the form did not pre-exist but evolved out of the characters and situations.[50] Montagu admitted the influence that Seldes had upon his aesthetics,[51] but he did disagree with Seldes's view that the 'genteel' aspects of comedy had ruined the form. For Montagu, the slapstick form should be renewed through innovation and development, a belief that was clearly reflected in the Wells collaborations.[52]

C.O.D.—A Mellow Drama

The Montagu films continued to work in the tradition of slapstick and parody but moved towards a more serious form of cinema. C.O.D.—A Mellow Drama (1929), a film made by Lloyd T. Richards, Desmond

71

Dickinson, Gerald Gibbs and Harcourt Templeman, takes this strategy even further. While the film parodies the techniques identified with German Expressionism, it nevertheless moves beyond mere parody and creates a rather distinct formal aesthetic.

The filmmakers were technicians at the Stoll Studios in Cricklewood and made the film as a diversionary experiment when sound equipment was being installed. In stating that the film mocks Expressionism, I use the term in a similar way to Kristin Thompson: it emphasizes overall visual composition and tends to lend expressivity to the body, and also turns it into a purely compositional element.[53] I would add to this the use of low-key lighting as a major trait, which led to the ominous shadows and silhouettes. This feature was remarked on by many critics at the time. C.A. Lejeune, for example, wrote: 'The little shadow showman, the silhouette cutter, who spreads this new film before our eyes, might well stand for the spirit of German art in the kinema. To him, the substance is a shadow, the shadow alone catching the true soul of substance [...].'[54]

C.O.D. uses the familiar codes of heavy shadows and dark silhouettes and plays upon their ambiguous nature, especially the way that they obscure visual objects. It also takes to extremes the way Expressionist films often used the body as a compositional element by obscuring any facial characteristics of the characters within the film, and using an excessive amount of close-ups, which tend to fragment and abstract the human frame. The film is built on a formal system of ambiguities, matched by the content of the film, a kind of murder mystery story. The story revolves

3. The exaggeration of 'Expressionist' style employed to emphasize ambiguity within *C.O.D.—A Mellow Drama* (frame grab)

around a package, whose contents are never revealed but whose importance is unquestioned.

The film belongs to parody in the sense that it clearly draws on well-established forms and exaggerates them for effect. Yet there are no slapstick jokes or elements of social satire in the film; neither are there any attacks upon nationalism. Rather, the film takes a more respected element of an identifiable European film style and parodies it. In this sense it is closer in spirit to Oswell Blakeston's *I Do Like to Be Beside the Seaside*, though the unavailability of this print does not allow me to make any precise comparison between the two films.

However, the status of *C.O.D.* as a 'parody' is not at all straightforward: the manner by which it builds on the techniques that it borrows and constructs something different means that it can be construed as more serious in intent. Its formal structure is based around fragmentation and narrative compression. The film's use of fragments means that we rarely see the full figure of any person on the screen and, even if we do, their characteristics become blurred. The film images are thus a succession of fragments by which the human frame is transformed into a series of visual motifs. This certainly conforms to the manner by which Expressionism, to paraphrase Thompson, turns the body into a purely compositional element. But in *C.O.D.* this is achieved in a different manner from many German narrative films. No characterization is employed in this film, and this tends to dehumanize the human frame to an even greater extent than in Expressionist films. Instead, the visual field is turned into a compositional agglomeration of codes that play a part in the central mystery at the heart of the narrative. The rapid editing of shots of feet, legs and the backs of heads, and the employment of unusual angles to construct an ambiguous series of visual images, is threaded together by the parcel, whose trajectory the narrative follows. By using the parcel as a symbol of continuity and encoding visual signs as clues, the film manages to construct an elliptical narrative in which only the essential aspects pertaining to the mystery remain.

C.O.D., then, is certainly rooted in the deconstructionist mode of filmmaking in that it plays upon well-known film techniques and draws attention to them through exaggeration. But it also to some extent deflects this attention through the way in which it constructs a narrative of clues that attempt to draw the spectator into the mystery of the story. It can also be seen as drawing upon what were seen as specifically filmic means of artistry: close-ups, variation of angle, rapid cutting and atmospheric lighting (which may have been borrowed from the theatre and photography but which were accepted as filmic by many cinéastes). It therefore extended the range of the inter-referential films that I have already discussed by moving away from slapstick and into a more serious domain.

Conclusion

This chapter has demonstrated that sensitivity to formulae and an anti-British prejudice were important reasons why a self-consciously 'serious' alternative cinema was slower to emerge in Britain than in some other countries. Nevertheless, parody and burlesque offered an outlet through which to vent frustrations about the state of British film production.

Towards the end of the 1920s the attitude towards British films slowly altered, though many negative perceptions remained. In line with this slow alteration, *C.O.D.* and Montagu's burlesques incorporate elements that hint at new aesthetic paradigms, but they do so within the framework of parody. As these filmmakers were connected in some way to the Film Society they managed to have their films screened there, but they were virtually ignored within *Close Up*. While the films can be connected to alternative discourses, they did not fit into the most privileged canons that such discursive frameworks established.[55] Because parody was light-hearted and overtly intertextual, it did not fit into the modernist vision of a serious, original product of artistic vision. And yet a parodic film such as *C.O.D.* shared many features with other British films that were conceived as attempts to produce serious artistic visions. Its use of fragmentation and abstraction of the human figure in conjunction with rapid editing can be found—to different degrees—in films such as *Drifters, Everyday, Beyond This Open Road* (1934) and *Camera Makes Whoopee* (1935). These films are covered in the following chapters and constitute a more accepted 'modernist' form of independent British filmmaking.

3

Drifters and the Emergence of an Alternative British Cinema

In contrast to the parodic strain of cinematic deconstruction, the end of the 1920s also witnessed an emergence of a new form of modernist British cinema that broadly fitted into the frameworks of alternative discourse, and which regularly screened at film societies. As mentioned earlier, in line with the interest in some Soviet films, particularly those by Eisenstein, British cinéphiles began to locate cinematic art in terms of objective movements. That is, the shooting of external location footage, particularly that which had an edge of documentary realism, became important. Earlier in the 1920s cinematic art tended to be located within the subjective and the interior, as this was recognizably seen to be transforming the mechanical apparatus of the cinema and imprinting it with an artistic stamp. With montage theory, however, 'realistic' footage could be manipulated in post-production so that art merged with realism in a manner that was seen as more 'cinematic' than the theatrical-influenced German Expressionist films.

One British writer who began to formulate such an aesthetic merging of modernism and realism earlier than many others was John Grierson, who initially did so outside Britain. Grierson's views, though, did share many of the concerns that were evident within British alternative discourse. It was Grierson's debut film, *Drifters*, that fitted into cultural frameworks that were slowly beginning to call for a new form of modern British cinema, a cinema that combined artistry and modernist aesthetics with documentary realism. In this chapter I will outline some of Grierson's discourse before considering *Drifters* as the first serious British film that resonated within the network of alternative British film culture.

Grierson's Discourse

John Grierson may have become associated with the theory and practice of realism over the years, but his earlier writings demonstrate a blending of realist approaches and more modernist notions central to alternative culture. It is no surprise, then, that Grierson joined the Film Society in 1931; the documentary movement then played a crucial role in the development of alternative film culture throughout the 1930s.

While in America in the mid-1920s, where he was studying mass communications, Grierson wrote several articles on modern art for the *Chicago Evening Post*, and undertook a report on the film industry for Famous Players Lasky.[1] The articles reveal that Grierson was interested in many aspects of modern art, such as Vorticism and Futurism, because he thought that these movements were expressive of the modern age. They expressed, in abstract form, what he thought were symbols of modern life: objective movement and change.[2] Far from being a simple 'realist', Grierson was deeply interested in questions of form and individual creativity.[3] What he did oppose was art that was excessively 'inward' and thus cut off from what he called the 'objective rhythms of everyday life'.[4]

In part, Grierson was influenced by objective science: Positivism— which was based on the study of objective and quantifiable data—was the most influential philosophical school in America in this period.[5] Grierson had also read the influential Behaviourist psychologist John B. Watson while he was at university.[6] Behaviourism was the positivist branch of psychology that stressed the study of objective behaviour and went so far as to claim that consciousness did not exist. Grierson combined Behaviourist objectivism with a belief that, underlying objective reality, there was a deeper, 'spiritual' reality. According to Ian Aitken, this spiritual aspect of Grierson's aesthetics derived from his interest in idealist philosophy.[7] The Behaviourist influence meant that Grierson largely remained hostile to cinematic attempts to portray subjective psychology.

During the early days of the Film Society, Grierson himself was already engaging in artistic criticism that shared features similar to those evident within its programme notes: a distinction between surface and depth, the artistic individual expressing him or herself, and art as the remoulding of reality into significant form. His earliest surviving writings on cinema— box office reports written for Famous Players Lasky—displayed his dual fascination with Hollywood as a mass communications medium and as an artistic centre. He admired Hollywood for managing to cater to the tastes of a large public, and believed that popular film was able to deal with 'universal' themes and magnify 'common emotions' on a grand scale. He also believed that Hollywood had developed sophisticated and uniquely cinematic technical standards that were brisk and visual, not slow or theatrical. He did not, however, think that there were enough 'quality' films made or that Hollywood was fully exploiting its strengths. Too often the films slipped into 'vulgarization' and 'petty hokum'.[8] They were also guilty of being sloppy, marred by a failure to hold a theme and realize the logic of character; too many films thus suffered from a lack of balance, coherence and consistency.[9] When noting the most important features of the Hollywood film, Grierson used terms familiar in alternative circles: visual composition, rhythmic structure and poetic overtones.[10]

Like other alternative aesthetes, although Grierson was extremely interested in popular cinema, he displayed contempt for some of its values and themes. He found the overall tone of Hollywood too vulgar, sensational and sentimental. Such hostility towards elements of popular culture often led to a misunderstanding of what really appealed to audiences: cinéphiles tended to pick out aspects of popular cinema that they liked and automatically assumed these aspects were most appealing to audiences. Thus Grierson attributed the success of Hollywood films to their naturalistic qualities and 'uniquely cinematic' elements. Two films that utilized the natural landscape—*The Covered Wagon* (Cruze) and *The Iron Horse* (Ford)—were the most popular American films in 1923 and 1924 respectively, which could have led Grierson to highlight the appeal of 'naturalism'.[11] Yet he conveniently ignored the popularity of genres such as the family melodrama and provided no evidence for the appeal of those qualities he favoured.

Like many other alternative aesthetes, Grierson also began to sketch a vision of British cinema that exploited national symbols representative of the modern world and which incorporated international formal developments. Likewise, he began to display increased antagonism towards the commercial cinema and instead thought that cinematic progress had more chance of prospering outside such a milieu. Grierson certainly developed his ideas in relation to changing contexts; his shifts can be more directly attributed to his specific tasks as an employee.

He first wrote directly on British cinema when he was employed by Stephen Tallents at the Empire Marketing Board (EMB) to compose a series of memoranda on British film problems.[12] In these, Grierson wrote that British films should be both poetic and popular, both national and international. He wrote that there were plenty of modern aspects of British life that would make excellent screen material:

> There are subjects aplenty in the progress of industry, the story of invention, the pioneering and developing of new lands and the exploration of lost ones, the widening horizons of commerce, the complexities of manufacture, and the range of communications: indeed in all the steam and smoke, dazzle and speed, of the world at hand, and all the strangeness and sweep of affairs more distant.[13]

He attacked what he saw as the more overt and parochial forms of patriotism because of their narrow outlook and lack of universal appeal, which he described as often being 'carried to the point of international indecency'.[14] Despite this attack on patriotism, Grierson's aesthetic view of British cinema was national, and thus continued the discursive tendency to think in terms of national movements, which were related to each other but also had their own distinctiveness. He thus stated: 'English production might easily add to the Russian intensity something of the English sense of moderation, and to the preoccupation with personal fortunes insisted on by the Americans something of the English sense, something of a sense of human importance.'[15]

Grierson eventually managed to get involved in production through making *Drifters* for the EMB. The practicalities of making films for a government-sponsored unit, and according to cinematic principles that he valued, led him to take a more marginal position in favour of what he would call 'documentary' films. Grierson also became somewhat hostile towards excessive experimentation. Yet he still continued to insist on the poetic and creative aspects of documentary filmmaking, so that film could reveal something on a deeper level than mere content, and could be distinguished from newsreels and ciné magazines, which were viewed as artistically insufficient. In line with the growth of social concerns, the artist now had to channel individual expression into an already defined purpose: communicating some of the abstract or concrete ideas underlying modern society.

Drifters: Production and Aesthetics

Grierson's work for the EMB eventually led to his producing and directing *Drifters*, a film designed to promote the herring-fishing industry. Grierson had to make a film on a specific subject yet was allowed a great deal of creative freedom. The film blended professional expertise with amateur enthusiasm and 'objective' material with creative interpretation. It was shot in the summer of 1928 and produced by New Era, a film company that specialized in short films, at a cost of only £2,948.[16] Basil Emmott, a professional cinematographer who worked in the British film industry, photographed it on 35mm stock.

Briefly summarized, *Drifters* begins with a short scene in which fishermen leave their small village and enter the 'modern', 'industrial' arena of the harbour, where they prepare their ships ready for the catch. The film then follows a single ship as it leaves the harbour, the camera mounted on the ship catching the view from it, and the action on it. We see the men cast two miles of nets; then, as they sleep, there are views of fish as they are caught within the nets. The men haul the nets in as a storm rises, and eventually the ship returns to the harbour. There follows a sequence showing the fish being sold and packaged on the market, and finally being loaded and transported away.

The film fits in with Grierson's ideas of an 'objective' drama of common life based around an action- and male-biased vision of the working classes. It dispenses with any psychological interplay between characters and instead shows ordinary actions as dramatic in themselves. The film is both an abstract depiction of objective reality and a poetic treatment of that

4. Fishermen casting nets in *Drifters* (picture from, and courtesy of, John Grierson Archive)

reality. Grierson treats nature, industry and humans as abstract material, lingering on the shapes and patterns they create. *Drifters* is also rhythmic in that drama is created through editing juxtapositions and tempo. These elements conform to the poetic, rhythmic and visual cinema that Grierson advocated in his writings.

The most noted influence on *Drifters* is Eisenstein's *Battleship Potemkin*, understandably, considering Grierson prepared the film for English-language screenings and mentioned it in many of his writings, and that the two films received their British premieres at the same Film Society screening on 10 November 1929. There are certainly similarities between the two films, in that *Drifters* uses montage for dramatic effect: in the absence of psychological characterization, montage serves as the motor that powers the film. *Drifters*'s negation of studio filming, its characterization and its adoption of (working-class) 'types' instead of 'actors' can also be seen as influenced by *Potemkin*. The parallels between the two films should not be overemphasized, however. I mentioned earlier that Grierson thought

5. A picturesque, silhouetted shot of a trawler, firmly encased within the natural landscape in *Drifters* (picture from, and courtesy of, John Grierson Archive)

that while the strengths of Soviet montage filmmaking should be adopted, there should be added something of the 'British sense of moderation'.[17] *Drifters* is clearly less intense in its pacing and action than *Potemkin*; while there are occasional moments of swift montage (especially during the storm), the editing is on the whole less rapid, as is the pace of actions within the frame.

Another very different film, yet a film also cited by Grierson as a chief influence, was Flaherty's document of an Inuit hunter, *Nanook of the North* (USA, 1922). Both films construct highly aestheticized images out of natural material: *Nanook* features strong contrasts between white and black, and occasionally represents characters as abstract specks on the landscape; *Drifters* features lingering, abstract shots of the sea and contains many silhouette shots. The two films also share a fascination with man's battle against, and relationship with, nature. Yet Grierson forsook the focus on an individual character and emphasized the rhythm of editing, in contrast to the more classical approach found in *Nanook*. Grierson also incorporated the machine into the man–nature relationship.

Nanook of the North was praised among artistic circles in America, and Grierson admired it for the way it offered alternatives to what he considered the negative aspects of commercial filmmaking.[18] The influence of avant-garde models, however, meant that *Drifters* evaded classical film conventions more than *Nanook*. It did so through fragmentary editing patterns that build up a symbolic drama of images rather than a character-driven plot. It is the interrelationship between man, machine and nature that fuels this symbolic drama. For example, the editing sequence that flits between abstract visions of sea and surf, followed by a ship's funnel emitting curlicues of billowing smoke, is associative montage that stresses connections between nature and industry. Likewise, there are many shots of birds and fish grouped together, cut with men casting herring nets; these emphasize the patterned and organizational similarities between different species. In a similar manner, the abstract and rhythmic properties of machinery—such as the mechanical motion of the turbine engine, or the revolving winch—are seen as an integral part of the overall process in which the fishermen participate, and are also admired for their abstract qualities. At one stage in the film, a close-up of the engine is eventually transformed by the superimposition of rippling patterns of the sea: these are not only abstract things that are fascinating in themselves, but are part of a global 'pattern'.

Such organization indicates that Grierson was combining abstraction with naturalism and objectivity. This inevitably connects *Drifters* with the 'city symphony' films of the period. Films such as *Berlin: Symphony of a City* (Ruttmann, Germany, 1927) and *Rien que les Heures* (Cavalcanti, France, 1926) combined avant-garde abstraction with more of an emphasis on 'objective' reality. City symphony films marked a merging of abstraction and social documentation, and were later mentioned by Grierson as valuable precedents to the documentary movement.[19] These films marked a shift towards social reality within abstract cinema, in which the outside world was structured through highly formalized compositions and rhythmic arrangements. *Drifters* does not focus as heavily on the urban environment, however: *Manhatta* (Strand and Sheeler, USA, 1921), for example, shows Manhattan's bridges as combinations of grids and lattices, buildings as angular formations, the smoke of funnels and chimneys as dense swirls. *Drifters* centres more around the battle between man and nature, and the interconnections between past and present.

The way in which *Drifters* concentrates on the interconnections between past and present—or tradition and modernity—reflects an evolutionary and rationalist creed. The evolutionary theme is highlighted in the film's opening titles, which read:

> The Herring fishing has changed. Its story was once an idyll of brown sails and village harbours—its story now is an epic of steel and steam.
> Fishermen still have their homes in the old time village—But they go down for each season to the labour of a modern industry.

The film then shows the fishermen's walk from their village to the modern, industrial harbour: they travel from the old to the new and are themselves symbols of the interconnectivity between old and new. While the film places itself on the side of modern progress, it stresses the organic links between past and present: these links highlight the evolutionary theme, itself a key component of 'progress'. I will return to this theme in more detail in Chapter 5.

Themes of evolutionary progress link Grierson's film to the ideological outlook of the Fabian Society, which espoused a gradualist and non-revolutionary form of socialism that should evolve in an organic manner.[20] It is relevant that many Fabian members, while opposing jingoistic attitudes, believed that European civilization was superior to the third world.[21] Such attitudes fitted into a nationalist-internationalist purview, which allowed Grierson to adopt imperialist attitudes without appearing excessively jingoistic; it is notable that Grierson himself was a member of the Fabian Society while at Glasgow University.[22] Evolutionary ideas can also explain why Grierson's film is so obsessed with both modern machinery and nature, and why man's battle against, and relationship with, nature was of central dramatic importance.

The Reception of *Drifters*

Drifters, as noted above, was first shown at the Film Society. According to Paul Swann, the filmmakers subsequently managed to secure extensive theatrical bookings.[23] Reviewers at the time generally saw the film as representing a new stage in British filmmaking. The leftist *Sunday Worker*, for example, proclaimed *Drifters* to be 'the best film that Britain has yet turned out'. Interestingly, the review went on to note the difference between *Drifters* and newsreels: its poetic, artistic properties and its 'touch of humanity'.[24] In the less politically concerned *Close Up*, Oswell Blakeston raved about the film's poetic force, hailing its combination of visual metaphors and rhythmic editing.[25] Looking over the many contemporary reviews of the film, it immediately becomes clear that it touched a nerve with the majority of British film critics, whether they moved in political or aesthetic circles, or were among the more artistically minded newspaper critics. It was seen as remarkable for its 'realistic' subject matter, its poetic qualities, its picturesque photography and its Soviet-style montage. The film was praised in a number of trade, daily and weekly papers of various ideological persuasions, both local and national, including the *Daily Mail*, the *Manchester Guardian*, the *Empire News*, the *Spectator*, the *Bioscope* and *Film Weekly*—a list that reflects the wide-ranging appeal of the film.[26]

Drifters tapped into the desire for a modernist form of British cinema, aware of artistic and international developments, yet specifically British and not parasitic upon familiar international styles. The film appeared in commercial cinemas and alternative outlets such as film societies: it exemplified an 'art film' that could appeal to a general audience (though whether it was liked by working-class audiences is open to question). It fitted the calls of many intellectuals for a film practice that merged experimentalism with dramatic coherency and 'balance'. It also fell between cheap amateurism and professionalism, both in terms of its budget and personnel (Grierson the amateur with artistic film credentials, Emmott the professional cameraman, shooting on 35mm). As I argued, although many people sought alternatives to the formulae of commercial filmmaking, amateur films were often judged technically deficient. *Drifters* clearly managed not to fall into this category for most reviewers.

The way that the film combined abstract aesthetics with a clear focus upon objective reality was also well received within intellectual circles. C.A. Lejeune praised the film because of the way that it used objective materials in an abstract and poetic manner. Criticizing commercial cinema's continual reliance upon literary and theatrical traditions, she wrote that man had 'stood in the way of development, blocking out from the cinema a combination of images in the rhythm of the abstract and inanimate that would give the directors' work a new and fuller meaning'.[27] She went on to add that she did not ask for a totally abstract cinema, but a cinema that accepted 'every scrap of material on its own merits, using evocative form, whether of man or machine, as an impartial basis for arrangement'.[28]

While the utilization of trawlers as subject matter could be hailed as an aesthetic option in some quarters, it could be perceived as a social choice in others. There were new workers' organizations forming around this time, and they generally saw commercial British cinema as ignoring the working classes as serious subjects, employing them only as figures of fun. For example, *Workers Cinema*, the official organ of the Federation of Workers' Film Societies, argued that commercial films represented

> A world in which the working class is permitted to intrude only to be insulted. The working class provides the comic relief. It provides the milieu for the crooks. It provides the surroundings to which the hero is relegated as a temporary punishment for sin, or as a hiding-place from 'the world'.[29]

This perception was undoubtedly overstated; nonetheless it contributed to the favourable reception of *Drifters*. In an age where class consciousness was on the rise through trade unions and workers' clubs, work itself became a central focus of an 'authentic' identity. The 'epic' construction of the process of work in *Drifters*, then, could be seen as treating the working classes as dignified. Unlike commercial cinema, this film was perceived as facing up to the realities of existence rather than escaping from them.

One of the few critics who did criticize *Drifters* was the American, H.A. Potamkin, who in *Close Up* perceptively bemoaned the lack of scrutiny in the film and the way that it dehumanized working men. While many British critics hailed the film's mix of objectivity and abstraction, for Potamkin this was evidence of a lack of insight into the human condition:

> Where are the people in his [Grierson's] film? He is more engrossed with the *independent graces* of fish in the water—well-done details in themselves but no part of the human process which the film was to be.

[...] The picture therefore is indeterminate [...] it is no re-vitalised revelation of human activity.[30]

Potamkin was confused by the critical fervour that had accompanied the film in Britain. His perception of the film encapsulated the problem of combining objective abstraction and an attempt to document working life.

Objectivity and the Working Classes

Potamkin had a point: Grierson's treatment of working-class trawler men in an 'objective' and abstract (or poetic) manner clearly does pose problems. On one level, the film was updating the modernist abstract film in a more 'humanist' manner. On another, it was creating an evolutionary drama of the tensions and interdependency of nature, man and machine in an industrial world. The strategy of abstracting concrete material ultimately dehumanized the men in the film, though, transforming them into geometrical shapes and functional objects.[31] Humans are often presented in fragments, so that their bodies are incomplete figures that contribute to the overall compositional balance of the film. They are like machinery in the way that they perform their tasks efficiently. It is no surprise that the men are mostly seen working; their only respite is through necessary functions, such as eating and sleeping. The film manages to objectify man, machine and nature, so that they constitute segmented parts of one, vast, interconnecting reality-machine.

By denying inner, psychological reality within the text, Grierson stressed the need for objective reality and actions to be presented in a way that reflected the (middle-class, intellectual) creative psychology of the individual. It was no coincidence that the physical, objective people in the film were working class: Grierson had already claimed in an earlier article that because cinema was a visual medium, it should concentrate on those who were 'physically expressive', such as children, animals, men at their craft, 'primitives and the like'.[32] This posited a differentiation between sedentary, psychological intellectuals who are able to create artistic works, and the working classes (as well as children, animals and 'primitives'), who are posited as 'objective' creatures. It is no surprise to learn that Grierson thought that there was a fundamental difference between the lower and middle classes, that they 'thought' in different ways.[33] This emphasis on action also partly explains the tendency of *Drifters* and other subsequent documentary films to focus on older, craft-based industries: such work showed the working man in a more physically expressive, 'objective' manner than, say, assembly-line labour in a factory. Ironically, the attempt to stress the continuation of craft in a world that was seen as becoming increasingly machine-like ultimately stressed the similarities between working men and machines.

This view of the working classes is inextricably connected to ideas of modernity and rationalization. The working classes were symbols of modernity; the rise in industrialized wage-labour and increased class-consciousness became marked features of the twentieth century, features that many 'modern' artists felt impelled to reflect. Many of the documentary filmmakers felt the need to bring the working classes to the screens because they saw this section of society as inextricably connected to 'objective' reality. Yet, what constituted objective reality was itself a subjective, or at least selective, matter. Documentary films often ignored employment in consumer industries and white-collar work as well as more repetitive, factory-line labour. At the time, however, shop and clerical work were growing faster than any other areas of employment in Britain and unskilled work was increasing faster than skilled or semi-skilled.[34]

So the documentary movement was constructing a selective, exclusionary vision of modernity, despite Grierson's insistence that the artist should have a broad outlook. This was due first, to the institutional framework in which such films were created. Most of these films were made for the government or for industrial sponsors, or both. They therefore had to avoid politically sensitive issues of exploitation or addressing workers' discontent. Therefore, the critique of such objectification of working subjects found in a film like Eugene Deslaw's *In the Shadow of the Machine* (Belgium, 1927) was absent. We also have to consider that these documentary filmmakers did not have an open choice of subject matter but were contracted to make films on specific matters. Second, the construction of modernity within this institutional framework was further skewed by what Grierson and other filmmakers considered interesting subject matter: the physical and 'dynamic' actions of man in more traditional working-class areas, which could be moulded into a 'poetic' film. Third, a masculine bias—which viewed consumption as 'feminine'—meant that filmmakers tended to emphasize men involved in the process of production.

While Grierson wanted to reflect the rhythms of everyday life, then, he did so in a discriminatory manner, which relegated what he regarded as 'feminine' aspects of everyday life to the outskirts of aesthetic representation. This can be illustrated by Grierson's remarks about the introduction of sound cinema, which he saw as feminine. He thought that sound would merely recreate 'trivial', everyday talk, thus destroying the artistic and poetic aspects of the silent film:

> The pathos of distance which comes with skylines may prove too tense—the abstraction which comes with silence may prove too remote—especially for the women audiences who hang like a millstone around the aesthetic neck of democracy. Living and thinking, as they do perforce, in a world of petty horizons and only too personal satisfactions, they will fall for chit-chat.[35]

Such a comment displays a subjective dislike of the 'feminine': the feminine was equated with talk, pettiness and inwardness; the male with action, dignity and externality. For all Grierson's emphasis on the objective, this passage shows how, ultimately, he was dressing up his subjective prejudices in objective (and binary) language, creating greater credibility for his own discourse. This masculine, traditionally inflected vision of modernity was something seemingly shared by many of the other members of the documentary movement (it is at least evident in their films). As contemporary feminist accounts of modernity have stressed, this has been a prevalent trait of modernist commentaries.[36] The inter-war period saw many challenges to the conventions and constraints that had defined femininity, leading to what has been called a crisis in masculinity. Mica Nava, for example, argues that the increasing freedom of women was often linked to consumerism, which therefore became encoded as feminine and passive by many male intellectuals.[37] The demarcation between passive/active, feminine/masculine, personal/public, then, can be seen as a displacement of rising male passivity in the face of increasing feminine freedoms: 'Concerns about "superfluous" women—who in the popular imagination were also "new" women: flappers, hedonists, feminists, workers, voters—can be read as an evidence of masculinity, of men's fear of being diminished, swamped and consumed.'[38]

Conclusion

Drifters was the first British film truly celebrated as a great work of art within native alternative film culture. One of the reasons for this was that it fitted into the broad discursive frameworks that had up until this point been formulated among such circles. It matched a number of evident trends: its focus on male working-class labourers, as well as on machinery in motion, met calls for a cinema that focused on 'modern' aspects of the nation; its use of montage reflected the acclaim that certain Soviet films were enjoying at the time, with a concomitant privileging of editing as an artistic cinematic technique. The manner in which such montage was incorporated into a slower paced structure, with a more 'picturesque' focus on landscape, meant that it also avoided what was thought to be 'uninspired imitation' of international influences.

In this sense, the film paved the way for the privileging of the documentary film movement as a native 'art' cinema, which therefore cemented its place within history. Although the documentary movement did gain a privileged place within this cultural milieu—and its status as a 'movement' was aided by such a position, as films produced within it thus came with a cachet—only some of these films were celebrated. The films that were the best received were those that were more self-consciously made as works of art (in the vein of *Drifters*) rather than more basic, straightforward 'informational' films, which actually constituted a large percentage of its output. Yet, while many of the films that followed in the line of *Drifters* (focusing on similar themes and/or subject matter) continued to be acclaimed, the introduction of sound complicated the state of filmmaking and hence modified attitudes towards film art. I look at some films that can be seen as working within a similar aesthetic template to *Drifters* in Chapter 5, but the next chapter will focus more specifically on the reaction in alternative film culture to sound.

4

Alternative Film Culture in the Shadow of Sound

In this chapter I will summarize some of the main trends of the alternative cultural network in light of the consolidation of sound cinema, as this was an event that profoundly rocked the views of many British cinéphiles. Many of the programmes of film societies, as well as attitudes towards cinema, continued the templates laid down in the 1920s. There were, however, some major transformations, particularly regarding opinions of commercial cinema. I will therefore examine discourse on cinema in *Close Up* during the 1930s until its demise in 1933, and also in two other influential 'alternative' journals of the period: *Film* (subsequently *Film Art*) and *Cinema Quarterly*. I will also look at some of the other main trends, such as exhibition. These major shifts in alternative culture in the 1930s will provide a contextual framework within which to assess a number of film productions.

Close Up: Sound and Disillusionment

In international alternative film culture, the introduction of sound was largely viewed as a serious setback for aesthetic as well as commercial reasons. Sound placed into question many ideas that cinéphiles had formulated about cinema. Numerous intellectuals had built up theories of film as an art in its own right, identifying aspects of the cinema seen as crucial to its 'identity'. Such components as montage, rhythm and fluid camera movement were isolated as developing cinema in a progressive and natural direction. That is, they were privileged as marking advances as well as conforming to a basic framework. The ontological properties formulated by film critics and theorists rarely took account of sound, though, because cinema was classified as a visual medium. One of the strengths of this was seen to reside in the presumed universality of the visual.

The advent of sound was therefore widely viewed as halting the artistic evolution of the medium, reducing mobility and aligning cinema more closely with the theatre. On a commercial level, sound threatened the very existence of a strong, independent film movement, in both production and exhibition. From the production aspect, most small-scale filmmakers could not afford to invest in sound equipment. On the exhibition side, many of the smaller film societies that had been established were unable to purchase the necessary equipment for projecting sound films. Thus an aesthetic and technical hostility towards the sound film arose. Whereas previously, many cinéphiles (especially in Britain) had placed much faith in technological progress for driving innovations essential to their vision of cinema, now many saw technology as deviating from the medium's organic development. Richard Abel, discussing the situation in France, has argued that whereas theory and criticism had previously seen itself as directing film practice, it was now straining to keep up with it: 'The theoretical positions that had been nurtured throughout the 1920s were now shaken, some almost shattered and others reconstituted anew. In this, French film theory and criticism seems to have been shaped by the pressure or rupture of several historical forces or events, none of which were uniquely French.'[1]

Many aesthetes rejected the 'talking' film and took up one of two broad positions. Some became disillusioned with the cinema and believed that its standards had irrevocably degenerated, others attempted to formulate innovative uses of sound. In the former category, a proportion remained firmly committed to the aesthetics of the silent cinema, while another group withdrew their interest from the medium altogether. In the latter category, some people were drawn to 'atypical' uses of sound that did not adhere to strict precepts of reproduced dialogue, whereas others advocated a more radical, contrapuntal use of sound, in which sound was edited so that it clashed with the visual track.[2] In *Close Up*, all of these attitudes were aired. Nevertheless, towards the end of its publication the journal as a whole became disillusioned with cinema, a stance that was in part influenced by the sound revolution.

Discussions of sound in the earlier editions of *Close Up* are almost entirely negative, with sound perceived as a threat to cinematic art. Thus Kenneth Macpherson wrote that sound was a 'monstrosity [...] descending full speed upon us'.[3] After *Close Up*'s publication in October 1928 of Eisenstein, Pudovkin and Alexandrov's manifesto on sound, though, many writers began to believe that sound could be used in an artistic manner as long as it was developed along a non-synchronous path. In the (now famous) Soviet manifesto, the writers argued that sound should be used in a creative manner, in counterpoint to the visual images.

This method of using sound would not only retain (and extend) creative editing strategies, it would also maintain cinema's internationalism and lead to a 'new *orchestral counterpoint* of sight-images and sound-images'.[4] By 1929 Macpherson was praising films that used sound in a creative manner, such as *Blackmail*.

Many *Close Up* writers in the late 1920s became interested in sound and prescribed ways in which it could be used creatively. There were always some critics who saw nothing but artistic deprivation heralded by the new technological revolution. Ernest Betts, for example, wrote: 'To have a running vocal commentary from the characters in a full-length film will utterly destroy its real eloquence, which lies in its silence.'[5] His view was that the addition of another dimension would dilute the overall power of a movie, by deflecting attention away from the medium's essential function, which he argued was to capture 'flowing forms of light and shade to a rhythmic pattern'.[6] Betts's anti-sound argument reflected his belief in an essential aesthetic function of cinema: sound, being a later addition to the cinematic apparatus, was viewed as an aesthetic intruder rather than an 'organic' development. This argument saw the cinema as a body, with sound an 'unnatural' prosthetic addition. The problem with such point of view was that it attempted to freeze organic life and thus repress the fact that bodies evolve in reaction to social, cultural or climactic change. It therefore made an erroneous assumption that cinema at this point was a natural and essential outcome of its own internal logic. Cinema, however, has always developed within an arena of social and cultural forces that in turn affect its 'evolution'.

Among the various modes of sound cinema promoted in the journal, contrapuntal sound became encoded as the most progressive, as the best way of adding another artistic dimension to the medium without harming other valued properties. H.A. Potamkin held up Alexandrov and Eisenstein's *Romance Sentimentale* (USSR, 1930) as exemplifying a creative use of sound. This film fulfilled a number of goals that Potamkin considered 'basic' in 'playing with sound', such as running the soundtrack backwards, or inscribing and designing the sound so that it could be cut to change or even be warped. Such strategies could dissociate sound from the instrument that produced it, and thus produce non-naturalistic, 'expressionist' noises.[7]

From a commercial angle it was undeniable that independent production—and the diversity of modes of film practice it more or less ensured—was threatened, at least in the short term. Even so, many of the aesthetic arguments over sound were questionable. They were usually guilty of dismissing the panoply of artistic thought that had gone into sound reproduction: in short, they simplified 'dialogue' films in a way that earlier anti-film critics simplified visual reproduction. Those who dismissed film often did so in simplistic terms, seeing it as merely reproducing what was in front of the camera. Cinéphiles themselves had defended cinema as being more than a mere representation: they claimed that the filmic process involved a whole host of creative decisions. This was an aspect they were blind to when it came to synchronized dialogue and natural sounds. As Rick Altman has highlighted, all types of recorded sound are representations of an original source.[8] The placing of the microphone, type of technical equipment used and treatments of sound are just a few of the choices that have to be made in deciding how sound is represented. Such a rudimentary sketch of the complexities involved in (merely) recording dialogue emphasize the false manner in which many theorists—even those who adopted a relatively 'progressive' stance—formed assumptions against sound. They tended to homogenize any adoption of synchronized sound into an undifferentiated mass.

Altman has accused those involved in early theoretical discussions of sound of engaging in and perpetuating two misleading notions.[9] First, there was an historical belief that treated sound as a late addition to cinema, when in fact it was an integral part of cinema from the beginning: this meant that instead of treating image and sound as simultaneous and coexistent, they were ordered chronologically.[10] Second, there was an ontological fallacy that reacted to the rapid universalization of sound by locating the essence of cinema within the visual and relegating sound to a supplementary position. In their eagerness to challenge a theatrical use of language, Altman has contended, intellectual aesthetes argued for the primacy of the visual: 'the historical and ontological fallacies are the prescriptive arguments of silent filmmakers intent on preserving the purity of their "poetic" medium.'[11]

Altman's points are perceptive and I think it is true that the prioritizing of the visual has influenced later film theory and led—at least until recently—to the relative lack of sophisticated analysis of sound in film studies. He does perhaps overstate his case, however. While music was part of the cinematic experience in its early years, there does not seem to be any evidence that people were as awed by sound as much as by the series of moving images. Although experiments in synchronized dialogue did occur from cinema's beginnings, they were marginal and hampered by synchronization defects and amplification problems.[12] These isolated experiments cannot therefore be seen as an integral part of the cinematic experience and it is perhaps erroneous to assume that sound and image were of equal importance from the very beginnings of cinema. It is possibly because of this slight disparity that cinéphiles favoured the visual and subsequently overlooked the complexity of sound reproduction.

Close Up did occasionally print more technical articles that focused on sound in a detailed manner. For example, Dan Birt's 'The Principles of Film Recording' discussed the technicalities and complexities of sound recording even at the most basic level, discussing the science of sound and looking at the different permutations of sound recording. He mentioned the different types of sound qualities that could be affected by what type of microphone was used, where it was placed, how the sound was mixed at the mixing panel, and how it could be manipulated through muting, amplification, fading and echoing. The prevailing trends in intellectual film criticism and theory meant these more detailed, technical analyses of sound were relatively scarce within the pages of *Close Up*.[13]

Despite printing serious considerations of sound as an important cinematic element, and even the occasional defence of the 'talking' film, the journal became increasingly hostile to the development of film in the early sound era. In 1930 H.A. Potamkin argued against those who dismissed speech in a homogeneous manner and stated that speech could itself be used aesthetically: 'Speech can be stylised, harmonised and unified into an entity with the visual image.'[14] He argued that it was wrong to take speech out of the cinema, since 'everything in life belongs to the cinema'.[15] He thus considered the denunciation of speech as excessive and also restrictive. Despite such arguments, the tone of *Close Up* became increasingly anti-sound, thus increasing its antagonism towards commercial cinema.

In fact, as Bordwell has demonstrated, there was not a fundamental shift between silent and sound film aesthetics. In the early stages of sound film, *Close Up*'s complaints were justified, as there was less variety of angles, less mobility of the camera(s) and a flatter depth perspective in Hollywood films because of the limitations of sound technology.[16] Yet by the end of 1931 this was changing and the fluidity of the talking picture was similar to that of an average silent Hollywood film. Both Bordwell and Barry Salt note that there was a rather innovative spirit active in the early 1930s: Bordwell writes that there was a 'vogue for flashy camera movements', while Salt argues it was 'a period when some of the brightest spirits were still very active in trying out new devices for narrative construction in the mainstream sound cinema'.[17] Despite this, *Close Up* largely remained hostile and did not seem to notice these stylistic continuities. It was as though they were perennially resentful of the insertion of dialogue into the film. This led to the journal's main editorial board becoming disenchanted with the cinema, ultimately causing the journal's demise. This growing disillusionment was heralded by the reduction of the journal from twelve issues a year to four from March 1931 onwards.

There were a number of reasons why *Close Up* became disillusioned with cinema, most of them to do with sound. The first was that the editors saw the unconscious element of cinema being lost. Macpherson and Bryher had encouraged contrapuntal or expressive uses of sound primarily because they saw this as the only way in which sound could represent unconscious processes. For them, the dominance of synchronized dialogue not only made cinema more static, but also returned it to the level of the conscious. Coming from a literary background, the editorial board of the journal tended to locate cinematic art in expressing what lay beyond words, thus representing an aesthetic realm outside literature. This ties in with Laura Marcus's claims that H.D.'s writings in *Close Up* were preoccupied with cinema as a medium capable of unlocking 'inner-speech'. H.D.'s conception of cinema was that it was a form of hieroglyphics, 'a thinking in pictures rather than words', a birth of a new visual language that could express the speech of the soul more adequately than spoken language.[18]

The second reason for *Close Up*'s disillusionment with cinema was the aforementioned reduction of internationalism. This was explicitly stated by Macpherson in the first quarterly edition of the journal:

> With the establishment of the talking film, the world situation with regards to films is completely altered. Whereas, during the period of silent films, world distribution was fluid, now films are becoming more and more tied up within national limits. Circulation has to an enormous extent come to an end.[19]

He cited an example of this in Switzerland, which during the silent period was an 'open market for the world', showing films from many different countries. With the advent of the talking film this ended, and French and German films began to be shown 'almost exclusively', because of language differences. This meant that recent converts to screen art would have their film diet limited to those spoken in their own language. As a consequence, Macpherson argued that *Close Up*, in order to 'continue as before' and cover international cinema, would have to be published less regularly. Rather than leaving foreign films solely in the hands of foreign correspondents, Macpherson announced that 'the editors and their representatives' would themselves travel to various countries so that *Close Up* did not become a 'hotch-potch of news'. The lack of 'enough relevant material' was cited as an additional reason for the reduction of output.

A third reason for the loss of interest was that the dream of a strong independent movement feeding into the commercial film industry and thus aiding its progression was—at least temporarily—crushed. The majority of commercial films were sound films, the majority of independent films were silent: they had thus grown further apart, rather than closer together. While Macpherson and Bryher had always privileged 'progressive' films made within a commercial climate, they also thought that an independent movement was crucial if commercial industries were to make 'artistic' innovations. With coordination between the two spheres in disarray, the journal tended to become more fiercely anti-commercial in the 1930s. Macpherson argued that:

> More and more expenditure will be required on the part of film executives, and the higher their costs soar, the more wary they will have to be. Experiment will be confined to technical change—wide screen, stereoscopy, etc. Not to ideas. They will see to it that the films remain sodden with banality and popular appeal. And what will [sic] the point of the independent cinematicist continuing for very much longer his experiments on 35mm. film stock, if there will be no place for his work in any cinema?[20]

With hopes of coordination dashed, the journal also lost hope of the mass public becoming attuned to 'artistic' films and thus became more dismissive towards the 'mass', who had flocked to sound films.[21]

The final reason I would cite for the journal's disenchantment is not related to sound. It is, rather, the poor critical reception that Macpherson's feature film, *Borderline* (1930), received. Before the critical failure of this film, which I will discuss in more detail in Chapter 7, Macpherson and Bryher had begun to take a more optimistic view towards sound, but after it the hostility towards commercial cinema as a whole was exacerbated.[22]

Macpherson's remaining articles tended to hark back nostalgically to the days of silent cinema. Disappointed with the increasing technological sophistication of commercial films and loath to accept low-budget, independent filmmaking as a suitable alternative, he attacked commercialism and excessive rationality, claiming that filmmakers should return to the days of 'primitives'. In an article written with Oswell Blakeston he bemoaned the fact that the magic and innovation of earlier cinema had been replaced by scientific precision and visual sophistication.[23] Yet, while

Blakeston developed a marginal cinematic trajectory out of such a belief, Macpherson lost interest in the whole medium.

Blakeston rethought his attitudes and started to adopt a more prescriptive tone. Obviously aware that 'independent' cinema was under threat by sound developments, he seemed to detect that the only way a creative alternative to commercial cinema could arise was through amateur filmmaking. However, aware that many amateur films fell into the 'home movie' variety of family snap-shots, or into the category of 'Hollywood imitation', Blakeston sought to give advice on making cheap, artistic movies.[24] He did not want Hollywood to colonize film practice, so his advice to amateur filmmakers can be seen as a way of keeping alternative methods alive. He also participated in the making of an abstract film, *Light Rhythms* (1929), which I will discuss in Chapter 6.

Bryher also lost interest in the medium, and H.D. had ceased to contribute to the journal. Realizing that the aesthetics of the silent film had been left behind, the main editorial team itself became mute, as if embodying what they thought the cinema should be. In conjunction, the journal itself reduced its written text, published more photographs (many of which were not related to film), and reviewed books on non-cinematic fields such as photography, literature and poetry. It is not surprising that the aesthetics most associated with the journal—namely a psychologically based conception of the medium—began to be eclipsed in alternative circles. As a result of such developments, the journal ceased publication in 1933.

Film Art and *Cinema Quarterly*

When *Close Up* ceased publication in 1933 many of its threads—especially its aesthetic concerns—were continued in the journals *Cinema Quarterly* (first published in 1932) and *Film Art* (first published as *Film* in 1933). The educational themes of *Close Up* were also covered in the journal *Sight and Sound* (first published 1932). This is representative of a greater fragmentation of interests within alternative film culture in the 1930s. In the 1920s, despite different emphases, there were broad similarities between aesthetes who were writing about film as a distinctive, modern and artistic medium. In the 1930s, along with the separation of aesthetic and educational coverage of film, there was also a growing political interest in film, as represented in papers such as *Workers Cinema* and *Kino News*, and the emergence of several workers' film societies. There were still many figures who continued to be interested in different areas, but the growing strength of alternative film culture inevitably brought conflicts of interest and a rise of more specialized concerns.

Cinema Quarterly and *Film Art* are the most important journals for this study because they both emphasized the aesthetic side of the cinema. They were, however, marked by major differences. While *Cinema Quarterly* took a broadly documentary line in stressing the social application of formalism, *Film Art* was less concerned with social considerations. This gap widened as the 1930s progressed, but there was no evident animosity between them, as can be gauged by the fact that some writers contributed to both. There were also a number of similarities between the journals: a willingness to promote amateur films and minority film organs; an interest in 'poetic' cinema; and a rather patronizing attitude towards the general cinema-going public.

Cinema Quarterly, an Edinburgh-based journal, was edited by Norman Wilson, with Forsyth Hardy as its review editor and Basil Wright as London correspondent. The journal was a staunch supporter of the documentary movement, but in its early years, at least, it was more than just a propagator of documentary ideas. In general, it was promoting 'alternative' and 'intelligent' international cinema. It also attempted to promote the diverse array of film societies and amateur filmmaking within Britain, even acting as a distributing agency for small British films without official distribution.

While *Cinema Quarterly* supported filmmaking that was allied to social purpose, in its first few years it also stressed the necessity of aesthetic, formalist concerns. It propounded, for the most part, an aesthetics that merged technical skill, a concern for subject matter and structural discipline. In its first editorial, Wilson argued that good technique was necessary, but not sufficient on its own; theme and plot had to be considered too.[25] He further stated that the journal stood for artistic sincerity, as opposed to commercial compromise. Because of this investment in the notion of sincerity (which also connoted 'independence'), Hollywood was now seen in largely detrimental terms, creating 'a world of its own which is so far removed from reality that anything its films attempt to say is utterly worthless'.[26] Artists were encouraged to go into the 'real world', but also to shape this world in a way that revealed something 'beneath the surface'. This led to a slight tension between the creative temperament of the artist and the social necessity of addressing what were considered to be important matters.

Films made in a cooperative manner within the documentary movement were celebrated as they represented collaborations between like-minded artists who shared a common goal. This was contrasted to the workings of the mainstream industry, whose commercial imperative was ultimately seen as compromising artistic sincerity. It must be noted that, despite the cooperative nature of the documentary movement being approved, *Cinema Quarterly* did still tend to attribute directorial control to a single person as a result of its adherence to the cult of the artist.

Film Art was first titled *Film*, but changed its name after only one edition. Its editorial board and purview, however, remained largely the same. Edited by B. Vivian Braun, its associate editors were Orlton West, Irene Nicholson, Robert Fairthorne and Edward Ashcroft, most of whom were filmmakers.[27] West occasionally contributed to *Close Up*; another *Close Up* regular, Oswell Blakeston, also contributed to *Film Art*. The main difference between *Film Art* and *Cinema Quarterly* was that *Film Art* did not demand a combination of formal experimentation and social purpose. *Film Art* considered content to be subordinate to form and only relevant in so far as it contributed to the formal properties of the film. Braun favoured films that were abstract because they relied 'entirely on form, and the form may absorb the subject matter'.[28] *Cinema Quarterly* was interested in the formal aesthetics of the cinema, but considered film to be 'a medium for the communication of ideas and the exposition of ideals', rather than an end in itself.[29] *Film Art* was interested in film itself and did not see any particular need to connect cinema to a wider social fabric. Replying to a letter from H.P.J. Marshall, who suggested that political content was essential within a work of art, Braun argued that form was far more important than political content and that the 'direct mixing of art and politics is fatal'.[30]

Another difference between the journals was that *Film Art* began to modify the hitherto strict adherence to aesthetic unity previously prominent within alternative film discourse. The belief that a truly satisfying work of art should be coherent, with every moment contributing to the greater whole, was still evident in *Cinema Quarterly*. *Film Art*, however, tended to diverge from this type of judgement. While its contributors may still have favoured films that satisfied all of their aesthetic preferences, they also paid much attention to films that only contained 'moments' of aesthetic beauty. They therefore began to focus more on fragments of films in isolation from the totality within which they were contained.[31] The journal tended to favour 'visual splendour', 'poeticism' and creative editing. If a film displayed occasional elements that fitted into these categories, it could be singled out for praise. Perhaps this was an attempt to move towards an evaluative aesthetics that was kinder to amateur productions, realizing that amateur films were made under different conditions to commercial films. In light of the increased hostility towards commercial filmmaking, this would make sense. Nevertheless, as I shall later demonstrate, the aesthetic preferences detectable in the journal did not totally move away from standards derived from commercial practice.

Another slight difference between the journals was the attitudes towards sound that dominated aesthetic evaluation. Both journals adopted views that were in accord with previous alternative discourse, but the difference between them was that whereas *Cinema Quarterly* generally accepted sound as a positive component of the cinema, *Film Art* did not, instead clinging to the view that the cinema was a visual art. Sound was quite clearly perceived as an unnecessary addition to the cinematic apparatus, one that had no relation to the fundamental properties of cinematic art. In addition, it was, like *Close Up*, clearly international in scope, which meant that it saw sound as a force that would strengthen national boundaries.[32]

Correspondents from several countries contributed to *Film Art*, which sought to retain international cooperation between 'independent' film artists. This was one of the reasons why it was no longer concerned with cooperation between the commercial and independent spheres; the independent spheres of filmmaking, often with insufficient financial resources to use sound, represented the last bastion of a pan-national film language. In this context, Braun thought that sound—if used at all—should be used as a visual adjunct.

Cinema Quarterly was more positive towards sound so long as it was used in a 'creative' manner. It therefore tended to criticize sound when it merely recorded dialogue, which shows that the journal was by no means realist in any straightforward sense. Most of the articles on sound in the journal discussed using sound in an expressive manner. The emphasis on personal artistry also demanded that creative thought should be put into the soundtrack. This line on sound meant that, while straightforward dialogue recording was frowned upon, sound was accepted as an essential component of the cinematic medium. Thus many aesthetes reconfigured the artistic nature of the medium in line with changing technology, in contrast to those writing for *Film Art*. Sound was considered a positive addition to the cinematic apparatus because it boosted the creative permutations of the medium. Anthony Asquith, for instance, argued that sound was not external to the properties of film art, but altered them; he recommended a rhythmic employment of both sound and vision.[33]

Despite these differences, the two journals were drawn to a similar range of films. Both admired Soviet 'montage' films, films by artists such as Pabst and Dreyer, some Surrealist films and, in particular, many of the more abstract films made within the British documentary movement (as well as many of the more formalist documentaries from other countries). *Cinema Quarterly's* preference for British documentary films was unsurprising: not only did many documentary filmmakers write for the journal, but films such as *Cargo From Jamaica* (Wright, 1933), *Liner Cruising South* (Elton, 1933), *Contact* (Rotha, 1933) and *Song of Ceylon* (Wright, 1934) merged formal concerns with 'social purpose'. While *Cinema Quarterly* praised the use of 'realistic' material in a creative and coherent manner, *Film Art* tended to single out what it viewed as the more 'poetic' moments in these films and ignored the subject of realism.

Both journals also paid attention to amateur events and organizations, indicating the growing interest by amateurs in formalist filmmaking. *Cinema Quarterly* was keen to promote amateur film activities because their independence from commercial concerns meant that they occupied a position of artistic 'sincerity'. In the first few issues of the journal it is clear, though, that it was not satisfied with the state of amateur production at that point in time. It was therefore interested in the amateur movement more for its potential than for its actual achievements. Thus, although much attention was paid to amateur film activities, it was mostly informational, rather than aesthetic, in tone. Not many reviews of amateur films were published, the exceptions only gaining a few lines of basic description.

Amateur films never received much in the way of positive critical analysis. In one sense it could be argued that—following on from coverage in *Close Up*—amateur films did not fit into the dominant aesthetic frameworks of alternative discourse. Despite the shift away from commercial cinema in the 1930s, along with the encouragement and growth of amateur filmmaking, it is clear that the journal was still swayed by notions of technical quality that had been established by commercial film production. The fact that amateur filmmakers did not have access to advanced technical equipment, along with the common perception that their aesthetic organization was lacking in care and orderliness, meant that they were rarely reviewed in a positive light. In 1935 Leslie Beisegel wrote that 90 per cent of amateur films were 'drivel', many of them just 'animated family album'-type films.[34] This notice did suggest that there were a *few* amateurs making good films, but that material conditions worked against a fully fledged, artistic amateur movement: 'Let us be thankful that there are amateur film-makers with something to say, who are more interested in cinema than in themselves. Unfortunately these film-makers are either lone workers, handicapped by lack of capital, or else small groups of semi-professionals who are soon absorbed by the film industry proper.'[35]

In the mid-1930s, *Cinema Quarterly* became slightly more pessimistic regarding the ability of the amateur movement to transform the cinema. In tandem with this shift, the journal also began to adopt a more realist line: it became more committed to documentaries that forsook aesthetic experiments and paid more attention to how content was represented in an already established formal manner. This is roughly in line with the development of Grierson's thought, since he too began to adopt a more hostile attitude towards experimentation, in accord with his earlier views. He believed that filmmakers should experiment with aesthetic form to discover a suitable means by which to represent content in a fresh way. When a suitable formal language had been discovered, however, there would be no more need for further experimentation.[36]

Cinema Quarterly eventually began to propose a less ambitious programme for amateur filmmakers. It warned them to avoid 'tawdry romantics and pseudo-aesthetics', and emphasized the importance of focusing upon more modest matters.[37] In short, amateurs should not copy Hollywood formulae, nor should they be too experimental; instead, they should make simple, small-scale documentaries. 'Artistry' would be limited to the fact that these films should be carefully thought out by single-minded, creative individuals. It was now that the journal began to devote itself to documentary films and separate them from more experimental, personal films.

As its editor Braun was actually involved in amateur filmmaking, it is not surprising that *Film Art* was also concerned with promoting an aesthetically grounded amateur film movement. Like *Cinema Quarterly*, it thought this was a possibility rather than an actuality. Many articles in the journal expressed some kind of dissatisfaction with the (then) current state of amateur filmmaking. Judith Todd wrote in the first issue that she thought this was partly because amateur production societies and amateur exhibition outlets were often separate. Thus one segment of the amateur film world was aesthetically aware but technically unaware, while the reverse was true for the other sector. Todd thought it imperative that film societies should begin to make films, in order to contribute more to alternative film culture: 'The 16mm camera in the right hands is no toy. The pity is that the film societies, in concentrating on the exhibiting side, have not made use of it for inexpensive, experimental work.'[38]

While the editorial board of *Film Art* made a concerted attempt to partake in a coordinated amateur film culture (see below), it nevertheless tended to favour those films that, if not made within a professional context, could draw upon more financial resources and rely upon a greater knowledge of technical expertise than most amateur filmmakers in Britain could afford. Even though *Film Art* managed to modify the strict adherence to aesthetic coherence and balance, its choices were still informed by notions of 'technical excellence'. This discursive framework even worked against the critical reception of films made by its own editorial members: Braun's *Exhilaration* (1934) and Braun and Nicholson's *Beyond This Open Road* did not even receive full reviews, while Nicholson's *Ephemeral* (1934) received only a lukewarm reception from Braun. He thought the film was a creative piece of cinema marked by a good sense of composition, but that it was ultimately slight and marred by technical faults.[39]

Film Art also tended to favour documentary films as best representing artistic filmmaking within Britain, as they merged 'technical quality' and formal experimentation. The journal was only drawn to those films that it thought displayed overtly aesthetic qualities, though, and was far less celebratory about the movement as a whole than *Cinema Quarterly*. Discussing the GPO Film Unit, Braun thought it provided good facilities for genuinely creative directors to experiment with film form, and when they were allowed to do so they produced good results. But he also thought that the overall restrictions of the unit were a hindrance to artistic achievement in some cases: much of the output was uninspired and lacked experimentation. Good films arose from the unit when creative directors were allowed to express themselves in an unfettered manner, but too often the unit restricted such possibilities. Braun was thus attacking what Rachael Low has called the large output of straightforward 'instructional' documentaries, as opposed to the more self-consciously aesthetic and 'poetic' documentaries.[40]

It is clear from the notices in these journals that there were plenty of films made by film societies or clubs interested in the aesthetic possibilities of the medium. Along with the marginalization of amateur filmmaking at the time, many of the films that experimented with the medium in a self-consciously aesthetic manner have been lost, so it is impossible to judge the formal characteristics of such films or the extent to which they might be described as experimental. Only a few 'formalist' films made on an amateur basis—some of Norman McLaren's early films, and Braun and Nicholson's *Beyond This Open Road*—still exist. These films gained more notice than many amateur films, but they still did not receive extensive praise. It seems that, while these journals were keen to celebrate an artistic and spiritual alternative to Hollywood and the commercial film industry, they were less willing to celebrate the alternative image qualities often produced by cheap film equipment. If they had been willing to re-evaluate standards of technical quality, then it might have transpired that more amateur films would have been celebrated. As it turned out, the documentary movement was seen as representing a more technically accomplished compromise between art and commerce.[41]

In the later 1930s the journals began to lose interest in amateur filmmaking. *Film Art* started to recommend working for industrial sponsors as the best opportunity to make artistic films outside the commercial industry. Sponsors such as the EMB, the GPO, the Gas Light and Coke Company and Shell-Mex were praised for their openness in allowing individuals to develop their skills, in addition to providing decent technical resources.[42] Having completed *Beyond This Open Road,* Braun left *Film Art* after a dispute with Irene Nicholson, who took over editorial control of the journal along with John Moore; Braun launched his own journal *New Cinema* (1935), which only lasted for one edition. *Film Art* still gave notice to film societies, but only in relation to exhibition activities. News on amateur productions had seemingly dried up. Even Nicholson herself had engaged in making a film for the *Trinidad Guardian.*[43] The journal continued until 1937, but it seems that at this point those people interested in strictly formalist filmmaking had fallen to a number insufficient to continue the journal.

In 1936 *Cinema Quarterly* underwent a significant change and was eventually renamed *World Film News.* The new journal shifted its base to London and it became an altogether different journal in tone, a change that did not please some of those associated with *Cinema Quarterly.* While *World Film News* did still act as an outlet for the documentary movement, it reduced the number of theoretical articles published and concentrated on the main strands of documentary filmmaking: straightforward 'instructional' documentaries and those documentaries that were moving towards a convergence with the narrative film.[44] The publication became more like a trade paper, with an emphasis on documentary rather than the commercial film world. Nevertheless, it did pay more attention to commercial films than did *Cinema Quarterly.*

Film Groups and Societies

In the late 1920s there was already a shift towards the privileging of a more 'realist' form of experimental cinema, as highlighted by the preference for Soviet features.[45] This, in line with the growing (if never total)

103

disillusion with commercial cinema apparent within critical writing, led to the increasing preponderance of documentary films within film society screenings. The Film Society, for example, showed a greatly increased number of documentary films in the 1930s, and began to show these as the 'main attractions', whereas that privilege had often previously been accorded to a narrative feature.

In the post-sound era it became increasingly difficult for independent, artistic films to be made outside the film industry because of the expense of attaining sound equipment. Many avant-garde or artistic filmmakers turned to sponsored documentary filmmaking, which could still be seen as 'independent' cinema because such films were made outside the commercial industry. The shift from a 'formalist' towards a more objective and political form of 'independent' filmmaking is highlighted by the emphases of the two major international, independent conferences of the late 1920s. According to Hans Richter, while the first conference at La Sarraz was mostly concerned with the art of the cinema, the second conference in Brussels recognized that 'the Avant-Garde as a purely aesthetic movement had passed its climax and was on the way to concentrating on the social and political film, mainly in documentary form'.[46]

In light of such developments, many film societies operating along similar aesthetic lines to the Film Society continued to emerge, but there also arose two types of societies that were different in intent: workers' societies and amateur film societies, both of which had started to form in the late 1920s but really took off in the 1930s. In addition, there were a number of amateur production groups, variously termed 'ciné societies', 'cine groups' and 'film clubs', in operation by the early 1930s.

Workers' film societies emerged to show films with a political or social bent, in contrast to the existing societies in Britain, which were perceived as being primarily aesthetic in nature. The key organization involved in the establishment of a network of workers' film societies was the Federation of Workers' Film Societies (FWFS), which was founded on 28 October 1929.[47] It was established to encourage the formation of workers' film societies, to supply equipment, to give advice and support and to encourage the production of workers' films, amongst other things. Ralph Bond immediately appealed for membership of his London Workers' Film Society (LWFS), which had its first screening in November 1929.[48] And yet, while the workers' societies may have been opposed to the aesthetic emphasis that they perceived as dominating some of the existing societies, there were considerable overlaps between such societies. Many members of the Federation were already involved in the Film Society or *Close Up*, including: Ivor Montagu (the Federation's chairman), John Grierson, Ralph Bond, Oswell Blakeston and Robert Herring. The Federation—whose distribution wing was the Atlas Film Company—also collaborated with *Close Up* in order to present that journal's petition against censorship to parliament in 1930.[49]

Several of the workers' film groups were affiliated to different left-wing organizations.[50] Probably the most productive of these were Kino and the Workers Film and Photo League (WFPL, later the Film and Photo League). Kino was set up in 1933 in order to exhibit Soviet films and workers' newsreels on 16mm;[51] in 1934 it began making its own films, mostly workers' newsreels.[52] The WFPL came into being in October 1934 and was an offspring of Kino and the Workers' Camera Club; it aimed to coordinate 'the activities of all workers, artists and technicians in films and photography'.[53] From 1935 Kino became Kino Ltd and concentrated on distribution (it maintained strong ties with the WFPL, distributing its productions).[54]

The workers' film groups, then, which also had their own publications—such as *Workers Cinema* and *Kino News*—created a network that was a part of the broader alternative film culture, but still had enough of its own distinctive aims to be called a specific sub-section of that culture. Amateur film groups were less specific in nature, though those groups that emerged primarily to produce small-scale films were different to the exhibition-led film societies. Nevertheless, some film societies did also produce their own films, even if these were not made on a regular basis. The Edinburgh Film Guild, for example, made a 16mm documentary of Edinburgh in 1932 (title unknown), while Preston Film Society also made two documentaries in the same year: *O* and *Pylons*.[55]

B. Vivian Braun, meanwhile, who was already editing *Film Art*, attempted to cover all bases of alternative film culture by forming a Sub-Standard Film Society in 1932, which stated its objectives as 'exhibiting and studying experimental, abstract and documentary films'.[56] Braun and Irene Nicholson also became involved in film programming at the Forum Cinema, London, where they showed a range of alternative fare.[57] In 1934 they set up a film art course, designed to study the aesthetics of the cinema.[58] This sold out, and a more practical course followed in the same year, covering scenarios, filming, montage and film theory.[59] Also in 1394, they formed a production company, First Cinema Unit, declaring that they made films for film societies and other specialist cinemas, advertising their recent film *Beyond This Open Road* (1934), and announcing that several productions were in preparation.[60]

Braun and Nicholson's First Cinema Unit was just one of several amateur production clubs to emerge in this period. The amateur production movement was given a boost in 1932, when the Institute of Amateur Cinematographers was founded to give advice to amateur filmmakers and to act as an amateur film exchange.[61] Another attempt to encourage an 'artistic' amateur movement came with the establishment of the Independent Film-Makers Association (IFMA) in 1933. With G.A. Shaw as its honorary secretary and J.C.H. Dunlop as its honorary treasurer, the association contained a number of prominent advisers from the documentary and commercial spheres, including John Grierson, Anthony Asquith, Stuart Legg, Andrew Buchanan, Paul Rotha and Basil Wright. It was formed 'to bring together and assist those who are interested in the production of Documentary, Experimental, and Educational films'.[62] The association functioned to put members in touch with each other, to give personal advice and provide a scenario service to filmmakers and to operate a film exchange for films made by members. It also proposed to run a summer production school each year.

During the early years of the amateur film publication, *Amateur Cine-World*, attention was given to ciné clubs producing artistic, experimental films (though such attention seemed to recede after the first few issues). Within these pages one can glimpse the amount of amateurs who were attempting to produce films. Societies such as the Bolton Amateur Cine Association, the Blackheath Film Club, the Leicester Amateur Cine Society, the Teeside Cine Club, the Cambridge Photographic Club Cine Group and the Civil Service Cine Society were amongst those engaged in producing films. A number of these were engaged in producing 'documentary' films, thus reflecting the widespread move to the documentary in alternative film culture, though there did exist other groups who were engaged in more 'abstract' film work. For example, the Cambridge Photographic Club Cine Group were reported as engaged in a production of 'a study in cinematic expression' entitled *Delirium*, which is described as psychological in tone.[63]

Conclusion

In contrast to the 1920s, there was a great deal of independent film production in the 1930s: the growth of alternative film culture since the mid-1920s had seen the rise of journals, film societies and film clubs, as well as distribution units and the important British Film Institute (which often provided technical assistance to first-time filmmakers). This stronger network, though containing diverse currents, nevertheless stimulated production. The rise of sound, and concomitant loss of faith in the rise of a commercial 'art' cinema, also would have stimulated the growth of small-scale production, as more efforts were put into the growth of such productions. The aesthetic reactions to the sound phenomenon can be linked to a number of productions that emerged: for example, the 'denial of sound' attitudes found within the pages of *Film Art* can broadly be connected to a number of small, independent productions that were shot without sound facilities. By contrast, some of the more 'artistic' films made within the documentary environment did have sound facilities, and often experimented with the use of sound, thus connecting to the calls for an 'expressive' application of sound in filmmaking. The next two chapters will thus look in detail at a number of diverse films that can be related to such templates.

It should not be assumed that commercial cinema somehow became disengaged from the cultural ripples started by the growth of alternative film culture. It may have been the case that general attitudes prominent within alternative discourse became more hostile towards commercial cinema and thus paid more attention to the margins. However, as I have also pointed out, aesthetic preferences were still marked by the admiration of qualities produced by 'professional' technical equipment. In this sense, it should come as no surprise that many people who participated in alternative cultural activities were active in the commercial film industry: for example, Anthony Asquith, Alfred Hitchcock and Thorold Dickinson. A detailed analysis of such work is, unfortunately, beyond the scope of this study. Over the next three chapters I will instead scrutinize a number of 'independent' (or, at least, 'semi-independent') films that were made in Britain during the 1930s.

5

Montage, Machinery and Sound

I argued in Chapter 3 that *Drifters* fitted into the frameworks of alternative discourse in British film culture. Into the 1930s, a number of films following in the line of *Drifters* also tended to be valued as 'good' British cinema: films that merged social realism with more abstract, poetic elements. These were films that fell outside the narrative illusionism of commercial cinema, but which nevertheless were not too cheaply made, and therefore were seen to avoid the pitfalls of 'amateurism'—in particular 'sub-standard' technical quality. In this chapter, I will focus on selected themes that arose within some of the more formal films that fall under a broadly social documentary mode. I will also consider some films made outside the documentary movement, but which also addressed pressing social issues in a self-consciously formal way (some films that emerged from the broad workers' movement). For a number of films made under the aegis of the documentary film movement it is also important that sound was often employed in a manner that was considered more creative than its standard application in commercial cinema, a theme that I will address in the final section.

Montage and Machinery; Tradition and Modernity

Drifters employed a technique—montage—that was very much favoured by alternative discourse, but it did so in a manner that was not seen as merely mimicking the aesthetic templates of other cinemas (in particular, Soviet montage films). It achived this through exploring what were recognized as 'particularly British' concerns, and one of the main features that it addressed was the industrialization of Britain and how this connected to tradition. This connection between tradition and modernity, and an emphasis upon the employment of montage techniques for expressive and poetic purposes, continued to be a feature of many films made within the documentary film movement.

108

An early compilation film made in the documentary movement, *Conquest* (1930), is an interesting experiment in terms of portraying links between tradition and modernity, though it does so in a much more ruthless manner than *Drifters*. Directed by Basil Wright, it was an educational film, not intended for theatrical release and part of a low-budget cycle of films geared towards training young, inexperienced staff whom Grierson had recruited from the film society milieu. (It was, however, shown at the Film Society.) These films, cheap to produce and assembled from pre-existing footage, were exercises in creative construction that bypassed any financial risk. *Conquest* was largely constructed from footage from American Westerns, primarily from Paramount,[1] and provided Wright with the opportunity to indulge in experimentation by editing various fragments of film together.[2] Wright recalled that he also cut in some material from *Turksib* (Turin, USSR, 1929), but these scenes had to be removed so he copied them instead. The most noticeable way in which *Turksib* influenced *Conquest* is through the rhythmic editing of titles for dramatic effect (with capitals and font sizes used to emphasize certain themes).

Conquest is one of the most blatantly imperialist films made in the documentary movement in the inter-war years. It is a vehement defence of the expropriation of land in the name of 'progress', achieved through cutting and subtitling. The material is edited in a way that constructs an historical, evolutionary narrative. It follows a conservative history of the United States, in which the destruction of Native Americans is seen as a justified and positive event. In general terms, the film is about the increasing sophistication of technology, the titles announcing: 'The implements of man are the instruments of his progress. Only by the continual invention of more powerful tools and mechanisms has the conquest of the wilderness been made possible.'

One particularly interesting aspects of *Conquest* is the manner by which it intertwines rhetoric concerning general technological and evolutionary progress with cinematic progress. When the film arrives at the invention of the train, it begins to speed up its editing pace and develop a more overtly rhythmic editing pattern: the train is seen as a giant power that helped conquer the distances of the prairie and herald the modern world. Concurrent with the sophistication of instruments, then, is the sophistication of aesthetic technique, namely rhythmic montage, which in 1930 was generally regarded as the pinnacle of cinematic technique in a variety of alternative film cultures. The moment of cinematic and technological ecstasy is heralded by the titles as they flash up 'MACHINERY' in an imposing manner. What follows is an abstract montage of machinery in motion: a cadence of wheels, moving landscapes as seen from a train, the blur of train tracks.

This glorification of the train as a symbol of technological (as well as imperial) magnificence was a continual trope in many different realms of silent cinema, and *Conquest* itself edits together different images of the train as represented in other films. As Lynne Kirby has pointed out, the train itself was a symbol of modernity that was inextricably linked with the emergence of the cinema in terms of social and perceptual paradigms.[3] She argues that discourses surrounding the railroad prefigured those surrounding the cinema in that rail travel had to legitimate itself as respectable and safe; she also argues that the train instituted new perceptual subjectivities.[4] The most famous perceptual transformations involved new experiences of space and time, which both the cinema and the railroad could compress: 'The speed of train travel created a temporal and spatial shrinkage and a perceptual disorientation that tore the traveler out of the traditional space-time continuum and thrust him/her into a new world of speed, velocity and diminishing intervals between geographical points.'[5]

In *Conquest*, machinery and motion not only allow for greater ease of living and greater mobilization, they are also the two processes essential to the creation of montage. Montage is here an act of creation that imposes a transformative energy on pre-existing film. It is also allied with the train in that montage is privileged as the major cinematic power in the film, while the train is seen as the major technological power. The train could bring spaces together just like montage, and both were forces that could excite viewers/passengers by offering them dynamic, machine-mediated visions.

Conquest, edited together out of pre-existing materials, displays more of a reliance upon Soviet montage techniques than many of the more acclaimed, formal documentaries emerging from the documentary film movement, though it does still share an interest in evolutionary progress, even if in a more ruthless fashion than many other documentaries. Nevertheless, even a more 'poetic' film like Paul Rotha's *Contact* (1933) is underpinned by a rather single-minded concern for technological progress, which is perhaps not surprising considering that it was a promotional film for Imperial Airways.[6] Yet, as was common in Britain during the 1930s, promotional work also offered opportunities to experiment with creative filmmaking. Rotha had at this point established himself as a figure on the alternative circuit through his book *The Film Till Now*, and he had already worked briefly with Grierson at EMB. *Contact*, however, was his first film as director.

Like *Conquest*, *Contact* features montage scenes of transport: edited, abstract details of wheels, shots of sea, surf and train tracks in motion, as well as larger shots of ships and trains moving. These images then give way to the coming of the aeroplane, the titles announcing that this is the next wonder of transport, the images backing this up through a lovingly composed pictorial montage of the plane in the air, views of the sky (a new abstract vision), and close-ups of the plane as an assemblage of machine parts.

The film then settles into a more leisurely rhythm, as the plane in mid-air is contrasted with the many images that can be seen from the plane: deserts, seas, mountains and famous landmarks of places such as Nairobi, Athens and Cairo. In this part of the film, the continuity of technology and nature is established: the technological progress of aeroplane construction can, by dint of the visual perspectives it facilitates, provide new ways to wonder at nature. This mode of filmmaking is reminiscent of early travel films, in which film was employed to provide visions of distant, exotic places.[7] The railroad in particular had a close relationship with this genre and cooperated with film companies to provide covert advertising.[8] Likewise, Rotha's film eventually settles into a rather picturesque travelogue, with the plane now updating the wonders of railway vision. The film was thus an opportunity to show people who were unable to afford the expense of air travel the panoramic sights generated by this new vision-machine.[9] On one level, then, the film is a simulated virtual reality in which the pleasures of tourism are promoted.

Although the film is rather leisurely paced, a more ruthless dynamic occasionally seeps through. For example, while nature is seen as a picturesque visual display, it nevertheless must give way to industrial development when required by economics, as heralded in the title that reads: 'distant airports must be built in the face of nature'. Thus nature, still retaining its charm, is giving way to the modern world. It is no surprise, then, that when the film follows the plane around the world, nature becomes a long-distance view, fading into the past.

The film attempts to paper over this underlying message by presenting the scenes of the plane flying around the world in a romantic manner. The photography is pictorial and the pace of the film becomes leisurely. Even the soundtrack uses compositions by classical figures such as Rossini and Mozart, which provide a 'symphonic' experience of the luxurious pleasures of air travel. Rotha constantly argued for the social importance of the documentary movement, and opined that 'Beauty and symphonic movement is [...] nothing in itself.'[10] Yet *Contact* seems to subordinate any social message to a series of aesthetically pleasing images.

Both *Contact* and *Conquest* tend to fetishize machinery, constructing loving montage sequences of abstract machine parts. Such a technique was evident in many films (including the aforementioned *Drifters*) connected to alternative film culture in this period, and reflects a machine aesthetic that was detectable within modernist art generally during this period. Such an aesthetic saw machines transforming the notion of 'beauty', instituting a new artistic paradigm. In contrast to many of the more 'traditional' aesthetic views, in which the introduction of machinery debased creative integrity, for some the machine heralded the dawn of a more 'functional' beauty. For example, in 1932 H.T. Pledge argued the case for this opinion. He did concede that many machines were 'ugly', but that this was only because of a 'mixture of incompatible styles'.[11] This led to a purist view of machines as aesthetic objects: 'there is beauty in any object which is completely functional—completely formed, down to the last detail of what has been pared away, on any clear and single purpose. Such beauty, to be sure, is apt to be very abstract.'[12]

The other essential element that contributed to the beauty of the machine was movement, for in movement one could admire the machine for its 'astonishing mechanical efficiency'.[13] At high speeds the motion of machines produces a blur and gives the viewer a 'primitive thrill' that is hypnotic.[14] In conclusion Pledge argued that even machines that are not beautiful as a whole could be admired piecemeal, for some 'bearish' machines have parts that are 'commonly excellent'.

The beauty in machinery was a subject for many photographers, who could capture the more abstract qualities of machines through isolating their elemental parts or through capturing the abstract blur of their motion.[15] Yet the segmentation inherent within the overall construction of large machines, and the movement they produced while in operation, were more obviously suited to filmmakers. In *The Film Till Now* Rotha had explained how the machine itself encapsulated aesthetic movement, and argued that cinema should also strive for this mechanical aestheticism:

> Perhaps the simplest, and incidentally the most impressive, form of movement in pictorial composition is a single repetitive motion. Its limited and monotonous repetition has immediate fascination. The knowledge that the movement can stray no further than its given path holds the mind of the spectator. A typical instance of this can be found in the motion of the crankshaft; a single allotted path which is followed again and again. [...] The constricted course and rhythm of a machine is not only compelling to watch but symbolical, also, of infinite thought.[16]

Yet the problem with many documentary films adopting this aesthetic, as I have pointed out in relation to *Drifters*, was that working-class men were also turned into machinery. For example, in *Contact*, there is a brief section representing workers involved in assembling an aeroplane, which in one sense presents working activities in a more stark light than *Drifters*. Occasionally, however, the presentation of material construction is punctuated by blurring the focus of the camera, so that representation is rendered non-figurative, before sharpening the focus again and revealing raw materials. This technique stresses the continuity between abstract and concrete processes, and between the working man and machine. As a commentator noted at the time: 'In his [Rotha's] close-up shots of hands and faces, close machinery and inspection, he has tried to convey this intimate connection between the worker and machine.'[17]

Contact aestheticizes working life in a way that subjects the human workers to the demands of Imperial Airways on the one hand, and the artistic objectives of Rotha on the other. This is reinforced by the manner in which the scenes of workers generally gain rhythmic dynamism, as they become edited in a 'symphonic' manner, along with close-ups of static machinery. It would seem that the need to blend the psychological creativity of the artistic, individual filmmaker with the objective imperatives of socially purposive filmmaking often led to contradictions within the films themselves. In fact, the need to impose an artistic vision often overrode and submerged the social objectives of the film text.

Other acclaimed formal documentaries such as *Industrial Britain* (Flaherty, UK, 1931) and *Coal Face* (Cavalcanti, UK, 1935) also evince this tendency to dehumanize workers through aligning them with machinery. *Industrial Britain* depicts the continuation of craft skills within an increasingly industrialized landscape.[18] The film cuts between different types of work (mining and glass-making, for instance), the machinery that aids such work and the overall environments that house the activities. In doing so, it focuses on all of these elements as concrete, functional, dynamic, abstract machinery. *Coal Face* is, on the face of it, a much more dour film than many of the other films mentioned, and does, at least partially, address the dangers of working in the mines. Nevertheless, the film still seems to place the working man within a machine aesthetic. Close shots of men digging in the cramped shafts emphasize the abstract qualities of their bodies in motion and their concrete, utilitarian functions. In a similar manner, a montage of close-ups of various industrial machines fragments their wholeness and emphasizes their geometric patterns, while rhythmically stressing their inexorable and regulated effectiveness. After a claustrophobic underground sequence, the film then pans from a long shot of an exterior of a mine past an expanse of sky, before finally settling on an isolated tree. The continuity—but also the contrast—between nature and industry is thus again stressed. Towards the end of the film we are shown trains transporting coal (with emphasis placed on the blur of the train track and the receding landscape in motion), which connects this specific unit with the wider interconnected units of the world.

In one sense, this construction of the working man as functional, effective machinery would have been influenced by the restrictions of producing films for sponsors, a situation that would have made the critique of working conditions rather difficult. This, however, is not the only explanation for the ways in which the working classes were constructed: such aesthetic representation is also an outcome of the manner by which filmmakers combined a formal, poetic organization of materials with a view of the working classes that was ideological (as mentioned in Chapter 3). There were, though, more critical comments on working-class conditions as well as on the general situation in which man is aligned with machinery. It is to the former that I now turn; the latter will be treated in the next chapter.

Left-Wing Politics and Aesthetics

A challenge to the representation of working men as functional, abstract units can be found in many of the films that emerged from the workers' film movements; this is unsurprising, considering that they were concerned with the exploitation of the working classes. Many films made in this environment, however, were not attempts to explore aesthetic territory, partly as a result of budgetary limitations, and also because many producers within this milieu were more concerned with transmitting messages than with the production of 'art'. For example, communist papers such as the *Plebs* often contained articles that expressed disdain for any kind of abstract or aesthetic experimentation because they were seen to detract from political objectives.[19] Paul Marris argues that, for the most part, working-class groups engaged in 'counter newsreels', which he describes as straightforward renderings of left-wing news (often news items overlooked by conventional newsreels).[20] However, there were a few films that attempted to merge the commitment to left-wing politics with formal experimentation, and I will focus upon *Bread* (Kino, UK, 1934) and *Hell Unltd* (McLaren and Biggar, UK, 1936) as two prominent examples of such experiments.

Produced by Kino on 16mm, and influenced by Eisenstein, *Bread* concerns the story of an unemployed resident who, desperate because of penury, steals a loaf of bread, but is spotted by police and viciously beaten. The film is interesting for the angle from which it approaches its subject matter and for its formal blending of fiction and documentary (it ends with footage from the 1934 Hunger March), as well as its rapid editing sequences. It is also notable that it individualizes a working-class character in a way the documentary film unit usually avoided. By doing so, it was able to construct a more sympathetic portrayal of the working classes, and avoided painting them in a reductive manner, as impersonal machines. At the same time as acknowledging the individual nature of human beings (with their faults, desires and needs), it demonstrated the need for such individuals to band together as a collective unit in order for the current injustices and inequalities to be overcome.

In contrast to the documentary films that I have discussed, *Bread* opts to turn not a sociological group of people but a systematic means of organization (capitalism) into a machine. In this case, however, the machine is not a noble, efficient unit, but a demonic force (as one would expect from the output of a communist alliance). This demonic force is constructed via narrative, montage and camera placement. As the unemployed man is seated in front of three people to be means-tested, the low-angle views of their faces—a kind of distorted point of view shot—highlight their intimidating nature. A rapid montage of their three faces further underlines this point, stressing the overall imbalance generated by the capitalist system. This is both an ideological and a psychological construction, portraying the man's rising state of mental tension. The sequence therefore encapsulates the film's merging of didactic and dramatic, ideological and psychological aspects.

There is another rapid montage sequence when the police catch the man after he has stolen some bread. A violent scene is represented via rapid editing of static images, including a low-angled close-up of a policeman wielding a truncheon, followed by an image of the unemployed man lying helpless upon the ground. The image of the policeman—representing defence of the existing state system—is demonized: his face eagerly anticipates the meting out of punishment, while the low angle and close shot exaggerate his menacing look. The actual violence, however, is portrayed in an overtly symbolic manner: two images of the policeman's face and his hand wielding the truncheon are intercut in rapid alteration to symbolize the violent act (the pace of the editing and the close framing all give this impression). It is a sequence that is manifestly influenced by Soviet-style montage.

Perhaps the most striking combination of formal experimentation and a direct political message in 1930s Britain was Norman McLaren and Helen Biggar's *Hell Unltd.* McLaren, of course, subsequently became a renowned abstract filmmaker, to whom I will return in the next chapter. He is not particularly noted for his political filmmaking, although he did also work as a cameraman on *Defence of Madrid* (Montagu, UK, 1936), a film documenting Franco's attack on the capital,[21] and his Oscar-winning film *Neighbours* (Canada, 1952) was also in some senses political.[22] Biggar was a sculptress and filmmaker; she was also a member of the Communist Party of Great Britain and made *Challenge to Fascism* the following year.[23] *Hell Unltd.* was not directly produced for a workers' film group, which may explain its more daring use of experimentation.[24] It was made with help from students and tutors at the Glasgow School of Art, and then distributed by both Kino and Glasgow Kino.[25]

Hell Unltd. uses animation, pixillation, stock shots and rapid montage in order to protest against speculation from profits in armaments. The film is a mixture of several of the currents that made up alternative film culture in the period: it is concerned with contemporary social problems, it employs a whole range of formalist techniques and it contains a documentary element in that it features stock footage of demonstrations. In short, it is a combination of documentary and abstract aesthetics, which partly reflects the radical political base of communist politics, and therefore delivers a bluntly 'concrete' message.

The film is extremely didactic, offering a message that wholeheartedly rejects warfare and the money spent on armaments. It also implores citizens to do everything that they can to protest against war. It employs animation—such as an armaments spending bar spilling out of a chart into a bloody mass—as well as titles and found footage (particularly of dead soldiers), to build up not only a negative portrayal of war, but also a picture of a corrupt government who bandy contradictory ideological messages. At one stage in the film a title reads 'prosperity is returning', followed by proclamations of economic wealth. This 'official' rhetoric, however, is then undermined by an animated sequence that shows a man listening to the radio, followed by a cut to models in his room watering plants that sprout monstrous growths like grenades and fighter planes. Here, animation and 'tricks'—by conventional methods connected to illusion (actuality footage was connected to reality)—are associated with a deeper, unspoken 'truth'.

6. Helen Biggar's animated plasticine figures, used to symbolize hidden truths in *Hell Unltd.* (photo from the Billie Love Historical Collection, courtesy of Anna Shepherd)

Although *Hell Unltd.* may seem slightly naive in its politics in that it fails to address the issue of what would happen if nobody confronted fascism, it does address serious issues, such as the undemocratic operations of supposedly democratic governments, and the underhand ways they carry out their business. It does not shy away from attacking particular targets (it names companies implicated in profiteering from war), and although it may be dogmatic and propagandistic, it also questions any 'innocent' or 'transparent' representation, placing doubt on the ability of images to be equated with 'truth'.

So, while many of the workers' newsreels looked at news from a different ideological angle, *Hell Unltd.* reflects upon the construction of ideology itself. Through its overt dogmatism (which aligns the constructed text with a specific point of view), and its inversion of hierarchical codes (refusing to accept, for example, that actuality footage is necessarily more accurate or truthful than animation or other 'manipulated' techniques), it asserts that all filmic texts are constructions from a specific ideological or institutional position. It therefore manages to be at once dogmatic and sceptical about the circulation of images in everyday life, especially official newsreels.

Outside the documentary movement, then, the ability to work free from sponsorship restrictions, as well as a more explicitly left-wing stance,

7. Diplomats at a peace conference in *Hell Unltd.* (photo from the Billie Love Historical Collection, courtesy of Anna Shepherd)

meant that a more critical examination of exploitation could be probed, and this was sometimes done in formally adventurous ways. Within *Bread*, there was an exploration of individual subjective dissatisfaction, in contrast to the objectification of the working-class body so prominent in some of the documentary films; while in *Hell Unltd.* there was a direct engagement with political issues in a formally experimental manner that was markedly different from the more 'poetic', leisurely montage strategies evident within a number of documentary films.

It was the more 'poetic' style—gentle montage combined with pictorial cinematography and careful framing—that was most privileged in alternative critical discourse. I will now go on to consider how such a style was combined with the use of sound in an 'expressive' manner, focusing in particular on *Song of Ceylon* (Wright, UK, 1934), which also probed the connections between tradition and modernity, and which was particularly well received within alternative culture.

Sound/Artistry

Despite the fact that 'expressive' uses of sound were called for in some alternative writings, it was only within the documentary film movement that sound was used outside the commercial industry, as the costs were largely too great for independent filmmakers. The GPO Film Unit, however, obtained a Visatone sound system in 1934 and Grierson encouraged staff to experiment with the use of sound to some extent. It was in *Song of Ceylon*, directed by Basil Wright and co-directed by composer Walter Leigh, that one of the most complex and ambitious sound-vision experiments can be found. Leigh was a student of Paul Hindemith in Germany and may have been inspired by his mentor's experimentation with sound.[26] Conceptualizing film sound, Leigh argued that the soundtrack should be carefully and thoughtfully composed of four separate elements: music, synchronized natural sound, counterpoint natural sound and sound effects. The first was seen as emotional, the second informational, the third expressive and the fourth atmospheric. Leigh argued that these elements should be combined to make a 'sound-score which has a definite shape, and not only is an accompaniment to the visuals, but adds an element which they do not contain'.[27]

Song of Ceylon was a four-part documentary (originally conceived as four separate films) sponsored by the Ceylon Tea Board and was, in effect, made to advertise an imperial business enterprise. The filmmakers' interest in experimenting with the medium, however, led to the production of an extremely aesthetic view of Ceylon life that, while never totally papering over its imperial underpinnings, offers a poetic and rather complex aesthetic meditation on Ceylon, its religious life and its relation to modernity. The first part of the film portrays the religious rituals of native Buddhists, the second shows the working life of natives, the third deals with the introduction of modern communication technologies into the country and the last part shows the coexistence of tradition and modernity. Filmed over three months in Sri Pada (Adam's Peak), the Buried Cities (comprising Anuradhapura, Polonnaruwa and Sigiriya) and Kandy, the film is typical of early documentaries' implicit connection with discovering and reconstructing 'otherness'. Many of the British documentaries filmed the working classes as noble aliens, fascinating yet safely distant behind the screen, but *Song of Ceylon* harks back to Robert Flaherty's fascination with 'exotic' cultures. This construction of otherness is reinforced by the fact that Basil Wright actually recruited actors to reconstruct Sinhalese life.

In the first section of the film, carefully framed compositions, pans and the edited sequence of images contribute to a romantic portrayal of a cultural tradition inextricably linked to natural processes. The ceremony on Adam's Peak, a centre of Buddhist pilgrimage for over two hundred years, continues this emphasis, seen as integral to the country's character. This section of the film, which follows a group of natives walking up towards the mountain in order to pray, occasionally makes use of quick cutting to stress conceptual connections and also to impose a rhythm upon the images. The accompanying sound flits between anthropological observation and sound montage. In addition to spoken commentary, music is sporadically interspersed throughout the film at various moments, blending traditional harmonic music played by Sinhalese dancers and drummers with the more dissonant gongs that represent the sounds of ritual ceremony.[28]

The dissonant parts of the soundtrack are still merged with the images in a harmonious way: the editing of sound and image thus creates a harmonic unity. The manner by which it does so seems to create a schism between surface and underlying relationships in the film. To take an example: towards the end of the first section, jarring gongs on the soundtrack accompany pans over the statue of Buddha, intercut with a bird flying over a silhouetted landscape. The 'feel' of this sequence is experimental, disconcerting even. Yet on a symbolic level, these aspects are a harmonic representation of the events of the island, which are seen to exist organically on a deep, rather than a surface, level. By contrast the commentary, although inextricably connected to the images superficially, is discordant on a deeper level. Ostensibly, the voice is describing the images that the viewer sees, thus creating a harmonic relationship between sound and image. Yet, more profoundly, the narration clashes because of the cultural fissure between the imperialist discourse and the Buddhist ceremony taking place. This gap is expressive of the unequal relations that existed between Britain and Ceylon. Britain at this point had ruled Ceylon since 1796 and the mannered accent ordering the apparently 'exotic' images is somewhat representative of imperialist disparity.[29] This imperialist discourse is, however, complicated by the fact that Wendt himself was actually a Burger—a descendant of Dutch colonists and the Sinhalese.[30]

The limitations of the sound recording equipment available meant that the film could not reproduce 'natural' sounds to accompany the images.[31] This means that when we do actually hear representations of the natives, we must consider that they are sound reconstructions put together in an English studio. In keeping with the rather experimental nature of the overall film, Leigh manipulated the reconstructions by mixing and treating them. This enabled him to cut the image and sound in rhythmic conjunction, and to treat the sound as texture. It also contributed greatly to the strange dialectic between tradition and modernity that is so central to the film. In a sense, the continual 'mutation' of found sound by Leigh signals the whole project of the film, as the 'exotic' and 'natural' is translated and modified by the western, modernist representational schema.

The third part of the film, 'The Voices of Commerce', is at once the most experimental section of the film and the most explicit admission of imperialist expansion. It immediately marks a sudden rupture with the previous two sections, as the chaotic sounds and modern machinery of industrial life abruptly contrast with the traditions and sounds of native life. Again, however, the rupture is only 'superficial'. On one level the complex collage of industrial noises contrasts with the previous sounds; yet there is continuity as both soundtrack elements are, on a formal level, similarly constructed. The difference lies in the actual pitch and quality of the sounds themselves: in the third section, Leigh blends together economic commentaries from different sources, plus the bleeps and crackles emitted by modern telecommunications systems, into a *musique concrète*-style format. The images that accompany these sounds also flit around via audio montage. Modern machines give way to views of natural landscapes, which move onto shots of natives working, followed by shots of people speaking on telephones and a pan along a telegraph wire. This series of contrasts continues throughout the section—allowing Wright to indulge in the vogue for fetishizing modern machinery—with images of natives working in tea fields contrasted with the modern sounds on the soundtrack.

On the one hand, this fiercely experimental sequence is chaotic and rather disconcerting. The experimentation could be justified in the sense that Wright and Leigh may have been attempting to represent the 'invisible'

8. A pan along a telegraph wire in *Song of Ceylon* emphasizes the importance of modern communications (frame grab, courtesy of Film Images)

processes of modern telecommunications systems and the new sets of spatial and temporal relationships that they gave rise to. In this sense, the experimentation could be seen as an attempt to represent what were seen as the remarkable new space–time configurations set in place by electronic communications. As Stephen Kern suggests, the telephone, telegraph and wireless created the ability to experience a multiplicity of distant events simultaneously. This itself had repercussions for conceptions of time and space, seen by artists and philosophers as undergoing compression.[32] This sequence can be taken to be an attempt to contract time and space and represent a new—and therefore rather confusing—map of contiguous relationships, which nevertheless is inscribed by unequal power relations.

On the other hand, chaos is contained on a deeper level: these sound–image clashes are eventually resolved through the manner by which machinery is eventually seen to coexist with native traditions. Machinery is therefore represented as an extension of these traditions, which can harmoniously coexist with them, as they too lived alongside nature and were themselves an extension of it. A form of evolutionary development is therefore proposed, as in *Drifters*.

This positing of evolutionary development is not, however, a linear progression whereby each innovation wipes out its precedent. *Song of Ceylon* expresses the need for developments to coexist with traditions; it even hints that the machines of modernity are paralleling older traditions. Through this logic the film is an audio-visual anticipation of Marshall McLuhan's ideas of the global village. McLuhan believed that the emergence and proliferation of new media such as radio and television meant that less literate, electronic templates that harked back to older, oral cultures were replacing existing paradigms. The electronic revolution, with its ability to connect people from all around the world, was heralding the re-emergence of a 'tribal, integral awareness'.[33] *Song of Ceylon* makes similar claims: transportation, modern communications and cinema itself, are re-establishing, rather than destroying, traditional forms of cultural expression. Many technological proponents wanted to overcome and coerce nature in order to advance civilization, an attitude that sparked alarm in many.[34] *Song of Ceylon* contains a message that, while nature must be manipulated and tampered with, it should also be respected. The film thus centred on a 'progressive' ideological discourse—the internationalization of the world and the abolition of restrictive barriers—without losing touch with more traditional concerns.

The final section of *Song of Ceylon* echoes the beginning of the film, thus reinforcing a circular mode of evolution, as opposed to a more ruthless model of linear progression.[35] Sound and editing are similarly constructed; the final shot pans over palm leaves, a direct reference to the opening shot. The final sequence, though, adds a layer of telecommunication beeps: thus preservation is stressed on the one hand, progression and modernization on the other hand. In the second section the commentary refers to the fact that it is considered dishonourable to work for hire, so the film does not completely paper over conflicts between tradition and modernity. However, this resistance to modernity is shown as misplaced, as the clash between modernist noise and traditional sounds become merged and blurred in the final section, emphasizing the prospect of continuity rather than disruption.

On the whole, the imperial underpinnings of the film were not remarked upon, with the exception of a review by Charles Day.[36] More likely was admiration for the formal properties of the film. For example, Graham Greene—who in addition to being a famous novelist was one of the most important film critics of the period—extolled the film as a major work of art.[37] This is not particularly surprising as the film is complex and develops one of the most sustained experiments in sound as expressed in the aesthetic discourse of the period: sound as expressive, fragmented, multi-dimensional and anti-theatrical.

Song of Ceylon, then, was 'progressive' in both a formal sense, and, to a lesser extent, in a social sense. It was more radical formally; socially it was embedded in the tradition of mild reformism. Though from a present-day perspective it is easy to dismiss it as imperialist, if we consider the context in which the film was made, it should be considered a rather ambiguous text. Entrenched in a film culture that was, to a large extent, reactionary and nationalist, and working for an imperialist sponsor, the film's attempts to look at a subordinated national culture in a positive light are far from jingoistic. I would disagree with William Guynn, who claims that the film critiques industrialization.[38] While the film does undoubtedly contain its critical elements—especially in the reference to working for hire as dishonourable—it eventually attempts to placate such criticisms by emphasizing the circular and preservative process of industrialization. As Guynn notes, the film takes liberties with the notion of 'documentary' in that it exoticizes the natives by constructing them for a western audience (Wright hired actors to play the part of natives in some scenes). Such cultures are, via a stereotypical focus on natives as primitive and natural, seen as inferior to western culture. At the same time, there is respect for their cultural traditions, a belief that such traditions should not be exterminated by industrialization, despite their inferiority to it.

Radical sound experimentation was never repeated to quite the same extent, though there were other films made in the documentary movement that did manage to experiment with sound and image combinations. In *Coal Face*, for example, although there are only very occasional moments of sound experimentation, these are nevertheless quite strikingly employed. After sounds of coalminers singing, their voices become broken into fragmented bits and synchronized with a monotone beat. This again is a strategy wherein man and machine become one, so that a mechanical rhythm predominates.[39]

Experimentation with sound in the documentary film movement was, however, not taken up in a sustained manner. It tended to be employed, as in *Coal Face*, within small sections of a film if at all. An example would be the rhythmic intonation that is used in *Night Mail* (Wright and Watt, UK, 1936), so that the human voice is transformed into a train-like cadence. More commonly, however, documentary films tended to use sound in more prosaic ways, as commentary voiceover, using sound as a rhetorical force capable of explaining accompanying images.

One of the few documentary films to use sound with an imagination comparable to that of *Song of Ceylon* was a rather atypical product of the movement: Cavalcanti's comedy-fantasy, *Pett and Pott* (UK, 1934), which was made with assistance from Humphrey Jennings and William Coldstream. Subtitled 'A Fairytale of the Suburbs', it is a mixture of blunt advertisement, narrative drama and formalist experimentation. It concerns the tale of two families who live next door to each other in a middle-class, suburban environment. The Petts are conventional, happy and have children; the Potts are depicted as unconventional and unhappy, without any children. Eventually, through comparing and contrasting these families, the film proceeds to demonstrate the advantages of having a telephone—it is a device that enables the Petts to foil a robbery.

The film constructs similarities and differences between the families through public and private divisions: while their public façade is identical, their private spaces are wildly divergent. After the film shows Mr Pett and Mr Pott leaving their houses wearing matching suits and bowler hats, there is a cut to the inside of a train carriage, with a symmetrically arranged shot of two rows of identically dressed men reading newspapers. There is then a shot of the papers, showing a story with the headline 'Another Suburban Burglary'. Another cut takes us to a woman waking in her bed to find a burglar in her house. She screams, accompanied by a dissonant pitch of sound that heightens her psychological turmoil. This sound merges with the noise of a train going through a tunnel, and there is a cut back to the inside of the train. Such a shot demonstrates the playful use of sound in an expressive and associative manner in the film.

Another striking use of sound, combined with a visually experimental scene, occurs when Mrs Pott trudges home on her own, carrying a large amount of groceries. As she makes her way up steep steps, gloomy, atmospheric sounds communicate her toil; a calendar is then shown and merged with this sequence. There is then a repetition of her trudge up steps in slow motion, as if to increase her plight. This is followed by a montage of a calendar going through the days, intercut with repeated shots of Mrs Pott trudging up the steps. Over the soundtrack there is a sparse, monotonous thudding of drums. This repetitious montage not only emphasizes the way that Mrs Pott is herself going through a traumatic and repetitious ritual, but also recalls a sequence in *Ballet Mécanique*, in which a woman's movement going up steps is looped.[40] *Pett and Pott* does not 'loop' the film moment, and this does not therefore have the feel of frustrating the desire to go beyond such a 'moment'. Rather it is both an economical expression of the narrative and a pattern of circular repetition (itself a core thematic aspect of the film).

The use of subtle, yet often expressive, sound and visual experimentation occurring at moments throughout *Pett and Pott* meant that it was a film that gained attention in critical writing, but only because of its use of sound. *Monthly Film Bulletin*, for instance, noted that the film should appeal to those with an interest in sound cutting.[41] In *Cinema Quarterly*, Forsyth Hardy pointed to the film as part of the GPO Film Unit's general experimentation with sound, and argued that films were now starting to develop much more expressive uses of sound.[42] *Pett and Pott* was seen as representing 'a complete departure from the traditional picture and the emergence of a sound film with an aural expressiveness related to, but not merely dependent on, the visuals'.[43] In contrast, the rest of the film did not warrant the same admiration and has come to be viewed by many involved in the documentary film movement as a superficial comedy.[44] This is probably because it very much diverged from the more poetic models that were favoured in critical frameworks, in which the dialectic of tradition and modernity was dramatized through montage strategies.

Conclusion

In this chapter I have analysed a number of films that were representative of certain trends in alternative filmmaking, particularly those linked with the documentary film movement. It was common for such films to merge social documentation, picturesque imagery (such as abstraction of nature or industrial components) and rhythmic editing strategies. In terms of the content of these films, they continued the tensions—evident in *Drifters*—between tradition and modernity, tensions that the films often sought to negotiate through advocating a gradual process of evolution. These films thus fitted into the broad discursive frameworks established during the 1920s. Yet, many of these films dehumanized working-class subjects, and this was something that many of the films made by the workers' film movement attempted to counter. If, however, there was a growing unease with excessive formal experiment within certain sectors of the documentary movement, there was even more hostility towards aesthetic exploration in the workers' film movements. Despite this, there were certain pockets of the workers' film movement that were merging aesthetic formalism and direct politics; this should come as no surprise given the overlaps between this movement and the wider (primarily aesthetically oriented) alternative film culture.

As I mentioned in the previous chapter, however, the consolidation of sound shifted concerns in alternative discourse. While there were not a great deal of independent sound films made, there were some that reflected concerns to create an expressive, rather than naturalist, sound fabric. Films such as *Song of Ceylon*, *Coal Face* and *Pett and Pott* featured some striking and creative moments of sound experiment. In the main, though, smaller experimental films continued to work without sound; I will address many of these in the next chapter, which focuses on more abstract filmmaking.

6

Mechanization and Abstraction

While the more formal and 'poetic' films made in the documentary film movement tended to be lauded more than other films by alternative critical discourse, there was nevertheless a number of significant and interesting films that lay outside this broad terrain. Some of these, including many films made by Len Lye, were actually made for the documentary film movement; others were made independently. The two most striking themes, or formal categories, that characterize these films are mechanization and abstraction. Abstraction of the image is quite straightforward, but mechanization is a broader term that I have used in order to refer to a number of films that addressed the rationalization of working life either through the content of the film or through the formal structure employed (or in some cases a combination of both).

Mechanical Rhythms

According to Siegfried Geidion, the inter-war period was a time when mechanization penetrated 'the intimate spheres of life' within industrialized societies.[1] A key development in the mechanization of everyday life was the growth of 'scientific management': Taylorism was an ergonomic philosophy that became most successfully reified in the assembly line at Henry Ford's factory in Highland Bell, which was fully operational by 1910.[2] According to Peter Wollen, Taylorism 'heralded a new epoch in which the worker would become as predictable, regulated and effective as the machine itself'.[3]

In tandem with such developments, mechanization and rationality also greatly affected a range of artistic practices. Many artists—most notably the Constructivists and Futurists—celebrated the machine and rationality, and, as I have demonstrated, so did many of the documentary films, albeit in a less futuristic manner. Others, however, tended to be depressed by such developments. In 1923, for example, Hugo Von Hofmannsthal wrote despairingly of the society that the working people of Britain grew up in, of the

> work-day with its routine, in factory or shop, with the same mechanical motions to be gone through, the same hammering, the same rasping, the same vibrations, the same everlasting whirr of the wheels. And then the return home, where the same mechanical gestures are repeated: implements to which one becomes so accustomed that in the end they dominate and make a tool of him who uses them: the human being is no more than a tool amongst tools.[4]

For Hofmannsthal, Hollywood movies were valuable because they provided an escape from such drabness, but in the film that Hans Richter made with the Film Society, *Everyday* (1929), there is an attempt to critique the mechanization of everyday life and the escape that Hollywood provides, with the implication that they are both products of excessive rationality.

Everyday was remade for the Film Society's fiftieth anniversary celebrations, which poses an instant problem when having to judge this film, as the print available is the remade film. However, the evidence is that the visual track of the restored version is almost the same as the original version bar a few deletions near the end of the film (which reduced some repetitions). The major difference is the addition of a soundtrack, not originally present on the film because of the expense of sound equipment at the time. Richter added this soundtrack to the film when he was in America and it was eventually left unchanged during the film's restoration.[5] The film also features Sergei Eisenstein in an acting role, and Basil Wright and Len Lye were involved in the production. Nevertheless, for unknown reasons, Richter was unhappy with the film when it was originally made and it was not released.[6]

The film is a portrayal of a life in the day of London, focusing for the most part on drab work routines of an office environment. It begins with people getting out of bed and commuting, and ends with people going out in the evening after work. Patterned editing of fragmented bodies throughout the film suggests the negative ways in which people have been turned into machinery, while shots of yawning people intercut with clock faces denote the tyranny of time. *Everyday* makes an assault upon the machine of rational bureaucracy, a key feature of modernity that brings to mind the critiques of sociologists like Georg Simmel and Max Weber. Weber, for instance, criticized the 'purposive-instrumental' functionalism (*Zweckrationalitat*) that was a key feature of modernity, as he believed that rather than leading to the liberation of humanity, it would lead to the 'creation of an "iron cage" of bureaucratic rationality from which there is no escape'.[7]

Although the opening sequence of the film suggests that these bodies are objective elements akin to machine parts, it then goes on to show the ill fit between this conception of human beings and their experiences. Tension begins to build as the bored workers look at the clocks and the editing gradually increases speed. The clock is a central motif in the film, linked as it is to the regulation of work. One contemporary writer, Lewis Mumford, saw the clock as the key machine of the industrial age, but also felt it was linked to oppressive demands over humans, replacing their 'natural' rhythms with more 'mechanical' rhythms.[8] Earlier commentators such as George Beard, writing in the late nineteenth century, thought that the 'unnatural' demands of standardized time wrought havoc upon the human central nervous system.[9]

When a lunch break occurs in the film an exaggerated display of relief is configured through a scene in which—via stop-motion photography—food begins to move around. Here, inanimate objects assume lifelike properties and revolt against daily routine, thus expressing the sublimated desires of the workers. This echoes an earlier Richter film, the Dadaist *Ghosts Before Breakfast* (Germany, 1928), in which a series of objects—such as cups and hats—take on a life of their own. Richter had said that this expressed 'a personal view of mine that things are also people'.[10] At the same time, people have become 'things', a process that Richter denounces. His focus upon objects becoming animate is a trope that expresses rebellion against completely fixed positions. In *Everyday*, this trope becomes a symbol of the fact that, although clockwork mechanization has invaded the bodies of these workers, it has not taken them over completely.

After work has finished we see workers visit either a show or the cinema. We see people watching glamorous women dancing in choreographed movements or sequences at the cinema of lovers embracing. These scenes provide relief from the working day; yet Richter suggests that these diversions are themselves machine-like extensions of mundane work, different only to the extent that they are wrapped up in glamorous packaging. The dancers, for example, are shown to be moving in a rather mechanical manner, and in the cinema shots Richter constructs a montage of kiss scenes and cuts them together in a way that exaggerates the factory-like nature of Hollywood filmmaking. For example, he rapidly cuts between different angled shots of two lovers embracing, thus overtly signalling the functional nature of shot/reverse-shot conventions.

Richter then focuses on a worker at an audience and probes his subjective mind. We see him looking tired at the show, intercut with him getting into bed and dreaming (of superimposed hands), intercut with various shots of repetitive office work that we have already seen. He jumbles these shots in order to cut across temporal moments and thus suggest that all of these mechanical actions blur into one undifferentiated mass. It would seem, then, that Richter was suggesting that the segmentation of rational bureaucracy is only an illusory veil that barely covers up the endless monotony and repetition of everyday life in the modern world.

Such repetition is then further emphasized as Richter repeats the day. Many of the previous scenes recur but at a quicker pace, as if suggesting the tension building up in the humans who have to go through these actions. Shots of large machines in motion are superimposed on workers at the office, stressing the machine–man analogy. Workers at a cigarette factory and telephone operators are also intercut with the office workers: different working environments, similar repetitious actions. The daily routine of going to work is repeated many times, the pace building all the time. Towards the end the pace is almost frantic, suggesting an unhealthy build up of nervous tension.

In *Everyday* the formal pattern of the film is the prison-machine within which the workers are locked, and it thus determines their patterns of behaviour to a certain extent. Such formal organization again echoes Weber's argument that the bureaucratic system abstracts man and conceptualizes him as an abstruse ideal. Weber argued that a 'fully developed bureaucratic apparatus stands to [...] other forms in much the same way as a machine does to non-mechanical means of production.' This bureaucratic machine increases in efficiency by excluding 'all love, all hatred, all elements of purely personal sentiment—in general, everything which is irrational and avoids calculation'.[11]

Yet the occasional moment of subjectivity and the build up of tension in *Everyday* suggest that humans cannot completely be turned into machines. In the attempt to do so in a rigid manner—as in Fordism—there is a tension generated between the functional and the spiritual dimensions of the human being. There will thus always be a friction between the private and public role of the individual. The film does not describe in any overt manner what the results of excessive rationality will be, but its intense acceleration of editing indicates a rather stressful, unhealthy tension.[12]

In contrast to *Everyday*, Norman McLaren made a couple of films reflecting mechanization that are more ambiguous in tone, stranded between satire and celebration of mechanical life. McLaren, who is widely known for the later animation films that he made in Canada at the National Film Board, made his first publicly shown film, *Seven Till Five* (1933), for the Glasgow School of Art Kine Society, which had at the time only recently formed.[13] Other people involved in the making of the film were editor Stewart McAllister and camera operator Willie McLean.[14] McLaren himself has remarked on how he was influenced by the films of Eisenstein and Pudovkin, which he saw at the Glasgow Film Society.[15]

Seven Till Five depicts a day in the life at an art school, though in the fragmented and segmented manner that it portrays events, the school seems to function like a machine. As in *Everyday*, there is a specific link connecting the clock and rationality: in between the shots of the clock there are patterned scenes showing a labouring workforce. The cutting pace is set at a regular tempo, with recurrent close-ups magnifying tasks being performed. Individuality may have collapsed into mass movements of a highly predictable nature, but these movements are nonetheless seen as fascinating. They are abstract, geometric patterns that reveal the aesthetic moments of everyday life. The only deviations from this regulated structure are occasional stop-motion scenes, such as full plates being transformed into empty plates at lunch; such a technique is used, therefore, to summarize routines in a succinct manner.

There are elements of *Seven Till Five* that could be taken as attacking rationality through parody, and the film is not in any way a straightforward celebration of rationality. In this sense, the deconstructive aspects of British alternative film culture can be seen to have infected McLaren. His oeuvre is characterized by a kind of mocking distance, and it is telling that he was drawn to modern art by a cartoon in *Punch* that satirized art's pretensions.[16] Although McLaren remained interested in modern art, he was never entirely happy with what he saw as the air of restrictive dogma that surrounded it.[17] Considering these facts, *Seven Till Five* seems detached from any statement about rationalization and mechanization, and at the same time serious about creating a piece of 'art'. It explores themes of modernity but does not seem to tackle the subject from any definite 'position': such themes merely provide a structural template by which to order everyday life aesthetically.

Seven Till Five draws heavily on Soviet montage techniques, parody films and documentary films, the first two of which I have already elaborated upon; the influence of documentary films is evident in its focus upon people at work, shaped creatively in an abstract manner. It is probably the blend of 'serious' documentary aesthetics and more light-hearted, parodic aesthetics that imbues the film with its ambiguities. It is interesting that the film also fragments the human body on many notable occasions for artistic effect. This recalls an earlier parody film discussed in the previous chapter, *C.O.D.—A Mellow Drama*. As noted above, *C.O.D.* built up an almost self-sufficient aesthetic of its own through excessive fragmentation and ellipsis; it was therefore stranded between parody and a distinct style. It could be argued that *Seven Till Five* also sits within this uneasy category. So while alternative film writing and production shifted towards more serious concerns in the 1930s, parodic aesthetics were still evident. A similar aesthetic of fragmented editing and parodic aesthetics is also apparent in Richard Massingham's *Tell Me if it Hurts* (1934), which explores the paranoia of a man visiting the dentist.

In McLaren's next film, *Camera Makes Whoopee* (1935), the themes of *Seven Till Five* are expanded upon with more emphasis upon tricks, enabled by McLaren's acquisition of a ciné Kodak camera, which allowed for easy production of pixillation, double exposure, split screen and fade in/fade out.[18] Both *Everyday* and *Seven Till Five* bear comparison with Dziga Vertov's *The Man With the Movie Camera* (USSR, 1929) with their 'day in the life' structure. *Camera Makes Whoopee*, however, is more similar to Vertov's film as it merges this structure with self-reflexivity. Attention is drawn to the camera as a protagonist within the film, as a constructor of visual possibilities. McLaren has said of his early years:

> I used to think of the camera as my instrument. Your camera is your instrument and you have to use it. Of course, being a beginner I wanted to use it fully—use every knob that was on it—and I over-used it of course. But I was just obsessed with technique.[19]

Camera Makes Whoopee is again set in an art school, but differs in structure. It is in two parts: the first part, like McLaren's previous film, focuses on the creative personnel of the art school at work; the second part extends the canvas of the first film by focusing upon what they have created—sets for the art-school ball. The constant foregrounding of the camera is a meditation upon the specific cinematic reality under construction, and a celebration of the camera itself, which afforded McLaren more freedom to 'compose' filmed action.

The first movement of the film is very similar to *Seven Till Five*, though there are also differences. The main one is that the ordered, fragmented elements in *Camera Makes Whoopee* eventually begin to pile on top of one another in a more chaotic, less regulated fashion. This more haphazard aesthetic informs the second section of the film, which further revels in a more abstract, disordered celebration of visual effects. In one sense this is influenced by the fact that we are now watching the performance of the art-school ball, which is a creative presentation, rather than a mere construction. The structure of the second movement is therefore less mechanistic, as it is concerned with capturing the spirit of display and enjoyment (of the performers and the audience), as opposed to laborious working methods. This section visually summarizes aesthetic sensation, approaching a synaesthetic mode: close-ups of instruments being played bleed into elaborate superimpositions that become increasingly more frenetic; visual tricks such as animated 'dancing octaves' are employed, along with spirals and matrices; animation is blended with live-action photography in order to attempt a visual representation of the ball itself.

Although the film does follow a strict structure (the end echoes the beginning, it is in two movements, there is patterned editing), it allows greater freedom within this structure for a more spontaneous type of movement. So we can postulate two specific articulations that advance on the themes of *Seven Till Five*: first, the fact that the film focuses on entertainment as well as work means that the structure becomes looser, by attempting to represent the 'subjective' enjoyment of the ball; second, the fact that McLaren has acquired more sophisticated technical equipment with which to work means that he was, in a sense, 'showing off' by experimenting with these effects. It is this aspect of the film that was most likely responsible for Grierson's criticism of the film as disorganized.[20]

The connections with *The Man With the Movie Camera* exist on a number of levels, even though McLaren claims not to have been aware of that film. Vertov was influenced, via Constructivism, by the 'machine aesthetic'. Constructivism was a movement that attempted to reflect the changing status of art in an industrialized world: it saw the artist as an engineer whose job was to produce useful objects that would contribute to the creation of a new society; in this manner parallels were drawn between aesthetics and industry.[21] *The Man With the Movie Camera* reflects this not only in some of its lingering shots of machines and factory workers, but also in the manner by which Vertov segmented his montage into thematic units. He thought of the film not merely as a sum of recorded facts, but a 'higher mathematics of facts'.[22] This machine aesthetic is, as argued previously, evident in both of McLaren's first two films through their structure; in *Camera Makes Whoopee* it is also evident in the foregrounding of the machinery of construction—the camera. Machinery informs both the structure and the content of *The Man With the Movie Camera* and *Camera Makes Whoopee*, and both are connected by self-reflexivity, in which the notion of construction itself is highlighted. In addition, certain elements of *The Man With the Movie Camera* seem to inform McLaren's film, specifically the stop-motion anthropomorphizing of the camera; the use of dance via superimposition, which creates a dynamic sense of visual movement; and the 'day in the life' format.

The mechanical aspects of rationalization even cast a shadow over some films that may not at first glance seem particularly related to such themes. An example is B. Vivian Braun and Irene Nicholson's *Beyond This Open Road* (1934), a depiction of the leisure time that people enjoy through various modes of transportation. A backdrop of modern work informs the film and its formal structure is representative of this. Titles at the beginning make this clear, claiming that in the week most people work in drab factories or offices, but at the weekend they have a chance to leave the suburbs and head out onto the open road 'and beyond'.

The film taps into leisure as a modern phenomenon: a fixed, time-restricted mode of free time defined in opposition to work. This type of structured leisure time is a particular phenomenon that arose in tandem with the Industrial Revolution.[23] In the twentieth century mass manufacturing led to an increase in transport ownership, which facilitated visits away from the home.[24] *Beyond This Open Road* looks at the possibility of escape from the heavily structured workplace through the exploration of free time. It is still related to mechanical aesthetics in that it is underpinned by rationalization, on thematic and formal levels. At the beginning of the film, for example, we are introduced to people leaving their houses, and are then shown modes of transport segmented into montage fragments: bicycle and motorcycle wheels, car grilles, walking feet. The film depicts various journeys out into the countryside, with the majority of time allotted to depicting people at leisure: rather quick shots of people jumping in water give way to slower-paced, more pictorial displays of people lazing in the sun. The film ends, though, with journeys home: a quick-fire echo of the travelling out, but with a focus on the dark skies, which seem to represent the foreboding return of working life ahead.

Beyond This Open Road is split roughly into four parts; its first section is an introduction of fragments, focusing on aspects of transport. This includes the human and is representative of the modernist blurring between man and machine. The second part is fast, focusing on the motion of the journey. For the most part this excitement is kept in check by the formalist regularity of montage, but it also includes an element of excess and danger.[25] The third segment is still swiftly edited but relatively leisurely, focusing on pleasure and relaxation via composition and absorption in

9. Self-consciously 'artistic' framing in *Beyond This Open Road* (frame grab)

patterns within the frame. The fourth part is a return to the second, only shorter and darker. This structure, with its slow–fast–slow–fast motion, is itself slightly machine-like (mimicking acceleration and deceleration). Its absorption in the pleasures of leisure time is differentiated from other aspects (aesthetic absorption as against rhythmic control), as leisure itself was differentiated from work. Leisure is seen to be rather homogeneous, organized in a mechanical manner, yet in relation to working time it becomes free and subjectively fulfilling.

Abstract Aesthetics

In contrast to the films that I have discussed thus far, there were a number of films made in this cultural environment that were more abstract in nature. In one sense these abstract films represent a rupture with rationalization, although Siegfried Geidion has argued that abstract art is nevertheless still related to rationalization in two ways. First, many abstract artists attempted to represent movement in a non-figurative manner, a practice that Jules-Étienne Marey and Eadweard Muybridge had been engaged in when developing motion studies in the late nineteenth century. Second, abstract art can also be seen as a reaction against the mechanized straitjacket of excessive rationalization, and was to some extent negatively influenced by it.[26]

This abstract mode of filmmaking was not, though, encouraged by the dominant discourses of British alternative film culture. This meant that, while there was by no means a completely restrictive framework within which to operate, there was a growing tendency to dismiss certain activities. The elevation of the aesthetic wing of documentary filmmaking in alternative discourses meant that 'non-objective' filmmaking was not looked upon favourably overall (even less so than it was in the mid- to late 1920s). The dominant mode of discourse was never entirely uniform, however, and there were opportunities for people not only to make abstract films, but also—as in the case of Len Lye—to have them favourably received. It was rare, though, for abstract films to be heralded as precursors of a widespread film style that was considered desirable. Much critical writing instead tended to view abstract films as laboratory experiments. Paul Rotha thought that the avant-garde was a 'testing ground for the instruments of film', while Caroline Lejeune wrote of the French avant-garde: 'it may achieve little in itself, but suggests a hundred jumping-off places for thought'.[27]

One of the few film critics who did champion abstract filmmaking was Oswell Blakeston, who was involved in the production of *Light Rhythms* (1930), a relatively early British abstract film. As we have seen, Blakeston had worked on an earlier film, *I Do Like to Be Beside the Seaside* (1927), which belonged to a selection of parodic experiments made in the mid- to late 1920s. *Light Rhythms*, made in collaboration with American photographer Francis Bruguière, typifies a general shift by alternative film culture: a move from a deconstructive, mocking aesthetics towards a more serious attempt at constructing an accepted form of alternative British cinema. Bruguière had already been involved in early American avant-garde filmmaking, having collaborated with Dudley Murphy and the dancer Adolph Bolm on *Danse Macabre* (1922), a filmed version of a ballet, which included experimental moments.[28]

If we look at the figure of Oswell Blakeston in relation to film criticism and filmmaking, we are presented with a concrete embodiment of this shift. In his first few years at *Close Up*, Blakeston's criticism was marked by a refusal to engage in any prescriptive valuations, a scathing attitude towards British filmmaking and a gently mocking tone towards any excessive pretensions. By 1930, the idea of creating a serious, modernist form of British cinema had ceased to be a joke. In line with this trend, Blakeston began to write prescriptive articles that encouraged a serious, low-budget, experimental cinema. *Light Rhythms* should be seen in this context.

In addition to *Light Rhythms*, Blakeston and Bruguière collaborated on an advertisement film called *Empire Buyers are Empire Builders* (1931),[29] an abstract advertisement for the EMB, whose title is apparently formed by gradual streaks of light against a moving abstract background.[30] These films thus marked a shift towards more abstract and serious concerns for Blakeston: indeed, *Light Rhythms* was an attempt to carve out new cinematic forms. The contribution of Bruguière was a major determining factor in the aesthetic make-up of these films: they were based on his work in the photographic medium. Yet Blakeston was central in translating these photographic ideas into the medium of film.

Blakeston's activities are indicative of a general modernist artistic culture in Britain that was forging interconnections between painting, literature, photography and film. He also wrote poetry and collaborated with Bruguière on a photographic book entitled *Few Are Chosen* (1931), in which Blakeston's text provided an accompanying poetic narrative to Bruguière's abstract photographic imagery.[31] Bruguière also collaborated with E. McKnight Kauffer on posters and advertisements, creating a series of abstract poster advertisements for Shell Oil and the British Postal Service.[32]

Light Rhythms was based on Bruguière's photographic experiments in which he made cut-outs from paper and manipulated light to form abstract patterns. The film is approximately five minutes in length and explores the illusion of movement created by light patterns. In the film each frame is static, and focuses on the abstractions caused by the variation of light on a cut-out figure. The static form is held for approximately ten seconds and then a new form is superimposed to create a different pattern (all the time varied by the manipulation of light). Fade outs bridge new cuts and the film proceeds through the combination of old and new forms in varying combinations.

The film is underpinned by a rather rigid, mathematical formal system that is not clearly evident when viewing the film. This is because within the frame the level and pace of illumination varies considerably, while the frame transitions themselves are executed in a fluid manner. The light in the frame can obscure and reveal different aspects of paper configurations, so that an apparently stark surface is transformed into a more complex and elaborate pattern. At other times a range of different lights move around the frame at a rapid pace and become the main, flickering attraction within the frame. In combination, the movement and level of light and the different paper patterns create a shifting array of abstract permutations.

In a piece about the film written for *Architectural Review*, Mercurius claimed that the film deviated from previous film practice 'in that it receives its animation from the movement of light on static form, and not from the movement of form in static light'.[33] He added that the viewers'

10. Paper cut-outs and moving light create abstract patterns in *Light Rhythms*
(frame grab)

interest 'is held by the pattern created by the rhythmic operations of this
process, as the light is revealed in its passage and gradations and subtleties
of tone'.[34]

The film would seem to fit into a 'dominant' modernist form of
avant-gardism. It was a film that used familiar experimental techniques
and attempted to give them a new twist, thus aspiring to a notion of
'originality' that Rosalind E. Krauss has seen as central to the avant-garde
project.[35] It employed the familiar method of working with only abstract
forms and created a rhythmic dance of non-objective material. The film in
some respects can be allied to Lazslo Moholy-Nagy's light experiments.
Moholy-Nagy had built a light–space modulator, a machine containing
thirty light-bulbs of various colours producing a series of different light
permutations. Using this, he made a film, *A Light Play in Black-White-
Grey* (Germany, 1930), which created abstract movement through light.
Although he subsequently worked in England, he did not continue this
form of abstract filmmaking, although curiously his light–space modulator
found its way into the beginning of the GPO scientific documentary
The Coming of the Dial (Legg, 1933). The two films Moholy-Nagy made
in England in this period were both documentaries: *The Life of a Lobster*
(co-directed with John Mathias, 1935), a documentary on lobster-fishing
made for Alexander Korda, and *New Architecture at the London Zoo* (1936),
a showcase documentary co-funded by the Museum of Modern Art, the
architecture department at Harvard University and the Zoological Society
of London.[36]

Blakeston, however, does not appear to have made any more films,
demonstrating the difficulty of making abstract or 'non-objective' film in
Britain during this period. The only figure to have made a number of such

films is the New Zealand-born Len Lye. Lye can actually be linked to Blakeston: Blakeston championed his films in *Close Up* and Lye designed the cover and provided illustrations for Blakeston's book of poetry, *Death While Swimming* (1932). Lye's work in Britain was marked by a playfulness and lack of pomposity that could be seen as a continuation of the 'humorous' aspects of alternative film culture in Britain. Lye also illustrates the plight of the abstract filmmaker in Britain in this period. Although people seemed to realize his talent and appreciate his films (unusual for an abstract filmmaker in Britain), the films didn't fit into any recognizable framework and therefore caused problems in terms of how they were interpreted.

Lye had moved to Britain in 1926, where he joined the modernist group of British artists the Seven and Five Society, with whom he exhibited. He had already begun to develop a style of 'doodling' based around his interest in kinetic energy, and so the medium of film appealed to him because of its qualities of movement.[37] He made his first film as early as 1929: *Tusalava* was, as I have mentioned, funded by the Film Society with assistance from Robert Graves, Norman Cameron and Sidney Bernstein.[38] *Tusalava* contained around 4,400 drawings in total, a feat that Lye called 'pretty interminable'.[39] Yet he also described how he became locked in a process of absorption, and how important he felt it was to become preoccupied with 'the aesthetic feeling of this stuff'.[40] This sense of a physical aesthetics—as opposed to an intellectual one—involving the absorption of body and mind, was something that would inform Lye's work; it is possibly why he was not easily understood by alternative circles, given their heavily intellectual bias. *Tusalava* only received a few screenings, including a Film Society showing on 1 December 1929 (programme 34); according to Roger Horrocks and Wystan Curnow many of its first viewers did not know what to make of it, but it was praised by the art critic Roger Fry.[41]

Blakeston was one of the few other critics to praise *Tusalava* and attempt to interpret it.[42] The film is quite difficult to describe because it is more about movement than narrative. When attempting to define or describe the film it is also hard to avoid imposing some kind of narrative upon it. It involves a number of dots and circles that mutate into various shapes and patterns, some completely abstract, some more concrete (such as a humanoid figure). The freedom of using animated, amorphous shapes allowed Lye to create an experience of movement for the viewer, relatively free from the strictures of rational logic.

Lye was working in a tradition of modernist abstract filmmakers that included Hans Richter and Walter Ruttman, though there are specific elements within *Tusalava* that differentiate Lye from such predecessors. As Horrocks and Curnow have pointed out, a great difference between Lye's films and films made by abstract filmmakers such as Richter was that the latter tended to 'aim for clean lines and steady movements', while Lye tended to see the 'jittery-ness' of shapes.[43] It is this aspect of Lye's shapes—determined most notably by his interest in doodles and his studies of tribal designs and cave paintings—which imbue them with a more organic character.

Apart from its Film Society screening *Tusalava* does not appear to have been shown widely on the alternative circuit. Although the Film Society did show a number of abstract films, these were by no means the most influential of their screenings, and it seems that in 1929 there were not enough people interested in abstract animation for Lye to establish himself fully within the 'minority' film world. At this time the majority of adherents to film art were interested in concrete issues and the possibilities of editing; most forms of abstraction were incorporated into such frameworks. In this sense, Lye was an anomaly, and it is no surprise that he was more appreciated by the fine arts crowd than by cinéphiles. Consequently Lye did not make another film for five years. This was despite the fact that he had planned to make another two sections of *Tusalava*.[44]

Lye found it hard to attract sponsors for his filmmaking, and only made one more film before joining the GPO Film Unit—*Experimental Animation* (or *Peanut Vendor*) (1933)—which was a three-minute puppet film sponsored by Sidney Bernstein.[45] It was after making this film that he began to experiment with the technique of painting directly onto celluloid, which he is now credited with pioneering.[46] In order to satisfy sponsorship requirements, Lye had to include advertising slogans in his first film for the GPO—*A Colour Box*—made in 1935.[47] He managed to do this without relinquishing his abstract objectives, however. Lye experimented with different kinds of paint that would not peel away but were transparent enough to produce bright colours when projected.[48] He then used tools such as a camel-hair brush and a fine-toothed comb to build up colour textures on the filmstrip. Rather than following one line of movement, Lye presented a mass of complex and jumbled movements through painting directly onto celluloid. This has the added effect of creating a greater sense of off-screen space, as if the patterns are streaming in and out of the frame. Further, the dynamic abstract shapes seem to dance to the popular Cuban music that made up the soundtrack.[49] Towards the end of the film, GPO letters are inscribed on the film, combining with the other shapes, followed by a few slogans advertising the postal service.

11. A still from *A Colour Box*, in which Lye painted directly onto the film strip
(frame grab, courtesy of Film Images)

According to David Curtis, *A Colour Box* was seen 'by a larger public than any experimental film before it, and most since'.[50] Although cinemas were originally reluctant to show the film, Sidney Bernstein eventually launched it at his Granada chain and it became popular with general audiences.[51] It aroused considerable critical interest and while not all responses were positive, many were; the *Sunday Mercury* announced: 'You've not seen a colour film till you've seen a Len Lye effort.'[52] It may seem strange that this film, which with the exception of the end titles was more abstract than *Tusalava*, proved popular whereas *Tusalava* did not. Its reception must be considered in conjunction with its popular music and its use of colour. *A Colour Box*, only four minutes long, may have seemed strange, but it was not a solemn or overtly 'intellectual' film. Its colour—so vividly employed—would have proved a novel element and, along with its 'bouncy' soundtrack, it was a 'fun' abstract picture. *Sight and Sound* certainly thought so, remarking that the 'reinforcements of sound and colour have stirred the abstract film to a new, more lively vitality. Hitherto but a silent and bloodless shadow it now springs forth startlingly real and self-complete.'[53] Elsewhere, Robert Herring wrote of how the film used colour effectively in a non-realistic manner, creating a dance of colour.[54]

Despite this popularity, Lye did not gain sustained critical acclaim in alternative circles. In artistic film journals there was appreciation of his work, but never extensive writing about it. Perhaps this kind of work just did not fit into the overall climate of such a culture: *Cinema Quarterly* was devoting much of its attention to social realist experiments, while *Film Art* chiefly focused on photographic and editing techniques as the sources of true artistry. Within artistic circles Lye was mostly praised by figures from the fine art domain, such as Roger Fry and Paul Nash.[55] In many ways this has to be related to the general boundaries that existed between the fine art world and the film world. Philip Dodd has argued that there has been a long tradition of placing histories of art and film in separate categories without noting the connections, a tradition that undoubtedly derived from the boundaries that existed at the time.[56] There was a smattering of fine artists who ventured into film and vice versa, and there was interest in abstract films that relied upon fine art techniques, but critical attention was most consistently devoted to films that were encased in either dramatic or poetic frameworks. Even in the aforementioned article by Herring, which was a sustained attempt to grapple intellectually with *A Colour Box*, the author had to admit that the film was 'impossible to describe'.[57]

The majority of people who constructed the 'alternative' discourses about film in Britain were, on the whole, from a more literary tradition and often felt uncomfortable dealing with those films that crossed over into the terrain of fine art. Oswell Blakeston, who was interested in literature, fine arts, photography and film, is a rare exception, as is Humphrey Jennings. Paul Rotha was also involved in art design when he worked for a commercial film company, but his writings on film display many of the traits that characterized what can be called the dominant perception of film within alternative circles. Although Grierson supported the work of Lye, his many writings about films tended to overlook this kind of filmmaking.

Other artists who crossed disciplinary boundaries when working in Britain tended to veer towards experimentation with more 'realistic' material. For example, Hans Richter, Laszlo Moholy-Nagy, William Coldstream and Humphrey Jennings were all in their respective ways drawn to an experimental-documentary form of filmmaking in Britain. E. McKnight Kauffer made geometric designs for film, as in *The Lodger*, but he did not make self-contained abstract films, nor did he write about the topic in film journals (despite designing the logo for *Cinema Quarterly*). *Film Art*, although championing formalism for its own sake, nevertheless more consistently promoted films that formally arranged 'photographic' material. The manner by which they praised Lye's films without sustained critical analysis of his work implied that they had difficulty in understanding these films. Ironically, the abstract films of Lye and, to a lesser extent McLaren, were the films that would so easily fit into later surveys of avant-garde filmmaking of this period, thus demonstrating how changing cultural frameworks affect the meanings and values of art works.

Because Lye was attempting to tap into what he termed the 'old brain' and thus bypass rational consciousness, he shared concerns with the surrealists. Lye thought that the surrealists were too literary, though, in that they placed excessive emphasis on intellectual and rational signifiers.[58] But the absence of rational explanations meant that Lye's films were hard to come to terms with. Perhaps in reaction to this confusion Lye eventually began to take a more rigorously theoretical line in his own work. In 1935, in conjunction with Laura Riding, he published 'Film-Making', his first theoretical piece about his work in a British journal.[59] Lye had already engaged in writing and had indeed published a book, *No Trouble*, in 1930. While that work was characterized by an attempt to stretch language into elliptical, rhythmic shapes, 'Film-Making', was more straightforward and explanatory. In it Lye and Riding adopted a self-conscious engagement with the principles of cinematic form and expressed their frustrations with the excessive (literary) mediation that blocked an approach to filmmaking (and viewing) that was more direct and physical.

It is no surprise that Lye eventually incorporated more realistic material into his work. At the same time, while reacting to 'objective' contextual pressures, he still managed to retain an idiosyncratic approach to film form and experiment with movement and colour. This is evident in *Rainbow Dance* (1936), also made for the GPO Film Unit.[60] In this film Lye used Gasparcolor film stock, a type of stock that contained three layers of film dye on the celluloid and which could be manipulated according to levels of exposure. Lye shot the film using black-and-white sets, which allowed him to codify the overall colour scheme of the film.[61] This method also meant that Lye could emphasize contrasts between background and foreground colours, using colour in a 'fantastic', rather than realistic, sense. He could also use deregistration effects on the colour stock at certain moments, thus producing the 'colour echoes' that appear in the film.[62]

At the same time, the representations caught on the film, however 'fantastic', are more concretely connected to real-life signifiers than those of his previous films. A human dancer—Rupert Doone—was used in the film, and much of the film consists of photographed material. But Lye completely transformed this footage through extremely complex colour coding and by superimposing stencil patterns.[63]

It seemed that Lye's theoretical articles did at least attract more sensitivity to his working methods and his abstract form of filmmaking. *Rainbow*

Dance received an extensive review in the pages of *Sight and Sound*, the reviewer carefully elaborating the technical processes of the film and then evaluating its aesthetic quality.[64] The film was favourably reviewed, the writer arguing that without abandoning the 'tradition established by *A Colour Box*', Lye 'skips and capers into fresh and more extensive territory'.[65] Lye's use of non-naturalistic colour is praised, but although admiring Lye's attempt to diversify, the reviewer ultimately felt that the film was not quite as good as *A Colour Box*. Whereas that film was full of movement, the addition of a third dimensional perspective to *Rainbow Dance* meant that the backgrounds imbued the film with a comparatively static quality.

Rainbow Dance—through its use of strictly formal colours and its almost synaesthetic visual effects—is partly influenced by 'absolute film', and can be connected to a musical use of colour, traceable back to eighteenth-century experiments with 'colour-music'.[66] Indeed, in an article written in 1936 Lye betrays such an influence in his appeals to move away from literary meaning and to tap into a purely sensational relationship with the viewer, by developing his argument through musical analogies.[67] On the other hand, *Rainbow Dance* shows the increased contextual pressures to experiment with forms that had some concrete connections, as opposed to forms that were totally abstract and solely about movement. Lye thus managed to combine 'absolute' and 'concrete' modes, retaining many of his visible signatures, such as the dance of squiggly lines and the moving dance of circular forms. This method would be taken even further in his next film, *Trade Tattoo* (1937), which used Technicolor rather than Gasparcolor, and which transformed pre-existing GPO footage. After this, Lye would vacillate between making live-action films and 'direct' films, or a combination of the two.

Lye's experiments in non-objective filmmaking were almost unique in Britain at this time apart from the aforementioned *Light Rhythms*. Norman McLaren also dabbled in this area of filmmaking, though it would be some time before animated abstract film became his preferred mode of filmmaking. His first film—subsequently destroyed—was entirely abstract and painted directly onto film with a brush and coloured inks;[68] his only surviving 'abstract' film of this period is *Polychrome Fantasy* (1935), made in collaboration with W.H. Finlayson and T.D. Allen. Although this film is not completely abstract, covering as it does a dance by art students, the concrete aspects of the film seem to be secondary to the abstract processes.[69] The film mixes live action with elaborate, animated abstractions.

Yet, in contrast to Lye, McLaren's abstract filmmaking activities were somewhat restricted when he worked for the GPO Film Unit, in that he mostly made straightforward educational films.[70] The exception to this is *Love on the Wing* (1938), an animation promoting the postal service in which a series of two-dimensional white images continually mutate against a moving, multiplane coloured background. The sexual overtones of this film were considered 'too erotic and too Freudian' by the GPO minister at the time.[71] These Freudian overtones may not have been apparent to McLaren when he made the film, but possibly arose from his interest in surrealism.[72] Terrence Dobson interestingly connects the film to surrealism through its play of associations and its reluctance to completely forgo representational imagery (the surrealists wanted to map the unconscious by using recognizable images). He also links the film to the work of Emile Cohl, who pioneered the use of transforming simple linear images into other images.[73]

Another strain of abstract filmmaking of a rather different order was the educational abstract films made by Robert Fairthorne and Brian Salt. Fairthorne was on the editorial board of *Film Art*, and was interested in film aesthetics; Salt was an educational filmmaker employed by Gaumont-British Instructional, and who had previously made a film entitled *Euclid 1.32*.[74] Together they explicitly attempted to merge the aesthetic and educational aspects of filmmaking. The only surviving film that they made along these lines is a rather curious artefact entitled *The Equation X+X=0* (1936). This cross-disciplinary anomaly is essentially a visual demonstration of an equation, in which a series of geometrical forms are generated by mathematical permutations. While the film is a visual demonstration of an equation, the film—according to Fairthorne—could be appreciated as a purely abstract series of movements. There were also a number of other films that utilized geometric animation for education purposes: James Fairgrieve made a number of such films, including *Movement of Rain in a Thunderstorm* (1933), which was a scientific demonstration of weather patterns.[75] Specialist educational filmmaking companies, such as British Instructional, also made other films in the same vein.[76]

Conclusion

As this chapter has demonstrated, there was a significant flowering of abstract filmmaking in Britain during the 1930s, reflecting the influence of Continental abstract films, but also inflected by more specific concerns and motifs. In particular, aspects of mechanization informed the formal structure of many films, so that works such as *Everyday* and *Seven Till Five* are jerkier in structure than the 'smoother', more 'poetic' films that were covered in the previous two chapters. There was also an interest in more abstract filmmaking, as evident in *Light Rhythms*, but more particularly in many of the films produced by Len Lye. Nevertheless, the films of Lye also indicate the difficulty of making 'non-objective' films in a cultural milieu that was informed by aesthetic preferences marked by dramatic principles and/or documentary imagery (a demand to represent 'real life', however aestheticized). While Lye's films were admired, then, he was an exceptional figure in the sense that his films did not constitute stylistic templates that had any impact, at least in the immediate future.

Thus, even though Lye's abstract films were admired for their innovative qualities, they were not easily understood using existing aesthetic frameworks. They were therefore never unequivocally promoted as great cinema in the way some of the more poetic documentaries such as *Drifters* and *Song of Ceylon* were, even though they did have their admirers. Nevertheless, these films did tangentially connect with the discursive frameworks of alternative criticism: for example, the abstraction of Lye's films could fit in with the growing dominance of what I have called a modernist, 'objective' aesthetics. It is no surprise that Grierson—who was a supporter of Lye on an institutional, if not discursive level—admired much modernist art because he believed that the abstractions of Cubism, for example, represented the dynamism and abstract energies of an increasingly industrialized world. By contrast, films that attempted to explore the psychological states of fictional protagonists—what I would term 'subjective' film—existed even further outside the frameworks of alternative cultural taste during the 1930s, despite the fact that many such films were favoured in the mid-1920s. In the next chapter I look at one particular 'subjective' film—*Borderline*—and attempt to explain why it was not well received when it was made.

7

Borderline: Subjectivity and Experimentation

In this final chapter I will discuss a single film, *Borderline* (1930), that was made by the key editorial team behind the journal *Close Up*. The reason that this film will be treated alone is twofold: first, it is one of the few independent, avant-garde narrative features made in this period; and second, it was connected to *Close Up*, which has been seen as a particularly influential journal. Nevertheless, when the film was released, it was somewhat out of kilter with the dominant frameworks of alternative discourse. By 1930—the year in which *Borderline* was released—the editorial core of *Close Up* was becoming somewhat disillusioned with the cinema, and their fiercely anti-British stance was becoming eclipsed (even in other writings in the journal itself) by demands for artistic films that merged international trends with specifically British themes. Kenneth Macpherson, Bryher and H.D. were the chief contributors to the film and were also the figures (along with Oswell Blakeston) who most distanced themselves from such discourse. This is a key factor in understanding the lack of attention paid to the film by intellectual circles at the time of its release.

   In contrast to its reception at the time of its release, the film has become rehabilitated somewhat, at least in academic circles.[1] This renewed interest in the film should be linked, at least in part, to the fact that the film involved H.D. and Paul Robeson, and has thus been reassessed within the context of inter-war modernism and studies of racial representation. In this chapter I will focus on some more contemporary writings on the film, but will also discuss the reasons for it being so neglected in the early 1930s.

Background and Narrative

Borderline was the first feature-length film to be produced by the POOL group, who had previously made three short films: *Wing Beat* (1927), *Foothills* (1929) and *Monkey's Moon* (1929). Unfortunately, the first two of these only exist in fragmentary form, and the third film has been lost.[2] *Wing Beat* was described in the first issue of *Close Up* as a 'film of telepathy';[3] two stills from the film were also published in the magazine. The film investigated the idea of telepathic communication and featured Macpherson and H.D. Anne Friedberg has written that the film uses superimpositions, out-of-focus shots and iris masks to represent thought. *Foothills* featured H.D. as a city woman who visits the countryside and grows bored, and was thus an alternative take on Murnau's *Sunrise* (1927). *Monkey's Moon* was a documentary about Macpherson's pet douroucoulis monkeys.

Borderline was a much more ambitious project in comparison to these three films. It was longer, more costly and featured a well-known figure, Paul Robeson, who at this time was already a successful stage actor and concert singer. Nor was the film intended only for private screenings. Along with Robeson, the major acting personnel consisted of Eslanda Robeson (Paul's wife), H.D. and Gavin Arthur. According to Susan Stanford Friedman, Macpherson was introduced to the Robesons through Robert Herring.[4] Both Herring and Macpherson were extremely interested in the Harlem Renaissance. In fact, Macpherson had attempted in 1929 to enlist poet and writer Langston Hughes, political activists Walter White and Elmer Carter—all of whom wrote for the black journal *Opportunity*—to write for *Close Up*.[5] While the first two refused, Carter did write a short letter that was published in a special edition of *Close Up* devoted to the 'negro' and the cinema. This fascination with black culture was, for Macpherson, charged with homoerotic desire; according to Friedman he started to pursue liaisons with young black men in 1929.[6]

The film also featured, in minor roles, Bryher, Robert Herring, Charlotte Arthur and Blanche Lewin. Principal photography took around a fortnight, and the whole film was completed in six and a half weeks.[7] Bryher has subsequently written that the film cost around £2,000 to make, but notes she wrote regarding expenses in 1930 suggest the cost was closer to £1,000.[8] Macpherson rented out a derelict theatre to shoot the interior sequences, which were lit with carbon arc lamps; he used a Debrie camera with six lenses and shot the film with Kodak panchromatic film stock (more sensitive to tone values than orthochromatic stock).[9] The cast worked free of charge on the film but did have their expenses covered. The film eventually gained its first showing at the Academy cinema in London on 13 October 1930.[10]

While Macpherson was promoted as the sole creative force behind the film—especially so in a long pamphlet about the film written by H.D.—it has been argued that Bryher and H.D. also contributed significant input. Friedman has claimed that Macpherson was sick when *Borderline* was being edited, so this task, an extremely important and central aspect of the film, was left to H.D. and Bryher.[11] Macpherson did, though, carry out a number of other important tasks, such as writing the scenario, direction and cinematography, while Bryher acted as assistant by keeping a record of shots and changing the carbons.[12]

The film's narrative centres around two couples. Thorne (Gavin Arthur) and Astrid (H.D.) are a white couple, he a dipsomaniac, she a neurotic; Pete (Paul Robeson) and Adah (Eslanda Robeson) are a mixed-race couple. At the outset of the film Thorne, Astrid and Adah are staying at a room in a non-specific European location. Although Thorne and Astrid are a couple, Thorne has been having an affair with Adah. Adah, however, finds out that her husband Pete has been working in a hotel café in the town and they resume their relationship. When Pete reunites with Adah, tension erupts between Thorne and Astrid. Thorne eventually decides to leave Astrid and accidentally kills her in the tussle that ensues from her resistance to such a move. During these incidents, Pete is subject to racist comments from Astrid and an old lady. After the death of Astrid, these racist feelings lead to Pete being ordered out of town, and Thorne is acquitted of murder.

The narrative of the film is a device that orients and orders the images and is a background that supports the exploration of many themes. The most obvious theme is racism, but the film also looks at the mutability of identity, sexuality and relationships. It is also, of course, an exploration of the mind.

Mental Representation and Film Form

While the narrative of *Borderline* is simple, the formal structure of the film is rather complicated and disorienting. The POOL group were evidently aware of this, as they printed a 'libretto' to accompany screenings of the film.[13] This libretto indicates that a foreknowledge of the story was necessary, so viewers were not engaged in merely trying to work out what was going on. Rather, they would have been provided with prior knowledge in order to concentrate on the visual aspects of the film and the attempts to go inside the characters' minds. The film aims to fully explore 'borderline' themes: Adah is on the borderline of two relationships and of racial identity; Thorne is on the borderline of addiction; Astrid is on the borderline of mental stability; Pete (as well as Adah) is on the borderline of social acceptability. The film is therefore grounded in a strong conceptual framework. As Jean Walton and Anne Friedberg have pointed out, this liminal metaphor also structures binary divisions between white and black,

149

homosexual and heterosexual, civilized and primitive, and so on.[14] The film explores these binary divisions as well as the murky 'borderline' territory that lies between them.

Perhaps the two most overt influences on the film are, as Friedberg has argued, psychoanalysis and Soviet montage.[15] Bryher, H.D. and Macpherson were especially interested in psychoanalysis and believed the cinema could visually represent thoughts and intellectual matters in a universally understandable manner. The cinema could be allied to psychoanalysis in its ability to isolate everyday objects and charge them with great significance. Friedberg also notes that one of *Close Up*'s heroes, G.W. Pabst, had based his film *Secrets of a Soul* (Germany, 1926) on psychoanalysis. She argues there is a central difference between the two films: Pabst's film was 'mostly a narrative illustration of the therapeutic powers of psychoanalysis';[16] *Borderline* was, according to Macpherson, an attempt to take film 'into the minds of the people in it, making it not so much a film of "mental processes" as to insist on a mental condition'.[17]

The attempt to represent mental processes led to *Borderline* being a rather fragmented and 'difficult' affair. The construction of space in the film is sometimes disconcerting: as the film is more concerned with mapping interior space, there is a paucity of establishing shots. While the geographic location of the film is 'realistic' rather than 'fantastic', it is often used as a metaphorical signifier of mental conditions, which makes the film quite difficult to read at times. Roland Cosandey has elaborated on this point and argued that the narrative of the film is 'completely determined by the movement of emotional states, on the level of acting as well as on the level of narration'.[18] He explains that the film never uses the 'distinctive signs of passage from an exterior state, serving as referent, to the interior states—fantasy, reminiscence, vision, dream'. This leads him to conclude that subjectivism guides the film's narrative and constitutes an 'objective system'.[19]

Cosandey's analysis of the film is perceptive and I would agree with most of his argument. I do think, however, that we can add a few more nuances to his account. For example, subjectivism certainly does seem to guide a significant portion of the film, but it does not quite constitute an 'objective system'. Rather, the film seems to waver between subjectivism and objectivism (another binary opposition we can add to those previously mentioned): as H.D. wrote, the film 'is a modern attempt to synchronise thought and action'.[20] It also uses distinctive signs to mark the passage from exterior to interior states on occasion: for example, the use of 'clatter montage' is a clear sign that mental processes are being portrayed. While these are coded as explicitly subjective, other scenes are more confusing. There are some scenes that take place in a bar of the inn where Thorne, Astrid and Adah are staying. These scenes involve a barmaid (played by Charlotte Arthur), a pianist (Gavin Arthur), the landlady (Bryher) and an old woman (Blanche Lewin). Some of these scenes seem extracted from the main narrative and relate to it in a metaphorical manner. The one in which the barmaid cavorts from behind the bar in a rather maniacal way, with a knife clenched between her teeth, feels superfluous to the narrative. It is posited as a symbolic action and is contrasted to the intercut scene in which Thorne eventually kills Astrid with a knife. The film, then, has three levels of articulation: 'realistic' or 'objective' narrative, renderings of 'interior' events, and a symbolic system that uses visual images as poetic metaphors.

The use of 'clatter montage'—a term used by Eisenstein to describe the rapid montage of film strips in order to almost create an effect of superimposition—and symbolic interpolations clearly aligns the film with Eisensteinian thought, especially his conception of 'overtonal montage'.[21] Friedberg rightly notes that Macpherson inflected Eisenstein's theory of overtonal montage with psychoanalysis, shifting his physiological focus. The physiological aspects of Eisenstein's theory did remain, however, in the more poetic symbolism within the film. The use of symbolic interpolations are not always psychological and are often in accord with Eisenstein's conception of editing according to 'a-dominant' principles, in which symbolic ideas—rather than narrative logic—guide editing, leading to 'intellectual overtones' within the film.[22] The use of 'clatter montage' was thus formally derived from Soviet practice, but on the whole it was inflected in a psychological direction.

In addition to Friedberg's argument that *Borderline* merges psychoanalysis and Soviet montage, I would contend that the film is also informed by humanism. I suggested in Chapter 1 that *Close Up* partly interpreted the specific political issues dealt with in Soviet films through a humanist, as well as psychoanalytical, filter, and I would argue that *Borderline* works in the same vein. *Borderline* thus focuses upon the personal relationships of human beings and takes place in a realistic environment that is nevertheless stripped of any specificity. This tends to emphasize that the location transcends 'real' time and place. And while political themes such as racism and homosexuality inform the film, its humanist underpinnings dilute the political edge that such themes may carry, as I shall demonstrate in discussion of these issues. In this sense I would agree with Cosandey when he writes that '*Borderline*'s approach to racism has nothing to do with a practical position, but represents above all the act of an artist attentive to the problems of being human.'[23]

The Borderline Between Tradition and Modernity

While previous articles on *Borderline* have covered a range of issues, work placing it in the milieu of alternative film culture has been rare and brief. Although there were some key differences between the aesthetic underpinnings of *Borderline* and those of the more privileged areas of alternative film culture at the time of its release, the film does still share some common themes that I have already mentioned, which loosely align it with some of the documentary films.

Close Up's hostility towards British culture and its exile status have probably been the major reason why scholars have previously situated *Borderline* within an international, rather than national, context. Yet, strange as it may seem, the film was promoted as a British film. The invitation to the trade show announced that the film 'has been directed, photographed and largely acted by British people', and insisted that '*Borderline* is a British film'.[24] Such rhetoric reveals that the filmmakers were consciously engaged in a project of transforming British film culture: their attacks on it were paving the way for their intervention in it; they also may have been hoping that a distributor would have picked the film up for quota purposes.

The main theme that aligns *Borderline* with some of the other films I have discussed is the link between tradition and modernity, understandable in that these themes permeated most areas of alternative discourse. Yet, whereas these themes were explicit in films like *Drifters* and *Song of Ceylon*, in *Borderline* they underpin the film in a subtler manner. The more overt linkages between past and present can actually be found in H.D.'s pamphlet on the film. In this pamphlet it is clear that Macpherson is being promoted as a director marked by both traditional and modernist traits. This construction is most clearly elaborated when H.D. compares Macpherson, rather exaggeratedly, to Leonardo da Vinci: 'This name connotes mechanical efficiency, modernity and curiosity allied with pure creative impulse. The film *per se*, is a curious welding of mechanical and creative instincts.'[25] She reiterates that the film is artistic both in a modern, 'filmic' sense and in an 'actual, historic, conventional' sense.[26] This conception of the film—and of Macpherson himself—as an amalgamation of past and present was a central trope of alternative filmmaking in Britain. It reflected the desire not only to legitimate the mechanical medium of film with artistry but also, conversely, to legitimate 'older' artistic values within an increasingly technological world.

Although themes of tradition and modernity connect *Borderline* with documentary films in the inter-war period, major differences still separated them. First, *Borderline* places great emphasis upon subjective events, while the documentary films tended to concentrate on objective events. Second, documentary films were keen to stress the continuity of tradition, but nevertheless tended to place faith in scientific progress. The POOL team, on the other hand, were more ambivalent about science. They were positive about the technological breakthroughs it had produced, but seemed to be less positive about excessive rationality. As 'creative artists' they held firmly to ideas about artistic inspiration that were almost supernatural in character. Numinous ideas permeated the thought of H.D., who was drawn to Eleusinian mysticism (and used the word 'runic' in her *Borderline* pamphlet several times).[27] Such ideas can also be found in an article that Robert Herring wrote for *Close Up*, entitled 'A New Cinema, Magic and the Avant-Garde', in which he proposed that cinema casts a spell over its audience.[28] It should not be forgotten that *Wing Beat* was also an exploration of telepathy; Macpherson, Bryher and H.D. may have been drawn to psychoanalysis because it was scientifically grounded, yet they also paid a great deal of attention to the secret mysteries of the mind. It was, therefore, a science that still accepted the illogical and creative realities of an internal world.

It is surprising that this 'magical' aspect of *Borderline* has been overlooked. It certainly could help to explain some of the more obscure sections of the film. For example, in the scene in which Thorne decides to leave Astrid, a rapid montage sequence shuffles images of his suitcase and Astrid's face. This constitutes an internal rendering of Astrid's mind: the suitcase, a symbol of Thorne's imminent departure, is intercut with her face to indicate her point of view; the rapid flickers indicate mental tension generating within her mind. Suddenly, Astrid falls to the ground and we see Thorne, as though this is a point-of-view shot, looking at her supine body, which appears dead. This sequence is intensely dramatic and seems to exceed any simplistic, 'objective' rendering of physical actions. Though this may be interpreted as an objective event, the manner in which it occurs, and the specific cinematic coding of the event, indicates that something more is going on. This is emphasized when Thorne goes over to the body and is startled when Astrid suddenly rises, in an exaggeratedly dramatic manner.

One interpretation of this scene is that it is a moment when subjective and objective registers become somewhat blurred within the film. While

(left) 12. Thorne's point-of-view shot of Astrid, lying motionless on the floor as though dead in *Borderline* (courtesy of BFI)
(right) 13. Astrid, however, suddenly raises her head, as though coming back from the dead (courtesy of BFI)

the 'clatter montage' denotes Astrid's subjective impressions, there are no such clearly marked codes to tell us that we then enter Thorne's mind. The shot of Astrid lying on the floor could, though, be seen as his subjective, unconscious image of her dead body (representing a wish fulfilment) as well as an objective image of her collapsing through mental exhaustion. The reason no subjective markers are used here, then, is because it is a moment when the objective and the subjective overlap. Alternatively, considering the interests of the POOL group in numinousness, the sequence could be considered a supernatural and subjective rendering in which Thorne, in a moment of clairvoyance, 'sees' Astrid dead (an event that will occur soon after this moment). Astrid stirring in an exaggeratedly dramatic manner can therefore be read as Thorne witnessing a resurrection (hence his startled reaction).

Race and Difference

The subject of race has attracted much attention in coverage of *Borderline*, specifically in relation to how 'white' modernism became interested in issues of 'blackness'. The Harlem Renaissance—encompassing a broad array of black American artists and political figures—was the central focus of white intellectuals' interest in black culture during the 1920s and 1930s. Many commentators have noted how white modernist culture often appropriated 'blackness' as a symbolic weapon that opposed stifling bourgeois conventions. Nathan Higgis has argued that black culture was

154

appropriated by whites 'to fulfil their own psychic needs',[29] while James De Jongh writes: 'In its racial transformation, Harlem had become the embodiment of an idea, for by its very existence Harlem posed a challenge to contemporary limits and cultural terms within which personal being for both blacks and whites were imagined and defined.'[30]

It was common for white writers to stereotype blackness as primitive and natural, as opposed to white civilization and sophistication.[31] This kind of thinking about 'blackness' informed Macpherson's—and many other *Close Up* writers'—interest in black culture and fed into *Borderline*. Such thinking can be discerned in the special 'negro' edition of *Close Up*, as well as in the article Macpherson wrote for Nancy Cunard's substantial anthology of black culture, *Negro*, first published in 1934. In the issue of *Close Up* focusing on 'negro' cinema, Macpherson's editorial proclaimed 'the only way to understand people is in their essence'.[32] He therefore homogenized the black race in a manner not evident when discussing white culture: white culture had never previously been defined by skin colour.

Macpherson extended this argument in 'A Negro Film Union—Why Not?', his contribution to *Negro*. In this essay, he argued that much black literature was 'genteel', a consequence of both the negro's essentialism being diluted by the print medium and of the way in which white censorship muted 'blackness'. In order for a 'quintessential negro cinema' to develop, argued Macpherson, a 'negro film union' should be constructed so that blacks could work out their own film language.[33] Macpherson may have been advocating a progressive message here in that he called for black filmmakers to construct their own representations. At the same time, he relied upon universal notions of blackness as necessarily 'authentic', as opposed to civilization, which is why the 'negro' becomes diluted in print compared to the 'opulence' of black music and the 'atavistic pull' of black dancing.[34]

Macpherson's essay is revealing in that it shows how he was himself occupying a position bordering essentialism and relativism, an extension of the tradition/modernity dualism within which *Close Up* often operated. While the discourse in *Close Up* often inherited humanist traditions, it also tended to go against these traditions at various points in order to rail against convention. Thus, Macpherson wavers between explaining the 'genteel' nature of black literature from an essentialist position (it is not fitted to their nature) and explaining it from a relativist position (the current structures of society dilute it). This fluid characteristic of discourse can also be found in H.D.'s *Borderline* pamphlet: one moment she proclaims that there are no fixed artistic standards, the next moment she relies upon a transcendent and universal notion of 'beauty'.[35] This fluid nature of discourse is also evident in *Borderline* and is, I would argue, an important feature of the film. However, within the discourse of *Close Up*, essentialism was often predominant over relativity, thus reducing and limiting its potentially disruptive impact. In the same manner, the fluid aspects of *Borderline* are generally subservient to fixed and transcendent universals.

In the film Pete and Adah are endowed with pure qualities, and connected with nature, especially when they are shot against vast backdrops of mountains, clouds and waterfalls. Thorne and Astrid, on the other hand, are unstable and connected to the claustrophobia of their hotel room; Thorne's alcohol consumption signifies his degenerate state. This binary structure is not fixed, however, and fluidity is hinted at. Adah is involved in both black and white relationships and seems to occupy a borderline position between these two states. At the same time, however, there exist essential, unchanging qualities to the characters that negate this flexibility. For instance, the characters contain similar attributes throughout; they are never inconsistent. Fluidity is therefore a feature of the film, but a set of deeper structures contains it. Thus Adah, who crosses into the realm of both races, is described as 'mulatto'; her 'essential' identity is mixed, so she can therefore mix. Pete, on the other hand, can only mix with the 'mulatto'—not white—woman, as he has racial connections with her. Therefore, race is fluid on one level, distinct on another.

Jean Walton has briefly remarked that, although Macpherson posited a 'universal "human mind" whose labyrinthine nature is shared by male and female, black and white', in practice the film 'distinguishes greatly among the minds it "probes"'.[36] Pete's mind is only entered to connote his 'natural' placidity, in opposition to the turbulent minds of the white characters, while Adah 'remains very much a cipher'. Walton argues that 'the asymmetry between "black" and "white" emerges from the POOL group's racial understanding of Freudian psychoanalysis.'[37] Though I would not deny such claims, I think it is important to be aware of the humanist dimension that filtered the group's psychological thought. Walton is correct when she argues that such a psychoanalytic component results in black being equated with natural sexuality, white with repressed (civilized) sexuality. But this distinction is not merely psychoanalytical; according to Richard Dyer it was a distinction prevalent at the time, made amongst both blacks and whites.[38] Therefore, such essentialist dualisms should not be condemned too heavily from contemporary perspectives; at the same

14. *Borderline:* Pete (Paul Robeson) shot against the sky to emphasize his links with nature

time, it is important to recognize such discursive structures as they fed into *Borderline*.

In *Borderline*, blackness is equated with emotion as against intelligence, so that the black person is seen as naive and simple, in structural opposition to whiteness. This leads to an ambivalent representation of the 'mulatto' woman, because she is stranded between such fixed identities. Pete is always represented as the good/positive character, yet he is also seen as simple in comparison to the white characters. While their rapid montage sequences denote a mish-mash of subjective impressions, it is debatable whether the montage sequences associated with Pete even denote his subjectivity. These sequences depict trees, clouds and mountains, more or less implying that these are symbolic interpolations connecting Pete with nature. Therefore, even though white subjectivities are encoded as degenerate, they are still more complex and powerful than black subjectivities. Adah, meanwhile, lacks any specific identity whatsoever, her subjectivity not even hinted at. Because she is neither white nor black, she exists in a kind of flicker world, vacillating between both categories but never entering either (she also causes the subsequent grief). As Jean Walton has written: 'While Adah [...] signifies a structural and thematic link between black and white, her interiority is not adequately explored. She becomes the untheorised ground, or excluded middle, on which the black/white opposition of *Borderline* is predicated.'[39]

Sexuality and Desire

The theme of sexuality is another 'progressive' theme that *Borderline* deals with, but it does so less overtly than with the race theme. The main characters all represent racial tensions in an explicit way, but at the same time their relationships are heterosexual: Thorne is paired with the two women; Adah with the two men; Astrid with Thorne and Pete with Adah. Walton has argued that homosexuality does, however, play a central role in the film and cannot be disconnected from the themes of race and sexual difference. She points out that there are more overtly signified homosexual characters: the manageress and the barmaid are codified as a lesbian couple, while the piano player is codified as gay.[40] Her reasons for these interpretations are that the manageress, played by Bryher, is 'butch', and that the barmaid 'dances, flirts with patrons and affectionately ruffles the manageress's hair'. This interpretation is reinforced by the fact that, in one scene, they are framed in a two shot with the barmaid's arm around the manageress's shoulder. The piano player, meanwhile, is seen as gay as he 'gazes longingly at Pete, or at the picture of him propped on his piano, flourishes a long cigarette-holder, sometimes dances the Charleston across the room'.[41]

There are two other levels of homosexuality that inform the film, according to Walton: the homosexuality of the filmmakers, which is implicitly represented in the film, and the sublimated homosexuality of the main character, Thorne. Though Thorne is involved with two different women in the film, Walton argues that there are moments in the film that signify a sublimated desire for Pete. The first time is when he bursts into Pete's room to discover Pete and Adah together. Walton writes that Pete and Thorne engage in a drawn-out staring match, which has homoerotic undertones, emphasized by the fact that the pianist (who has a photo of Pete on his piano) has rushed up behind Thorne, along with the manageress. When Pete knocks on the door of Thorne and Astrid's room just after Astrid has been killed, Thorne locks the door quickly. There is then a clatter montage of the two hands on each side of the door, a scene that Walton interprets as continuing the homoerotic coupling of the former scene. The difference is that the 'black space' where Pete lives is easily penetrated by whiteness, whereas the reverse is not true. This coupling is metaphorically consummated at the end of the film when Pete and Thorne sit on the hillside together, shake hands and smile at each other.[42]

Walton connects this interpretation to the themes of race and psycho-analysis. She argues that the main white pair are civilized and negatively encoded: they have neuroses engendered by the repression of their desires, represented through the occasional flickers of subjective montage. The black pair are 'natural' and heterosexual, free from the affliction of neurotic repression. The minor white characters are, according to Walton, civilized and 'mentally stable': this is because they are homosexual and have not repressed these desires.[43]

Much of this argument is persuasive, but some points warrant further consideration. The first of these is the problematic way in which psychoanalysis is used to defend homosexuality as positive in comparison to heterosexuality. Walton cites Freud's analysis of da Vinci's homosexuality, which he considered to be healthily channelled into artistic activity, while his repression resulted in his neurosis. She argues that the POOL team would have been aware of this (note H.D.'s rather exaggerated comparison of Macpherson with da Vinci) and that it would have influenced their treatment of homosexuality within *Borderline*. Walton's reading of the film is heavily influenced by the personal interests of the filmmakers themselves, but perhaps does not take into account the institutional milieu in which they had to operate. Bryher, H.D. and Macpherson may all have had homosexual tendencies, but rarely did they discuss homosexuality in their written work in any explicit manner.[44] Homosexuality in this period was against the law and those who practised were liable for imprisonment. Therefore, the social restrictions of the time pushed homosexuality undercover; likewise, in *Borderline*, the theme becomes implicit, not overtly displayed. This repression of desire leads to the state of neurosis, which is explored in the film.

The white characters are aligned with the civilization/neurosis axis, upon which homosexuality could be attached as an implicit adjunct. If this is so, then we might ask why the minor characters are, according to Walton, 'mentally stable'. Here I would have to disagree with her and argue that the barmaid's dipsomania and rather manic actions, as well as the pianist's occasionally odd behaviour, do not signify mental stability. If we do not go into their minds via clatter montage in order to probe their neuroses, this is not particularly connected with their stability; rather it is a result of their minor status in the film. In contrast, as Walton has pointed out, the black characters are aligned with nature/stability/heterosexuality. If Adah was placed upon the racial borderline, then Thorne is placed upon the sexual borderline (an implication of homosexuality, but nothing explicit) in contrast to Astrid, who does not seem to have homosexual inclinations. Thus white is equated with sexual vacillation, whereas black is equated with sexual stability. Once again, fluidity is opened up in one sense, closed down in another.

Perhaps the most overt indication of homosexuality is in Macpherson's direction of Paul Robeson: his body is captured in semi-naked statuesque poses and is the centre of almost fetishistic attention. As Michael O'Pray has written: 'Often shot in tight close-up from a low angle, Robeson's face takes on the quality of an icon, of a creature who rises passively above the emotional mire of the other characters, who stands outside the narrative space almost.'[45]

While blackness is codified as 'straight', it can still be appropriated as an object of white desire. Such appropriation of blackness as a fetishistic and essentialized object neatly encapsulated the way in which many white intellectuals appropriated 'blackness' out of personal interest. The black person is thus an exotic 'other' who is positively connected with nature and is a figure of noble stability within the flux of 'white' modernity. This construction can be partially aligned to the manner by which documentary filmmakers constructed the working classes and colonial subjects as fetishistic 'others', through low-angled, close-up compositions, in order to connote naturalism and nobility.

The Reception of *Borderline*

Although the filmmakers may not have expected *Borderline* to be a commercial success, they were hoping that it could be appreciated beyond the realms of their private circle. This would have fitted in with their ideas about attempting to broaden the appeal of 'intelligent' cinema. The fact that the film was also reviewed in a trade paper, the *Bioscope*, as well as in the *Evening Standard*, the *Observer* and the *Manchester Guardian*, shows that the filmmakers had invited journalists who might possibly promote the film. The *Bioscope* announced that the film was being offered for public exhibition and that it had received an 'A' certificate from the BBFC.[46] Such hopes, however, went unfulfilled. The film was not well received and was not widely shown. Cosandey has managed to discover that the film played in nine cinemas: in London, Brussels (at the second International Congress of Independent Cinema, 1930), Barcelona, Neuchatel, Berlin (two locations), Glasgow, Amsterdam and New York.[47] The only additional screening I have been able to trace is at the Edinburgh Film Guild, on 13 March 1932.[48] Surprisingly, the film was not even shown at the Film Society.

The reviews of the film were negative. Not unexpectedly, the *Bioscope* was hostile towards the experimental and apparently disorderly nature of the film. The reviewer complained of Macpherson burying his intentions in an 'agglomerate [sic] of weird shots and queer situations, worked out around a dissolute set of unsympathetic characters. He thinks too much of close-up and not enough of border-line. The result is a wholly unintelligible scramble of celluloid eccentricity.'[49]

Even Caroline Lejeune, a reviewer much more receptive to experimental and 'artistic' filmmaking, was unimpressed by the film in her review for the *Observer*. Despite praising Macpherson and the writers of *Close Up* for excellence in film appreciation, she did not think that the film lived up to their ambitions. She thought that it was too ambitious and that it lacked control, which resulted in a formless, incoherent picture:

> Finite it may be in the mind of its makers who have the written word and the drawn sketch as supplement and corollary, but to the public, facing it without pre-conception, the film is formless—urgent perhaps, but urgent in chaos, lacking that single broad stream of creation, whether of theme, or mood, or simply rhythm, along which any work of art must travel towards its implicit end.[50]

These reviews reveal that the film was perceived as confusing and chaotic. Cosandey has argued that it was because the film followed a completely subjective orientation that it so baffled the critics.[51] I would only partially agree: I do think that the attempts to probe the subjective minds of the characters in the film were a major reason for its poor reception. However, I have argued that the film was not a complete objectification of subjective (il)logic. I therefore think that there are other explanations for the film's negative reception.

In Britain the emphasis upon subjectivism was, I think, too strong and was not in tune with the changing aesthetic predilections of alternative film culture. By the time that *Borderline* was released, there was a marked preference for the objective movements found in documentary films. In these films, psychological processes were not represented, they just informed the creation of the film through the 'artistic' mind of the filmmaker. So, while the film was not completely dominated by subjective considerations, the emphasis placed upon this aspect would have been out of step with the cultural zeitgeist.

The way in which *Borderline* attempted to merge subjective, objective and metaphorical registers also meant that it was rather unpredictable and disjunctive. This affected the film's British reception, as discourse privileged those films that were marked by coherence, where filmic elements related organically to the whole. In *Drifters*, experimentation is incorporated into a very orderly structure; in *Borderline* this is not the case, a point reflected in Lejeune's criticism of the film. *Borderline*'s formal arrangement even went against the critical frameworks that were most prominent in *Close Up* itself. Lejeune also picked up on this aspect, arguing that *Borderline* 'is not the stuff to which the true Macpherson would extend patronage'.[52]

It could therefore be argued that *Borderline* was not just a critical failure but a failure in terms of the filmmakers' own objectives. In their criticism, Macpherson and Bryher were continually appealing for experimental films that were nevertheless coherent and which could potentially appeal to an audience beyond specialist circles. If the film was an extension of their critical interventions within film culture, then it was an attempt to merge the radical and the coherent (and thus to forge a borderline position). Yet, unlike the themes of race and gender in *Borderline*, in which fluidity is ultimately contained by fixed distinctions, the radical aspects of the film (subjective representations, metaphorical encodings) tend to overwhelm the more traditional aspects (coherent storyline, overriding 'realism'). In this sense, radical disjunction was not successfully contained inside a more stable framework. It may be that this was due to the inexperience of the filmmakers, in that they lacked the skills to incorporate their ambitious ideas into a coherent structure. However, although this worked against them at the time, it has more recently worked in their favour. In the last couple of decades, critics have received the film more positively; its complexity and difficulty is more in tune with late twentieth-century notions of avant-gardism than the more restrained experimentation found in many documentary films of the 1930s.[53]

Conclusion

In the 1930s the representation of personal and psychological events became something of a minority affair in alternative and independent film culture. This is in some ways extraordinary when one considers that the psychological inwardness of German art cinema was regarded as the pinnacle of artistic creativity by British cinéphiles only five years earlier. This shows that while many ideas about cinema persisted within alternative film culture, others were changing rapidly, a result of the swift technological and aesthetic changes that were occurring in the broader social climate, as well as the relatively nascent state of film criticism and theory.

The growing antipathy towards psychological films meant that fewer independent filmmakers made subjectively oriented films; even if they did, they were less prone to be well received and therefore unlikely to find a place in film histories. The only independent film that seems to share any affinities with *Borderline* is Brian Desmond Hurst's *The Tell-Tale Heart* (1934). While this film is very different from Macpherson's, especially regarding montage strategies, it does share a preoccupation with the distinctions and overlaps between subjectivity and objectivity. An adaptation of Edgar Allan Poe's story, it concerns a cataleptic man who suffers from visual hallucinations. The film insistently probes the mind of this man to the extent that it becomes confusing to us whether what we see is real or hallucination. It seems to suggest that, for this man, subjective and objective realms are inseparable, implicitly questioning any simplistic, 'objective' representation. The dividing line between objective and subjective was never clear cut, as demonstrated in the reception of Eisenstein's films, which were considered aesthetically objective by Grierson, yet construed as acutely psychological by *Close Up*'s editors. While the aesthetics of Eisenstein were built upon complex psychological ideas, however, he rarely tried to delve into the mind of subjective states. It was this preoccupation with subjective states, and an almost numinous fascination with the powers of the mind, that became marginalized by the growth of the documentary movement.

Conclusion

This book has primarily been concerned with investigating the activities within alternative film culture; the commercial film industry has largely functioned as a symbol of what was considered negative, an imaginary 'other' that fed into the identity of those reacting against it. Nevertheless, it would be simplistic in the extreme to think of these two fields as totally opposed and distinct. While hostility did exist between these camps, there were also overlaps, interconnections and mutual influences. One obvious example is that many cinéphiles were alerted to the art of cinema through viewing films made within a commercial context. For these aesthetes, commercialism was not an absolute, but something that had an impact on filmmaking by degrees. It was, it should be remembered, excessive commercialism, rather than commercialism per se, that was to be resisted. In much the same way that the boundaries between art and commerce were not fixed, the markers between alternative film culture and the British film industry were also permeable. As I have mentioned, particularly within the mid-1920s it was hoped that non-commercial, artistically minded film activities—viewing, writing and discussion—would affect the commercial film industry.

Looking in detail at the extent to which this occurred is beyond the scope of this present book, and would in fact perhaps entail a separate book in itself. Nevertheless, there were some signs that alternative film culture did have an effect on commercial British cinema, which demonstrates how the 'alternative' and 'mainstream' are not mutually exclusive spheres. The Film Society, for example, had a number of prominent members who were involved in directing and producing British commercial films: these included Anthony Asquith, Michael Balcon, Adrian Brunel, Alfred Hitchcock and Victor Saville. Within commercial film production, a move towards brisker editing, more economical use of titles and a willingness to undertake stylized visual and/or sound experiments are some of the traits that can be connected to the impact of alternative film culture, even if we cannot solely attribute such trends to a single factor.

The films discussed in this book, however, fall under the rubric of 'independent' cinema.[1] As should be clear from the number of such films that I have mentioned in the preceding pages, experimental filmmaking in inter-war Britain was far more vibrant than has sometimes been acknowledged. It may be the case that such activities were not on a par with those of France, for example, but this does not negate their significance. They are valuable in that they represent the first real flowering of sustained, experimental filmmaking in this country, thus forming a crucial part of an alternative tradition.

These experimental, independent films were variegated in nature, yet there were some patterns detectable across such productions. In the mid- to late 1920s, for example, there was a marked tendency for parody and satire in the few such films that were produced. As the broader alternative culture became stronger and more established, the films themselves not only increased in number, but also gained more confidence and seriousness. The output of the 1930s was marked, as were a number of films made in other countries, by a merging of experimental techniques with a social purpose. A selection of films emerging from the documentary film movement is the most obvious manifestation of such a tendency. Films made outside this milieu also on occasion bore such traits, like a few films connected with the workers' movement. The influence of the 'machine aesthetic' also played an important role in shaping a number of films. On a formal level, for example, this fascination was evident in regulated, rhythmic editing, which reflected machine-like efficiency, while on the level of content the trope of machinery in motion was a common feature. Despite the occurrence of common themes and tropes, this should not lead us to overlook the variety of filmmaking that was taking place in this period.

Such diversity may have robbed many of these films of a stable identity, which was crucial to their approval at the time in alternative film culture, as it has subsequently been. Yet we need to revise our ideas of what constitutes modernist filmmaking, detaching it—at least to some extent—from national styles and connections with already established modernist artists. These lead to assumptions that this was not a period in which modernism flourished in British cinema. To cite an example: Sarah Street claims that modernist experiment in this period was limited, one reason being that artists, by and large, turned their backs on film in this country.[2] Why should experimentation, or cinematic modernism, be measured by the extent to which modernist artists established in other media participated in film? This would seem to fly in the face of those who at the time wanted to establish cinema as an art on its own terms. This type of thinking may be misguided when taken to the extreme—in the sense that it leads to a quest for purity that unfairly dismisses overlaps with other media—but it does at least lead away from approval by proxy (that is, this film is important because it has connections to reputable painters). In light of such considerations, the lack of modernist artists making films should not be seen as connected to a lack of experiment within British filmmaking. As I have shown, there was plenty of modernist exploration of the medium, but it was not bestowed with the immediate validity accorded to many French avant-garde films. Neither did those films made outside the documentary movement (and some made within it) cohere into a nationally specific movement.

In an age, however, where the specificity of the national is increasingly being questioned, perhaps it is time to re-evaluate these films, and the culture at large (despite its nationalist trappings), as presciently international. The films themselves may be seen as hybrid objects, constituted of a plurality of different, sometimes seemingly incompatible, influences. This makes them difficult to categorize in any neat and tidy manner, but fascinating nonetheless. In fact, my own method of grouping these films together—through nationality and links to a specific culture— should be seen as convenient rather than essential. They have allowed me to assess a range of films as linked, but which in actuality were marked by a number of differences as well as internationalist influences.

The fact that independent, experimental filmmaking increased during the 1930s shows how important the broader 'film culture' was, thus justifying a need to look not solely at film texts, but the context out of which they emerged. With films made on a small scale such as these, a surrounding alternative culture of exhibition, distribution and critical discourse served as an important base that influenced more films to be made, and offered spaces where they could potentially be exhibited. This broader, alternative 'film culture' was important not just for promoting, and giving a voice to, filmmakers working outside the mainstream, but also for a number of other reasons, which link it to some areas currently being researched in film studies.

First, British alternative film culture was a key site of the development of cinéphilia, the intense and passionate attachment to cinema as a popular art form that encourages rituals (the Sunday Film Society screenings with attendant debates) and writings. Recently, following Susan Sontag's article on the death of cinéphilia, and a subsequent re-articulation of film culture through various Internet platforms, the topic of cinéphilia has gained increasing attention.[3] It is often discussed as a particularly striking phenomenon of the 1950s and 1960s, and it is also now generally acknowledged that it was a practice that emerged in the inter-war period. While British alternative film culture formed the context out of which independent and experimental films emerged, it was also a broader platform for expressing the love of a new art form.

The passionate attachment to cinematic culture led to a celebration of a wide variety of different films, while critical engagement with these films fed into the construction of a suitable lexicon that enabled this medium to be discussed as 'art'. Screenings and attitudes to film expressed in writings from this period are important in that they have shaped conceptions of what constitutes good cinema, and what types of films are worthy of preservation. Thus issues of 'the canon' and 'taste cultures', concerns of contemporary film studies, were crucial components of alternative film culture in inter-war Britain.[4] This was the first cultural formation to attempt systematically to change the ways that films circulated within everyday life. The ephemeral film object needed to be rendered enduring, capable of being studied as a text, if it was to be plucked from the oblivion that 'mass culture' had assigned it. Cinema needed to be historicized, infused with a narrative of progress, so that values could be assigned and then placed within a temporal lineage. This involved a curious blending of tradition and modernity, of low and high culture. Traditional notions of artistic worth needed to be retained in order to bestow this medium with cultural value, yet its modernity could also be employed as the sign of a radical art, capable of original modes of aesthetic registration. This cultural milieu was undoubtedly operating within the frameworks of 'high culture', but it was also attracted to the popular nature of the medium, albeit in a rather ambiguous manner: cinema's blending of the high and the popular was one of its appeals.

In this sense, alternative film culture in this period fed into a number of important developments within subsequent film culture: film education, film preservation and the need to provide sites where a diverse array of films can be seen. Debates about cultural exhibition have continued to play an important role for film cultures, so that Hollywood domination can be kept at bay. 'Quality' versus 'quantity' arguments, crucial to the discursive construction of cinematic artefacts, continue to this day, even if in reconfigured forms. Although, from a contemporary perspective, some of the attitudes evident from this study may seem rather elitist, they were still key contributors to the serious consideration of cinema as a powerful cultural force that itself led to the formation of film studies courses within the academy. While the ways in which films are approached have been broadened significantly, as have the films deemed worthy of attention, the underlying sense that cinema is important is something that most people involved in film appreciation and education still share. Alternative film culture in inter-war Britain was a vital force in institutionalizing such a belief, at a time when it was far from gospel.

Notes

Introduction

1 Various accounts of avant-garde or experimental filmmaking (the terms tend to be used interchangeably) written between the late 1960s and the late 1980s can be found in the following works, some of which focus on more specific movements or types of filmmaking (such as abstract filmmaking or Cubist film): David Curtis, *Experimental Cinema: A Fifty Year Evolution* (London: Studio Vista, 1971); Phillip Drummond, Deke Duisinberre and Al Rees (eds), *Film as Film: Formal Experiment in Film 1910–1975* (exhibition catalogue; London: Hayward Gallery, 1979); Stephen Dwoskin, *Film Is: The International Free Cinema* (Woodstock and New York: The Overlook Press, 1975); John G. Hanhardt, 'The Medium Viewed: The American Avant-Garde Film', in *A History of the American Avant-Garde Cinema* (exhibition catalogue; New York: American Federation of Arts, 1976); Rudolf Kuenzli (ed.), *Dada and Surrealist Film* (New York: Willis Locker and Owens, 1987); Standish D. Lawder, *The Cubist Cinema* (New York: New York University Press, 1975); Malcolm Le Grice, *Abstract Film and Beyond* (London: Studio Vista, 1977); P. Adams Sitney, 'Introduction' in P. Adams Sitney (ed.), *The Avant-Garde Film* (New York: New York University Press, 1978); Parker Tyler, *Underground Film: A Critical History* (New York: Grove Press, 1969). In terms of 'exceptions', these are mentioned very briefly, but usually include some examples from the USA (Curtis, Dwoskin and Tyler mention a few US examples); Britain (Curtis very briefly, Dusinberre, 'The Other Avant-Gardes', in Drummond, Dusinberre and Rees, *Film as Film*); Netherlands (Dusinberre) and Poland (Dusinberre).

2 Ian Christie, 'The Avant-Gardes and European Cinema Before 1930', in John Hill and Pamela Church Gibson (eds), *The Oxford Guide to Film Studies* (Oxford: Oxford University Press, 1998), p. 453.

3 Hanhardt, 'The Medium Viewed', p. 21.

4 A.L. Rees, *A History of Experimental Film and Video* (London: BFI, 1999), p. 1.

5 Clement Greenberg, 'Avant-Garde and Kitsch', in Clement Greenberg,

Collected Essays and Criticism: Volume 1, Perceptions and Judgments 1939–1944 (Chicago: University of Chicago Press, 1986), pp. 6–11.

6   This is outlined by Murray Smith, 'Modernism and the Avant-Gardes', in Hill and Church Gibson, *The Oxford Guide to Film Studies*, p. 395.

7   Rees, *A History of Experimental Film and Video*, pp. 2–3.

8   See ibid. See also Michael O'Pray (ed.), *Avant-Garde Film: Forms, Themes and Passions* (London: Wallflower, 2003).

9   Richard Abel, *French Cinema: The First Wave, 1915–1929* (Princeton: Princeton University Press, 1984).

10 Quoted in Abel, *French Cinema: The First Wave*, p. 241. Originally from 'Le Repertoire et l'avant-garde du cinema', *Cinea-cine-pour-tous* 31 (17 February 1923), p. 5.

11 This should not imply that the 1960s ciné clubs only privileged a narrow range of films: the first three *Film Culture* Independent Film Awards demonstrate the variety of films favoured within such an environment: *Shadows* (1959, winner of the first award), *Pull My Daisy* (1959, winner of the second award) and *Primary* (1960, winner of the third award). See 'Appendix: The Independent Film Award', in P. Adams Sitney (ed.), *Film Culture Reader* (New York: Cooper Square Press, 2000), pp. 423–29.

12 Christie, 'The Avant-Gardes and European Cinema Before 1930', p. 450.

13 Peter Bürger, *Theory of the Avant-Garde* (Minneapolis: University of Minnesota Press, 1984).

14 Andreas Huyssen, 'The Hidden Dialectic: Avantgarde-Technology-Mass Culture', in Andreas Huyssen, *After the Great Divide: Modernism, Mass Culture, Postmodernism* (Bloomington: Indiana University Press, 1983); Paul Willemen, 'An Avant-Garde for the Nineties', in Paul Willemen, *Looks and Frictions: Essays in Cultural Studies and Film Theory* (London: BFI, 1994).

15 Abel, *French Cinema: The First Wave*, pp. 241–51.

16 Ibid., p. 241.

17 Ibid., p. 249. For selected writings from this period, see Richard Abel (ed.), *French Film Theory and Criticism 1907–1939: Volume 1, 1907–1929* (Princeton: Princeton University Press, 1988).

18 Abel, *French Cinema: The First Wave*, pp. 251–60.

19 Ben Davis, 'Beginnings of the Film Society Movement in the U.S.' *Film & History* 24: 3–4 (1994), p. 8; Jan-Christopher Horak, 'The First American Film Avant-Garde, 1919–1945', in Jan-Christopher Horak (ed.), *Lovers of Cinema* (Madison: University of Wisconsin Press, 1995), p. 20. Davis notes that there was actually an earlier film society operating in 1919 in Woodstock, though this only ran for a short period (p. 8).

20 Horak, 'The First American Film Avant-Garde', pp. 20–24. For a detailed discussion of small theatres showing 'artistic' and international films, see Tony Guzman, 'The Little Theatre Movement: The Institutionalization of the European Art Film in America' *Film History* 17 (2005), pp. 261–84.

21 Ibid., pp. 26–27. Such activities fed into the creation of the Museum of Modern Art's Film Library, which preserved and exhibited films. For a detailed investigation of MoMA's Film Library, see Haidee Wasson, *Museum Movies: The Museum of Modern Art and the Birth of Art Cinema* (Berkeley and Los Angeles: University of California Press, 2005).

22 For a detailed overview of developments across Europe during this period, see Malte Hagener, *Moving Forward, Looking Back: The European Avant-Garde and the Invention of Film Culture, 1919–1939* (Amsterdam: Amsterdam University Press, 2007)

23 Hagener, *Moving Forward, Looking Back*, pp. 88–89. For detailed discussion of the discourses on cinematic art in Germany during this period, see Sabine Hake, *Cinema's Third Machine: Writing on Film in Germany 1907–1933* (Lincoln: University of Nebraska Press, 1993); and Anton Kaes, 'The Debate About Cinema: Charting a Controversy' *New German Critique* 40 (Winter 1987), pp. 7-33.

24 Scott MacDonald, 'Introduction', in Scott MacDonald, (ed.), *Cinema 16: Documents Toward a History of a Film Society* (Philadelphia: Temple University Press, 2002), p. 2.

25 In Spain, for example, the film journal *Nuestro Cinema* was a key journal for critics and avant-garde figures: see Nuria Triana, *Spanish National Cinema* (London and New York: Routledge, 2003), pp. 24–27. In Poland the Praesens Group based in Warsaw, composed of painters, sculptors and architects, promoted progressive ideas in film form by organizing occasional screenings and publishing statements on film in their monthly periodical; articles on film also appeared in *Linia*, and filmmakers the Themersons published two editions of a journal *The Artistic Film* in the early 1930s: see Dusinberre 'The Other Avant-Gardes', pp. 55–57. The movement in Canada was not established until the mid-1930s, see Germaine Clinton, 'The Canadian Federation of Film Societies', in Cecile Starr (ed.), *The Film Society Primer* (New York: American Federation of Film Societies, 1956), pp. 71–73.

26 See Ian Christie and Richard Taylor (eds), *The Film Factory: Russian and Soviet Cinema in Documents* (Cambridge, MA: Harvard University Press, 1988); Denise J. Youngblood, *Movies for the Masses: Popular Cinema and Soviet Society in the 1920s* (Cambridge: Cambridge University Press, 1992), pp. 35–50.

27 According to Denys J. Wilcox, the Bloomsbury painters began to dominate the group at the end of the period 1910–19: see Denys J. Wilcox, *The London Group 1913–39: The Artists and their Works* (Aldershot: Scolar Press, 1995), p. 20.

28 Frances Spalding, *British Art Since 1900* (London: Thames and Hudson, 1986), p. 61.

29 Surrealism influenced Paul Nash, Edward Wadsworth and Edward Burra; Constructivism affected the work of Ben Nicholson and Barbara Hepworth.

See Susan Compton, 'Unit One—Towards Constructivism' and Andrew Causey, 'Unit One—Towards Surrealism', both in Susan Compton (ed.), *British Art in the Twentieth Century: The Modern Movement* (London and Munich: Royal Academy of Arts and Prestel-Verlag, 1986).

30 Deke Dusinberre's article 'The Avant-Garde Attitude in the Thirties' is the only piece thus far to have looked at a number of such elements as interconnected. That article is an important intervention and has served as crucial inspiration for my own work, yet it was limited by its length. It was originally published in Don Macpherson (ed.), *Traditions of Independence: British Cinema in the Thirties* (London: BFI, 1980).

Chapter 1

1 Rachael Low, *The History of the British Film 1918–1929* (London: George Allen and Unwin, 1971), pp. 241–42; also see Kenton Bamford, *Distorted Images: British National Identity and Film in the 1920s* (London and New York: I.B.Tauris, 1999), pp. 79–81.

2 See, for example, Geoff Brown, 'Sister of the Stage: British Film and British Theatre' and Brian McFarlane, 'A Literary Cinema? British Films and British Novels', both in Charles Barr (ed.), *All Our Yesterdays: 90 Years of British Cinema* (London: BFI, 1986). Also see various essays in Alan Burton and Laraine Porter (eds), *Scene-Stealing: Sources for British Cinema Before 1930* (Trowbridge: Flicks, 2003).

3 Gerry Turvey, for example, has claimed that screenwriters Elliot Stannard and director Harold Weston were thinking carefully about the ways in which literary sources should be adapted in cinematic terms from at least 1914 onwards. See Turvey, 'Enter the Intellectuals: Elliot Stannard, Harold Weston and the Discourses on Cinema and Art', in Burton and Porter, *Scene-Stealing*, pp. 85–93. Dismissals of British cinema of this period as literary and theatrical have also undergone subsequent revision. Perhaps the most extensive analysis of British cinema of the 1920s from such a revisionist perspective is Christine Gledhill's *Reframing British Cinema 1918–1928: Between Restraint and Passion* (London: BFI, 2003).

4 See 'Imogen' in *Bioscope*, 14 August 1924, p. 27, who bemoans the general neglect of films within newspapers and the fact that the medium is not treated in a sufficiently serious manner.

5 Letter from Ivor Montagu to Kenneth Macpherson, 14 January 1928, from Ivor Montagu Special Collection, item 143: Correspondence with Kenneth Macpherson. This letter concerns the idea of Montagu writing an article on Russian films for *Close Up*.

6 For a more detailed look at Barry's writings, see Haidee Wasson, 'Writing Cinema into Daily Life: Iris Barry and the Emergence of British Film

172

Criticism', in Andrew Higson (ed.), *Young and Innocent: Cinema and Britain 1896–1930* (Exeter: University of Exeter Press, 2002).

7 Some of her reviews are reprinted in Anthony Lejeune (ed.), *The Caroline Lejeune Film Reader* (Manchester: Carcanet, 1991).

8 For a detailed discussion of Montagu's critical practice see Gerry Turvey, 'Towards a Critical Practice: Ivor Montagu and British Film Culture in the 1920s', in Higson, *Young and Innocent*.

9 Low, *The History of the British Film, 1918–1929*, p. 20. For more on Mycroft and his film writing for the *Evening Standard* (between 1923 and 1926), see Vincent Porter, 'The Construction of an Anti-Hollywood Aesthetic: The Film Criticism of Walter Mycroft in the 1920s', in Alan Burton and Laraine Porter (eds), *Crossing the Pond: Anglo-American Film Relations Before 1930* (Trowbridge: Flicks, 2002), pp. 71–81.

10 Hugh Miller, 'An Independent Film Theatre?', *Evening Standard*, 1925, from Film Society Special Collection, item 11: Press Clippings Relating to the Film Society 1925–95; the clipping only has the year in which the article was written. Vincent Porter has written that Walter Mycroft had suggested establishing a film society in an *Evening Standard* article in 1924, which shows that a number of people were thinking about the same idea in the early 1920s. See Porter, 'The Construction of an Anti-Hollywood Aesthetic', p. 78.

11 Miller, 'An Independent Film Theatre?'.

12 Caroline Moorehead, *Sidney Bernstein: A Biography* (London: Jonathan Cape, 1984), pp. 21–22.

13 See Ivor Montagu, 'The Film Society, London' *Cinema Quarterly* 1: 2 (Winter 1932), pp. 42–46.

14 Low, *The History of the British Film, 1918–1929*, p. 33.

15 *Bioscope*, 18 October 1923, p. 54; George Pearson, *Flashback: The Autobiography of a British Film-maker* (London: George Allen & Unwin, 1957), p. 121.

16 Ivor Montagu saw *The Cabinet of Dr. Caligari* when he was at Cambridge University, and also contributed film criticism to university magazines. See Alan Lovell, Sam Rohdie and Peter Wollen, 'Interview with Ivor Montagu' *Screen* 13: 3 (Autumn 1972), p. 72. Rachael Low writes that there existed university film clubs with an emphasis on amateur production: the Cambridge Kinema Club was set up by Peter Le Neve Foster in 1923 and an Oxford University Film Society was established by Evelyn Waugh and Terence Greenberg in 1924. See Low, *The History of the British Film, 1918–1929*, p. 34, and Amy Sargeant, 'Elsa Lanchester and Chaplinism', in Burton and Porter, *Crossing the Pond*, p. 97.

17 Low, *The History of the British Film, 1918–1929*, p. 34.

18 Film Society Special Collection, item 2: Constitution and Rules of the Film Society Limited.

19 Performances were held approximately once a month. There was a three-month break in the summer.

20 Members such as Sidney Bernstein—cinema proprietor—could also advise the Society on a number of legal issues and help them to obtain cinemas for showings. See Moorehead, *Sidney Bernstein*, p. 23.

21 It is not clear why three different prices were charged, though the programme notes do state that concessions were given to people involved in the making of films.

22 Kauffer was an artist who was influenced by Cubism and Vorticism. He joined the London Group in 1917 and was also a member of Wyndham Lewis's short-lived Group X. He applied his art to a number of commercial pieces throughout the 1920s and 1930s.

23 Adrian Brunel Special Collection, box 165, item 5: untitled. Wells, son of H.G., was a fellow director of the company, which was officially established in 1927. Also see Ivor Montagu Special Collection, item 40a: Brunel and Montagu.

24 Adrian Brunel Special Collection, box 211: untitled. Other companies they provided a service for included Gainsborough, W&F Film Service, Wardour Films Ltd, and Western Import Co. Ltd.

25 Film Society Special Collection, item 15: Correspondence Related to Films Shown at Film Society Performances.

26 The Film Society Programme notes, performance 1, Film Society Special Collection, item 5: The Film Society Programme Notes. All subsequent programme note references are from this source.

27 This is generally credited as *Why Broncho Billy Left Bear Country* (1913).

28 The film was actually released in 1915.

29 Barry Salt, *Film Style and Technology: History and Analysis* (London: Starword, 1983), pp. 197–99.

30 For further details, see Kristin Thompson, 'Dr. Caligari at the Folies-Bergère', in Mike Budd (ed.), *The Cabinet of Dr. Caligari: Texts, Contexts, Histories* (New Brunswick: Rutgers University Press, 1990), pp. 127–36.

31 Thomas Elsaesser, *Weimar Cinema and After: Germany's Historical Imaginary* (London: Routledge, 2000), pp. 1–61.

32 These are aspects that have been attributed to more traditional accounts of German Expressionist film. See, for example, John D. Barlow, *German Expressionist Film* (Boston: Twayne, 1982), p. 25.

33 Hake, *Cinema's Third Machine*, p. 113.

34 For a discussion of the combination of the traditional and the new in Weimar cinema, see Elsaesser, *Weimar Cinema and After*, pp. 62–66.

35 See Mike Budd, 'The Moments of *Caligari*', in Budd, *The Cabinet of Dr. Caligari*, p. 55. Tony Guzman has also detailed how the film was extremely popular among the small-cinema circuit in the USA. See Guzman, 'The Little Theatre Movement', p. 262.

36 Hake, *Cinema's Third Machine*, p. 163.

37 Kristin Thompson and David Bordwell, *Film History: An Introduction* (New York and London: McGraw-Hill, 1994), p. 115.

38 Thompson, 'Dr. Caligari at the Folies-Bergere', pp. 149–56. Although Thompson says that not all intellectual reaction to *Caligari* was positive, it was highly praised by prominent figures such as Louis Delluc and Abel Gance.

39 Ivor Montagu, 'Present Day Russia and the Film', *Kinematograph Weekly*, 12 November 1925, p. 52.

40 Second Annual Report (1926–27), Film Society Special Collection, item 24.

41 See Stuart Macintyre, *A Proletarian Science: Marxism in Britain, 1917–1933* (Cambridge: Cambridge University Press, 1980); John Lucas, *The Radical Twenties* (Nottingham: Five Leaves, 1997); Raymond Plant, 'Social Thought', in C.B. Cox and A.E. Dyson, *The Twentieth Century Mind: History, Ideas and Literature in Britain: Volume 2, 1918–1945* (London: Oxford University Press, 1972), pp. 77–90.

42 See Abel, *French Cinema: the First Wave*, pp. 260–74.

43 Third Annual Report (1927–28), Film Society Special Collection, item 24.

44 See, for example, Tom Ryall, *Alfred Hitchcock and the British Cinema* (London, Athlone, 1996; first published 1986), pp. 13–14.

45 Despite the fact that these films represented only a very small output of the respective countries' films.

46 Many of Grierson's articles acknowledging his admiration for various aspects of Soviet cinema can be found in the chapter entitled 'The Russian Example', in Forsyth Hardy (ed.), *Grierson on Documentary* (London: Faber & Faber, 1966; expanded version of book first published in 1946). Hitchcock famously discusses the influence of Pudovkin in François Truffaut, *Hitchcock* (New York: Simon & Schuster, 1984; first published in French in 1966; first English translation published 1968), p. 214.

47 The lectures by Eisenstein and Pudovkin were reported in *The Times*, the *Daily Express*, and the *Daily Telegraph*. See Film Society Special Collection, item 11: Press Clippings Relating to the Film Society 1925–95.

48 Gerry Turvey, '"That Insatiable Body": Ivor Montagu's Confrontation with British Film Censorship' *Journal of Popular British Cinema: Forbidden British Cinema* 3 (2000), p. 33.

49 See Film Society Special Collection, item 20: London County Council Correspondence.

50 Ivor Montagu, *The Youngest Son: Autobiographical Sketches* (London: Lawrence and Wishart, 1970), pp. 323–24.

51 Memorandum to the London County Council (1929), from Film Society Special Collection, item 20.

52 Film Society Special Collection, item 20.

53 Letter dated 20 February, 1930, Film Society Special Collection, item 20.

54 Montagu, *The Youngest Son*, p. 320.

55 Ivor Montagu, *The Political Censorship of Films* (London: Victor Gollancz, 1929), p. 21 and passim.

56 Fourth Annual Report (1928–29), Film Society Special Collection, item 24.

57 *Bioscope*, 24 September 1925, p. 38.

58 For Barry's response, see *Bioscope*, 1 October 1925, p. 43.

59 Ralph Bond, 'Acts Under the Acts' *Close Up* (April 1930), pp. 278–79. The LCC rejected a licence application for the London Workers' Film Society to show *Potemkin* on two occasions: November 1929 and January 1930; Moorehead, *Sidney Bernstein*, p. 26.

60 G.A. Atkinson, *Daily Telegraph*, 17 March 1931, in Film Society Special Collection, item 11. Although Atkinson was an original member of the Film Society, he had fallen out with a large number of its personnel after they accused him of taking money to write favourable reviews. See Moorehead, *Sidney Bernstein*, p. 26.

61 On 7 February 1929, in relation to the Film Society screening of *The End of St. Petersburg*, Sir Robert Thomas asked the home secretary, Sir W. Joynson-Hicks, if he was aware of the Film Society presenting the film. He asked whether he was to take any action over the rumoured hissing of the national anthem and the cheering of the words 'all power to the Soviet'. Joynson-Hicks replied that the Film Society had assured him that the national anthem was properly received by the audience, and that a colleague in attendance had confirmed this. He concluded: 'I have drawn the attention of the London County Council to the exhibition of this film, and they will no doubt consider whether it comes with the condition referred to. I am disposed to think, from information that has reached me independently, that such incidents as occurred have been exaggerated, and I do not contemplate any further action in the matter.' From *Parliamentary Debates: Official Report* (fifth series, vol. 224), cols 1926–27.

62 Film Society Special Collection, item 16: Russian Films.

63 Huntley Carter, 'Labour and the Cinema' *Plebs* (November 1930), reprinted in Macpherson, *Traditions of Independence*, pp. 135–38.

64 See the Fifth (1929–30) and Sixth (1930–31) Film Society Annual Reports in Film Society Special Collection, item 24.

65 Programme notes for Edinburgh Film Guild can be found in *Twenty-one Years of Cinema: A Twenty-first Anniversary Retrospect of the Work of the Edinburgh Film Guild* (Edinburgh: Edinburgh Film Guild, 1950). The programmes were shown at the Caley cinema: see Forsyth Hardy, 'The Film Society Movement in Scotland', in Starr, *The Film Society Primer*, p. 75.

66 'The Federation of the British Film Societies' *Cinema Quarterly* 1: 2 (Autumn 1932), p. 46.

67 Margaret Hancock, 'The Federation of Film Societies', in Starr, *The Film Society Primer*, p. 78.

68 Peter Cargin (ed.), *An Introduction to the British Federation of Film Societies*, BFI Film Society Unit pamphlet (London: BFI, 1989), pp. 8–9.

69 Hardy, 'The Film Society Movement in Scotland', p. 76.

70 See letter from Ivor Montagu to Robert Aran (organizer of the Independent Congress in La Sarraz) on 1 May 1929, in which this information is reported. In Ivor Montagu Special Collection, item 30: International Congress of Independent Cinema, La Sarraz; and Hardy, 'The Film Society Movement in Scotland', p. 76.

71 'BFI: Aims and Objectives' leaflet, Film Society Special Collection, item 32: Correspondence With Other Film Societies.

72 Film Society Special Collection, item 32.

73 Initially, the Society gave the NFA its collections for safe-keeping on a temporary basis, but as it never recommenced activities after the war, the collection remained there. See Penelope Houston, *Keepers of the Frame: The Film Archives* (London: BFI, 1994), p. 42.

74 Wasson, 'Writing Cinema into Daily Life', p. 322. Barry wrote for the *Spectator* between 1923 and 1927 and for the *Daily Mail* from 1925 to 1930.

75 See, for example, Iris Barry, 'The Cinema, American Prestige and British Films', *Spectator*, 11 July 1925, and 'Of British Films', *Spectator*, 14 November 1925. Also see her 'A National or International Cinema?', *Bioscope*, 28 February 1924. Barry's criticisms of a 'parochial' conception of nationality and her subsequent calls for a more internationally aware mode of national cinema were also made by Michael Balcon (another Film Society member). See, for example, Balcon, 'British Film Production: Is the General Conception Too Narrow?', *The Film Renter and Moving Picture News*, 3 January 1925, in Adrian Brunel Special Collection, box 112, item 3.

76 Ivor Montagu, 'Old Man's Mumble: Reflections on a Semi-centenary' *Sight and Sound* 44: 4 (1975), p. 224.

77 Film Society programme notes, performance 1.

78 Film Society programme notes, performance 88.

79 Film Society programme notes, performance 44.

80 Gilbert Seldes, *The 7 Lively Arts* (New York: Sagamore Press, 1957; first published 1924), ch. 2.

81 For overviews on criticism in these countries, see Abel, *French Film Theory and Criticism 1907–1939: Volume 1*; and Hake, *Cinema's Third Machine*.

82 See Henri Daimant-Berger, 'The Découpage' (1919), in Abel, *French Film Theory and Criticism 1907–1939: Volume 1*, pp. 185–88.

83 Such ideas can be traced back to even earlier writings on the art of cinema by Vachel Lindsay and Hugo Munsterberg. See Vachel Lindsay, *The Art of the Moving Picture* (New York: Liveright, 1978; first published 1915); Hugo Munsterberg, *The Film: A Psychological Study* (New York: Dover Publications, 1970; first published 1916).

84 Chris Baldick, *The Social Mission of English Criticism 1848–1932* (Oxford: Clarendon Press, 1983), p. 20.

85 David Bordwell, *On the History of Film Style* (Harvard: Harvard University Press, 1997), p. 23.

86 Oswell Blakeston replaced H.D. as the silent era began to wane.

87 This was the first book to be published by POOL. They also published *Why Do They Like It?* (Territet: 1927), a reflection on British public school education by E.L. Black (a pseudonym used by Bryher's brother, John Ellerman Jr); *Civilians* (Territet: 1927), an account of civilian sacrifice in the First World War by Bryher; *Gaunt Island* (Territet: 1927), the second novel by Kenneth Macpherson; *Through a Yellow Glass* (London: 1928), a look at the film studios by Oswell Blakeston; *Anatomy of Motion Picture Art* (Territet: 1928), an aesthetic survey of cinema by Eric Elliott; *Film Problems of Soviet Russia* (Territet: 1929), Bryher's survey of Soviet cinema; *Extra Passenger* (Territet: 1929), a novel about British studio life by Oswell Blakeston; *Does Capital Punishment Exist?* (Territet and Dijon: 1930), a pamphlet on capital punishment by Hanns Sachs; and *The Light-Hearted Student* (Dijon: 1930), a German-teaching text by Bryher and Trude Weiss. Details taken from James Donald, Anne Friedberg and Laura Marcus (eds), *Close Up 1927–1933: Cinema and Modernism* (London: Cassell, 1998), appendix 3, p. 318.

88 Bryher was the daughter of Sir John Reeves Ellerman, who was a shipping magnate and international financier. When he died his estate was estimated by *The Times* at £17 million. See Donald, Friedberg and Marcus, *Close Up*, p. 315.

89 Roland Cosandey, 'On Borderline' *Afterimage* 12 (Autumn 1985).

90 Kenneth Macpherson, 'As Is' *Close Up* 1: 4 (October 1927), p. 16.

91 Lucas, *The Radical Twenties*, pp. 177–78.

92 She wrote that 'had it not been for the commercial encouragement found in the States during the past ten years, cinematography might still be in a very backward condition', Bryher, 'Defence of Hollywood' *Close Up* 2: 2 (February 1928), p. 45.

93 Kenneth Macpherson, 'As Is' *Close Up* 1: 2 (August 1927), p. 14.

94 See, for example, Kenneth Macpherson, 'As Is' *Close Up* 2: 2 (February 1928), p. 11.

95 Bryher, 'G.W. Pabst: A Survey' *Close Up* 1: 6 (December 1927), p. 60.

96 These articles were called 'Continuous Performance'.

97 Kenneth Macpherson, 'As Is' *Close Up* 3: 3 (September 1928), p. 6.

98 H.D., 'Russian Films' *Close Up* 3: 3 (September 1928), pp. 27–29.

99 Robert Herring, 'Film Imagery: Eisenstein' *Close Up* 3: 6 (December 1928), pp. 20–30.

100 Sergei Eisenstein, 'The Fourth Dimension of the Kino', part 1, *Close Up* 6: 3 (March 1930), pp. 184–94, and part 2, *Close Up* 6: 4 (April 1930), pp. 253–68.

101 Kenneth Macpherson, 'Introduction to the Fourth Dimension of the Kino', *Close Up* 6: 3 (March 1930), p. 175.

102 Kristin Thompson, 'Eisenstein's Early Films Abroad', in Ian Christie and Richard Taylor (eds), *Eisenstein Rediscovered* (London: Routledge, 1993).

103 Youngblood, *Movies for the Masses*, p. 156. Youngblood writes that most Soviet

films ran for two to three weeks in first-run theatres, while 'avant-garde' films 'frequently disappeared from the screen in a week or less' (p. 18). There were, however, a few exceptions to this. *Strike*, for instance, ran for three weeks at a first-run cinema.

104 Marc Allegret was announced as Paris contributor in the second issue (February 1927); in May 1927 Robert Herring was announced as London editor; in March 1928 Symon Gould was announced as New York correspondent and Clifford Howard as Hollywood correspondent; in January 1929 Freddy Chevally was announced as Geneva correspondent; in March 1929 Andor Kraszna-Krauss was announced as Berlin correspondent; in May 1929 Jean Leneaur became a second Paris correspondent. In the 1930s Pera Attasheva became Moscow correspondent and Trude Weiss Vienna correspondent, while H.A. Potamkin replaced Gould as New York correspondent.

105 Kenneth Macpherson, 'As Is' *Close Up* 2: 6 (June 1928), pp. 5–12.

106 For example, articles on low-budget and amateur filmmaking were written by head of the Manchester Film Society Peter Le Neve Foster, 'Two Film Snags' *Close Up* 3: 6 (December 1928), pp. 61–63; Adrian Brunel, 'Experiments in Ultra-Cheap Cinematography' *Close Up* 3: 4 (October 1928), pp. 43–46; and the Film Guild of London's Orlton West, 'Russian Cutting' *Close Up* 5: 3 (June 1929), 57–59.

107 'As Is' *Close Up* 2: 6 (June 1928), pp. 5–12. *The Life and Death of 9413* was also known as *Hollywood Rhapsody*.

108 J.A. Hardy, 'Comment and Review' *Close Up* 1: 3 (September 1927), pp. 70–71.

109 Hugh Castle, 'Some British Films' *Close Up* 5: 1 (July 1929), p. 43.

110 Bryher, 'How I Would Start a Film Club' *Close Up* 2: 6 (June 1928), pp. 30–36. Although Bryher used the word 'English' here, I do not think that this makes much difference, for the journal used the words 'English' and 'British' interchangeably.

111 Orlton West, 'Bits and Pieces' *Close Up* 5: 3 (September 1929), pp. 231–33.

112 The failure of this movement is documented in Leslie B. Duckworth's article, 'The Future of the Amateur Film Movement' *Close Up* 8: 1 (March 1931), pp. 52–54.

113 Although Macpherson never adopted a realist aesthetic and remained attached to formal experimentation in connection with subjective experience, and never adopted an explicitly political line within the journal, he did support the workers' movements. He was a founding member of the Federation of Workers' Film Societies in 1929. However, as he never wrote about working-class issues, it may be surmised that his interest in the workers' film movements stemmed more from the fact that they were showing Soviet films and thus exposing them to a wider audience.

114 'Comment and Review' *Close Up* 5: 4 (October 1929), p. 347.

115 Ernest Betts, *Heraclitus, or the Future of Films* (London: Dutton, 1928), p. 13.

116 Ibid., p. 59.

117 Eric Elliott, *Anatomy of Motion Picture Art* (London: POOL, 1928).

118 Duncan Petrie, 'Paul Rotha and Film Theory', in Duncan Petrie and Robert Kruger (eds), *A Paul Rotha Reader* (Exeter: University of Exeter Press, 1999), p. 51.

119 Paul Rotha, *The Film Till Now* (London: Vision Press, 1963), p. 313.

120 Ibid., p. 318.

121 Ibid., p. 362.

122 Ibid., p. 101.

Chapter 2

1 Adrian Brunel, *Nice Work: The Story of Thirty Years in British Film Production* (London: Forbes Robertson, 1949), pp. 57–65.

2 Ibid., p. 90.

3 Adrian Brunel, 'Experiments in Ultra-Cheap Cinematography' *Close Up* 3: 4 (October 1928), pp. 43–46. The film was distributed by Novello-Atlas Renters, which Brunel was involved in running. This firm also handled *The Man Without Desire*.

4 Rachael Low, *The History of the British Film, 1918–1929* (London: George Allen and Unwin, 1971), p. 288.

5 For an analysis of such literature, see Robert Fraser, *Victorian Quest Romance: Stevenson, Haggard, Kipling and Conan Doyle* (Plymouth: Northcote House, 1998).

6 Roger Sabin, *Comics, Comix and Graphic Novels: A History of Comic Art* (London: Phaidon Press, 1996), p. 14.

7 Brunel, *Nice Work*, pp. 38–47.

8 John Stevenson, *British Society 1914–45* (London: Penguin, 1990). Stevenson writes that war was promoted as 'an affair of great marches, great battles, quickly decided. [...] Those who thought differently were not generally believed' (p. 49).

9 John Lucas writes that the war brought with it 'a deep sense of vulnerability, of defences broken down. Britain—or England—was no longer immune from the demonic forces of history', Lucas, *The Radical Twenties*, p. 41.

10 See the *Sunday Pictorial*, 3 February 1924, for full programme details.

11 Margaret Dickinson and Sarah Street, *Cinema and State: The Film Industry and the British Government 1927–1984* (London: BFI, 1985), p. 14.

12 Andrew Higson, *Waving the Flag: Constructing a National Cinema in Britain* (Oxford: Clarendon Press, 1995), p. 33. Christine Gledhill discusses such tensions—between calls for British pictures to move closer to US methods of 'analytical editing', and more established filmmaking practices based upon a range of pictorial forms—in *Reframing British Cinema*, pp. 51–57.

13 Low, *The History of the British Film, 1918–1929*, p. 288.

14 Brunel, 'Experiments in Ultra-Cheap Cinematography', pp. 43–46.

15 Luke McKernan, *Topical Budget: The Great British News Film* (London: BFI, 1992), pp. 68–69.

16 Guy Phelps, *Film Censorship* (Letchworth: Garden City Press, 1975), p. 32.

17 Annette Kuhn, *Cinema, Censorship and Sexuality, 1909–1925* (London and New York: Routledge, 1988), especially chs 7 and 8.

18 Jay Leyda, *Kino: A History of the Russian and Soviet Film* (London: George Allen and Unwin, 1983), pp. 170–92.

19 Montagu, *The Youngest Son*, pp. 283–303.

20 Brunel, *Nice Work*, p. 114.

21 The film screening was advertised in *Workers Cinema* 1: 1 (November 1931), p. 4.

22 Adrian Brunel, *Film Production* (London: Newnes, 1936), p. 37.

23 Brunel, *Nice Work*, passim.

24 Rosalind Krauss, *The Originality of the Avant-Garde and Other Modernist Myths* (Cambridge, MA, and London: MIT Press, 1986), pp. 161–63.

25 Thomas Elsaesser, 'Dada/Cinema?', in Kuenzli, *Dada and Surrealist Film*, p. 20.

26 Ibid., p. 19.

27 Kenneth Macpherson, 'As Is' *Close Up* 6: 1 (January 1930), p. 2. Macpherson accused many French cinéastes of 'movieosophy', described as blind devotion to a set of accepted conventions.

28 Virginia Woolf, 'The Cinema' *Arts* (June 1926), reprinted in O'Pray, *The British Avant-Garde Film*, pp. 33–36.

29 Sargeant, 'Elsa Lanchester and Chaplinism', p. 97.

30 Mercurius, review of *I Do Like to Be Beside the Seaside*, *Architectural Review* (June 1930), p. 341.

31 Mercurius, review of *I Do Like to Be Beside the* Seaside.

32 See George Kitchin, *A Survey of Burlesque and Parody in English* (Edinburgh: Oliver & Boyd, 1931); V.C. Clinton-Baddeley, *The Burlesque Tradition in the English Theatre After 1660* (London: Methuen & Co., 1973); Mark Hallett, *The Spectacle of Difference: Graphic Satire in the Age of Hogarth* (New Haven, CT, and London: Yale University Press, 1999).

33 John Hawkridge, 'British Cinema From Hepworth to Hitchcock', in Geoffrey Nowell-Smith (ed.), *The Oxford History of World Cinema* (Oxford: Oxford University Press, 1996), p. 32.

34 McKernan, *Topical Budget*, p. 67. Andy Medhurst has noted that parody was a trend of British silent comedy and that the Pimple films stood out as the most prolific satires of contemporary events and fashions: Andy Medhurst, 'Music Hall and British Cinema', in Barr, *All Our Yesterdays*, p. 173.

35 Christine Gledhill, 'Wit and the Literate Image: The Adrian Brunel/A.A. Milne Collaborations', in Alan Burton and Laraine Porter (eds), *Pimple, Pranks and Pratfalls: British Film Comedy Before 1930* (Trowbridge, Flicks, 2000), p. 87.

36 For a good discussion of 'high' and 'low' comedy in relation to class at the turn of the century, see Henry Jenkins, *What Made Pistachio Nuts? Early*

Sound Comedy and the Vaudeville Aesthetic (New York: Columbia University Press, 1992), pp. 26–58.

37 Ibid., p. 86.

38 See Ivor Montagu, *With Eisenstein in Hollywood* (Berlin: Seven Seas, 1968), pp. 18–19. Lanchester brought in her long-term partner Charles Laughton, whom she would soon marry.

39 Montagu, *With Eisenstein in Hollywood*, pp. 20–23.

40 Ivor Montagu Special Collection, item 24: Correspondence on Wells' Comedies. The films were distributed by Ideal Pictures.

41 Ivor Montagu Special Collection, item 24.

42 Ivor Montagu Special Collection, item 24. Another reason for the company's bankruptcy was the extra expense incurred when the films were originally exported to Germany with English, rather than German, titles. The negatives were returned and had to be retitled, finally arriving in Germany in 1931, the year the company went bust.

43 Montagu, *With Eisenstein in Hollywood*, p. 23. The films had been held up to meet Ideal's output requirements in the second quota year. Angle Pictures did not have the financial resources to add sound to the pictures. See Ivor Montagu Special Collection, item 24.

44 *Daily Mail*, 14 July 1929, in Ivor Montagu Special Collection, item 25: Clippings on Wells' Comedies.

45 *Bioscope*, 18 September 1929, in Ivor Montagu Special Collection, item 25.

46 See, for example, a review of *The Pathetic Gazette* in *Bioscope*, 9 October 1924, in which the experimentation is seen as fitting into the framework of the burlesque/parody genre.

47 Letter from Ivor Montagu to Robert Aran, 1 May 1929, Ivor Montagu Special Collection, item 30: International Congress of Independent Cinema, La Sarraz. Aran was president of the Congress. I have yet to trace any other mentions to films made by Alex Stewart.

48 Rees, *A History of Experimental Film and Video*, pp. 29–30. The Surrealist Group listed Méliès, Chaplin and Mack Sennett in their list of 'things to see' in 'Some Surrealist Advice' (1951), reprinted in Paul Hammond (ed.), *The Shadow and Its Shadow: Surrealist Writing on the Cinema* (Edinburgh: Polygon, 1991), pp. 51–52.

49 Rees, *A History of Experimental Film and Video*, p. 30.

50 Seldes, *The 7 Lively Arts*, p. 23.

51 Ivor Montagu, 'Old Man's Mumble', p. 221.

52 See Turvey, 'Towards a Critical Practice'.

53 Kristin Thompson, *Eisenstein's Ivan the Terrible: A Neoformalist Analysis* (Princeton: Princeton University Press, 1981), p. 173.

54 C.A. Lejeune, review of *Warning Shadows*, *Manchester Guardian*, 24 November 1924.

55 Oswell Blakeston criticized *C.O.D.* for being a light-hearted trifle that

amounted to nothing. See *Close Up* 4: 6 (May 1929), p. 88. Even Blakeston's own parody, *I Do Like to Be Beside the Seaside* was virtually ignored in the journal.

Chapter 3

1   These articles are collected in the John Grierson Archive (held at the University of Stirling), G1A.3: Extracts from Chicago Newspapers, and G1A.5: 1–7: Extracts from Motion Picture News. For another overview of these writings, see Ian Aitken, *Film and Reform: John Grierson and the Documentary Film Movement* (London: Routledge, 1990), pp. 59–89.

2   He also believed that philosophy, psychology, logic and political science were Vorticist, as they expressed 'the mental feeling of the time'. See Grierson, 'Saving Modern Art From its Friends', John Grierson Archive, G1A.3.

3   Grierson, 'The Personality Behind the Paint', John Grierson Archive, G1A.3.

4   Grierson, 'Of Whistler and the Light That Failed', John Grierson Archive, G1A.3.

5   Aitken, *Film and Reform*, p. 151.

6   John Grierson Archive, G1A.1: 1; Grierson's University Library Records.

7   Aitken, *Film and Reform*, inter alia.

8   Grierson, 'The Industry at a Parting of the Ways', *Motion Picture News*, 13 November 1926, p. 1842, John Grierson Archive, G1A.5: 2.

9   'The Product of Hollywood', *Motion Picture News*, 6 November 1926, p. 1756, John Grierson Archive, G1A.5: 1.

10 'Putting Punch in a Picture', *Motion Picture News*, 27 November 1926, and 'Putting Atmosphere in Pictures', *Motion Picture News*, 4 December 1926, John Grierson Archive, G1A.5: 4 and 5.

11 Richard Koszarski, *An Evening's Entertainment: The Age of the Silent Feature Picture, 1915–1928* (New York: Charles Scribner's Sons, 1990), p. 33.

12 In the reports, Grierson uses 'British' and 'English', without any apparent distinctions; I will follow his usage.

13 John Grierson Archive, G2A.2.15: 4: 'Notes for English Producers, Part One: Cinema and the Public', p. 12.

14 Ibid.

15 John Grierson Archive, G2A.2.15: 4: 'Notes for English Producers, Part Two: British Cinema Production and the Naturalistic Tradition', p. 18.

16 Paul Swann, *The British Documentary Film Movement 1926–1946* (Cambridge: Cambridge University Press, 1989), p. 33.

17 John Grierson Archive, G2A.2.15: 4: 'Notes for English Producers, Part Two: British Cinema Production and the Naturalistic Tradition', p. 18.

18 Patricia R. Zimmerman writes that *Nanook*, along with *Battleship Potemkin*, *The Gold Rush*, Murnau's *Sunrise* (USA, 1927) and Dreyer's *The Passion of Joan*

of Arc (France, 1928) became established in alternative American exhibition arenas in the mid- to late 1920s. See Zimmerman, 'Startling Angles: Amateur Film and the Early Avant-Garde', in Horak, *Lovers of Cinema*, p. 146.

19 John Grierson, 'Documentary (2)' *Cinema Quarterly* 1: 3 (Spring 1933).

20 Ian Britain, *Fabianism and Culture: A Study in British Socialism and the Arts 1884–1918* (Cambridge: Cambridge University Press, 1982), pp. 14–15.

21 Partha Sarathi Gupta, *Imperialism and the British Labour Movement, 1914–1964* (London: Macmillan, 1975), p. 12.

22 Forsyth Hardy, *John Grierson: A Documentary Biography* (London: Faber and Faber, 1979), p. 23. Other people active in alternative film circles, such as Adrian Brunel and Ivor Montagu, also belonged to the Fabian Society at some point. It should be noted that at university Grierson read Bertrand Russell, another Fabian member. Information from John Grierson Archive, G1A.1: 1: Grierson's University Library Records.

23 Swann, *The British Documentary Film Movement*, p. 33.

24 *Sunday Worker*, 3 November 1929, clipping from John Grierson Archive, G2.24:3.

25 Oswell Blakeston, 'A New Force in British Cinema' *Close Up* 5: 4 (October 1929), p. 320.

26 Many of these reviews are collected in John Grierson Archive, G2.24.

27 C.A. Lejeune, 'Is Man Necessary?', *Observer*, 27 July 1930, in John Grierson Archive, G2.24:21.

28 Ibid.

29 *Workers Cinema* (November 1930), p. 1, in John Grierson Archive, G2.24:20: Press Cuttings of Film and General Interest 1928–1933.

30 H.A. Potamkin, 'Movie: New York Notes' *Close Up* 7: 4 (October 1930), p. 250.

31 For a good account of the objectification of the working classes in documentary films, see Philip and Kathryn Dodd, 'Engendering the Nation', in Andrew Higson (ed.), *Dissolving Views: Key Writings on British Cinema* (London: Cassell, 1996), pp. 40–41.

32 John Grierson Archive, G2A.2.15: 4: 'Notes for English Producers, Part Two: British Cinema Production and the Naturalistic Tradition', p. 15.

33 Aitken, *Film and Reform*, p. 64.

34 Stevenson, *British Society 1914–1945*, pp. 182–87.

35 *Clarion* (June 1929), reprinted in Hardy, *Grierson at the Movies*, p. 28.

36 See Mica Nava, 'Modernity's Disavowal: Women, the City and the Department Store', in Pasi Falk and Colin Campbell (eds), *The Shopping Experience* (London, Thousand Oaks and New Delhi: Sage, 1997); Anne Friedberg, *Window Shopping: Cinema and the Postmodern* (Berkeley: University of California Press, 1993), passim.

37 Nava, 'Modernity's Disavowal'. For a discussion of various elements of mass culture encoded as feminine and thus inferior, see Andreas Huyssen, 'Mass

Culture as Woman: Modernism's Other', in Huyssen, *After the Great Divide*, pp. 44–62.

38 Nava, 'Modernity's Disavowal', p. 83. This reaction to increasing feminization has been acutely dissected in relation to the documentary movement by Kathryn and Philip Dodd, 'Engendering the Nation', passim.

Chapter 4

1 Richard Abel, *French Film Theory and Criticism 1907–1939: Volume 2, 1929–1939* (Princeton: Princeton University Press, 1988), p. 8.

2 See David Bordwell, *On the History of Film Style*, p. 36.

3 Kenneth Macpherson, 'As Is' *Close Up* 3: 1 (July 1928), p. 8.

4 Eisenstein, Pudovkin and Alexandrov, 'The Sound Film: a Statement', *Close Up* 3: 4 (October 1928), p. 12.

5 Ernest Betts, 'Why "Talkies" are Unsound' *Close Up* 4: 4 (November 1928), p. 23.

6 Ibid., p. 24.

7 H.A. Potamkin, 'Playing With Sound' *Close Up* 7: 2 (August 1930), p. 112.

8 Rick Altman, 'The Material Heterogeneity of Recorded Sound', in Rick Altman (ed.), *Sound Theory, Sound Practice* (London: Routledge, 1992), pp. 15–31.

9 Rick Altman, 'The Evolution of Sound Technology', in Elizabeth Weis and John Belton (eds), *Film Sound: Theory and Practice* (New York: Columbia University Press, 1985), pp. 44–53. Altman updates this to 'Four and a Half Film Fallacies' in Altman, *Sound Theory, Sound Practice*. Only the additional category of the 'representational fallacy' is applicable to this chapter, however (and I have already mentioned this).

10 Altman notes that Edison always conceived of sound and image as a synchronized pair, but that 'various influences delayed for decades the acceptance of his original concept' ('The Evolution of Sound Technology', p. 45). He also mentions Lee De Forest's early invention of the audition tube. It is worth commenting that the first successful presentations of synchronized sound processes were made at the Paris Exposition Internationale in 1900. Public reaction to these was not enthusiastic, according to Alan Williams. See Williams, 'Historical and Theoretical Issues in the Coming of Recorded Sound to the Cinema', in Altman, *Sound Theory, Sound Practice*, p. 127.

11 Altman, 'The Evolution of Sound Technology', p. 52.

12 Michael Chanan, *Repeated Takes: A Short History of Recording and its Effects on Music* (London: Verso, 1995), p. 71.

13 Dan Birt, 'The Principles of Sound Recording' *Close Up* 8: 3 (September 1931), p. 202.

14 H.A. Potamkin, 'Phases of Cinema Unity' *Close Up* 6: 6 (June 1930), p. 465.

15 Ibid., p. 465.

16 David Bordwell, 'The Introduction of Sound', in David Bordwell, Janet Staiger and Kristin Thompson, *The Classical Hollywood Cinema* (London: Routledge, 1985), p. 306.

17 Bordwell, 'The Introduction of Sound', p. 308; Salt, *Film Style and Technology*, p. 285.

18 Laura Marcus, 'The Contribution of H.D', in Donald, Friedberg and Marcus, *Close Up*, pp. 96–104.

19 Kenneth Macpherson, 'As Is' *Close Up* 7: 6 (December 1930), p. 367.

20 Ibid., p. 369.

21 Robert Murphy writes that in Britain the cinema-going public quickly established a preference for sound films. See Murphy, 'The Coming of Sound to the Cinema in Britain' *Journal of Historical Film, Radio, and Television* 4: 2 (1984), p. 157.

22 See also Friedberg, 'Introduction: Reading *Close Up*, 1927–1933', in Donald, Friedberg and Marcus, *Close Up*, p. 25.

23 Kenneth Macpherson and Oswell Blakeston, 'Manifesto' *Close Up* 9: 2 (June 1932), p. 93.

24 These ideological approaches to amateur film construction were promoted in the early amateur magazines, such as *Home Movies and Home Talkies*. Don Macpherson has argued that the film as 'family record' was the most popular type of amateur film, which largely stemmed from the family 'as both a dominant consumer unit, and as an object for active rememoration'. Small amateur film clubs, though, also began to make fictions ('Amateur Films', in Macpherson, *Traditions of Independence*, pp. 191–207).

25 Norman Wilson, 'Spectator' *Cinema Quarterly* 1:. 1 (Autumn 1932), p. 5.

26 Ibid., p. 5.

27 Braun and West were responsible for *Film* 1 (Autumn 1933). The other contributors joined from the second edition, when the journal became *Film Art*.

28 B. Vivian Braun, 'Towards True Cinema' *Film* 1 (Autumn 1933), p. 3.

29 Wilson, 'Spectator', p. 5.

30 B. Vivian Braun, 'Reply to a Letter by H.P. Marshall' *Film Art* 3 (Spring 1934), p. 30.

31 Deke Dusinberre has previously noted this 'selective encouragement of certain sequences' within *Film Art*. See Dusinberre, 'The Avant-Garde Attitude in the Thirties', in Macpherson, *Traditions of Independence*, p. 43.

32 The desire to evade national boundaries was the most overtly political dimension of the journal.

33 Anthony Asquith, 'Rhythm in Sound Films' *Cinema Quarterly* 1: 3 (Spring 1933), pp. 144–46.

34 Leslie Beisegel, 'Independent Film-Maker' *Cinema Quarterly* 3: 2 (Winter 1935), p. 125.

35 Ibid., pp. 125–26.

36 See Aitken, *Film and Reform*, p. 62.

37 Beisegel, 'Independent Film-Maker', p. 126.

38 Judith Todd, 'The Film Societies' *Film* 1 (Autumn 1933), p. 13.

39 B. Vivian Braun, review of *Ephemeral, Film Art* 5 (Winter 1934), p. 42. It is possible that this review by Braun led to the differences of opinion between him and Nicholson, resulting in him leaving the journal and forming *New Cinema*.

40 Rachael Low, *The History of the British Film: Documentary and Educational Films of the 1930s* (London: George Allen and Unwin, 1979), p. 81.

41 Brian Winston has also argued that both the documentary film group and left-wing film groups unquestioningly accepted an ideology in which 16mm was seen as amateur in relation to the 'professional', 35mm gauge. He argues that even those left-wing filmmakers who did use 16mm only did so grudgingly because of economic reasons. See Winston, *Technologies of Seeing: Photography, Cinematography and Television* (London: BFI, 1996), pp. 66–68.

42 Irene Nicholson, John C. Moore and Robert Fairthorne, 'Editorial' *Film Art* 9 (Autumn 1936), p. 6.

43 This film, made with Brian Montagu, was commissioned by the *Trinidad Guardian* to show the varied life of Trinidad. It was basically a promotional film for Trinidad, as opposed to a personal, amateur film. *Film Art* 7 (Spring 1936) showed stills of the film and announced that the film was about to commence production. See Irene Nicholson and John C. Moore, 'Editorial', p. 8. The next two editions carried stills from the film, which had yet to be completed or fully titled.

44 For more details on these trends in documentary filmmaking, see Ian Aitken, 'Introduction', in Ian Aitken (ed.), *The Documentary Film Movement: An Anthology* (Edinburgh: Edinburgh University Press, 1998), pp. 21 and 41; Andrew Higson, '"Britain's Outstanding Contribution to the Film": The Documentary-Realist Tradition', in Barr, *All Our Yesterdays*, p. 84; and Elizabeth Sussex, *The Rise and Fall of the British Documentary Movement* (Berkeley: University of California Press, 1978), pp. 79–111.

45 While many of these films were narrative features rather than documentaries, they were admired for their documentary-like scenes and can be seen as part of a continuum between commercial narrative cinema and documentary films.

46 Hans Richter, 'A History of the Avant-garde', in Frank Stauffacher (ed.), *Art in Cinema: A Symposium on the Avant-garde Film* (San Francisco: San Francisco Museum of Art, 1947), p. 18.

47 Bert Hogenkamp, *Deadly Parallels: Film and the Left in Britain, 1929–1939* (London: Lawrence and Wishart, 1986), p. 36.

48 Ibid., p. 36; The LWFS was followed by workers' film groups in Cardiff, Edinburgh, Glasgow and Liverpool.

49 Ivor Montagu Special Collection, item 75: Correspondence on Workers'

Film Societies. Atlas Film Company only lasted until 1932; according to Bert Hogenkamp this was due to the delayed effects of the 1927 Quota Act, Hogenkamp, '"Making Films With a Purpose", Film-making and the Working Class', in Jon Clark, Margot Heinemann, David Margolies and Carol Snee (eds), *Culture and Crisis in Britain in the Thirties* (London: Lawrence and Wishart, 1979), p. 258.

50 Victoria Wegg-Prosser writes that there were seven main producers and distributors of workers' films: WFPL/FPL, Kino, FWFS, the Workers' Film Association, the London Co-operative Society, Progressive Film Institute and the Socialist Film Council; Wegg-Prosser, 'The Archive of the Film and Photo League' *Sight and Sound* 46: 4 (Autumn 1977), p. 245.

51 In 1933, Kino won a court case brought by the police after showing *Battleship Potemkin*; this eventually led to amendments of the 1909 Cinematograph Act (which included non-flammable film stock as subject to censorship restrictions). Hogenkamp, *Deadly Parallels*, pp. 86–87.

52 Kino's first productions were *Bread* and *Hunger March*, produced in 1934 along with the first of its *Workers' Newsreels*. See Stephen G. Jones, *The British Labour Movement and Film, 1918–1939* (London and New York: Routledge and Kegan Paul, 1987), p. 177.

53 Hogenkamp, *Deadly Parallels*, p. 116.

54 Kino was the largest distributor of working-class films in the inter-war years. Jones, *The British Labour Movement and Film*, p. 179. Kino again set up a production group in 1936, but according to Hogenkamp this was not very productive due to financial restraints. Hogenkamp, '"Making Films With a Purpose"', p. 261.

55 See 'Achievement and Endeavour' (uncredited) *Cinema Quarterly* 1: 1 (Winter 1932), pp. 57–58.

56 Ibid., p. 57.

57 Advertisement, *Film Art* 2 (Winter 1933), p. 40. The films shown here do not seem to be first-run amateur films, however. Amongst the films that it planned to show were *Berlin*, *The General Line*, *Turksib*, *Romance Sentimentale*, Fischinger's 'Abstracts' and *Liner Cruising South*.

58 Advertisement, *Film Art* 3 (Spring 1934). This was a nine-week course, split into two groups: those with, and those without their own camera. Cost was three guineas.

59 Advertisement, *Film Art* 4 (Summer 1934). This course lasted ten weeks, and was split into three groups: beginners, ordinary and advanced. As part of the course, visits to film studios were arranged. The cost was three and a half guineas.

60 Advertisement, *Film Art* 5 (Winter 1934).

61 Advertisement, *Cinema Quarterly* 1: 1 (Winter 1932), p. 56.

62 'Notice of Formation of Independent Film-Makers Association' *Cinema Quarterly* 2: 1 (Autumn 1933), p. 70.

63 'What the Societies are Doing' *Amateur Cine World* (April 1934), pp. 38–39.

Chapter 5

1 According to Forsyth Hardy, 'Grierson persuaded Hollywood companies, particularly Paramount, to give him the use of material from such films as *The Covered Wagon, The Iron Horse* and *Pony Express* [. . .]'. Hardy, *John Grierson*, p. 58.

2 See Sussex, *The Rise and Fall of British Documentary*, p. 8.

3 Lynne Kirby, *Parallel Tracks: The Railroad and Silent Cinema* (Exeter: University of Exeter Press, 1997).

4 Ibid., pp. 19–73.

5 Ibid., p. 41.

6 It was partly funded by Shell-Mex and British Petroleum, and distributed by British Instructional Films. Imperial Airways was a company subsidized by the government, which up until the early 1930s had a monopoly in the civic aviation industry. At this point it faced competition from a host of new companies, as well as criticism for the fact that it spent too much time fostering empire communications at the expense of other routes (especially in Europe). See Derek H. Aldcroft, *British Transport Since 1914: An Economic History* (Newton Abbot: John Sherratt & Sons, 1975), pp. 56–58.

7 See, especially, Charles Musser, 'The Travel Genre in 1903–1904: Moving Towards a Fictional Narrative', in Thomas Elsaesser and Adam Barker (eds), *Early Cinema: Space, Frame, Narrative* (London: BFI, 1990), pp. 123–32.

8 Ibid., p. 128. Musser argues that these travelogue films eventually—through the need for novelty—introduced narrative elements within their frameworks. Rotha, who by this time was becoming opposed to the narrative film, conveniently ignored such narrative elements (at least as understood in a conventional, classical sense).

9 At this time air travel was a luxury only affordable by the rich, hence the broad appeal of experiencing simulations of air travel via film. See Aldcroft, *British Transport Since 1914*, p. 60.

10 Paul Rotha, *Documentary Film* (London: Faber and Faber, 1952; first published 1935), p. 153.

11 H.T. Pledge, 'Beauty in Machinery' *Architectural Review* (March 1932), p. 85.

12 Ibid.

13 Ibid.

14 Ibid.

15 Indeed, two photographs of machinery accompanied the Pledge article. Bruguière photographed a pump at Berkeley Court, while E.O. Hopp took a shot of Lots Road Power Station.

16 Rotha, *The Film Till Now*, p. 378.

17 '*Contact*: An Interview with Paul Rotha' *Sight and Sound* 2: 5 (Spring 1933), p. 110.

18 Basil Wright has said that *Industrial Britain* was based on the idea of 'the persistence of individual craftsmanship in the modern engineering type of industry that was developing. In other words, in the world of mass production the craftsman still counted.' Such a view encapsulated the idea of a traditionally based vision of modernity. See James Beveridge, *John Grierson: Film Master* (New York: Macmillan, 1978), p. 67.

19 See, for example, the articles reproduced in Macpherson, *Traditions of Independence*, pp. 135–43.

20 Paul Marris, 'Politics and "Independent" Film in the Decade of Defeat', in MacPherson, , *Traditions of Independence*.

21 *Defence of Madrid* was produced by the Progressive Film Institute (PFI), another major workers' film organization that produced, distributed and exhibited films. Set up by Ivor Montagu in 1935, the PFI worked in parallel to Kino; whereas Kino distributed and exhibited 16mm films, PFI took care of 35mm film. Although it did not produce many films, those produced have been considered to be some of the more important films emerging from the movement, such as *Spanish ABC* (1938) and *Peace and Plenty* (1939). See Jones, *The British Labour Movement and Film*, pp. 178–79.

22 It was influenced by McLaren's experience of the effects of war in China when he was working there for UNESCO. See Valliere T. Richard, *Norman McLaren: Manipulator of Movement* (East Brunswick: Associated University Presses, 1982), p. 80.

23 Don Macpherson, 'Introduction: The Labour Movement and Oppositional Cinema', in Macpherson (ed.), *Traditions of Independence*, p. 89.

24 Although both McLaren and Biggar were members of Glasgow Kino, the film was made independently. Hogenkamp, '"Making Films With a Purpose"', p. 266.

25 Hogenkamp, *Deadly Parallels*, p. 151.

26 Stanley Sadie (ed.), *The New Grove Dictionary of Musics and Musicians: Volume 8* (London: Macmillan, 1990), pp. 573–87.Hindemith was a classical composer who gradually began to incorporate an eclectic range of styles into his compositions, such as jazz, music hall and cabaret. He also, on occasion, veered into dissonant noise, and included the use of a siren in his work *Kammermusik no. 1* (1922). Hindemith also began to experiment with discs played on variable-speed turntables in the 1930s, when John Cage and Edgar Varèse were making similar trials. He can, therefore, be indirectly linked to *musique concrète*. See Chanan, *Repeated Takes*, p. 140.

27 Walter Leigh, 'The Musician and the Film' *Cinema Quarterly* 3: 2 (Winter 1935), p. 74.

28 These gong sounds were put together in the GPO studio, using experimental

techniques such as recording with a swinging microphone. Leigh, 'The Musician and the Film', p. 74.

29 In 1929, only a few years before the film was shot, the areas in Ceylon where tea was cultivated were divided into 1,200 estates with British companies owning approximately 80 per cent of these. See Lennox A. Mills, *Ceylon Under British Rule, 1795–1932* (London: Frank Cass & Co., 1964), p. 253.

30 Martin Stollery, *Alternative Empires: European Modernist Cinemas and Cultures of Imperialism* (Exeter: University of Exeter Press, 2001), p. 192.

31 The GPO Film Unit had a British Visatone system, which was relatively cheap at £1,050. See Swann, *The British Documentary Film Movement*, p. 54.

32 Stephen Kern, *The Culture of Time and Space, 1880–1918* (Cambridge, MA: Harvard University Press, 1983), pp. 67–68.

33 Marshall McLuhan and Quentin Fiore, *War and Peace in the Global Village* (New York: Bantam, 1968), p. 25 and passim.

34 Carolyn Marvin, *When Old Technologies Were New: Thinking About Electric Communication in the Late Nineteenth Century* (New York: Oxford University Press, 1990), pp. 114–21.

35 This circular logic of the film was noted in a contemporary review by Graham Greene in *Spectator*, 4 October 1935, reprinted in Greene, *The Graham Greene Film Reader: Mornings in the Dark* (London: Carcanet, 1993).

36 Day thought that the film's third section avoided the fever and conflict of the meeting between imperial powers and native traditions. Charles Day, 'Review of *Song of Ceylon*' *Cinema Quarterly* 3: 2 (Winter 1935), p. 110.

37 Greene, *The Graham Greene Film Reader*.

38 William Guynn, 'The Art of National Projection: Basil Wright's *Song of Ceylon*', in Barry Keith Grant and Jeanette Sloniowski (eds), *Documenting the Documentary: Close Readings of Documentary Film and Video* (Detroit: Wayne State University Press, 1998).

39 The blurring between men and machines in *Coal Face* has been noted by John Corner, *The Art of Record: A Critical Introduction to Documentary* (Manchester: Manchester University Press, 1996), p. 62.

40 Cavalcanti would have been well acquainted with the film, since he had worked with Léger designing the elaborate sets for L'Herbier's *L'Inhumaine* (1923), the year before *Ballet Mécanique* was made.

41 W.F., review of *Pett and Pott*, *Monthly Film Bulletin* 1: 11 (December 1934), p. 105 (it is not clear who the writer of this review is).

42 Other GPO films released around the same period that experimented with sound are *Cable Ship* (Legg and Shaw, 1934), *6.30 Collection* (Anstey and Watt, 1934), *Under the City* (Shaw, 1934) and *Weather Forecast* (Spice, 1934). See Swann, *The British Documentary Film Movement*, p. 54.

43 Forsyth Hardy, 'Developing Sound' *Cinema Quarterly* 3: 1 (Autumn 1934), pp. 39–40.

44 See especially Sussex, *The Rise and Fall of British Documentary*, pp. 51–52.

Chapter 6

1   Siegfried Geidion, *Mechanization Takes Command: A Contribution to Anonymous History* (New York: Oxford University Press, 1955), p. 41.

2   Steven Tolliday, 'Management and Labour in Britain 1896–1939', in Steven Tolliday and Jonathan Zeitlin (eds), *The Automobile Industry and Its Workers: Between Fordism and Flexibility* (Cambridge: Polity Press, 1986), p. 30.

3   Peter Wollen, 'Cinema/Americanism/the Robot' *New Formations* 8 (Summer 1989), p. 8.

4   Hugo Von Hofmannsthal, 'A Substitute For Dreams' *London Mercury* 9: 50 (December 1923), p. 177.

5   Ivor Montagu Special Collection, item 336: Correspondence Between Ivor Montagu and Hans Richter. No date is revealed for when Richter added the soundtrack.

6   See Ivor Montagu Special Collection, item 336: Correspondence Between Ivor Montagu and Hans Richter.

7   Quoted in Richard J. Bernstein (ed.), *Habermas and Modernity* (Cambridge: Polity Press, 1985), p. 5.

8   See Lewis Mumford, *Technics and Civilization* (London: Routledge & Kegan Paul, 1967; first published 1934), p. 15. For good analyses of clocks in relation to working patterns and the surrounding debates, see Gerhard Dohrn-van Rossum, *History of the Hour: Clocks and Modern Temporal Orders*, trans. Thomas Dunlap (Chicago and London: University of Chicago Press, 1996), especially chs 2–7; and E.P. Thompson, 'Time, Work-Discipline and Industrial Capitalism' *Past and Present* 38 (December 1967).

9   Kern, *The Culture of Time and Space*, p. 15.

10 Quoted in Curtis, *Experimental Cinema*, p. 27.

11 Max Weber, 'The Development of Bureaucracy and its Relation to Law' (1922), in *Max Weber, Selections in Translation*, ed. W.G. Runciman, trans. E. Mathews (Cambridge: Cambridge University Press, 1978), pp. 350–51.

12 This reflected very real tensions between mechanization and human workers. Ford's stringent working methods created intense worker dissatisfaction and led to complaints about inhuman conditions. Without union protection many people left their jobs; at the end of 1913 labour turnover was 370 per cent at the plant. Ford countered this unrest through his famous 'five-hour day', in which wages were massively increased in return for productivity and strict behaviour. He also rationalized the workplace more tightly and hired more supervisors to oversee production. See Tolliday, 'Management and Labour in Britain 1896–1939', pp. 30–31.

13 Terrence Dobson, 'The Film Work of Norman McLaren' (unpublished PhD thesis; University of Canterbury, New Zealand, 1994), p. 36.

14 Dai Vaughan, *Portrait of an Invisible Man: The Working Life of Stewart McAllister, Film Editor* (London: BFI, 1983), p. 17.

15 Dobson, *The Film Work of Norman McLaren*, p. 8.

16 Ibid., p. 3.

17 Ibid., p. 29.

18 Ibid., p. 38. Dobson writes that this camera was given to McLaren after *Seven Till Five* had won the Victor Saville Award at the second Scottish Amateur Film Festival in 1934.

19 Maynard Collins, *Norman McLaren* (Ottawa: Canadian Film Institute, 1976), p. 66. McLaren has denied being aware of the work of Vertov during his early filmmaking years, which is rather surprising considering that he was a member of the Film Society.

20 Grierson remarked: 'Technically it's very competent, but artistically it's nothing but a jumble and a mess. It's got no form or organization, it's got no development, and it's totally zero as far as being a work of art.' Quoted in James Beveridge, *John Grierson*, p. 80.

21 Vlada Petrić, *Constructivism in Film: The Man With the Movie Camera: A Cinematic Analysis* (Cambridge: Cambridge University Press, 1987), p. 5.

22 Quoted in ibid., p. 72.

23 Michael Argyle, *The Social Psychology of Leisure* (London: Penguin, 1996), pp. 20–21. Before the Industrial Revolution the distinctions between work and leisure were not so clear cut; much non-work activity would have consisted of meaningful, ritualistic activities, such as religious occasions. Though peasants would have frequented inns in order to drink and socialize, there was no strict temporal separation between leisure and working hours.

24 Stevenson, *British Society, 1914–1945*, pp. 390–92.

25 This may be related to the very real dangers of the road at the time. In 1934, the year the film was made, there were 7,300 road deaths. Stevenson, *British Society, 1914–1945*, p. 390.

26 Geidion, *Mechanization Takes Command*, pp. 107–14. One must be wary of accepting such an argument in any simplistic manner. After all, Klee and Kandinsky were both abstract artists who were part of the Bauhaus movement, which involved attempts to merge art and industry.

27 Rotha, *The Film Till Now*, p. 296; C.A. Lejeune, *Cinema* (London: Alexander Maclehose, 1931), p. 154.

28 For a discussion of the film, see William Moritz, 'Americans in Paris: Man Ray and Dudley Murphy', in Horak, *Lovers of Cinema*, pp. 123–25.

29 In an EMB memorandum in 1930, the film is scheduled for production at a cost of £57. From John Grierson Archive, G2A.2:8: Creation of a Small Empire Marketing Board Producing and Editing Unit.

30 James Enyeart, *Bruguière: His Photographs and his Life* (New York: Alfred A. Knopf, 1977), p. 93.

31 Ibid., pp. 75–76.

32 Ibid., p. 93.

33 Mercurius, 'Light Rhythms' *Architectural Review* (March 1930), p. 154.

34 Ibid. Jack Ellit, who worked with Len Lye, provided the film with a musical soundtrack.

35 Krauss, *The Originality of the Avant-Garde*, pp. 161–63. As I have already noted, Krauss sees modernist-vanguardist discourse as characterized by the attempt to forge original pathways.

36 Jans-Christopher Horak, *Making Images Move: Photographers and the Avant-Garde* (Washington and London: Smithsonian Institution Press, 1997), pp. 131–34.

37 Wystan Curnow and Roger Horrocks (eds), *Figures of Motion: Len Lye, Selected Writings* (Auckland: Auckland University Press, 1984), pp. ix–xiii; Andrew Bogle, 'Len Lye's Paintings', in *Len Lye: A Personal Mythology* (book accompanying exhibition; Auckland: Auckland City Art Gallery, 1980), p. 12.

38 Roger Horrocks, *Len Lye: A Biography* (Auckland: Auckland University Press, 2001), p. 92.

39 Ibid., p. 91; Wystan Curnow, 'Len Lye and Tusalava: Interview' *Cantrills Filmnotes* 29/30 (February 1979), p. 38.

40 Ibid., p. 40.

41 Horrocks and Curnow, *Figures of Motion*, p. xiv.

42 Blakeston interpreted the film as a metaphorical story of an artist being attacked by outside forces and placed the film within a tradition of abstract art, mentioning Kandinsky as a possible precursor. See Oswell Blakeston, 'Comment and Review' *Close Up* 6: 2 (February 1930), p. 155.

43 Horrocks and Curnow, *Figures of Motion*, p. xiv.

44 Lye made drawings for the film, some of which appeared in *Architectural Review*. One drawing from the proposed second part of *Tusalava* appeared at the 1936 International Surrealist Exhibition held in New Burlington Galleries as a photogram. It was turned into a batik on silk and entitled *Pond People* (1930). See Michel Remy, *Surrealism in Britain* (Aldershot: Ashgate, 1999), p. 60; and Bogle, 'Len Lye's Paintings', p. 20.

45 Horrocks and Curnow, *Figures of Motion*, p. xiv.

46 Earlier examples are thought to have been made, but have not survived. William Moritz has written that the Italian painter Arnaldo Ginna made some films painted directly onto celluloid in the period 1911–12; he also writes that the German psychologist Hans Lorenz Stoltenberg, in his book *Pure Light Art and its Relationship to Music* (1920), claimed to have experimented with painting directly onto film. See William Moritz, 'Norman McLaren and Jules Engel: Post-Modernists', in Jayne Pilling (ed.), *A Reader in Animation Studies* (Sydney: John Libbey, 1997), p. 106.

47 Originally this film was set to a verse from *The Tempest* and was entitled *Full Fathom Five*. See Horrocks, *Len Lye*, p. 136.

48 He finally settled on a range of lacquer paints. See ibid., p. 136.

49 Jack Ellit made a chart for the music of Dan Barretto and Lye painted

images directly onto clear film beside the soundtrack. See Horrocks, *Len Lye*, pp. 137–38. Horrocks claims that Lye generally associated different sounds with different shapes, but did not follow a strict code.

50 Curtis, *Experimental Cinema*, p. 36.

51 Horrocks, *Len Lye*, p. 138.

52 *Sunday Mercury*, 8 December 1935, quoted in Curnow and Horrocks, *Figures of Motion*, p. xiv.

53 A. Vesselo, review of *A Colour Box, Sight and Sound* 4: 15 (Autumn 1935), p. 117.

54 Robert Herring, 'Technicolossal' *Life and Letters Today* 13 (1935), pp. 194–96.

55 Paul Nash praised Lye in 'The Colour Film', in Charles Davy (ed.), *Footnotes to the Film* (New York: Oxford University Press, 1937).

56 Philip Dodd, 'Modern Stories', in Ian Christie and Philip Dodd (eds), *Spellbound: Art and Film* (exhibition catalogue; London: BFI, 1996), pp. 34–38.

57 Herring, 'Technicolossal', p. 196.

58 Lye is included in Michel Remy's *Surrealism in Britain*, and, considering that he was exhibited at the International Surrealist Exhibition in 1936, he cannot strictly be disconnected from the movement.

59 Len Lye and Laura Riding, 'Film-Making' *Epilogue* 1 (1935); reprinted in Curnow and Horrocks, *Figures of Motion*.

60 In between *A Colour Box* and *Rainbow Dance*, Lye made *Kaleidoscope* (1935), a film sponsored by the Imperial Tobacco Company, which experimented with stencils; and *Birth of a Robot* (1936), a more collaborative film that included input from Humphrey Jennings. The latter film was a puppet film sponsored by Shell-Mex and BP Ltd.

61 Len Lye, 'Experiment in Film Colour' *World Film News* (December 1936), p. 33.

62 Ian Christie, 'Colour, Music, Dance, Motion. Len Lye in England 1927–44', in Jean-Michel Bouhours and Roger Horrocks (eds), *Len Lye* (Paris: Éditions du Centre Pompidou, 2000), p. 189.

63 Ian Christie notes that Doone was involved in the Group Theatre, which had parallels with Meyerhold's biomechanics in that they wanted to revive the theatre as an 'art of the body'. He suggests that *Rainbow Dance* should be seen as a continuation of the 'ballet-spectacle' as celebrated by Léger. Ibid., pp. 189–90.

64 It would seem that Lye's own article in *World Film News*, which explicated his technical methods, influenced the attempts to understand his working methods. *Film Art* also printed a moderately detailed review of the film that incorporated the same technical details. See Robert Fairthorne, review of *Rainbow Dance, Film Art* 10 (Spring 1937), p. 38.

65 A. Vesselo, review of *Rainbow Dance, Sight and Sound* 5: 19 (Autumn 1936), p. 83.

66 See Wulf Hurzogenruth, 'Light-Play and Kinetic Theatre as Parallels to Absolute Film', in Drummond, Dusinberre and Rees, *Film as Film*.

67 Len Lye, 'Notes on a Short Colour Film' *Life and Letters Today* 13 (1935), pp. 197–98; reprinted in Curnow and Horrocks, *Figures of Motion*, pp. 49–51.

68 The untitled film was made in 1933 and was chewed up by a film projector; see Richard, *Norman McLaren*, p. 43. Richard writes that McLaren painted onto film as he could not at the time afford a film camera.

69 In *Camera Makes Whoopee* the abstract processes seem to be incorporated within a dominant concrete framework.

70 In 1937 he made *Book Bargain*, a film about the telephone directory, as well as *News for the Navy*. In 1938 he contributed a sequence to Massingham's *Mony a Pickle*, and in 1939 he made *The Obedient Flame* for the Gas Board. See McLaren filmography in *Film Dope* 38 (December 1987), p. 3.

71 David Curtis, *Norman McLaren* (Edinburgh: Scottish Arts Council Catalogue, 1977), p. 13.

72 Dobson, *The Film Work of Norman McLaren*, p. 88.

73 Ibid., p. 88.

74 Robert Fairthorne, 'Abstract Films and the Mathematicians' *Film Art* 9 (Autumn 1936), p. 19. I cannot trace the date for *Euclid 1.32*, though it is presumably 1935 or 1936.

75 Fairgrieve also made *Illustration of Elementary Functions (Versions A and B)* (1933), *Movement of Air in a Circular Cyclone Crossing Britain* (1934) and *Spinning* (1938).

76 For an overview of such films see R.A. Watson, 'Teaching Physics With Films' *Sight and Sound* 6: 21 (Spring 1937), pp. 35–37.

Chapter 7

1 It now seems to be undergoing further recuperation, particularly because of its exploration of race and because it stars Robeson. In 2005 Courtney Pine was commissioned to write a new score for the film as part of the BFI's 'Black World' initiative, a nationwide series of events and projects celebrating black culture. The live score was premiered at the Tate Modern on 28 May 2006. Criterion has since released *Borderline* on DVD as part of their *Paul Robeson: Portraits of the Artist* box set, with the accompanying Pine soundtrack. The BFI also released the film on DVD in 2007 with the Pine soundtrack.

2 Anne Friedberg reassembled *Wing Beat* and *Foothills* in 1979 after discovering them amongst H.D.'s papers at Yale. They are kept at the Museum of Modern Art in New York. See Anne Friedberg, 'Introduction: *Borderline* and the POOL Films', in Donald, Friedberg and Marcus, *Close Up*, footnote 1, p. 332.

3 Notes accompanying a still from the film in *Close Up* 1: 1 (July 1927), p. 16.

4 Susan Stanford Friedman, *Penelope's Web: Gender, Modernity, H.D.'s Fiction*

(Cambridge: Cambridge University Press, 1990), p. 13. Thomas Cripps claims that Macpherson wrote to Eslanda in February 1930 to discuss the Robesons' participation in the film. See Cripps, *Slow Fade to Black: The Negro in American Film 1900–1942* (New York: Oxford University Press, 1977), p. 209.

5 Ibid., pp. 208–9. *Opportunity* was the house journal of the National Urban League, a civil rights movement that aimed to eliminate racial segregation and discrimination.

6 Friedman, *Penelope's Web*, p. 17.

7 See Bryher Papers (Beinecke Rare Book and Manuscript Library, Yale University Library), item 5628: Borderline Notes.

8 Bryher Papers, Borderline Notes; and Bryher, *The Heart to Artemis: A Writer's Memoirs* (London: Collins, 1963), p. 261.

9 Bryher, *Heart to Artemis*, p. 264.

10 Bryher Papers, item 5636: Borderline ticket.

11 Friedman, *Penelope's Web*, p. 18.

12 Bryher, *Heart to Artemis*, p. 264.

13 Anne Friedberg has reproduced the libretto in 'Writing About Cinema: Close Up' 1927–1933' (unpublished PhD thesis; New York: University of New York, 1983), p. 150.

14 Friedberg, 'Introduction: Borderline and the POOL Films', p. 218; Jean Walton, 'White Neurotics, Black Primitives and the Queer Matrix of Borderline', in Ellis Hansen (ed.), *Out Takes: Essays on Queer Theory and Film* (Durham, NC, and London: Duke University Press, 1999), p. 245.

15 Anne Friedberg, 'Approaching *Borderline' Millenium Film Journal* 7–9 (Autumn/Winter, 1980–81).

16 Ibid., p. 132.

17 Kenneth Macpherson, 'As Is' *Close Up* 3: 5 (November 1930), p. 294.

18 Roland Cosandey, 'On Borderline', p. 76.

19 Ibid., p. 76.

20 H.D., 'The Borderline Pamphlet', in Bonnie Kime Scott (ed.), *The Gender of Modernism: A Critical Anthology* (Bloomington and Indianapolis: Indiana University Press, 1990), p. 123. This pamphlet was originally published anonymously in order to promote *Borderline*.

21 Eisenstein uses this term in 'A Dialectical Approach to Film Form', which Anne Friedberg references in her 'Introduction: Borderline and the POOL Films', p. 220. H.D. described these clatter montage sequences as almost like 'super-imposition, but subtly differing from it', achieved by 'the meticulous cutting of three and four and five inch lengths of film and pasting these tiny strips together', H.D., 'The Borderline Pamphlet', p. 119.

22 While Eisenstein did stress 'psycho-physiological' principles, the psychological basis of this argument was conceived in terms of the effect on the mental state of the viewer, rather than a representation of a character's psychological state.

23 Cosandey, 'On Borderline', p. 80.

24 Bryher Papers, item 5636: Borderline ticket.

25 H.D., 'The Borderline Pamphlet', p. 112.

26 Ibid., p. 116.

27 Friedman, *Penelope's Web*, p. 10.

28 Robert Herring, 'A New Cinema, Magic and the Avant-Garde' *Close Up* 4: 4 (April 1929).

29 Quoted in James De Jongh, *Vicious Modernism: Black Harlem and the Literary Imagination* (Cambridge and New York: Cambridge University Press, 1990), p. 11.

30 Ibid., p. 15.

31 Ibid., ch. 1; Richard Dyer, *Heavenly Bodies: Film Stars and Society* (London: BFI, 1986), pp. 79–88.

32 Kenneth Macpherson, 'As Is' *Close Up* 2: 2 (February 1928), p. 85.

33 Kenneth Macpherson, 'A Negro Film Union—Why Not?', in Nancy Cunard (ed.), *Negro: An Anthology* (New York: Frederick Ungar, 1974), pp. 106–7.

34 Ibid., p. 206.

35 H.D., 'The Borderline Pamphlet', p. 114.

36 Jean Walton, 'Nightmare of the Uncoordinated White-folk: Race, Psychoanalysis and *Borderline*' *Discourse* 19: 2 (Winter 1997), p. 93.

37 Ibid., p. 92.

38 Dyer, *Heavenly Bodies*, pp. 75–77.

39 Walton, 'Nightmare of the Uncoordinated White-folk', p. 95.

40 Ibid., p.245.

41 Ibid., p. 246.

42 Ibid., pp. 252-258.

43 Ibid., p. 246.

44 Susan Stanford Friedman discusses H.D.'s repression of her homosexuality in '"I Had Two Loves Separate": The Sexualities of H.D.'s *HER*', in Susan Stanford Friedman and Rachael Blau (eds), *Signets: Reading H.D.* (Madison: University of Wisconsin Press, 1990), p. 208. She links this to the general social condemnation of homosexuality at the time.

45 Michael O'Pray, 'Borderline' *Art Monthly* 116 (1988), p. 36.

46 *Bioscope*, 15 October 1930, p. 21.

47 Cosandey, 'On Borderline', p. 82. The film's release was delayed in America as it was seized by customs. According to Anne Friedberg this was because its theme of miscegenation was considered taboo. See Friedberg, *Writing About Cinema*, p. 184.

48 *Twenty-one Years of Cinema*, p. 13.

49 Review of *Borderline*, *Bioscope*, 15 October 1930, p. 21.

50 Caroline Lejeune, review of *Borderline*, *Observer*, 19 October 1930, p. 20.

51 Cosandey, 'On Borderline', p. 76.

52 Lejeune, review of *Borderline*, p. 20.

53 Peter Wollen, for example, has written that *Borderline* 'remains the one outstanding British avant-garde film of the period.' See Wollen, 'The Last New Wave: Modernism in the British Films of the Thatcher Era', in Lester Friedman (ed.), *Fires Were Started: British Cinema and Thatcherism*, (Minneapolis: University of Minnesota, 1993), p. 39. Wollen also mentions the film in a broader international survey of the avant-garde film in 'Together' *Sight and Sound* 6: 7 (July 1996).

Conclusion

1 I use independent here in a broad, contextual sense. Thus, documentary films were often seen as independent in that they offered far more artistic freedom than was common in the film industry. So although they were dependent on sponsorship, which to different degrees shaped and compromised their work, documentary filmmakers could still be seen as independent.

2 Sarah Street, *British National Cinema* (London and New York: Routledge, 1997), p. 155.

3 See, for example, Jonathan Rosenbaum and Adrian Martin (eds), *Movie Mutations: The Changing Face of World Cinephilia* (London: BFI, 2003) and Marijke de Valck and Malte Hagener (eds), *Cinephilia: Movies, Love and Memory* (Amsterdam: University of Amsterdam Press, 2005). Susan Sontag, 'The Decay of Cinema', *New York Times*, 25 February 1996, p. 60.

4 Peter Wollen argues that the archive has always played a 'key role in taste and canon formations', in 'The Canon', in Peter Wollen (ed.), *Paris Hollywood: Writings on Film* (London and New York: Verso, 2002), p. 211. Let us not forget that the Film Society provided the core of the original collection held by the major British film archive, the NFTVA.

Bibliography

Archive Materials

Adrian Brunel Special Collection
Anthony Asquith Special Collection
Film Society Special Collection
Ivor Montagu Special Collection (all held at the BFI library)
John Grierson Archive Papers (held at the University of Stirling)
Bryher Papers (held at the Beinecke Rare Book and Manuscript Library, Yale
University)

Contemporary Newspapers, Trade Papers and Periodicals

*Amateur Cine World; Bioscope; Cinema Quarterly; Cinema Review; Close Up;
Daily Express; Daily Mail; Daily Sketch; Daily Telegraph; Evening News; Evening
Standard; Experimental Cinema; Film/Film Art; Film Culture; Harper's Magazine;
Kinematograph Weekly; Kino News; Life and Letters Today; London Mercury;
Monthly Film Bulletin; News Chronicle; Observer; Spectator; Sight and Sound; The
Times; Workers Cinema; World Film News*

Books, Articles in Journals, Theses and Pamphlets

Abel, Richard, *French Cinema: The First Wave 1915–1929* (Princeton: Princeton
University Press, 1984)
—— (ed.), *French Film Theory and Criticism 1907–1939: Volume 1, 1907–1929*
(Princeton: Princeton University Press, 1988)
—— (ed.), *French Film Theory and Criticism 1907–1939: Volume 2, 1929–1939*
(Princeton: Princeton University Press, 1988)
Aitken, Ian, *Film and Reform: John Grierson and the Documentary Movement*
(London: Routledge, 1990)
—— (ed.), *The Documentary Film Movement: An Anthology* (Edinburgh: Edinburgh
University Press, 1998)

——, 'Introduction', in Aitken (ed.), *The Documentary Film Movement*

Aldcroft, Derek H., *British Transport Since 1914: An Economic History* (Newton Abbot: John Sherratt & Sons, 1975)

Allen, Robert C., *Horrible Prettiness: Burlesque and American Culture* (Chapel Hill: University of North Carolina Press, 1991)

Altman, Rick, 'The Evolution of Sound Technology', in Weis and Belton (eds), *Film Sound*

—— (ed.), *Sound Theory, Sound Practice* (New York and London: Routledge, 1992)

——, 'Four and a Half Film Fallacies', in Altman (ed.), *Sound Theory, Sound Practice*

——, 'The Material Heterogeneity of Recorded Sound', in Altman (ed.), *Sound Theory, Sound Practice*

Anderson, Benedict, 'Introduction', in Gopal Balakrishnan (ed.), *Mapping the Nation* (London and New York: Verso, 1996)

Argyle, Michael, *The Social Psychology of Leisure* (London: Penguin, 1996)

Armes, Roy, *A Critical History of British Cinema* (London: Secker & Warburg, 1978)

Armstrong, Nancy, 'Modernism's Iconophobia and What it Did to Gender' *MODERNISM/modernity* 5: 2 (April 1998)

Arnold, Matthew, *Culture and Anarchy* (Cambridge: Cambridge University Press, 1988; first published 1869)

Baldick, Chris, *The Social Mission of English Criticism 1848–1932* (Oxford: Clarendon Press, 1983)

Bamford, Kenton, *Distorted Images: British National Identity and Film in the 1920s* (London and New York: I.B.Tauris, 1999)

Barlow, John D., *German Expressionist Film* (Boston: Twayne, 1982)

Barr, Charles (ed.), *All Our Yesterdays: 90 Years of British Cinema* (London: BFI, 1986)

——, *English Hitchcock* (Moffat: Cameron & Hollis, 1999)

——, 'Introduction: Amnesia and Schizophrenia', in Barr (ed.), *All Our Yesterdays*

Barry, Iris, *Let's Go to the Movies* (New York: Arno Press, 1972; originally published 1926)

Benjamin, Walter, 'The Role of Art in the Age of Mechanical Reproduction', in Walter Benjamin, *Illuminations*, ed. Hannah Arendt, trans. Harry Zorn (London: Fontana, 1992)

Bergfelder, Tim, 'The Production Designer and the *Gesamtkunstwerk*: German Film Technicians in the British Cinema of the 1930s', in Higson (ed.), *Dissolving Views*

Bernstein, Richard J. (ed.), *Habermas and Modernity* (Cambridge: Polity Press, 1985)

Berry, David, *Wales and Cinema: The First Hundred Years* (Cardiff: University of Wales Press, 1994)

Betts, Ernest, *Heraclitus, or the Future of Films* (London: Dutton, 1928)

Beveridge, James, *John Grierson: Film Master* (New York: Macmillan, 1978)

Blakeston, Oswell, *Through a Yellow Glass* (London: POOL, 1928)

Bogle, Andrew, 'Len Lye's Paintings', in *Len Lye: A Personal Mythology* (book accompanying exhibition; Auckland: Auckland City Art Gallery, 1980)

Bond, Ralph, 'Cinema in the Thirties: Documentary Film and the Labour Movement', in Clark, Heinemann and Snee (eds), *Culture and Crisis in Britain in the Thirties*

Bordwell, David, *Making Meaning: Inference and Rhetoric in the Interpretation of Cinema* (Cambridge, MA: Harvard University Press, 1989)

——, *On the History of Film Style* (Harvard: Harvard University Press, 1997)

——, 'The Introduction of Sound', in Bordwell, Staiger and Thompson, *The Classical Hollywood Cinema*

——, Kristin Thompson and Janet Staiger, *The Classical Hollywood Cinema: Film Style and Mode of Production to 1960* (London: Routledge, 1985)

Bouhours, Jean-Michel and Roger Horrocks (eds), *Len Lye* (Paris: Éditions du Centre Pompidou, 2000)

Bourdieu, Pierre, *Distinction: A Social Critique of the Judgement of Taste* (London: Routledge, 1992)

Bradbury, Malcolm, 'The Cities of Modernism', in Bradbury and McFarlane (eds), *Modernism 1890–1930*

—— and James McFarlane (eds), *Modernism 1890–1930* (Harmondsworth: Penguin, 1976)

—— ——, 'The Name and Nature of Modernism', in Bradbury and McFarlane (eds), *Modernism 1890–1930*

Britain, Ian, *Fabianism and Culture: A Study in British Socialism and the Arts 1884–1918* (Cambridge: Cambridge University Press, 1982).

Brown, Geoff, 'Sister of the Stage: British Film and British Theatre', in Barr (ed.), *All Our Yesterdays*

Brunel, Adrian, *Film Production* (London: Newnes, 1936)

——, *Nice Work: The Story of Thirty Years in British Film Production* (London: Forbes Robertson, 1949)

Bryher, *Film Problems of Soviet Russia* (London: POOL, 1929)

——, *The Heart to Artemis: A Writer's Memoirs* (London: Collins, 1963)

Buchanan, R.A., *The Power of the Machine: The Impact of Technology From 1700 to the Present* (London: Penguin, 1994)

Budd, Mike (ed.), *The Cabinet of Dr. Caligari: Texts, Contexts, Histories* (New Brunswick: Rutgers University Press, 1990)

——, 'The Moments of *Caligari*', in Budd (ed.), *The Cabinet of Dr. Caligari*

Bürger, Peter, *Theory of the Avant-Garde* (Minneapolis: University of Minnesota Press, 1984)

Burton, Alan, 'The Emergence of an Alternative Film Culture: Film and the British Consumer Co-operative Movement Before 1920' *Film History* 8: 4 (1996)

—— and Laraine Porter (eds), *Pimple, Pranks and Pratfalls: British Film Comedy Before 1930* (Trowbridge: Flicks, 2000)

—— —— (eds), *Crossing the Pond: Anglo-American Film Relations Before 1930* (Trowbridge: Flicks, 2002)

—— —— (eds), *Scene-Stealing: Sources for British Cinema Before 1930* (Trowbridge: Flicks, 2003)

Callaghan, John, *Socialism in Britain Since 1884* (London: Basil Blackwell, 1990)

Canudo, Ricciotto, 'Reflections on the Seventh Art' (originally published in 1923), in Abel (ed.), *French Film Theory and Criticism 1907–1939: Volume 1*

Cargin, Peter (ed.), *An Introduction to the British Federation of Film Societies* (BFI Film Society Unit pamphlet, London: BFI, 1989)

Carter, Huntley, *New Spirit in the Cinema* (London: Harold Shaylor, 1930)

Causey, Andrew, 'Unit One—Towards Surrealism', in Susan Compton (ed.), *British Art in the Twentieth Century: The Modern Movement* (London and Munich: Royal Academy of Arts and Prestel-Verlag, 1986)

Chanan, Michael, *Repeated Takes: A Short History of Recording and its Effects on Music* (London: Verso, 1995)

Christie, Ian, 'The Avant-gardes and European Cinema before 1930', in Hill and Church Gibson (eds), *The Oxford Guide to Film Studies*

——, 'Colour, Music, Dance, Motion. Len Lye in England, 1927–44', in Bouhours and Horrocks (eds), *Len Lye*

——, 'French Avant-garde Film in the Twenties: From "Specificity" to Surrealism', in Drummond, Dusinberre and Rees (eds), *Film as Film*

—— and Philip Dodd (eds), *Spellbound: Art and Film* (exhibition catalogue; London: BFI, 1996)

—— and Richard Taylor (eds), *The Film Factory: Russian and Soviet Cinema in Documents* (Cambridge, MA: Harvard University Press, 1988)

—— —— (eds), *Eisenstein Rediscovered* (London: Routledge, 1993)

Clark, Jon, Margot Heinemann, David Margolies and Carole Snee, *Culture and Crisis in Britain in the Thirties* (London: Lawrence and Wishart, 1979)

Clinton, Germaine, 'The Canadian Federation of Film Societies', in Cecile Starr (ed.), *The Film Society Primer* (New York: American Federation of Film Societies, 1956)

Clinton-Baddeley, V.C., *The Burlesque Tradition in the English Theatre After 1660* (London: Methuen & Co., 1973)

Collins, Maynard, *Norman McLaren* (Ottawa: Canadian Film Institute, 1976)

Colls, Robert and Philip Dodd (eds), *Englishness: Politics and Culture 1880–1920* (Beckenham: Croom Helm, 1986)

Compton, Susan (ed.), *British Art in the Twentieth Century: The Modern Movement* (London and Munich: Royal Academy of Arts and Prestel-Verlag, 1986)

——, 'Unit One—Towards Constructivism', in Compton (ed.), *British Art in the Twentieth Century*

Cook, Pam (ed.), *Gainsborough Pictures* (London and Washington: Cassell, 1997)

Corner, John, *The Art of Record: A Critical Introduction to Documentary* (Manchester: Manchester University Press, 1996)

Cosandey, Roland, 'On Borderline', trans. Deke Dusinberre, *Afterimage* 12 (Autumn 1985)

Cripps, Thomas, *Slow Fade to Black: The Negro in American Film, 1900–1942* (New York: Oxford University Press, 1977)

Curnow, Wystan, 'Len Lye and *Tusalava*: Interview' *Cantrills Filmnotes* 29/30 (February 1979)

—— and Roger Horrocks (ed.), *Len Lye, Figures of Motion: Selected Writings* (Auckland: Auckland University Press, 1984)

Curtis, David, *Experimental Cinema: A Fifty Year Evolution* (London: Studio Vista, 1971)

——, *Norman McLaren* (Edinburgh: Scottish Arts Council Catalogue, 1977)

Daimant-Berger, Henri, 'The Decoupage', in Abel (ed.), *French Film Theory and Criticism: 1907–1939: Volume 1*

Davies, Tony, *Humanism* (London: Routledge, 1997)

Davis, Ben, 'Beginnings of the Film Society Movement in the U.S.' *Film & History* 24: 3–4 (1994)

De Jongh, James, *Vicious Modernism: Black Harlem and the Literary Imagination* (Cambridge and New York: Cambridge University Press, 1990)

de Valck, Marijke and Malte Hagener (eds), *Cinephilia: Movies, Love and Memory* (Amsterdam: University of Amsterdam Press, 2005)

Dickinson, Margaret, *Rogue Reels: Oppositional Film in Britain, 1945–90* (London: BFI, 1999)

—— and Sarah Street, *Cinema and State: The Film Industry and the British Government 1927–1984* (London: BFI, 1985)

Dobson, Terrence 'The Film Work of Norman McLaren' (unpublished PhD thesis; Canterbury, NZ: University of Canterbury, 1994)

Dodd, Philip, 'Englishness and the National Culture', in Colls and Dodd (eds), *Englishness: Politics and Culture 1880–1920*

——, 'Modern Stories', in Christie and Dodd (eds), *Spellbound: Art and Film*

—— and Kathryn Dodd, 'Engendering the Nation', in Higson (ed.), *Dissolving Views*

Dohrn-van Rossum, Gerhard, *History of the Hour: Clocks and Modern Temporal Orders*, trans. Thomas Dunlap (Chicago and London: University of Chicago Press, 1996)

Donald, James, Anne Friedberg and Laura Marcus (eds), *Close Up 1927–1933: Cinema and Modernism* (London: Cassell, 1998)

Drummond, Phillip, 'Notions of the Avant-Garde', in Drummond, Dusinberre and Rees (eds), *Film as Film*

——, Deke Dusinberre and Al Rees (eds), *Film as Film: Formal Experiment in Film 1910–1975* (exhibition catalogue; London: Hayward Gallery, 1979)

Dusinberre, Deke, 'The Avant-Garde Attitude in the Thirties', in Macpherson (ed.), *Traditions of Independence*

——, 'The Other Avant-Gardes', in Drummond, Dusinberre and Rees (eds), *Film as Film*

Dwoskin, Stephen, *Film Is: The International Free Cinema* (Woodstock, NY: Overlook Press, 1975)

Dyer, Richard, *Heavenly Bodies: Film Stars and Society* (London: BFI, 1986)

Eagleton, Terry, 'The Ideology of the Aesthetic', in Stephen Regan (ed.), *The Politics of Pleasure* (Buckingham: Open University Press, 1992)

——, *The Function of Criticism* (London: Verso, 1994)

Elsaesser, Thomas, *Weimar Cinema and After: Germany's Historical Imaginary* (London: Routledge, 2000)

——, 'Dada/Cinema?', in Kuenzli (ed.), *Dada and Surrealist Film*

—— and Adam Barker (eds), *Early Cinema: Space, Frame, Narrative* (London: BFI, 1990).

Elliott, Eric, *The Anatomy of Motion Picture Art* (London: POOL, 1928)

Ellis, John, 'Terms for a Cinema in the Forties and Seventies' *Screen* 19: 3 (Autumn 1978)

Enyeart, James, *Bruguière: His Photographs and his Life* (New York: Alfred A. Knopf, 1977)

Foucault, Michel, *The Archaeology of Knowledge*, trans. A.M. Sheridan Smith (London: Tavistock, 1974)

Fraser, Robert, *Victorian Quest Romance: Stevenson, Haggard, Kipling and Conan Doyle* (Plymouth: Northcote House, 1998)

Friedberg, Anne, 'Writing About Cinema: *Close Up* 1927–1933' (unpublished PhD thesis; New York: University of New York, 1983)

——, *Window Shopping: Cinema and the Postmodern* (Berkeley: University of California Press, 1993)

——, 'Approaching *Borderline*' *Millenium Film Journal* 7–9 (Autumn–Winter, 1980–81)

——, 'Introduction: *Borderline* and the POOL Films', in Donald, Friedberg and Marcus (eds), *Close Up*

——, 'Introduction: Reading *Close Up*, 1927–1933', in Donald, Friedberg and Marcus (eds), *Close Up*

Friedman, Susan Stanford, *Penelope's Web: Gender, Modernity, H.D.'s Fiction* (Cambridge: Cambridge University Press, 1990)

——, '"I Had Two Loves Separate": The Sexualities of H.D.'s *HER*', in Susan Stanford Friedman and Rachael Blau (eds), *Signets: Reading H.D.* (Madison: University of Wisconsin Press, 1990)

Fulbrook, Mary, *Historical Theory* (London and New York: Routledge, 2002)

Geidion, Siegfried, *Mechanization Takes Command: A Contribution to Anonymous History* (New York: Oxford University Press, 1955)

Gledhill, Christine, *Reframing British Cinema 1918–1928: Between Restraint and Passion* (London: BFI, 2003).

——, 'Wit and the Literate Image: The Adrian Brunel/A.A. Milne Collaborations', in Burton and Porter (eds), *Pimple, Pranks and Pratfalls*

Greenberg, Clement, 'Avant-Garde and Kitsch', in Clement Greenberg, *Collected Essays and Criticism: Volume 1, Perceptions and Judgments 1939–1944*, ed. John O'Brian (London and Chicago: University of Chicago Press, 1986)

Greene, Graham, *The Graham Greene Film Reader: Mornings in the Dark* (London: Carcanet, 1993)

Gupta, Partha Sarathi, *Imperialism and the British Labour Movement, 1914–1964* (London: Macmillan, 1975)

Guy, Josephine M., *The British Avant-Garde: Theory of Politics and Tradition* (Hemel Hempstead: Harvester Wheatsheaf, 1991)

Guynn, William, 'The Art of National Projection: Basil Wright's *Song of Ceylon*', in Barry Keith Grant and Jeanette Sloniowski (eds), *Documenting the Documentary: Close Readings of Documentary Film and Video* (Detroit: Wayne State University Press, 1998)

Guzman, Tony, 'The Little Theatre Movement: The Institutionalization of the European Art Film in America' *Film History* 17 (2005)

Hagener, Malte, *Moving Forward, Looking Back: The European Avant-Garde and the Invention of Film Culture, 1919–1939* (Amsterdam: Amsterdam University Press, 2007)

Hake, Sabin, *Cinema's Third Machine: Writing on Film in Germany 1907–1933* (Lincoln: University of Nebraska Press, 1993)

Hallett, Mark, *The Spectacle of Difference: Graphic Satire in the Age of Hogarth* (New Haven, CT, and London: Yale University Press, 1999)

Hamilton, Ian, *The Little Magazines: A Study of Six Editors* (London: Weidenfeld and Nicolson, 1976)

Hammond, Michael, '"Cultivating Pimple": Performance Traditions and the Film Comedy of Fred and Joe Evans', in Burton and Porter (eds), *Pimple, Pranks and Pratfalls*

Hammond, Paul (ed.), *The Shadow and its Shadow: Surrealist Writings on the Cinema* (Edinburgh: Polygon, 1991)

Hancock, Margaret, 'The Federation of Film Societies', in Cecile Starr (ed.), *The Film Society Primer* (Forest Hills, NY: American Federation of Film Societies, 1956)

Hanhardt, John G., 'The Medium Viewed: The American Avant-Garde Film', in *A History of the American Avant-Garde Cinema* (exhibition catalogue; New York: American Federation of Arts, 1976)

Hansen, Miriam, *Babel and Babylon: Spectatorship in American Silent Film* (Cambridge, MA: Harvard University Press, 1991)

Hardy, Forsyth, (ed.), *Grierson on Documentary* (London: Faber and Faber, 1966; expanded edn of book first published 1946)

——, *John Grierson: A Documentary Biography* (London: Faber and Faber, 1979)

—— (ed.), *Grierson on the Movies* (London: Faber and Faber, 1981)

——, 'The Film Society Movement in Scotland', in Cecile Starr (ed.), *The Film Society Primer* (Forest Hills, NY: American Federation of Film Societies, 1956)

Harrison, Charles, *English Art and Modernism, 1900–1939* (New Haven, CT, and London: Yale University Press, 1994)

Hawkridge, John, 'British Cinema From Hepworth to Hitchcock', in Nowell-Smith (ed.), *The Oxford History of World Cinema*

H.D., 'The Borderline Pamphlet', in Bonnie Kime Scott (ed.), *The Gender of Modernism: A Critical Anthology* (Bloomington and Indianapolis: Indiana University Press, 1990)

Herring, Robert, *Films of the Year, 1927–28* (London: Studio Ltd, 1928)

Higson, Andrew, *Waving the Flag: Constructing a National Cinema in Britain* (Oxford: Clarendon Press, 1995)

—— (ed.), *Dissolving Views: Key Writings on British Cinema* (London: Cassell, 1996).

—— (ed.), *Young and Innocent: Cinema and Britain 1896–1930* (Exeter: University of Exeter Press, 2002)

——, '"Britain's Outstanding Contribution to the Film": The Documentary-Realist Tradition', in Barr (ed.), *All Our Yesterdays*

—— and Richard Maltby (eds), *'Film Europe' and 'Film America': Cinema, Commerce and Cultural Exchange, 1920–1939* (Exeter: University of Exeter Press, 1999)

Hill, John and Pamela Church Gibson (eds), *The Oxford Guide to Film Studies* (Oxford: Oxford University Press, 1998)

Hobsbawm, E.J., *Nations and Nationalism Since 1780: Programme, Myth, Reality* (Cambridge: Cambridge University Press, 1990)

Hogenkamp, Bert, *Deadly Parallels: Film and the Left in Britain, 1929–1939* (London: Lawrence and Wishart, 1986)

——, *Film, Television and the Left, 1950–1970* (London: Lawrence and Wishart, 2000)

——, 'Film and the Workers' Movement in Britain, 1929–39' *Sight and Sound* 45: 2 (Spring 1976)

——, '"Making Films With a Purpose": Film-Making and the Working Class', in Clark, Heinemann and Snee (eds), *Culture and Crisis in Britain in the Thirties*

Hood, Stuart, 'John Grierson and the Documentary Film Movement', in James Curran and Vincent Porter (eds), *British Cinema History* (London: Weidenfeld and Nicolson, 1983)

Horak, Jan-Christopher (ed.), *Lovers of Cinema: The First American Film Avant-Garde 1919–1945* (Madison: University of Wisconsin Press, 1995)

——, *Making Images Move: Photographers and the Avant-Garde* (Washington and London: Smithsonian Institution Press, 1997)

——, 'Discovering Pure Cinema: Avant-Garde Film in the 1920s' *Afterimage* 8: 1–2 (Summer 1980)

——, 'The First American Film Avant-Garde, 1919–1945', in Horak (ed.), *Lovers of Cinema*

——, 'Paul Strand and Charles Sheeler's *Manhatta*', in Horak (ed.), *Lovers of Cinema*

Horrocks, Roger, *Len Lye: A Biography* (Auckland: Auckland University Press, 2001)

——, 'Len Lye's Figures of Motion' *Cantrills Filmnotes* 31–33 (November 1979)

Houston, Penelope, *Keepers of the Frame: The Film Archives* (London: BFI, 1994)

Hunter, William, *Scrutiny of Cinema* (London: Wishart and Co., 1932)

Hurzogenruth, Wulf, 'Light-Play and Kinetic Theatre as Parallels to Absolute Film', in Drummond, Dusinberre and Rees (eds), *Film as Film*

Huyssen, Andreas, 'The Hidden Dialectic: Avantgarde-Technology-Mass Culture', in Andreas Huyssen, *After the Great Divide: Modernism, Mass Culture, Postmodernism* (Bloomington: Indiana University Press, 1983)

——, 'Mass Culture as Woman: Modernism's Other', in Andreas Huyssen, *After the Great Divide: Modernism, Mass Culture, Postmodernism* (Bloomington: Indiana University Press, 1986)

Jenkins, Henry, *What Made Pistachio Nuts? Early Sound Comedy and the Vaudeville Aesthetic* (New York: Columbia University Press, 1992)

Johnston, Claire, '"Independence" and the Thirties', in Macpherson (ed.), *Traditions of Independence*

Jones, Stephen G., *The British Labour Movement and Film, 1918–1939* (London and New York: Routledge and Kegan Paul, 1987)

Kaes, Anton, 'The Debate About Cinema: Charting a Controversy' *New German Critique* 40 (Winter 1987)

Kemp, Philip, 'Not For Peckham: Michael Balcon and Gainsborough's International Trajectory in the 1920s', in Cook (ed.), *Gainsborough Pictures*

Kern, Stephen, *The Culture of Time and Space, 1880–1918* (Cambridge, MA: Harvard University Press, 1983)

Kirby, Lynne, *Parallel Tracks: The Railroad and Silent Cinema* (Exeter: University of Exeter Press, 1997)

Kitchin, George, *A Survey of Burlesque and Parody in English* (Edinburgh: Oliver & Boyd, 1931)

Koszarski, Richard, *An Evening's Entertainment: The Age of the Silent Feature Picture, 1915–1928* (New York: Charles Scribner's Sons, 1990)

Krauss, Rosalind E., *The Originality of the Avant-garde and Other Modernist Myths* (Cambridge, MA, and London: MIT Press, 1986)

Kuenzli, Rudolf (ed.), *Dada and Surrealist Film* (New York: Willis Locker and Owens, 1987)

Kuhn, Annette, *Cinema, Censorship and Sexuality, 1909–1925* (London and New York: Routledge, 1988)

——, 'Recontextualising a Film Movement', in Macpherson (ed.), *Traditions of Independence*

Lapsley, Robert and Michael Westlake, *Film Theory: An Introduction* (Manchester: Manchester University Press, 1988)

Lawder, Standish D., *The Cubist Cinema* (New York: New York University Press, 1975)

Le Grice, Malcolm, *Abstract Film and Beyond* (London: Studio Vista, 1977)

Le Mahieu, D.L., *A Culture for Democracy: Mass Communication and the Cultivated Mind in Britain Between the Wars* (Oxford: Clarendon, 1988)

Leavis, F.R. and Denys Thompson, *Culture and Environment: The Training of Critical Awareness* (London: Chatto & Windus, 1933)

Lejeune, Anthony (ed.), *The Caroline Lejeune Film Reader* (Manchester: Carcanet, 1991)

Lejeune, C.A., *Cinema* (London: Alexander Maclehose, 1931)

Leyda, Jay, *Kino: A History of the Russian and Soviet Film* (London: George Allen and Unwin, 1983)

Lindsay, Vachel, *The Art of the Moving Picture* (New York: Liveright, 1978; first published 1915, rev edn 1922)

Lovell, Alan, 'The Documentary Film Movement: John Grierson', in Lovell and Hillier, *Studies in Documentary*

—— and Jim Hillier, *Studies in Documentary* (London: Secker and Warburg, 1972)

——, Sam Rohdie and Peter Wollen, 'Interview with Ivor Montagu' *Screen* 13: 3 (Autumn 1972)

Low, Rachael, *The History of the British Film, 1918–1929* (London: George Allen and Unwin, 1971)

——, *The History of the British Film: Documentary and Educational Films of the 1930s* (London: George Allen and Unwin, 1979)

——, *The History of the British Film: Films of Comment and Persuasion of the 1930s* (London: George Allen and Unwin, 1979)

——, *Film Making in 1930s Britain* (London: George Allen and Unwin, 1985)

Lucas, John, *The Radical Twenties: Writing, Politics and Culture* (Nottingham: Five Leaves, 1997)

Lyons, William, (ed.), *Modern Philosophy of Mind* (London: Everyman, 1995)

MacDonald, Scott, 'Introduction', in Scott MacDonald, (ed.), *Cinema 16: Documents Toward a History of a Film Society* (Philadelphia: Temple University Press, 2002)

McFarlane, Brian, 'A Literary Cinema? British Films and British Novels', in Barr (ed.), *All Our Yesterdays*

Macintyre, Stuart, *A Proletarian Science: Marxism in Britain 1917–1933* (Cambridge: Cambridge University, 1980)

McKernan, Luke, *Topical Budget: The Great British News Film* (London: BFI, 1992)

McLuhan, Marshall and Quentin Fiore, *War and Peace in the Global Village* (New York: Bantam, 1968)

Macpherson, Don (ed.), *Traditions of Independence: British Cinema in the Thirties* (London: BFI, 1980)

——, 'Introduction: The Labour Movement and Oppositional Cinema', in Macpherson (ed.), *Traditions of Independence*

Macpherson, Kenneth, 'A Negro Film Union – Why Not?', in Nancy Cunard (ed.), *Negro: an Anthology* (New York: Frederick Ungar, 1974)

Marcus, Laura, 'The Contribution of H.D', in Donald, Friedberg and Marcus (eds), *Close Up*

Marris, Paul, 'Politics and "Independent" Film in the Decade of Defeat', in Macpherson (ed.), *Traditions of Independence*

Marvin, Carolyn, *When Old Technologies Were New: Thinking About Electric Communication in the Late Nineteenth Century* (New York: Oxford University Press, 1990)

Mathews, Tom Dewe, *Censored* (London: Chatto & Windus, 1994)

Medhurst, Andy, 'Music Hall and British Cinema', in Barr (ed.), *All Our Yesterdays*

Miles, Peter and Malcolm Smith, *Cinema, Literature and Society: Elite and Mass Culture in Interwar Britain* (London: Croom Helm, 1987)

Mills, Lennox A., *Ceylon Under British Rule, 1795–1932* (London: Frank Cass & Co., 1964)

Mills, Sara, *Discourse* (London: Routledge, 1997)

Montagu, Ivor, *The Political Censorship of Films* (London: Victor Gollancz, 1929)

——, *With Eisenstein in Hollywood* (Berlin: Seven Seas, 1968)

——, *The Youngest Son: Autobiographical Sketches* (London: Lawrence and Wishart, 1970)

——, 'The Film Society, London' *Cinema Quarterly* 1: 1 (Autumn 1932)

——, 'Old Man's Mumble: Reflections on a Semi-centenary' *Sight and Sound* 44: 4 (Autumn 1975)

Moorehead, Caroline, *Sidney Bernstein: A Biography* (London: Jonathan Cape, 1984)

Moritz, William, 'Americans in Paris: Man Ray and Dudley Murphy', in Horak (ed.), *Lovers of Cinema*

——, 'Norman McLaren and Jules Engel: Post-Modernists', in Jayne Pilling (ed.), *A Reader in Animation Studies* (Sydney: John Libbey, 1997)

Mumford, Lewis, *Technics and Civilization* (London: Routledge and Kegan Paul, 1967; first published 1934)

Munsterberg, Hugo, *The Film: A Psychological Study* (New York: Dover Publications, 1970; first published 1916)

Murphy, Robert (ed.), *The British Cinema Book* (London: BFI, 1997)

——, 'The Coming of Sound to the Cinema in Britain' *Journal of Historical Film, Radio, and Television* 4: 2 (1984)

Musser, Charles, 'The Travel Genre in 1903–1904: Moving Towards a Fictional Narrative', in Elsaesser and Barker (eds), *Early Cinema*

Nash, Paul, 'The Colour Film', in Charles Davy (ed.), *Footnotes to the Film* (New York: Oxford University Press, 1937)

Nava, Mica, 'Modernity's Disavowal: Women, the City and the Department Store', in Pasi Falk and Colin Campbell (eds), *The Shopping Experience* (London, Thousand Oaks, CA, and New Delhi: Sage, 1997)

Nowell-Smith, Geoffrey (ed.), *The Oxford History of World Cinema* (Oxford: Oxford University Press, 1996)

O'Pray, Michael, 'Borderline' *Art Monthly* 116 (May 1988)

—— (ed.), *The British Avant-Garde Film 1926–1995* (Luton: University of Luton Press, 1996)

——, 'The British Avant-Garde Film in the Twenties and Thirties' (pamphlet accompanying the videos *History of the Avant-Garde: Britain in the Twenties* and *History of the Avant-Garde: Britain in the Thirties*; London: BFI, 2000)

——, 'Introduction', in O'Pray (ed.), *The British Avant-Garde Film 1926–1995*

Pearson, George, *Flashback: The Autobiography of a British Film-maker* (London: George Allen & Unwin, 1957)

Perkins, Roy and Martin Stollery, *British Film Editors: The Heart of the Movie* (London: BFI, 2004)

Petrić, Vlada, *Constructivism in Film: The Man With the Movie Camera: A Cinematic Analysis* (Cambridge: Cambridge University Press, 1987)

Petrie, Duncan, 'Paul Rotha and Film Theory', in Duncan Petrie and Robert Kruger (eds), *A Paul Rotha Reader* (Exeter: University of Exeter Press, 1999),

—— and Robert Kruger (eds), *A Paul Rotha Reader* (Exeter: University of Exeter Press, 1999)

Phelps, Guy, *Film Censorship* (Letchworth: Garden City Press, 1975)

Plant, Raymond, 'Social Thought', in C.B. Cox and A.E. Dyson, *The Twentieth Century Mind: History, Ideas and Literature in Britain: Volume 2, 1918–1945* (London: Oxford University Press, 1972)

Poggioli, Renato, *The Theory of the Avant-Garde* (Harvard: Harvard University Press, 1981)

Porter, Vincent, 'The Construction of an Anti-Hollywood Aesthetic: The Film Criticism of Walter Mycroft in the 1920s', in Burton and Porter (eds), *Crossing the Pond*

Pudovkin, V.I., *Film Technique and Film Acting* (London: Vision Press, 1974; first published 1929)

Rees, A.L., *A History of Experimental Film and Video* (London: BFI, 1999)

——, 'Cinema and the Avant-Garde', in Nowell-Smith (ed.), *The Oxford History of World Cinema*

Remy, Michel, *Surrealism in Britain* (Aldershot: Ashgate, 1999)

Richard, Valliere T., *Norman McLaren: Manipulator of Movement* (East Brunswick: Associated University Presses, 1982)

Richards, Jeffrey, *Thorold Dickinson: The Man and His Films* (London: Croom Helm, 1986)

——, 'British Film Censorship', in Murphy (ed.), *The British Cinema Book*

——, 'Modernism and the People: A View From the Cinema Stalls', in Keith Williams and Steven Mathews (eds), *Rewriting the Thirties: Modernism and After* (London and New York: Longman, 1997)

Richter, Hans, *The Struggle for Film: Towards a Socially Responsible Cinema*, trans. Ben Brewster (Aldershot: Scolar Press, 1986; first published in German 1976)

——, 'The Badly Trained Sensibility', in Sitney (ed.), *The Avant-Garde Film*

——, 'A History of the Avant-garde', in Frank Stauffacher (ed.) *Art in Cinema: a Symposium on the Avant-garde Film* (San Francisco: San Francisco Museum of Art, 1947)

Robertson, James, *The British Board of Film Censors: Film Censorship in Britain* (London: Croom Helm, 1985)

Rosenbaum, Jonathan and Adrian Martin (eds), *Movie Mutations: The Changing Face of World Cinephilia* (London: BFI, 2003)

Rotha, Paul, *Celluloid: The Film Today* (London: Longmans, 1931)

——, *Documentary Film* (London: Faber and Faber, 1952; first published 1935)

——, *The Film Till Now* (London: Vision Press, 1963; first published 1930)

——, *Documentary Diary* (London: Secker and Warburg, 1973)

Ryall, Tom *Alfred Hitchcock and the British Cinema* (London: Athlone, 1996; first published 1986)

Sabin, Roger, *Comics, Comix and Graphic Novels: A History of Comic Art* (London: Phaidon Press, 1996)

Sadie, Stanley (ed.), *The New Grove Dictionary of Musics and Musicians: Volume 8* (London: Macmillan, 1990)

Salt, Barry, *Film Style and Technology: History and Analysis* (London: Starword, 1983)

Samson, Jen, 'The Film Society', in Barr (ed.), *All Our Yesterdays*

Sargeant, Amy, 'Elsa Lanchester and Chaplinism', in Burton and Porter (eds), *Crossing the Pond*

Sayer, Derek, *Capitalism and Modernity: An Excursus on Marx and Weber* (London: Routledge, 1991)

Seldes, Gilbert, *The 7 Lively Arts* (New York: Sagamore Press, 1957; first published 1924)

Sexton, Jamie, The Audio-Visual Rhythms of Modernity: *Song of Ceylon*, Sound and Documentary Filmmaking', *Scope: An On-Line Journal of Film Studies* (May 2004), www.scope.nottingham.ac.uk

——, 'The Film Society and the Creation of an Alternative British Film Culture in the 1920s', in Higson (ed.), *Young and Innocent*

——, 'Grierson's Machines: *Drifters*, the Documentary Film Movement and the Negotiation of Modernity' *Canadian Journal of Film Studies* 11: 1 (Spring 2002)

——, 'Parody on the Fringes: Adrian Brunel, Minority Film Culture and the Art of Deconstruction', in Burton and Porter (eds), *Pimple, Pranks and Pratfalls*

Shotter, John, *The Cultural Politics of Everyday Life: Social Constructionism, Rhetoric and Knowing of the Third Kind* (Buckingham: Open University Press, 1993)

Sitney, P. Adams (ed.), *The Avant-Garde Film: A Reader* (New York: New York University Press, 1978)

—— (ed.), *The Film Culture Reader* (New York: Cooper Square Press, 2000)

Smith, Anthony D., *Nations and Nationalism in a Global Era* (Cambridge: Polity Press, 1995)

Smith, Murray, 'Modernism and the Avant-Gardes', in Hill and Church Gibson (eds), *The Oxford Guide to Film Studies*

——, 'Technological Determination, Aesthetic Resistance, or; *A Cottage on Dartmoor*: Goat-Gland Talkie or Masterpiece?' *Wide Angle* 12: 3 (July 1990)

Sontag, Susan, 'The Decay of Cinema', *New York Times*, 25 February 1996

Spalding, Frances, *British Art Since 1900* (London: Thames and Hudson, 1986)

Stam, Robert, *Subversive Pleasures: Bakhtin, Cultural Criticism and Film* (Baltimore and London: Johns Hopkins University Press, 1989)

Stevenson, John, *British Society 1914–45* (London: Penguin, 1990)

Stollery, Martin, *Alternative Empires: European Modernist Cinemas and Cultures of Imperialism* (Exeter: University of Exeter Press, 2001)

Street, Sarah, *British National Cinema* (London and New York: Routledge, 1997)

Surrealist Group, the, 'Some Surrealist Advice', in Hammond (ed.), *The Shadow and its Shadow*

Sussex, Elizabeth, *The Rise and Fall of the British Documentary Movement* (Berkeley: University of California Press, 1978)

Swann, Paul, *The British Documentary Film Movement 1926–1946* (Cambridge: Cambridge University Press, 1989)

Taylor, Richard, *The Politics of the Soviet Cinema 1917–1929* (Cambridge: Cambridge University Press, 1979)

Thompson, E.P., 'Time, Work-Discipline and Industrial Capitalism' *Past and Present* 38 (December 1967)

Thompson, Kristin, *Eisenstein's Ivan the Terrible: A Neoformalist Analysis* (Princeton: Princeton University Press, 1981)

——, *Exporting Entertainment: America in the World Film Market 1907–1934* (London: BFI, 1985)

——, 'Dr. Caligari at the Folies-Bergere', in Budd (ed.), *The Cabinet of Dr. Caligari*

——, 'Eisenstein's Early Films Abroad', in Christie and Taylor (eds), *Eisenstein Rediscovered*

—— and David Bordwell, *Film History: An Introduction* (New York and London: McGraw Hill, 1994)

Timms, Edward and Peter Collier (eds), *Visions and Blueprints: Avant-Garde Culture and Radical Politics in Early Twentieth Century Europe* (Manchester: Manchester University Press, 1988)

Tolliday, Steven, 'Management and Labour in Britain 1896–1939', in Stephen Tolliday and Jonathan Zeitlin (eds), *The Automobile Industry and its Workers: Between Fordism and Flexibility* (Cambridge: Polity Press, 1986)

Triana, Nuria, *Spanish National Cinema* (London and New York: Routledge, 2003)

Truffaut, François, *Hitchcock* (New York: Simon & Schuster, 1984; first published 1966)

Turner, Bryan, 'The Rationalization of the Body: Reflections on Modernity and Discipline', in Scott Lash and Sam Whimster (eds), *Max Weber, Rationality and Modernity* (London: Allen & Unwin, 1987)

Turvey, Gerry, 'Enter the Intellectuals: Elliot Stannard, Harold Weston and the Discourses on Cinema and Art', in Burton and Porter (eds), *Scene-Stealing*

——, '"That Insatiable Body": Ivor Montagu's Confrontation with British Film Censorship' *Journal of Popular British Cinema: Forbidden British Cinema* 3 (2000)

——, 'Towards a Critical Practice: Ivor Montagu and British Film Culture in the 1920s', in Higson (ed.), *Young and Innocent*

Twenty-One Years of Cinema: A Twenty-First Anniversary Retrospect of the Work of the Edinburgh Film Guild (Edinburgh: Edinburgh Film Guild, 1950)

Tyler, Parker, *Underground Film: A Critical History* (New York: Grove Press, 1969)

Vaughan, Dai, *Portrait of an Invisible Man: The Working Life of Stewart McAllister, Film Editor* (London: BFI, 1983)

Walton, Jean, 'Nightmare of the Uncoordinated White-folk: Race, Psychoanalysis and *Borderline*' *Discourse* 19: 2 (Winter 1997)

——, 'White Neurotics, Black Primitives and the Queer Matrix of *Borderline*', in Ellis Hansen (ed.), *Out Takes: Essays on Queer Theory and Film* (Durham, NC, and London: Duke University Press, 1999)

Wasson, Haidee, *Museum Movies: The Museum of Modern Art and the Birth of Art Cinema* (Berkeley and Los Angeles: University of California Press, 2005)

——, 'Writing Cinema into Daily Life: Iris Barry and the Emergence of British Film Criticism', in Higson (ed.), *Young and Innocent*

Weber, Max, 'The Development of Bureaucracy and its Relation to Law' (1922), in

Max Weber, *Selections in Translation*, ed. W.G. Runciman, trans. E. Mathews (Cambridge: Cambridge University Press, 1978)

Wegg-Prosser, Victoria, 'The Archive of the Film and Photo League' *Sight and Sound* 46: 4 (Autumn 1977)

Weiner, Martin J., *English Culture and the Decline of Industrialism 1850–1980* (Cambridge: Cambridge University Press, 1982)

Weis, Elizabeth and John Belton (eds), *Film Sound: Practice and Theory* (New York: Columbia University Press, 1985)

White, Eric Walter, *Parnassus to Let: An Essay About Rhythm in the Films* (London: Hogarth Press, 1929)

Wilcox, Denys J., *The London Group 1913–39: The Artists and Their Works* (Aldershot: Scolar Press, 1995)

Willemen, Paul, *Looks and Frictions: Essays in Cultural Studies and Film Theory* (London: BFI, 1994)

——, 'An Avant-Garde for the Nineties', in Willemen, *Looks and Frictions*

Williams, Alan, 'Historical and Theoretical Issues in the Coming of Recorded Sound to the Cinema', in Altman (ed.), *Sound Theory, Sound Practice*

Williams, Kevin, *Get Me a Murder a Day! A History of Mass Communications in Britain* (London: Arnold, 1998)

Williams, Raymond, *Culture and Society 1780–1950* (Harmondsworth: Penguin 1963)

——, *The Politics of Modernism: Against the New Conformists* (London: Verso, 1990)

Winston, Brian, *Claiming the Real: The Documentary Film Revisited* (London: BFI, 1995)

——, *Technologies of Seeing: Photography, Cinematography and Television* (London: BFI, 1996).

——, 'The Tradition of the Victim in Griersonian Documentary', in Alan Rosenthal (ed.), *New Challenges for Documentary* (Berkeley and Los Angeles: University of California Press, 1988)

Wolfe, Charles, 'Straight Shots and Crooked Plots: Social Documentary and the Avant-Garde in the 1930s', in Horak (ed.), *Lovers of Cinema*

Wolff, Janet, *Aesthetics and the Sociology of Art* (London: George Allen & Unwin, 1983)

Wollen, Peter, 'The Canon', in Peter Wollen (ed.), *Paris Hollywood: Writings on Film* (London and New York: Verso, 2002)

——, 'Cinema/Americanism/the Robot' *New Formations* 8 (Summer 1989)

——, 'The Last New Wave: Modernism in the British Film of the Thatcher Era', in Lester Friedman (ed.), *Fires Were Started: British Cinema and Thatcherism* (Minneapolis: University of Minnesota, 1993)

——, 'Together' *Sight and Sound* 6: 7 (July 1996)

——, 'The Two Avant-Gardes', in Peter Wollen, *Readings and Writings: Semiotic Counter Strategies* (London: Verso, 1982)

Woolf, Virginia, 'The Cinema' (1926), in O'Pray (ed.), *The British Avant-Garde Film, 1926–1995*

Youngblood, Denise J., *Movies for the Masses: Popular Cinema and Soviet Society in the 1920s* (Cambridge: Cambridge University Press, 1992)

Zimmerman, Patricia, 'Startling Angles: Amateur Film and the Early Avant-Garde', in Horak (ed.), *Lovers of Cinema*

Filmography

£5 Reward (Brunel, UK, 1920)

Armageddon (Woolfe, UK, 1923)

Ballet Mécanique (Léger and Murphy, France, 1924)
Battleship Potemkin (Eisenstein, USSR, 1925)
Battling Bruisers (Brunel, UK, 1925)
Berlin: Symphony of a City (Ruttmann, Germany, 1927)
Beyond This Open Road (Braun and Nicholson, UK, 1934)
The Birth of the Robot (Lye, UK, 1936)
Blackmail (Hitchcock, UK, 1929)
Blighty (Brunel, UK, 1927)
Bluebottles (Montagu, UK, 1928)
The Blunderland of Big Game (Brunel, UK, 1925)
Bookworms (Brunel, UK, 1920)
Borderline (Macpherson, UK, 1930)
Bread (Kino, UK, 1934)
The Bump (Brunel, UK, 1920)

C.O.D.—A Mellow Drama (Richards, Dickinson, Gibbs and Templeman, UK, 1929)
The Cabinet of Dr. Caligari (Weine, Germany, 1919)
Camera Makes Whoopee (McLaren, UK, 1935)
Cargo From Jamaica (Wright, UK, 1933)
Challenge to Fascism (Biggar, UK, 1937)
Champion Charlie (Chaplin, USA, 1916)
Coal Face (Cavalcanti, UK, 1935)
A Colour Box (Lye, UK, 1935)
The Coming of the Dial (Legg, UK, 1933)
Conquest (Wright, UK, 1930)
Contact (Rotha, UK, 1933)
The Covered Wagon (Cruze, USA, 1924)

217

Crossing the Great Sagrada (Brunel, UK, 1924)
Crossing the Great Sahara (Buchanan, UK, 1924)
Cut it Out (Brunel, UK, 1925)

Danse Macabre (Murphy, USA, 1922)
Daydreams (Montagu, UK, 1928)
The Death Ray (Kuleshov, USSR, 1925)
Defence of Madrid (Montagu, UK, 1936)
Dr. Turner's Mental Hospital (Penrose, UK, 1929)
Drifters (Grierson, UK, 1929)

Emak Bakia (Man Ray, France, 1926)
Empire Buyers are Empire Builders (Blakeston and Bruguière, UK, 1931)
Enthusiasm (Vertov, USSR, 1931)
Entr'acte (Clair, France 1924)
Ephemeral (Nicholson, UK, 1934)
The Equation X+X=0 (Fairthorne and Salt, UK, 1936)
Euclid 1.32 (Salt, UK, 1936)
Everyday aka *The Daily Round* (Richter, UK, 1929)
Exhilaration (Braun, UK, 1934)
Experimental Animation, aka *The Peanut Vendor* (Lye, UK, 1933)

The Fall of the House of Usher (Webber, USA, 1929)
Father Sergius (Protazanov and Volkoff, Russia, 1917)
Foothills (Macpherson, UK, 1929)

The Gaiety of Nations (Ahern and Sewell, UK, 1929)
Ghosts Before Breakfast (Richter, Germany, 1928)
Greed (Von Stroheim, USA, 1925)

Hell Unltd. (McLaren and Biggar, UK, 1936)
How Broncho Billy Left Bear Country (Anderson, USA, 1912)

I Do Like to Be Beside the Seaside (Blakeston, UK, 1927)
In the Shadow of the Machine (Deslaw, Belgium, 1927)
Industrial Britain (Flaherty, UK, 1931)
L'Inhumaine (Le Herbier, France, 1924)
The Iron Horse (Ford, USA, 1924)

Kaleidoscope (Lye, UK, 1935)
Kino-Eye (Vertov, USSR, 1924)

The Life and Death of 9413 (Florey and Vorkapich, USA, 1928)

The Life of a Lobster, aka *Lobsters* (Moholy-Nagy and Mathias, UK, 1935)
A Light Play in Black-White-Grey (Moholy-Nagy, Germany, 1930)
Light Rhythms (Blakeston and Bruguière, UK, 1931)
Liner Cruising South (Elton, UK, 1933)
The Lodger (Hitchcock, UK, 1927)
The Lost Patrol (Summers, UK, 1929)
Love on the Wing (McLaren, UK, 1937)

The Man With the Movie Camera (Vertov, USSR, 1929)
The Man Without Desire (Brunel, UK, 1923)
Manhatta (Strand and Sheeler, USA, 1921)
The Marriage Circle (Lubitsch, USA, 1924)
Monkey's Moon (Macpherson, UK, 1929)
Moors and Minarets (Brunel, UK, 1923)
Movement of Rain in a Thunderstorm (Fairgrieve, UK, 1933)

Nanook of the North (Flaherty, USA, 1922)
Neighbours (McLaren, Canada, 1952)
New Architecture at the London Zoo (Maholy-Nagy, UK, 1936)
Night Mail (Wright and Watt, UK, 1936)
Nju (Czinner, Germany, 1924)

October (Eisenstein, USSR, 1928)
Opus 2 (Ruttman, Germany, 1923)
Opus 3 (Ruttman, Germany, 1924)
Opus 4 (Ruttman, Germany, 1925)

The Passion of Joan of Arc (Dreyer, France, 1928)
Pathetic Gazette (Brunel, UK, 1925)
Pett and Pott (Cavalcanti, UK, 1934)
Polikushka (Sanin, USSR, 1923)
Polychrome Fantasy (McLaren, UK, 1935)

Rainbow Dance (Lye, UK, 1936)
Raskolnikov (Wiene, Germany, 1923)
Rien que les Heures (Cavalcanti, France, 1926)
Romance Sentimentale (Alexandrov and Eisenstein, USSR, 1930)
La Roue (Gance, France, 1922)

The Scarlet Woman: An Ecclesiastical Adventure (Greenbridge, UK, 1925)
Secrets of a Soul (Pabst, Germany, 1926)
Seven Till Five (McLaren, UK, 1933)
The Shimmy Sheik (Brunel, UK, 1923)

The Skin Game (Hitchcock, UK, 1931)
So This is Jolly Good (Brunel, UK, 1925)
The Somme (Wetherell, UK, 1927)
Song of Ceylon (Wright, UK, 1934)
Strike (Eisenstein, USSR, 1925)

Tell Me if it Hurts (Massingham, UK, 1934)
The Tell-Tale Heart (Desmond Hurst, UK, 1934)
A Temporary Lady (Brunel, UK, 1921)
The Tonic (Montagu, UK, 1928)
Topical Budget Ham Spray September 1929 (Penrose, UK, 1929)
Topical Gazette (Evans, UK, 1921)
Toto's Wife (Kearn, UK, 1924)
Trade Tattoo (Lye, UK, 1937)
Turksib (Turin, USSR, 1929)
Tusalava (Lye, UK, 1929)
Twice Two (Brunel, UK, 1920)
Typical Budget (Brunel, UK, 1925)

Waxworks (Leni, Germany, 1924)
Weather Forecast (Spice, UK, 1934)
Wing Beat (Macpherson, UK, 1927)

Index

NORTH WALES
PLEASURE STEAMERS

North Wales
Pleasure Steamers

ANDREW GLADWELL

AMBERLEY

First published 2012

Amberley Publishing
The Hill, Stroud
Gloucestershire, GL5 4EP

www.amberley-books.com

British Library Cataloguing in Publication Data.
A catalogue record for this book is available from the British Library.

ISBN 978 1 4456 0471 8

Typesetting and Origination by Amberley Publishing.
Printed in Great Britain.

Contents

The pleasure steamers that operated between Liverpool and North Wales were able to cruise past some of the most spectacular and dramatic scenery in the UK.

Acknowledgements

This book has been written to evoke the heritage and atmosphere of the well-loved pleasure steamers that once plied the North Wales coast from Liverpool. It is difficult to show every steamer that operated along the coast. The images therefore reflect to a great extent, the pleasure steamers that plied the coast in the years after the Second World War. Well-loved steamers such as the *St Trillo*, *St Seiriol* and *St Tudno* of post-war years, have therefore been given prominence along with steamers from the late 1960s as well as pleasure steamers from the twenty first century. In compiling this book I have been grateful for the help and co-operation of several individuals. In particular, I would like to thank Campbell McCutcheon for allowing me to use some of his wonderful material and for providing such splendid support.

Websites
For further information on paddle and pleasure steamers
www.heritagesteamers.co.uk

For cruises by the pleasure steamers *Waverley* and *Balmoral* in North Wales
www.waverleyexcursions.co.uk

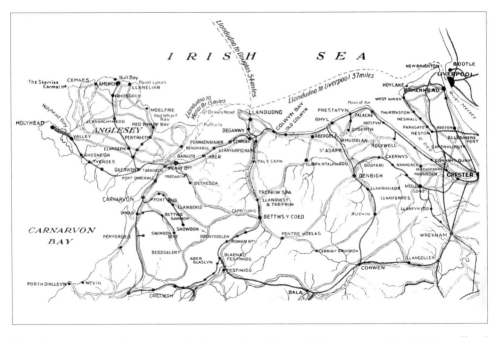

Map showing the cruising area of the Liverpool and North Wales steamers. North Wales offered some of the most scenic pleasure steamer cruises in the UK.

Introduction

Pleasure steamer cruises along the scenic North Wales coast from Liverpool disappeared during the 1960s. The outstanding beauty of North Wales and, in particular, the Menai Straits and Anglesey was, in its day, one of the most outstanding and scenic areas of the UK for enjoying the simple pleasure of taking a pleasure steamer cruise. It offered passengers a few hours at the seaside or enabled them to sample scenery away from that seen in everyday life of the industrial north of England. There was no finer grandstand to enjoy such a day as on one of the well-loved and stylish steamers of the Liverpool & North Wales Steamship Company of the 1950s and 1960s; *St Trillo*, *St Seiriol* and *St Tudno*.

Services between Liverpool and North Wales had their origin as far back as 1821 when the St George Steam Packet Company offered sailings. North Wales, like so many other areas around the UK, saw services expand and change during the Victorian era. Ever larger steamers with ever greater passenger facilities were built to compete with the expanding railway service along the North Wales coast. This increased competition ensured that steamers such as the *Bonnie Doon* heralded a new era of steamer services. Towards the end of the Victorian era in 1890, two large steamers, *Cobra* and *Paris*, were renamed and entered Norh Wales service and with the formation of the Liverpool & North Wales Steamship Company, a 'Golden Era' of North Wales cruising was about to begin.

The decades that followed saw some of the finest steamers to ever grace the Liverpool and North Wales route enter service. Perhaps the most majestic of them all was *La Marguerite*, which entered North Wales service in 1914. Her sheer size and magnificence immediately made her a great favourite. The inevitable cessation of services during the First World War was but a brief disruption to the North Wales service. Most of the steamer fleet saw war service during this time. The 1920s witnessed the entry into service of smart new steamers such as the *St Tudno* of 1926. The older paddle steamers were gradually replaced by these smart new turbine steamers of the inter-war years. The North Wales scene was then set for the carefree heyday of these steamers before the Second World War rudely interrupted day cruises to the North Wales coast once again.

With the ending of the Second World War, services soon got back to normal. The gallant trio of *St Trillo*, *St Seiriol* and *St Tudno* then once again provided carefree cruises from Liverpool to North Wales. The 1950s saw these steamers become very popular indeed. For most, it would seem that the steamers and the North Wales service would last forever. But, in common with all other areas of the UK, the Liverpool and North Wales route suffered from the ever-growing usage of the motor car as well as from the popularity of cheap foreign holidays by air. The long-standing habit of taking a holiday by steamer from Liverpool to North Wales was by then becoming less of a novelty. The steady trickle soon developed into a deluge. Tradition was fine, but for many, the flexibility of a motor car and its potential for providing a full sightseeing holiday was too much of a temptation. Traditional long-standing services therefore ceased in the early 1960s – was it the end of an era?

The cessation of services by the Liverpool & North Wales Steamship Company in 1962 didn't though mark the end of North Wales services. The well known company of P&A Campbell immediately set about continuing the service and continued doing this for around a decade with the *St Trillo* as well as with lesser known ships such as the *Queen of the Isles*. The 'White Funnel Fleet' was a brave and mainly effective attempt at keeping services going amidst a sea of ever-growing challenges. Services from Llandudno and Liverpool were also kept alive by the Isle of Man Steam Packet Company. By the mid-1970s, the paddle steamer *Waverley* had become the 'Last sea-going paddle steamer in the World' on her native Firth of Clyde. By the late 1970s, it became apparent that her traditional cruising area on the Firth of Clyde couldn't sustain her in the long term. It was at this stage that she was invited to attend the centenary of Llandudno Pier. After some deliberations, it was decided to do this and she visited North Wales for the first time in April and May 1978. This initial and somewhat unexpected visit was followed by several more. In 1986, *Waverley*'s consort, the *Balmoral*, entered her preservation career. *Balmoral* has been a regular visitor to North Wales each June since that date. Both steamers keep alive the tradition of the North Wales Company and allow passengers in the twenty-first century to admire the scenery of the Menai Straits and the North Wales coast from a viewpoint far removed from the predictability of the motorway. The spirit of the Liverpool and North Wales steamers is therefore still alive and we can still sample what passengers aboard the famous *St Trillo*, *St Seiriol* and *St Tudno* once experienced.

One

Heyday of the Paddle Steamers

MENAI SUSPENSION BRIDGE

88041

Paddle steamer services date back to 1821 in North Wales. Many famous and well-loved steamers such as *La Marguerite*, *Snowdon* and *St Tudno* plied between Liverpool and North Wales during the 'Golden Age' of Victorian and Edwardian times.

The North Wales service had it origins as far back as 1821 when the St George Steam Packet Company established services. Its steamers included the *St David* and *Prince Llewelyn*. Services were offered from the St Georges Dock at Liverpool to Beaumaris and Bangor as the traditional seaside resorts and their piers had yet to be developed. This company was replaced in 1843 by the City of Dublin Steam Packet Company. They took over the North Wales excursion business and operated their steamers *Erin-Go-Brach*, *Prince Arthur* and *Fairy*. As was common with the mid-Victorian era of paddle steamer operation around the rest of the UK, the period was typified by a large number of small and now forgotten steamer companies offering services. The next major development was the Liverpool, Llandudno & Welsh Coast Steamboat Company being formed in 1881 with their steamer *Bonnie Doon*. The company acquired the City of Dublin Steam Packet Company's steamers and trade in July 1881. This was a momentous event in North Wales service as it marked the start of a fully developed excursion service. This in turn was enlivened as North Wales resorts such as Llandudno and Colwyn Bay had developed into full-blown Victorian seaside resorts with piers, fine hotels, graceful promenades and shops to attract and cater for steamer passengers. 1890 was the next year of major development in North Wales. In that year the *Cobra* was acquired by the New North Wales Steamship Company and was renamed *St Tudno*. In 1891, the famous Liverpool & North Wales Steamship Company was formed after competition between the New North Wales Steamship Company and the Liverpool, Llandudno & Welsh Coast Steamboat Company Limited ended in the latter going into liquidation. The Liverpool & North Wales Steamship Company house flag was until 1905 or 1906, an ensign that was horizontally coloured (from top to bottom) red, white and blue. Upon the centre (white) strip were the letters 'N.W.S.S.C' in black. This was later changed to a white swallow tail with a blue St George cross with a yellow Prince of Wales feather emblem at the centre.

The paddle steamer *Columbus*. In the 1880s, tugs were often used for excursion services from Liverpool and the Lancashire coast to the Welsh coast. One of these operators was Mr Dodd of Liverpool. His family tugs named *Hercules* and *Columbus* took the poorly-paid working classes to the coast. More often than not, they were attracted to the bar rather than the scenery! The bar usually consisted of a trestle placed on some barrels under the awning of the aft deck of the vessel. The steamer service and perhaps prompted by the sale of liquor, made Dodd realise that a larger and more comfortable steamer was required and this resulted in the building of the *Snowdon*. (*J&C McCutcheon Collection*)

The North Wales steamers departed for North Wales from the Princes Landing Stage at Liverpool. This was around a twenty minute walk from Lime Street Station. The offices for the Liverpool & North Wales Company were located at 40 Chapel Street in Liverpool.

St Tudno was launched in April 1891 and could carry up to 1,061 passengers. She had a good career on the North Wales station of 22 years. She had a reputation for burning a great deal of coal.

St Elvies entered service in 1896. She was smaller than the uneconomic *St Tudno* but the North Wales Company wanted a steamer that was ultimately more economic. She was launched in April 1896 and was built by Fairfield's. She entered service at Whitsun that year with Captain Williams as her master. She could carry up to 991 passengers. Pleasingly, her coal consumption was around half that of the larger *St Tudno*. She had a speed of around 18.5 knots.

After service in the First World War during which time she had had the honour of carrying King George V, *St Elvies* re-entered service on the North Wales run on Whit Saturday 1919. Her triumphant return was short lived as just 24 hours later she hit Llandudno Pier, badly knocking over several passengers and alarming the pier master. Luckily, the steamer was unharmed but the pier for many years, had a broken pile named 'Elvies Pile'. This wonderful photograph shows one of the finest paddle steamers of the North Wales fleet.

The paddle steamer *St Elvies* had a good reputation as a sea boat. Originally, her funnels were a lot smaller until being enlarged in 1899. She had a varied schedule including Liverpool to Menai Bridge, Llandudno sailings as well as visits to Douglas on the Isle of Man and to Blackpool. In addition, she also cruised round the Isle of Anglesey. This cruise was some 170 miles long and took around eleven hours to complete. Between 1919 and 1930, *St Elvies* embarked upon an ambitious cruising programme in North Wales. She was particularly remembered for her Douglas sailings. In good weather, these were glorious but in more challenging seas, they became memorable for other reasons!

A postcard advertising the Colwyn Bay & Liverpool Steamship Company. The paddle steamer shown is the *Rhos Colwyn*.

The paddle steamer *St Elvies* in open sea. After being withdrawn from service, *St Elvies* was laid up at Birkenhead and demolition was completed at New Ferry in 1931. (*J&C McCutcheon Collection*)

Snowdon was perhaps one of the loveliest and most charming of all steamers to be placed in service in North Wales. Locally built by Laird of Birkenhead in 1892, she was 175 feet in length and had a width of 24.5 feet. She carried around 462 passengers. She was never built for speed and managed a service speed of 14 knots. *Snowdon* is shown here departing from Llandudno Pier. (*J&C McCutcheon Collection*)

The paddle steamer *St Trillo* reversing away from a North Wales pier around 1914. *St Trillo* has the distinction of being the very last paddle steamer to be purchased by the Liverpool & North Wales Company. She could carry up to 463 passengers and during her career in North Wales visited: Blackpool, Beaumaris, Bangor, New Brighton, Llanddwyn Island, Bangor, Rhyl, Rhos, Llandudno, Menai Bridge as well as several other smaller calling points. She ended her days as a hotel and duck shooting enterprise at the mouth of the Seville River. *St Trillo* was built by Barclay Curle at Glasgow in 1876. She was originally named *Carisbrooke* for Isle of Wight service. She was sold in 1906 to the Colwyn Bay & Liverpool Steamship Company. She was then re-sold a couple of times before finally being purchased by the Liverpool & North Wales Steamship Company and renamed *St Trillo*. After wartime service, she was returned to her owners at the cessation of hostilities but old age forced her sale in 1921. *St Trillo* was scrapped in 1935.

Snowdon's master for several years up to 1914 was Captain Highton. One eccentricity about Captain Highton was that he was a canary enthusiast and he kept, in good weather, a canary in a cage that he hooked on the small platform behind the bridge. The little canary would sing its song sheltered from the wind and bathed in the warm summer sun.

The rubber stamp of Mr J. H. Parry who was the representative of the Liverpool & North Wales Steamship Company at Rhyl.

Snowdon had a splendid promenade deck that was over 120 feet long and extended to the full width of the deck houses. Below the stern of the main deck was a particularly spacious and pretty passenger lounge along with a ladies' room where female passengers were looked after by an attentive stewardess.

Three Officers aboard the *Snowdon* in 1920. One of the proudest moments of the *Snowdon's* career was when she carried Princess Louise of Schelswig-Holstein on a cruise around Anglesey on 28 August 1902. A witty reporter in a local North Wales newspaper reported that Captain James Dodd, who was her master, should be created 'Lord Snowdon' in recognition of the cruise! (*J&C McCutcheon Collection*)

A rare deck view of the *Snowdon*. After service during the First World War, the little *Snowdon* re-entered service in July 1920. A well-loved trip at the time was the Sunday afternoon cruise from Liverpool to Blackpool return. This was under the command of Captain Williams of Port Dinorwic, who kept her spotlessly clean. 1931 saw the *Snowdon* withdrawn from service. Her last master was Captain Kearney and her fine bell was removed from her and placed on Menai Bridge pier. *Snowdon* had a service speed of 14 knots and sometimes cruised to Blackpool, Holyhead and Douglas as well as on her usual Liverpool to Menai Bridge and Llandudno to Caernarfon services. In 1930, she was based at Blackpool and undertook cruises in Morecombe Bay to replace the Isle of Man Steam Packet Company's *Tynwald*. In addition, she also operated cruises to Llandudno and Douglas from Blackpool. She was scrapped at the end of the 1931 season at Port Glasgow. This ended the life of one of perhaps the most charming of all North Wales steamers. (*J&C McCutcheon Collection*)

A stern view of the *Rhos Colwyn*. She operated between Rhyl, Rhos and Llandudno and continued to operate until 1911. She was then sold for breaking up. (*J&C McCutcheon Collection*)

St Elian off of Rhyl Pier. The pier opened in 1867 and was designed by James Brunlees at a cost of around £15,000. It soon became a popular calling point for the North Wales pleasure steamers. The pier contained the usual seaside pier attractions such as tea rooms, concert rooms, restaurants as well as private baths. Like many other exposed piers, it suffered regularly with ships damaging the structure. The early 1900s saw a series of fires and storms cause further damage. It was closed at the time of the First World War and soon after became more derelict. A large section was then demolished meaning that steamers would no longer be able to call. Rhyl Pier therefore had a very short life as a calling point for the North Wales pleasure steamers. (*J&C McCutcheon Collection*)

Queen of the North arriving at Llandudno Pier. Liverpool, as well as the bustling Lancashire resorts of Blackpool and Southport, offered steamer services to Llandudno Pier and the North Wales coast. Blackpool was perfectly positioned to offer some of the most stunning coastal cruises in the UK. The Lake District and North Wales coastlines were clearly visible at most times from the resort. The *Queen of the North* was a popular steamer running from Blackpool's Central Pier. (*J&C McCutcheon Collection*)

A steamer passing Beaumaris with the splendour of the North Wales mountains behind. In the old days, a seaman would ring the ship's bell to warn latecomers that the steamer would soon be departing. At the end of his first peal, he would pause and then follow this with one ring, then two, then three.

The *Snowdon* arriving at Llandudno Pier. Early steamer services in North Wales included several smaller steamers and rival operators. *Snowdon* was one of the smallest and most charming of these. North Wales also became known for the large and somewhat majestic paddle steamers that operated on it. These included the *St Tudno*, *St Elvies* and perhaps the most famous of all – *La Marguerite*.

Page from an early steamer guide showing *La Marguerite* at Beaumaris. (*J&C McCutcheon Collection*)

A steamer arriving at the graceful Bangor Pier. Work began on the construction of Bangor Garth Pier in 1893. The pier was 1,550 feet long and was designed by J. Webster at a cost of around £17,000. It was opened on 14 May 1896 by Lord Penrhyn. It soon became a popular calling point for the many paddle steamers from Blackpool, Southport, Liverpool and Llandudno. Like many other piers, it faced a period of decline and inevitable threat of demolition before it was listed as Grade II*. Bangor Garth Pier is one of the finest and least spoilt traditional seaside piers in the UK. During the early 1900s, Victorian and Edwardian confidence and engineering were invincible. For the owners at the time, it felt as if services would forever grow and flourish. The appetite for a day at the seaside by paddle steamer was one of the favourite occupations of the Victorian and Edwardian masses. This was of course the height of the British Empire, when the great northern industrial towns were at the height of their productivity. The working masses relished the chance to get away to the seaside and the closeness of Liverpool to the industrial heartland of the north gave it something of a never-ending market for steamer services to distant seaside resorts such as Llandudno. It must be remembered that at this time, most of the working classes would have had no holiday pay and so the only means of getting away for most people would be one family day at the seaside. The one special day of the year would therefore see them endeavour to have the very best day that they could afford. They saved their money and intended to enjoy themselves to the full. The boom in steamer services in North Wales was echoed by the revolutionary service and marketing of Alfred Aslett for the Furness Railway on the other side of Morecambe Bay. This was indeed a boom time for the seaside and its pleasure steamers. (*J&C McCutcheon Collection*)

25

LIVERPOOL & NORTH WALES
JULY & AUGUST SAILINGS, 1912

DAILY SAILINGS (Sundays Included)
From PRINCE'S LANDING STAGE (Weather and other circumstances permitting).

"ST. TUDNO,"   "La Marguerite," (Fitted with Wireless Telegraphy.)   "SNOWDON,"

"ST. ELVIES,"   "ST. TRILLO,"   "ST. ELIAN."

"LA MARGUERITE"
(Fitted with Wireless Telegraphy.)   WILL SAIL DAILY   (Fitted with Wireless Telegraphy.)

FRIDAYS "ST. TUDNO."

Leaving LIVERPOOL	10 45 a.m.	Leaving MENAI BRIDGE	3 30 p.m.
" LLANDUDNO	1 0 p.m.	" BANGOR	3 45 "
" BEAUMARIS	2 0 "	" BEAUMARIS	4 0 "
" BANGOR	2 20 "	" LLANDUDNO	5 15 "
Arriving MENAI BRIDGE	2 30 "	Arriving LIVERPOOL	7 30 "

Colwyn Bay. Regular Daily Service between Llandudno and Colwyn Bay (Rhos Pier) in connection with the Liverpool Steamers, leaving Llandudno for Rhos immediately after arrival of Liverpool Steamer. For Extra Sailings, Fares and particulars of connections, see Special Bills.

Carnarvon, Port Dinorwic & Liverpool. Daily, commencing 22nd July, until further notice (Sundays and Bank Holiday excepted).—Leaves Carnarvon at 1·0 p.m. for Menai Bridge, and returning immediately after arrival of Liverpool Steamer, due Menai Bridge at 2·30 p.m.

Extra Trips by "St. Tudno," "St. Elvies" or "Snowdon"
(BANK HOLIDAY EXCEPTED).

	SUNDAYS (Cheap Fares)		Fris., Sats., and Mons (except Aug. 5th) also Tues. Aug. 6th.			MONDAYS (except Aug. 5th) also Tues., Aug. 6th.	SATURDAYS.
Leaves	St. Tudno or St. Elvies.	Snowdon		Leaves			
LIVERPOOL	11 10 a.m.	2 15 p.m.	2 15 p.m.	MENAI BRIDGE		6 30 a.m.	8 30 a.m.
LLANDUDNO (arr) (dep)	1 30 p.m.	5 0 "	4 25 "	BANGOR		7 0 "	8 40 "
BEAUMARIS		6 0 "	4 30 "	BEAUMARIS		7 0 "	9 0 "
BANGOR		7 0 "	5 30 "	LLANDUDNO		8 0 "	10 0 "
Arrives MENAI BRIDGE		7 15 "	5 50 "	Arrives LIVERPOOL		10 15 "	12 15 noon
		7 30 "	6 0 "				

AFTERNOON EXCURSIONS, Liverpool and Llandudno. Passengers leaving Liverpool in the Afternoon as above, and returning same day, must disembark at Llandudno, and return by Steamer leaving Llandudno at 5·15 p.m., due in Liverpool at 7·30 p.m. 3/- Return (Saloon 1/- extra). Half Day Fares Sundays at 11·10 a.m., as above ; Llandudno 3/- Return (Saloon 1/- extra).

BANK HOLIDAY SAILINGS, Monday, Aug. 5th.

A.M. 9·0	"ST. TUDNO" for LLANDUDNO (due 11·15 a.m.) and ROUND ANGLESEY, due back Llandudno 5·30 p.m. and Liverpool about 8·0 p.m. 150 MILES' SAIL or 6½ HOURS AT LLANDUDNO.
A.M. 9·30	LLANDUDNO & MENAI STRAITS TRIP. "ST. ELVIES" from LIVERPOOL, calling at LLANDUDNO, thence to BEAUMARIS, BANGOR & MENAI BRIDGE. Due back in Liverpool about 8 p.m. SIX HOURS ON SHORE AT LLANDUDNO.
A.M. 10·45	"LA MARGUERITE" for LLANDUDNO, BEAUMARIS, BANGOR and MENAI BRIDGE. Due back about 7·30 p.m.

SPECIAL DAY FARES FROM LIVERPOOL (Pier Dues included)—

		1st Return.	2nd Return.
Llandudno		5/-	3/6
Beaumaris, Bangor and Menai Bridge		6/-	4/6
Round Anglesey		7/-	4/-

Excellent Catering on board these Steamers, under Company's Management ; Luncheons, Dinners, Teas of First-class Quality, and all Refreshments at Moderate Prices.
Special Reduced Boat Fares for Parties of 10 or more if previously arranged at Agents or at Office.
PRIVATE CABINS may be booked in advance for "La Marguerite," "St. Tudno" and "St. Elvies."

All Tickets are issued and Goods carried subject to the Company's Conditions of Carriage, as exhibited at the Company's Office and on the Steamers.

FARES (including Pier Dues) between—	DAY Return 1st	DAY Return 2nd.	WEEK END Return 1st.	WEEK END Return 2nd	ORDINARY FARES. 1st Saloon S'gle. R'tn.		2nd Saloon S'gle. R'tn.		CONTRACTS (Pier Dues excluded)
Liverpool & Llandudno	5/-	3/6	5/9	4/3	4/-	6/6	3/-	5/-	Monthly Ticket £1 10 0 £1 15 0
Liverpool and Colwyn Bay	5/6	4/-	6/-	4/6	4/6	6/6	3/6	5/-	Fortnightly " 1 1 0 1 5 0
Liverpool & Beaumaris, Bangor or Menai Bridge	6/-	4/-	6/9	4/9	5/-	8/-	3/6	6/-	Weekly " 0 13 6 0 16 0
Liverpool and Carnarvon	..	..	7/3	5/3	5/6	8/6	4/-	6/6	Contract Tickets issued only at the Company's Office.
Llandudno & Beaumaris, Bangor or Menai Bridge	3/-	2/-	..	..	2/-	3/6	1 6	2/6	Luggage in Advance.—Arrangements are made in connection with the Globe Express for passengers residing in Liverpool and Suburbs to have their Luggage collected and delivered at Llandudno, Beaumaris, Bangor or M. Bridge, at a charge of 1/6 per package.
Children over 3 and under 12 years Half Fare.		Available Day of Issue only.	Week End Return Tickets Available between Friday and Tuesday		Ordinary Return Tickets are available until end of Season.				Calls must be given at Company's Office, when booking Tickets.
All Tickets may be obtained alongside Steamer.									

Bicycles 1/3 (Motors 1/- extra) single journey, including Pier Dues.   Passengers allowed 1 cwt. Personal Luggage free of charge.

For all further particulars apply to any of the Company's Agents, or to The Liverpool and North Wales
S.S. Co. Ltd., T. G. BREW, Secretary, 40 Chapel Street, Liverpool.   Telephone—5955 Central.
OFFICIAL GUIDE, with Special Map, 2d (post free).

ALTERED SAILINGS for SEPTEMBER (See Special Bills).

ISLE OF ANGLESEY TRIPS by "ST. TUDNO," from Liverpool on Sunday, August 4th, Monday (Bank Holiday), 5th, and Wednesday, 7th (9-0 a.m.), Thursday, 8th (9-45 a.m.), Sunday, 18th, and Wednesday, 21st Aug. (9-15 a.m.) Due back each day about 8-15 p.m. (For further trips, see special Bills.)

Handbill from 1912 advertising sailings in North Wales by steamers such as the majestic *La Marguerite* as well as the beautiful little *Snowdon*. This was the pinnacle of North Wales services with steamers serving eight different locations. Passengers were alllowed to carry up to one hundredweight of luggage each.

Snowdon cruising in the Menai Straits around 1910. *Snowdon* took around 2.75 hours on the Liverpool to Llandudno run and she was patronised by the more genteel type of passenger. In 1899 following prolonged dispute between Dodd and the North Wales Company, Dodd became a director when the North Wales Company took over *Snowdon*. The company then adopted the pale primrose funnel colour of the *Snowdon*. (*J&C McCutcheon Collection*)

La Marguerite was perhaps the most magnificent of all North Wales pleasure steamers. She was purchased for North Wales service after starting her career on the Thames. She undertook her first North Wales cruise on 12 May 1904. She operated the Liverpool to Llandudno and Menai Bridge service during her career and was over 341 feet long making her the largest pleasure steamer to have ever operated in the Menai Straits. *La Marguerite* was certainly a palatial steamer especially for first class passengers. She had a large social hall with a ladies boudoir as well as cabins for those affected by the voyage. On the upper deck were six state cabins, a grand saloon as well as a large and luxurious smoking room and a huge dining saloon. Second class passenger accommodation was equally good with a large dining saloon on the lower deck and various saloons and refreshment rooms forward.

La Marguerite was a fine steamer. She had large bunkers capable of holding 100 tons of coal, which burned at 8 tons per hour at full speed. *La Marguerite* had two large yellow funnels with a black hull and white and gold paddle boxes. She served during the First World War and carried some 360,000 troops and steamed over 52,000 miles during the conflict. *La Marguerite* had a massive crew of 95 in pre-war days. The majority of these were employed in the catering department. This number declined a little after the First World War. Mr Fraser was the first Chief Engineer of *La Marguerite* in North Wales. He was succeeded by Mr McEwen in 1909 and he was replaced by Mr Balbirnie.

Passing under the Menai Suspension Bridge was one of the cruise highlights for North Wales steamer passengers. The bridge was designed by Thomas Telford and was completed in 1826. Before this time, cattle had to swim across the straits and passengers had to be ferried across by rowing boat. After the bridge had been finished, the journey time from London to Holyhead decreased. This made a saving of around nine hours.

After the First World War and reconditioning, *La Marguerite* was ready for the 1919 season. She burned coal heavily which meant after a day return from Liverpool to Menai Bridge she had to be re-bunkered (some 100 tons) between 8.00 p.m. and 9.00 a.m. the following morning. Engine trouble plagued her during the 1920s. It looked unlikely that she would pass the survey after 1925 and it was then decided to withdraw her from service. She made her final cruise on 28 September 1925 and was met by enthusiastic crowds at all her calling points. Many of her passengers had travelled up from London for this special event. Captain Highton was her master for her final North Wales season but, for most of her career, *La Marguerite* was under the command of Captain 'Bandy' Young. This small goatee-bearded man was well known on the North Wales run and he knew all of the tricks on how to manoeuvre her alongside Llandudno or Liverpool.

STEAMBOAT EXCURSIONS.

During the summer there is a daily service of boats to and from Menai Bridge, Beaumaris, Llandudno, and Liverpool. A boat runs two or three times a day between Bangor and Carnarvon. There are also excursions to Douglas (I. of Man) and back, to Blackpool and back, and round the Isle of Anglesey.

Queen of the North at Bangor Pier *c.* 1910. This steamer was a well-known paddle steamer from the bustling resort of Blackpool. Blackpool was ideally situated to take advantage of some of the most scenic cruises in the UK with the Lake District to the north and the scenic splendours of North Wales to the south. It was also possible for passengers from somewhere such as Bangor to sample the many delights of Blackpool. (*J&C McCutcheon Collection*)

St Elvies with flags and bunting flying departing from Liverpool for her very last cruise. The *Snowdon* can be seen making her approach to the pier. *St Elvies* like many steamers had a short life before being broken up in 1920. She was though a lucky steamer with a more or less unblemished career on the North Wales service. By 1923, over 350,000 passengers were using the steamers of the Liverpool & North Wales Steamship Company between May and September each year. By the late 1920s and early 1930s, pleasure steamer services in North Wales would change dramatically with the arrival of new turbine steamers to replace the older but perhaps more graceful paddle steamers. The confidence of the late Victorian and Edwardian Era was now to be replaced with a more realistic and modern world where luxury and size would be replaced by economy and efficiency. One era was ending but another was about to start.

Two

Arrival of the Turbine Steamers

The *St Tudno* along with the other turbine steamers provided pleasure steamer cruises during the 1930s heyday of North Wales services.

The newly-built turbine steamer *St Tudno* cruising in the Menai Straits. The General Strike and National Coal Strike of 1926, had a huge effect on the coal-fired paddle steamers as well as other forms of transport such as trains. The Liverpool & North Wales Company managed to source supplies of coal for the latter part of the season. This limited supply was allocated to *St Elvies* and *Snowdon*. Luckily, the *St Tudno* that had been completed that year, was oil-burning and therefore was unaffected by coal shortages. The company though had to lay on motor coaches from the main Lancashire mill towns to reach to steamer departure points as train services were limited.

St Tudno passing well-kept gardens at Vale Park, New Brighton. The town had its own ferry pier to land passengers predominantly from Liverpool. This ferry pier opened in 1867 and had a floating-stage joined by two iron bridges. In 1953, 2,907,000 people cruised to New Brighton. But, by 1971, when most people were travelling by car, this had dropped to around 300,000. The final boat sailed from New Brighton on 26 September 1971. The town also had the New Brighton Promenade Pier. This was positioned next to the ferry pier on the north side. It was opened on the 7 September 1867. It was 550 feet long and had a width of 70 feet. The entrance to the promenade pier was through the turnstiles on the ferry pier and people entered as they came off the ferries. (*J&C McCutcheon Collection*)

THE S.S. "ST. TUDNO" ARRIVING AT PIER FROM BANGOR, LLANDUDNO.

87

St Tudno arriving at Llandudno's landmark pier on a cruise from Bangor. The full unspoilt splendour of the pier can be seen in this image. Walter MacFarlane of Glasgow created the structure using iron castings made at the Elmbank Foundry in Glasgow. It was designed by Charles Henry Driver and James Brunlees. (*J&C McCutcheon Collection*)

The *St Tudno* was 329 feet in length with a gross tonnage of 2,326 tons. She ran her trials on 22 April 1926 and attained the speed of 19.25 knots. She was built by Fairfield's on the River Clyde. On her maiden voyage she departed from Liverpool amidst a great deal of celebration and was greeted on arrival at Llandudno and Menai Bridge by large amounts of bunting and rockets. *St Tudno* was built as the replacement for the majestic *La Marguerite*. She was launched by Madge McMahon on 2 February 1926. Madge was the daughter of the Managing Director of the North Wales company. *St Tudno* was quickly fitted out and made her maiden voyage from Liverpool to North Wales on Saturday 22 May 1926. Captain Highton was her master at the time.

The Menai Bridge with a steamer about to pass under it. John Hughes was the well-loved pier master at Menai Bridge for over 54 years. It was said that he never failed to meet the Liverpool steamer at his pier. The Hughes family at Menai Bridge offered around a century of service to the steamers with John Hughes succeeding his father in 1908, who had in turn served since 1878. After his retirement, John was succeeded by his son Dennis, thereby carrying on a long and proud family tradition.

St Tudno off of the Orme. *St Tudno* was requisitioned at the start of the Second World War and spent most of the war as an accommodation vessel at Sheerness in Kent. She was returned to North Wales ready for the 1946 season. She made her first post-war sailing on 8 June 1946. (*J&C McCutcheon Collection*)

St Tudno leaving the beautiful shoreline to embark on a cruise during her heyday. *St Tudno* recommenced her post-war sailings and for a decade, it seemed as if nothing had changed from pre-war days. By the late 1950s, things had deteriorated and her advancing age meant that her life would be short-lived. (*J&C McCutcheon Collection*)

The Tudno at 2,326 tons was the largest steamer built for service on the North Wales coast. She could carry an amazing 2,493 passengers. The St Tudno had beautifully decorated lounges decorated in trianon grey as well as having a fine oak-panelled dining saloon. St Tudno also offered a wide range of bars, cafeterias and refreshment bars as well as three private cabins. The St Tudno could steam at up to 19 knots.

St Tudno departing from Llandudno Pier. On 5 July 1955, the Lord Mayor of Liverpool accompanied a large civic party from the Mersey to Llandudno aboard the St Tudno to commemorate the linking of Liverpool and Llandudno by regular steamer services. They were met by a civic party at Llandudno upon arrival. (J&C McCutcheon Collection)

Passengers enjoying a cruise on the *St Tudno* during the 1940s or 1950s. The twin-screw turbine steamer St Tudno initially met with little interest from regular Liverpool and North Wales passengers when she entered service in 1926. But, as time moved on, the attitude of regular passengers changed. The 318-feet-long St Tudno later became a favourite steamer as can be seen in this photograph. St Tudno had a very shallow draft despute her massive size. This was required in the more limited conditions of the Menai Strait. This had the effect of making her very uncomfortable in lively conditions. From 1946 onwards, St Tudno experiences many excellent seasons as men were demobbed after the Second World War. Passengers were very keen to re-live the happy North Wales pleasure steamer memories of pre-war days. This soon ended, though, as the motor car and a myriad of other attractions tempted the once-loyal passenger away. St Tudno galliantly soldiered on until her final sailing on 16 September 1962. She left the Mersey for the final time on 13 April 1963 and was broken up in Belgium in May 1963. (*J&C McCutcheon Collection*)

St Elian cruising off of Puffin Island. The second *St Elian* was built in 1919 by J. C. Tecklenborg of Wesermunde in Germany. On arrival in North Wales in 1922, she opened up long forgotten cruises to places such as Bardsey Island and a more frequent service was operated to Blackpool (North Pier) and Holyhead. Her versatility also meant that she operated round Anglesey cruises as well as half day cruises to Liverpool. Short sea cruises as well as cruises from Liverpool to Beaumaris were also offered. The *St Elian* wasn't an attractive steamer on the North Wales station and had few admirers. In addition, she had a terrible tendency to create seasickness. Tommy Roberts, who was piermaster at Llandudno for many years, swore that he'd seen passengers waiting on the pier to embark 'shoot the cat' merely by observing the antics of the *St Elian* alongside the pier! *St Elian* also had a nasty tendency to emit a horrendous mix of smuts and boiling water over passengers as they waited to disembark from the steamer. A safety valve pipe was behind the funnel and was positioned perfectly to dispense the evil discharge when pressure built up when going alongside a pier. As a result, claims from upset and dirty passengers were plentiful! (*J&C McCutcheon Collection*)

Captain Dop, the master of the *St Tudno*, posing aboard the steamer. In her later years, a cafeteria was positioned on the main deck. She also had a dining saloon. In addition, refreshment bars were located on the main deck forward and aft and on the upper deck. A shop was located on the upper deck and soft drinks and ices were located on the upper deck. Lastly, tea kiosks were located in the main lounge and on the promenade deck. (*J&C McCutcheon Collection*)

An aerial view of the popular *St Tudno*. She was quickly refitted after the war. This allowed the North Wales Company to make some changes internally. The main one was getting rid of first and second class accommodation and making the steamer a one class ship. The result of this was a new self-service cafeteria as well as a soft drinks bar. The number of private cabins was also reduced to three from five. There were two dining saloons on the lower deck that accommodated 20 or 73 passengers whereas the main dining saloon could accommodate 110 diners. There was also a barber shop. Loudspeakers were also installed in 1946 to broadcast music during cruises as well as to make regular announcements. *St Tudno* occasionally helped with rescues along the often lively North Wales coast. One was in 1949 when three men were rescued from the *Gypsey Meg*.

A steamer alongside Llandudno Pier. Llandudno Pier was built at a cost of £30,000 and took just over a year to construct. The pier opened on 1 August 1877. When built, it was 1,234ft in length and was initially made up of a traditional seaside promenade deck with a 60ft 'T' shaped pier head. The shore end of the pier took an additional six years to complete. Facilities included a grand pavilion, swimming pool and an extension that passed the Grand Hotel to the promenade. This work took the piers overall length to a very impressive 2,295ft.

Poster advertising sailings from Llandudno Pier during the 1954 season. In the mid to late 1950s, the pier master at Llandudno was Captain Tom Roberts. After his death in 1957, Mr Edwards replaced him in the role. (*J&C McCutcheon Collection*)

An impressive view of the *St Seiriol* reversing away from a North Wales pier. The 1950s saw a few changes to the schedule of the *St Seiriol* such as a cruise from Llandudno to the Skerries close to Holyhead. Her main work though was between Llandudno and the Isle of Man as well as regular half-day trips between Liverpool and Llandudno.

A Liverpool & North Wales Steamship Company deckhand poses cheerfully for the camera around the late 1950s. In 1955, a legendary figure of the North Wales Steamship Company, 'Chippy' Hughes died at the age of 82. 'Chippy' was the well-known carpenter of the *St Tudno* and had been employed by the North Wales Company since 1896. This must have been some kind of record. During the 1955 season, the return fare between Liverpool and Llandudno was 12s 6d, whilst the fare to Menai Bridge was fifteen shillings. Special cheaper fares were offered on Fridays in June and September for a reduced fare of ten shillings to Llandudno or to Menai Bridge. Season tickets cost £10. (*J&C McCutcheon Collection*)

St Seiriol during her later years of service along the North Wales coast.

St Seiriol alongside Menai Bridge Pier on 6 June 1957. *St Seiriol* was the smaller sister of the *St Tudno*. She was completed in 1931 and made her maiden voyage to North Wales on 23 May 1931. She was a particularly good sea boat which made her perfect for the Llandudno to Douglas service. These were regularly undertaken once or twice a week. She also helped with Liverpool to Llandudno services on a regular basis as well as offering short sea cruises from Llandudno as well as the Menai Bridge cruise. (*J&C McCutcheon Collection*)

St Seiriol cruising in the River Mersey on 4 September 1957. *St Seiriol* was 270 feet long with a width of 37 feet and had a service speed of 18.5 knots. Her bell had been transferred from the *St Elvies*. (*J&C McCutcheon Collection*)

St Seiriol approaching Llandudno Pier. Llandudno Pier, with a length of 2,295ft, is Wales's longest pier and the fifth longest in England and Wales. It is unusual as it has two separate entrances. The first is on the promenade at North Parade and the second is at the pier's original entrance in Happy Valley Road. The area between the two entrances houses the Grand Hotel. (*J&C McCutcheon Collection*)

St Seiriol is fully decked with flags on Coronation Day on 2 June 1953. *St Seiriol* would make the ever-popular crossing from Llandudno to Douglas on the Isle of Man during the 1950s in around 3.5 hours. Once ashore, passenger had around three hours ashore to give them time to travel on the horse-drawn tramway or they could visit a nearby beauty spot before buying their Manx kippers and catching the steamer back home to Llandudno. (*J&C McCutcheon Collection*)

Cambrian Prince tied up alongside Llandudno Pier in May 1956. The Liverpool & North Wales Company operated with virtually no competition. But, in this month, the small motor vessel named *Cambrian Prince* began running a programme of trips from Llandudno Pier. She was a former Fairmile 'B Class' vessel and had been built at Maldon in 1941. Before North Wales service, she was the motor yacht *Lepanto*. Her time at Llandudno was short-lived and she took up service at Torquay during the following year as *Kiloran II*. (*J&C McCutcheon Collection*)

St Seiriol at Menai Bridge Pier in September 1948. After the Second World War, *St Seiriol* was converted into a one class ship and a self-service cafeteria was created from the old second class dining saloon. A year later in 1947, *St Seiriol* finished her round Anglesey cruise and instead took up the Isle of Man service. She also took up a new and short-lived service from Llandudno to Holyhead. The post-war refit also included the fitting of modern radio and navigation systems which helped on the Irish Sea runs. On a more practical level, central heating was fitted in the various saloons for the comfort of passengers. (*J&C McCutcheon Collection*)

St Seiriol berthed at Holyhead on 1 September 1949. *St Seiriol*, like most other seaside pleasure steamers, saw service during the Second World War. She had just departed from Liverpool towards North Wales when war was declared on Sunday 3 May 1939. Now at war, the *St Seiriol* carried on to Llandudno to disembark her passengers before returning to Liverpool to await war duties. In her wartime grey, she bore the distinction of being the first ship to arrive at Dunkirk to embark troops from the beaches. During the evacuation, *St Seiriol* went to help the well-loved River Thames paddle steamer *Crested Eagle*, which was ablaze. She managed to rescue 150 badly burned troops from the stricken steamer. The part played at Dunkirk by the *St Seiriol* was later commemorated in a carved wooden plaque aboard the steamer. After Dunkirk, *St Seiriol* spent the rest of the war on less dramatic duties transporting troops on the Clyde and to Northern Ireland. *St Seiriol* made the first post-war cruise to the Menai Straits on Good Friday, 19 April 1946. Captain Dop, as well as several other crew that had been at Dunkirk, accompanied her on that day. Fairfield's had refitted the *St Seiriol* at the conclusion of hostilities. (*J&C McCutcheon Collection*)

North Wales bought together a wonderful mixture of impressive steamers, spectacular scenery and idyllic piers. This view shows the wonderful pier at Bangor with steamer passing during the post-war heyday. The *St Seiriol* could carry up to 1,556 passengers between Liverpool and North Wales but was slightly slower (half a knot) than the *St Tudno*. *St Seiriol* was particularly well-loved for her cruises to Douglas on the Isle of Man. She was driven by turbine engines and fuelled by oil. (*J&C McCutcheon Collection*)

The *St Silio* soon after her entry into service flying the Liverpool & North Wales Steamship Company house flag. *St Silio* was built for local cruises from Llandudno and initially, it was intended to name her *St Tysilio*. *St Silio* initiated several new cruises such as those to and from Amlwch as well as along the Manchester Ship Canal with a rail return. *St Silio* was 149 feet long with a speed of 12 knots. Her impressive promenade deck extended for 94 feet and she had a large lounge bar that was 44 feet long. *St Silio* made her maiden voyage to North Wales on Wednesday 27 May 1936. Just three brief years later, she was requisitioned for war service at Liverpool. She was later used to ferry troops on the Clyde.

A starboard view of the *St Trillo* cruising amidst the scenic splendour of North Wales and the Menai Straits during her heyday. The 1956 season opened on 19 May. The master of the *St Trillo* that season was Captain Owen Owens who was formerly Chief Officer of the *St Tudno*. (*J&C McCutcheon Collection*)

A fine looking *St Trillo* passing the impressive scenery close to Llandudno. The sailing from Menai Bridge to Llandudno was very attractive. On leaving Menai, passengers could admire the scenic splendours of Snowdonia or Anglesey on either side as well as the impressive suspension bridge. On the right, they would then pass Bangor with its fine pier and then view picturesque Beaumaris on the left-hand side. Leaving Menai, the steamer would pass Puffin Island. Numerous seagulls, puffins and seals were to be seen. The Great Orme would then be viewed with its lighthouse and caves before Llandudno Bay and the pier would come into view. (*J&C McCutcheon Collection*)

Lady Orme and the *St Silio* passing close to the Little Orme. *Lady Orme* had been built in 1888 as *Fusilier* for service at Oban. She operated her first North Wales season as *Lady Orme* in 1935. After a spell away in 1936, she returned to North Wales in 1937 before being withdrawn and later scrapped in 1939. (*J&C McCutcheon Collection*)

St Trillo approaching the landing stage at Liverpool later in her career. (*J&C McCutcheon Collection*)

St Silio on Liverpool landing stage along with the *Manxman* around 1936. *St Trillo* was originally built as the *St Silio* and was built by Fairfield's. She became the first diesel passenger ship of the Liverpool and North Wales service. After the Second World War, it was announced that *St Silio* would thereafter be known as *St Trillo*. The newly-named *St Trillo* undertook her first post-war sailing on Sunday 19 May 1946. Captain McNamee was master of the *St Silio* and later of the *St Trillo* from her entry into service until 1955, when he died. He was succeeded by Captain Owen Owens before he too died. *St Trillo* eventually became the last of the 'big three' steamers to survive before being withdrawn in the late 1960s. (*J&C McCutcheon Collection*)

Three

Decline & The Final Years

St Trillo at Caernarfon. The glory days of the Liverpool & North Wales Steamship Company were over by the late 1950s. By the early 1960s, the unthinkable had happened and the company had ceased trading. The great tradition was though carried on valiantly by P&A Campbell. (*J&C McCutcheon Collection*)

Passengers enjoying a cruise on the *St Trillo* at Caernarfon. *St Trillo* had one of the longest careers of any North Wales steamer. (*J&C McCutcheon Collection*)

St Trillo at Llandudno on 29 August 1957. The impressive Grand Hotel can be seen at the shoreward end of the pier. Steamer services in North Wales came to an early end on 9 September 1957 due to the damage of a propeller aboard the *St Seiriol*. (*J&C McCutcheon Collection*)

THE LIVERPOOL
& NORTH WALES
40 Chapel Street

STEAMSHIP
COMPANY LTD
Liverpool 3

SEASON 1952

★

SAILINGS FROM LLANDUDNO AND MENAI BRIDGE

★

Programme for cruises from Llandudno and Menai Bridge during the 1952 season. Regular morning cruises were offered towards the Great Orme and Puffin Island as well as return cruises to Liverpool with time ashore.

Llandudno Pier and posters advertising steamer services in 1953. Just a year later, in 1954, the Liverpool & North Wales Company announced that it would be operated on a non-profit making basis. Therefore any profits would be ploughed back into the business. Ultimately, this was unsuccessful and the company ceased trading less than a decade later. (*J&C McCutcheon Collection*)

A stewardess posing on the deck of the *St Seiriol* whilst off duty during the late 1950s. Stewards of the Liverpool & North Wales Company wore smarts liveries of royal blue and white jackets. The dining rooms could hold up to 200 passengers at one sitting. You could also relax in a deckchair. Special deck stewards served coffee, tea and a variety of special North Wales 'Hi-Hat' ice creams to those passengers that just wanted to relax and to enjoy the splendid passing scenery. (*J&C McCutcheon Collection*)

Daily Sailings to Llandudno and Menai Bridge from Liverpool

(SUBJECT TO ALTERATION WITHOUT NOTICE)

To Monday, 14th September, 1959

SUNDAYS INCLUDED

From PRINCES LANDING STAGE LIVERPOOL (weather and other circumstances permitting)

"ST. TUDNO" OR "ST. SEIRIOL"

Leaving		Each Day	Leaving		Each Day
LIVERPOOL		10.45 a.m.	MENAI BRIDGE ...		3.45 p.m.
LLANDUDNO	due	1.05 p.m.	LLANDUDNO	dep	5.15 p.m.
MENAI BRIDGE	due	2.40 p.m.	LIVERPOOL ...	due	7.40 p.m.

N.B.—Passengers for Bangor, Caernarvon, Beaumaris, and other Anglesey Resorts—Crosville Bus Service from Menai Bridge.
DAILY THROUGH BOOKINGS FROM ALL PRINCIPAL RAILWAY STATIONS.

FARES—One Class Only.	DAY EXCURSION	PERIOD	SINGLE
Liverpool and Llandudno	16/-	18/6	12/-
Liverpool and Menai Bridge	19/-	20/-	15/-

CHILDREN OVER 3 AND UNDER 14 YEARS HALF FARE.   ABOVE FARES INCLUDE 9d PIER TOLLS

DAY TRIP PARTIES, SINGLE OR RETURN, SPECIALLY CATERED FOR AT REDUCED FARES IF PREVIOUSLY ARRANGED.
CATERING—LUNCHEONS — TEAS   CAFETERIA, BUFFETS AND REFRESHMENT BARS.
PRIVATE CABINS may be booked in advance.

INTERCHANGE BOAT AND RAIL ARRANGEMENTS (BANK HOLIDAY EXCEPTED)

Passengers holding Day or Period Steamer Tickets have the option of returning by Rail on surrendering the Return Half Boat Tickets and on payment of the undermentioned rates, receiving single ticket to destination.

From **LLANDUDNO** (Day 8/6, Period 6/6)   From **MENAI BRIDGE OR BANGOR** (Day 10/4, Period 8/4)

Rail Passengers can return by steamer on payment of following supplementary charges at the Steamship Booking Offices, Pier Gates :   Llandudno 9/-, Menai Bridge 11/-

Tickets may be obtained alongside vessels or in advance at Travel Agencies or Company's Office.
Bicycles 3/6 single journey, including Pier Tolls.
Passengers allowed 1-cwt. Personal Luggage free of charge. Luggage in Advance for Llandudno or Menai Bridge, or vice versa, 5/6 per package, collected and delivered (Local Liverpool area, 6 3 per package).
All Tickets are issued, Passengers and Goods carried, subject to the Company's Conditions of Carriage as exhibited at the Company's Offices and on the Vessels.

For all further particulars apply Travel Agencies, or—

The Liverpool & North Wales S.S. Co. Ltd.

Souvenir Guide 1/-   ## 40 Chapel Street, Liverpool 3   Telephone: CENtral 1653-1654

FOR AFTERNOON SAILINGS SEE OTHER SIDE

4 (1)

Handbill advertising cruises from Liverpool to Llandudno and Menai Bridge during the summer of 1959 aboard the *St Tudno* or *St Seiriol*. The 1959 season saw a number of operational difficulties. *St Tudno* had trouble with her steering gear in late August and the *St Trillo* was taken off service in June with engine problems.

A deck scene aboard the *St Trillo* off of South Stack at Holyhead in 1961. The 1961 season was opened by the *St Seiriol* and the *St Trillo* in late May. The *St Trillo* sustained damage to her bow when she collided with the *St Seiriol* in the Menai Straits on Sunday 28 May. (*J&C McCutcheon Collection*)

Dennis Hughes - the Menai Bridge Pier master aboard the *St Trillo* off of Caernarfon Pier in the early 1960s. Those years saw many changes in personnel. On 31 March 1962, John Hughes, the popular pier master at Menai Bridge, retired after 54 years in post. He was succeeded the following day by his son Dennis, who is shown in this photograph. (*J&C McCutcheon Collection*)

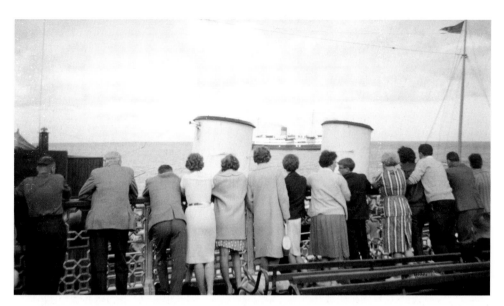

A familiar view of Llandudno Pier as passengers and the public watch to see the steamer arrive at the pier head. The *St Trillo* is at the landing stage and a Manx steamer is passing off of the pier. (*J&C McCutcheon Collection*)

St Trillo in choppy seas. By 1962 things had become choppy for the company as well. A scheme was launched to try and save the steamer after the Liverpool & North Wales company had gone into liquidation. An offer of £17,500 was made for the *St Trillo* but this was rejected by the liquidators of the company. (*J&C McCutcheon Collection*)

THE LIVERPOOL & NORTH WALES STEAMSHIP COMPANY LTD.
40 CHAPEL STREET, LIVERPOOL, 3.

TUESDAY, 2nd SEPTEMBER, 1958

SPECIAL EVENING CRUISE

By M.V. " ST. TRILLO "

Leaving LLANDUDNO PIER ..... 6-45 p.m.   Due Back ..... 8-0 p.m.

The arrival of the ship at Llandudno will be

TELEVISED

by B.B.C. "WISH YOU WERE HERE"

RETURN FARE **2/6**   Children over 3 and under 14, 1/3

ALL TICKETS ARE ISSUED, PASSENGERS AND GOODS CARRIED SUBJECT TO THE COMPANY'S
CONDITIONS OF CARRIAGE, AS EXHIBITED AT THE COMPANY'S OFFICES AND ON THE VESSELS

Llandudno Advertiser Ltd., Printers

By 1958, television was becoming one of the best ways to advertise your steamers and the areas that they covered. This handbill promoted a cruise by the *St Trillo* that was filmed as part of the popular television programme 'Wish You Were Here'.

THE LIVERPOOL & NORTH WALES STEAMSHIP COMPANY LTD.
40 CHAPEL STREET, LIVERPOOL, 3.

SATURDAY, 9th AUGUST, 1958

SPECIAL SAILINGS
Llandudno to Menai Bridge
On the occasion of visit by
H.M. The Queen to Anglesey

By " ST. TRILLO "

Leaving
LLANDUDNO PIER ..... 9-30 a.m.   *Due*
MENAI BRIDGE ..... 11-0 a.m.

By "ST. TUDNO"

Leaving
MENAI BRIDGE ..... 3-45 p.m.   *Due*
LLANDUDNO PIER ..... 5-0 p.m.

RETURN FARE **6/6**   Children over 3 and under 14, 3/3

ALL TICKETS ARE ISSUED, PASSENGERS AND GOODS CARRIED SUBJECT TO THE COMPANY'S
CONDITIONS OF CARRIAGE, AS EXHIBITED AT THE COMPANY'S OFFICES AND ON THE VESSELS

Llandudno Advertiser Ltd., Printers

Handbill advertising special sailings between Llandudno to Menai Bridge as part of the visit to Anglesey by HM The Queen in August 1958. The North Wales service was very much affected by the industrial changes in Lancashire and Yorkshire. In 1959, the number of passengers carried on the North Wales service dropped from that of 1958. This was blamed on the slump in the cotton industry.

An Officer and passengers posing on Llandudno Pier around 1962. Llandudno Pier was lucky in that it retained its Victorian and Edwardian buildings. The pier head was a fine and wide viewing point for those interested in North Wales steamers. Adjacent refreshment rooms provided fine facilities for those waiting for the steamers. (*J&C McCutcheon Collection*)

Two passengers hold up the name pennant of the *St Trillo* at Port Dinorwic. (*J&C McCutcheon Collection*)

Daily Sailings to Llandudno and Menai Bridge from Liverpool

(SUBJECT TO ALTERATION WITHOUT NOTICE)

Commencing Saturday, 4th June to Sunday, IIth September, 1960

SUNDAYS INCLUDED

From PRINCES LANDING STAGE LIVERPOOL (weather and other circumstances permitting)

"ST. TUDNO" OR "ST. SEIRIOL"

Leaving		Each Day		Leaving		Each Day	
LIVERPOOL	... ...	10.45 a.m.		MENAI BRIDGE	...	3.45 p.m.	
LLANDUDNO	due	1.05 p.m.		LLANDUDNO	dep	5.15 p.m.	
MENAI BRIDGE	due	2.40 p.m.		LIVERPOOL	...	7.40 p.m.	due

N.B.—Passengers for Bangor, Caernarvon, Beaumaris, and other Anglesey Resorts—Crosville Bus Service from Menai Bridge.
DAILY THROUGH BOOKINGS FROM ALL PRINCIPAL RAILWAY STATIONS.

FARES—One Class Only.

	DAY EXCURSION	PERIOD	SINGLE
Liverpool and Llandudno	16/-	18/6	12/-
Liverpool and Menai Bridge	19/-	20/-	15/-

CHILDREN OVER 3 AND UNDER 14 YEARS HALF FARE.   ABOVE FARES INCLUDE 9d PIER TOLLS

DAY TRIP PARTIES, SINGLE OR RETURN, SPECIALLY CATERED FOR AT REDUCED FARES IF PREVIOUSLY ARRANGED.
CATERING—LUNCHEONS — TEAS   CAFETERIA, BUFFETS AND REFRESHMENT BARS.
PRIVATE CABINS may be booked in advance.

INTERCHANGE BOAT AND RAIL ARRANGEMENTS (BANK HOLIDAY EXCEPTED)

Passengers holding Day or Period Steamer Tickets have the option of returning by Rail on surrendering the Return Half Boat Ticket and on payment of the undermentioned rates, receiving single ticket to destination.
From LLANDUDNO (Day 10/3, Period 7/9)   From MENAI BRIDGE OR BANGOR (Day 12/9, Period 11/9)
Rail Passengers can return by steamer on payment of following supplementary charges at the Steamship Booking Offices, Pier Gates : Llandudno 9/-, Menai Bridge 11/-

Tickets may be obtained alongside vessels or in advance at Travel Agencies or Company's Office.
Bicycles 3/6 single journey, including Pier Tolls.
Passengers allowed 1-cwt. Personal Luggage free of charge. Luggage in Advance for Llandudno or Menai Bridge, or vice versa, 5/6 per package, collected and delivered (Local Liverpool area, 6/3 per package).
All Tickets are issued, Passengers and Goods carried, subject to the Company's Conditions of Carriage as exhibited at the Company's Offices and on the Vessels.

For all further particulars apply to Travel Agencies, or—

The Liverpool & North Wales S.S. Co. Ltd.
40 Chapel Street, Liverpool 3

Souvenir Guide 1/-   Telephone: CENtral 1653-1654
(1)   **FOR AFTERNOON SAILINGS SEE OTHER SIDE**

The 1960 season was opened by the *St Tudno* on 4 June but the timetable was soon disrupted by the shipping strike in July. *St Seiriol* had trips cancelled on 9 and 10 July. Although things were resolved later in the month, problems re-occurred in mid-August.

St Tudno alongside a pier around 1957. In that year the *St Tudno* opened the North Wales service on 8 June. The season lasted until 16 September when the *St Seiriol* closed the season. (*J&C McCutcheon Collection*)

Advertisement for Hi-Hat ice creams. This ice cream was made in Wales and was supplied aboard the three steamers during the late 1950s. Many passengers that travelled on the North Wales steamers around 1960 will remember the many local foods that were supplied by local companies. In the days before distribution by a central wholesaler, a myriad of local bakers, butchers and other companies regularly delivered their goods freshly to the steamers. 'Foulds' baked the pies, 'Hansons' supplied the milk and 'Barker & Dobson' supplied chocolates and sweets.

enjoy a **Hi-Hat ICE CREAM**

On sale on board this ship and throughout North Wales

HI-HAT—WALES' OWN ICE CREAM

Timetable for Liverpool and North Wales services around 1960. In 1960, reduced price fares were offered for works and office outing from Llandudno if they had travelled from Liverpool or beyond by train or motor coach. A cruise was offered from Llandudno to Menai Bridge allowing an hour ashore to admire the famous suspension bridge before heading back to Llandudno by steamer. A special fare of eight shillings was offered for this cruise that took place during an afternoon.

Mr Jones, the Second Officer on the *St Seiriol*. He eventually became pier master at Llandudno in 1963. Close to Llandudno is the Marine Drive. This is a four-mile scenic drive round the base of the Great Orme from Llandudno's north shore to the west shore and shows spectacular views of the sea and mountains. It must also have given stunning views of the steamers in their heyday. (*J&C McCutcheon Collection*)

THE ST. TUDNO AT MENAI BRIDGE PIER.

M.109. A.W.H.

St Tudno at Menai Bridge Pier. The late 1950s and early 1960s witnessed a number of presentations to mark long service with the Liverpool & North Wales Company. In September 1960, aboard the *St Tudno* at Menai Bridge, Captain Robert Dop was presented with a gift to mark 41 years with the company. Regular passengers had collected £22 to buy him a table lamp to show their appreciation. His retirement came aboard the *St Tudno* a week later. Robert Dop was born in 1895 and spent his entire working life at sea. Forty of those years were with the Liverpool & North Wales Steamship Company. Perhaps his greatest moment was when he commanded the *St Seiriol* when she became the first ship to reach the beaches at Dunkirk in May 1940. After retirement, he served as pier master at Llandudno before taking full retirement in 1968 due to health problems.

St Trillo cruising in the Menai Straits. The straits vary in width from 1,300ft (from Fort Belan to Aber Menai Point) and 3,600ft (from Traeth Gwyllt to Caernarfon Castle). They narrow to around 1,600ft in the middle reaches between Port Dinorwic and Menai Bridge before broadening again. The different tides at the two ends of the straits cause strong currents to flow in both directions through the straits at different times thereby creating dangerous conditions. One of the most dangerous areas of the straits is known as the 'Swillies' between the two bridges. The entrance to the straits at the Caernarfon end is also hazardous because of the frequently shifting sand banks that make up Caernarfon bar.

63

Captain Kennedy posing with Mr Davies (in wing collar) aboard the *St Seiriol*. Mr Davies was retiring at that time after an incredible 51 years service. (*J&C McCutcheon Collection*)

An ever-popular cruise by steamers such as the *St Seiriol* was the scenic coastal cruise from the Llandudno. This took around two hours and passed the Great Orme with its caves and lighthouse before passing Puffin Island and then on towards Anglesey. The majestic sight of Snowdonia could be seen during part of the cruise. A good accompaniment to the scenic cruise was to have a meal aboard one of the steamers. The Liverpool & North Wales Steamship Company was proud of the high standard of catering offered aboard its vessels. During the late 1950s, luncheon could be purchased for eight shillings. This comprised of soup, then either grilled fish or roast joints with vegetables. A dessert of fruit and ice cream or cheese and biscuits completed the meal. High tea was also offered for seven shillings. This comprised of fried fish and chips or kippered herring with salad. A pot of tea along with bread, butter and preserves completed the meal. Cakes and pastries were served as extras.

NORTH WALES COAST

LA MARGUERITE

· OFFICIAL GUIDE ·
WITH MAP AND PHOTO VIEWS
· PRICE TWO PENCE ·

1. Official guide for North Wales services offered by the Liverpool & North Wales Steamship Company in 1923. This guide gave passengers a full description of the various routes offered by the company as well as advertisements for local hotels and shops. A number of photographs were also included to show the scenic splendours of the cruises offered.

2. *La Marguerite* was unique in having a sun deck which was reserved for first class passengers. This extended for two thirds of the ship's length. During the First World War, *La Marguerite* had a small deck house fitted as an anti-submarine post. After the war, it was placed on Llandudno Pier as the pier master's office. Before 1914, *La Marguerite*'s port and starboard lights were miniature lighthouses mounted on the paddle boxes. Passenger accommodation aboard *La Marguerite* was splendid. It contained what was reckoned to be the finest first class dining saloon ever known and had square port holes. It also included several first class private cabins, a beautiful first class drawing room, a fine smoking room and a large smoke room popularly known as the 'Black Hole'.

3. The Blackpool paddle steamer *Bickerstaffe* departing from Llandudno Pier around 1910. *Bickerstaffe* was named after Sir John Bickerstaffe, who was the entrepreneur behind the building of the famous Tower.

4. *La Marguerite* departing from Beaumaris Pier. 1904 saw the arrival of perhaps the largest and most magnificent steamer to grace the North Wales coast – *La Marguerite*. She was originally based on the River Thames, but her sheer size made her uneconomic. Rather surprisingly, she then found herself operating from Liverpool. She became successful and her North Wales career lasted until 1925. *La Marguerite* was known as the most popular excursion steamer in the United Kingdom at the time of her purchase by the Liverpool & North Wales Steamship Company. It was boasted at the time that she was unsinkable. She had eleven water-tight compartments and was licensed to carry up to 2,077 passengers on the North Wales run.

5. *St Tudno* arriving at Menai Bridge Pier. Menai Bridge is a small town situated on the Isle of Anglesey in North Wales. It overlooks the Menai Straits and lies close to the Menai Suspension Bridge. It's the third largest town on the island and occupies the area of the former parish of Llandysiliogogo. It's likely that a settlement has existed at the site of Menai Bridge since Roman times because this is the shortest crossing of the Menai Strait.

6. *Snowdon* had quite large bunkers and could carry around 80 tons, of which between 1 and 1.5 tons were used each hour. *Snowdon* had quite small paddle wheels and more often than not had a large awning placed over the promenade deck. She was one of those magical little steamers that became a firm favourite from the start and ran from Liverpool to Llandudno and Caernarfon as well as Blackpool, Holyhead and Douglas.

7. *St Elvies* cruising amid the splendid scenery of North Wales. Along with the other steamers, *St Elvies* had a black hull with white and gold paddle boxes and yellow funnels. Originally, these funnels were smaller and had black tops but later they were replaced by a taller set and painted all yellow in 1899. *St Elvies* undertook the main Liverpool to Menai Bridge run and round Anglesey. She also operated the North Wales to Isle of Man trip as well as trips to Blackpool. *St Elvies* was a well-liked and efficient steamer and could complete the Liverpool to Llandudno trip in an impressive 1.75 hours.

A Welsh Maid. Menai Bridge.

8. The Menai Straits is the most picturesque cruising area of North Wales. The scenic beauty is further enhanced by the two fine bridges that link the mainland to the Isle of Anglesey. The suspension bridge shown in this image was described as one of the most beautiful bridges in the world.

9. Pleasure steamer services between Liverpool and North Wales were relatively short-lived. They offered some of the finest coastal cruising in the UK, with the undoubted highlight being the Menai Straits, with the famous bridges. Majestic steamers such as *La Marguerite* and *Snowdon* gave way to the well-loved *St Tudno*, *St Seiriol* and *St Trillo* before the end of services during the 1960s.

10. The *St Tudno* was one of the most popular of all the North Wales pleasure steamers. Her cruises during the 1940s and 1950s are still remembered fondly today by countless former passengers.

11. *St Seiriol* made her last North Wales sailing from Llandudno to Douglas on Wednesday 6 September 1961. She was then withdrawn as she was more expensive to run than her fleetmates – her engines were in poor condition after her lengthy war service. She just didn't offer the flexibility required as the fleet faced harsh economic challenges in a shrinking market. Regular passengers were sad to see the withdrawal of this popular steamer.

12. The *St Trillo* during her Liverpool and North Wales heyday. The 1961 season saw the *St Trillo* change visually. Her usual and attractive black hull was replaced with one painted a light shade of green with dark green boot topping. This led to many of her regular enthusiasts naming it 'seasick green'! They also made many references to the rhyme 'The owl and the pussy cat put to sea in a beautiful pea green boat'! For some reason, her hull was repainted a more satisfying dark blue during the following season!

13. The *St Trillo* lasted into the late 1960s and provided wonderfully scenic cruises between Llandudno and Menai Bridge, and passing around the Great Orme and through Conway Bay. Towards the end of her career, she saw further service on the Bristol Channel in addition to North Wales.

14. Souvenir guide for the Liverpool & North Wales steamers, dating from around 1959. As well as describing the scenery to be seen during the cruise, it also advertised many well-known Liverpool stores and businesses such as Coopers Department Store.

15. *St Seiriol* passing through the Menai Straits, viewed from Penmon Point on Anglesey.

16. Passengers enjoying the *St Trillo* while cruising in the Menai Straits, close to the Britannia Tubular Bridge, on 24 July 1965. The bridge is 1,841 feet long. At this point, the Menai Straits are around 1,100 feet wide. Towards its centre is the Britannia rock, which can be seen at low water. (*J&C McCutcheon Collection*)

17. *St Trillo* cruising in the Menai Straits, close to the Britannia Tubular Bridge, on 24 July 1965. Menai Bridge marks the narrowest part of the Menai Straits. The bridge carries the London to Holyhead railway across the Menai Straits and opened in 1850. The bridge is supported by a central (Britannia) tower along with two side towers. (*J&C McCutcheon Collection*)

18. *St Trillo* cruising in the Menai Straits, close to the Britannia Tubular Bridge, on 24 July 1965. The nearby Menai Bridge Pier was opened by David Lloyd George MP on 10 September 1904. The tide through the Menai Straits rises around 20 feet and the tidal race is significant. The distance between the tubes of the bridge and the high water mark is around 101 feet. The stone used for constructing the bridge came from Penmon, close to Beaumaris. The bridge was designed by the famous railway engineer Robert Stephenson and cost £621,865 to construct. (*J&C McCutcheon Collection*)

19. Brochure advertising North Wales services from the Princes Stage at Liverpool by the *St Tudno* during the 1962 season. Its clear that the company were doing all that they could at the time to attract passengers with numerous inducements, including combined services with train or coach and catering facilities.

Above: 20. *St Trillo* in the Menai Straits on 24 September 1965. Officer Williams is on the bridge. The Menai Straits was described as 'a trip up the Rhine in miniature'. (*J&C McCutcheon Collection*)

Right: 21. Handbill advertising combined services by the White Funnel Fleet and Crosville Motor Services during the 1963 season. Services were advertised by motor coach from towns a 50-minute distance from Llandudno. A great many passengers were attracted from the holiday camps at Prestatyn, Rhyl (Winkups Camp) and Robin Hood Camp.

NEW

CROSVILLE
MOTOR SERVICES LIMITED

Coach and Steamer Service

PRESTATYN RHYL and ABERGELE

to

LLANDUDNO

Connecting with Sailings by
White Funnel Fleet Vessel "St. Trillo" to

MENAI BRIDGE

MONDAYS and THURSDAYS

also

Special "MUSIC AT SEA" Cruise from Llandudno on Sunday Evenings

Full Details Overleaf

Crosville Motor Services Ltd., Head Office, Crane Wharf, Chester.

22. *Balmoral* departing from Llandudno with the Little Orme in the distance. You can see in this image the former large, open car deck at the stern. This was a favourite sun trap for North Wales passengers. It was converted to a dining saloon when the *Balmoral* entered her preservation career in 1986. (*J&C McCutcheon Collection*)

23. *Balmoral* departing from Llandudno Pier during her 'White Funnel' years with the Little Orme in the distance. (*J&C McCutcheon Collection*)

24. *Waverley* about to pass the *Liverpool Pilot* on 19 April 1980.

25. *Balmoral* at Menai Bridge Pier in 1986. *Balmoral* has had a long and distinguished cruising career since entering service in 1949. Originally built for service between Southampton and Cowes on the Isle of Wight, she later operated on the Bristol Channel before becoming the highly successful consort to *Waverley* in 1986.

26. *Balmoral* cruising in glorious weather in the Menai Straits around 2005. The sheer beauty of the area can be fully appreciated in this photograph.

27. *Balmoral* cruising in the Menai Straits in 2005. *Balmoral* has changed a great deal since she first cruised in North Wales as part of the 'White Funnel Fleet'. In recent years, she has been re-engined and restored to her 1940s glory with the help of Heritage Lottery Fund grants. *Balmoral* is now the only regular large pleasure steamer to visit North Wales.

28. North Wales, and in particular the Menai Straits, offers some of the best coastal cruising in the UK. This view of the majestic Menai Suspension Bridge was taken from the well-loved *Balmoral* in 2005.

29. The *Balmoral* was once able to offer quite a notable season of cruises in North Wales during the late 1980s and 1990s. But with the loss of Blackpool North Pier, Morecombe Jetty and ongoing problems with Llandudno Pier, only Menai Pier and Caernarfon Pier are able to offer cruises, as seen here on the 2011 handbill.

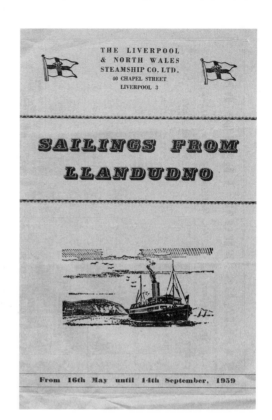

Programme advertising cruises from Llandudno during the 1959 season by the North Wales Company. Services changed very little during the 1950s.

It's always good to see photographs showing officers and crew working and relaxing aboard the steamers. Here the Bosun and Vic Howe (Second Officer) are smiling at the camera on the *St Tudno* in 1958. (*J&C McCutcheon Collection*)

A group of boy scouts waiting to join the steamer at Llandudno pier in about 1960. (*J&C McCutcheon Collection*)

Posters advertising steamer sailings at the gates of Llandudno Pier around 1960. By 1961, fares between Liverpool and Llandudno had increased to eighteen shillings for the return trip. The fare to Menai Bridge had risen to twenty one shillings and a season ticket had risen to £13. 16 June 1961 saw Captain W. Pritchard take command of the *St Tudno*. He was formerly her mate. On 13 August 1961, the *St Tudno* collided with a small boat at Menai Bridge whilst manoeuvring. The four occupants of the small boat either jumped or were thrown overboard by the incident and were luckily all saved without major injury. (*J&C McCutcheon Collection*)

Captain Robert Dop's brother posing cheerfully on the deck of the *St Tudno* in 1957. During the 1962 season, *St Tudno* operated the Liverpool to Llandudno and Menai Bridge service daily (except Fridays in June, July and September). The catering on the North Wales steamers during the 1962 season was reported to be of very good quality. (*J&C McCutcheon Collection*)

St Trillo alongside Caernarfon Pier. This image shows the small size of the *St Trillo*. Despite her size, *St Trillo* offered a good mix of open deck and enclosed passenger accommodation.

St Trillo approaching Llandudno on 30 July 1958. The *St Trillo* had three masters during her career with the North Wales Company. From 1936 to 1939 and from 1946 to 1955, her master was Captain John McNamee. He was succeeded by Captain Owen Owens who was master for just the 1956 season before he died. He was replaced by Captain Williams. (*J&C McCutcheon Collection*)

Enthusiasts stand next to *St Trillo*. *St Trillo* was lucky as she was the only one of the large steamers to survive. She continued to serve the North Wales coast for several more seasons during the 1960s. (*J&C McCutcheon Collection*)

THE LIVERPOOL & NORTH WALES STEAMSHIP CO. LTD.
40 CHAPEL STREET, LIVERPOOL, 3.

SPECIAL SAILINGS FROM

LLANDUDNO

SUN. 3rd JUNE to FRI. 8th JUNE, 1962
m.v. "ST. TRILLO"

A.M. 10.45	**MORNING CRUISE** Due back **12.15** p.m.	FARES INCLUDING PIER TOLLS **4/6**
P.M. 2·30	**MENAI BRIDGE** Due **4.0** p.m. (Return **4.30** p.m. due back **6.0** p.m.) ——— **Out by boat, return by Crosville bus.**	DAY RETURN **8/6** SINGLE **6/-** **10/-** Children 5/-

(Weather and other circumstances permitting)
(SUBJECT TO ALTERATION WITHOUT NOTICE)
Children over three and under fourteen years, half fare.
Buffet and Refreshment Bar on board.
Tickets at Company's Office, Pier Gates, Llandudno or on board the Vessel.
All tickets are issued, passengers and goods carried, subject to the Company's
conditions of carriage as exhibited at the Company's Offices and on the vessels.
7 (1)

Handbill advertising special sailings from Llandudno aboard the *St Trillo* in June 1962. The journey to Menai Bridge was 16 nautical miles in length. The upper deck of the *St Trillo* ran the whole length of the ship. *St Trillo* was the first diesel-engined passenger ship to operate on the North Wales service.

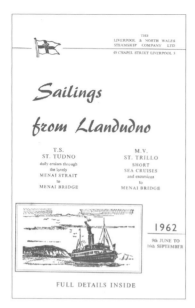

1962 was the final year for the Liverpool & North Wales Steamship Company. The faithful and well-loved *St Tudno* and the *St Trillo* made their final sailings for the Liverpool & North Wales Company on Sunday 16 September 1962 – the final day of the season as shown on this handbill. *St Seiriol* was laid up in 1962 because she was 'not up to requirements and needed a great deal spending on her'. She was sold for £12,000 less expenses. *St Seiriol* was sold to Belgium shipbreakers in October 1962. She departed for the breakers at Ghent on 13 November 1962, towed by the tug *Ebro*.

The large turbine steamers or motor ships were synonymous with Liverpool and North Wales services. On 2 November 1962, a notice of a meeting for creditors of the Liverpool & North Wales Company was announced for the 19 November. A further announcement stated that the Isle of Man Steam Packet Company would take up the Liverpool to Llandudno sailings but not the sailings as far as Menai Bridge. On 9 November 1962, a writ of attachment was fastened to the mast of the *St Tudno* by solicitors acting on behalf of clients run down by the steamer in the August of that year. This resulted in a judgment against the Liverpool & North Wales Company for £575 12s 6d on 11 November. At the meeting of creditors on 19 November, liabilities were admitted to be £91,918 with assets estimated at £83,350. This showed a deficiency of around £8,500. The main creditor was the bank (£59,000) with other main amounts being oil (£4,472) and Cammell Laird (£3,300). The trading loss for 1962 amounted to around £30,000. The once proud Liverpool & North Wales Company therefore went into voluntary liquidation. A sad event was later marked on 11 September 1963 when the former offices of the Liverpool & North Wales Company at 40 Chapel Street Liverpool were sold for £7,200. A chapter had closed on Liverpool and North Wales sailings. (*J&C McCutcheon Collection*)

Four

The Campbell Years &
Revival of Services

From the 1960s onwards, Liverpool and North Wales witnessed a number of pleasure steamer operators keen to rekindle happy memories of the Liverpool & North Wales Steamship Company. One of the most famous of these has been the regular visits of the well-loved *Balmoral* seen here on a cruise in 2005.

St Trillo decked with flags on her first trip to Llandudno under ownership of P&A Campbell on 1 June 1963.

P&A Campbell's booking office advertising sailings in the Menai Straits on the first day of operations under their control on 1 June 1963.

Sidney Clifton Smith Cox (second from right) with guests at Menai Bridge Pier on the final day of the 1963 season. This was the first season under management by P&A Campbell.

A view of the deck of the *St Trillo* as she approached Caernarfon at 5.30 p.m. on Saturday 24 July 1965. The following year saw no fare increases for the *St Trillo* in North Wales. Her timetable was more or less identical to the 1965 season with four round Anglesey cruises. She also acted as a tender to the liner *Gripsholm* in early May. (*J&C McCutcheon Collection*)

Passengers disembarking from the *St Trillo* at Caernarfon on Saturday 7 August 1965. (*J&C McCutcheon Collection*)

St Trillo loading passengers at Caernarfon during the mid-1960s. (*J&C McCutcheon Collection*)

ROAD AND SEA CRUISE

THE ONLY TRIP OF ITS KIND ON THE NORTH WALES COAST

OUT BY ROAD

To Menai Bridge or Llandudno on the regular services operated by Crosville via Conway, Penmaenmawr, Llanfairfechan and Bangor.

BACK BY STEAMER

Via the Menai Strait.

Apart from the magnificent scenery, the trip is a splendid tonic, the benefits of which will be enjoyed for days afterwards.

1st JULY to 12th SEPTEMBER, 1963

FARES · ADULT **10/-** RETURN · CHILD **5/-** RETURN
(Available day of issue only)

Special Return Fare of 8/6 (Child 4/6) on Last Sailing each Day from Llandudno or Menai Bridge.

TIME TABLE

STEAMER

		MTh a.m.	MTWF p.m.	Th p.m.	MTF p.m.	Th p.m.
LLANDUDNO (Pier)	Dep.	10 30	2 30	4 45	6 15	8 15
MENAI BRIDGE (Pier)	Arr.	12 0	4 0	6 15	7 45	9 45

ROAD

		p.m.	p.m.	p.m.	p.m.
MENAI BRIDGE (Post Office)	Dep.	12 17	4 32	6 37	7 56
BANGOR (Town Clock)	Arr.	12 29	4 44	6 49	8 8
BANGOR (Town Clock)	Dep.	12 33	4 53	7 5	8 33
LLANDUDNO (Clonmel Street)	Arr.	1 43	6 3	8 18	9 43

ROAD

		NSu a.m.	a.m.	p.m.	p.m.
LLANDUDNO (Clonmel Street)	Dep.	7 10	10 30	2 30	4 30
BANGOR (Town Clock)	Arr.	8 20	11 40	3 40	5 40
BANGOR (Town Clock)	Dep.	8 30	11 45	4 0	5 45
MENAI BRIDGE (Post Office)	Arr.	8 42	11 57	4 11	5 57

STEAMER

		SuTWF a.m.	MTh p.m.	MTWF p.m.	Th p.m.
MENAI BRIDGE (Pier)	Dep.	9 0	12 15	4 30	6 30
LLANDUDNO (Pier)	Arr.	10 30	1 45	6 0	8 0

MTh—Monday and Thursday   Th—Thursday   NSu—Not Sunday
MTWF—Monday, Tuesday, Wednesday and Friday.   SuTWF—Sunday, Tuesday, Wednesday and Friday.   MTF—Monday, Tuesday and Friday.

The road timings shown offer the most suitable connection, but passengers may trave on any other journey to suit their convenience. There is a 20 min. frequency between Llandudno and Menai Bridge, Last Bus from Llandudno 8-50 p.m. — Last Bus from Menai Bridge 9-51 p.m.

New operator – new look handbill! 13 May 1963 was a sad day in the North Wales Company's history when a poignant sale of fittings from *St Tudno* and *St Seiriol* was held in Liverpool. Many enthusiasts gathered to buy a memento of their favourite steamers. The following day saw the contents of the Head Office at 40 Chapel Street sold. These sales marked the end of an era as the heritage accumulated in the ships and company offices was dispersed. Enthusiasts went away with a souvenir to accompany the many happy memories of the steamers and the people that made them steam.

St Trillo passing through the 'Swillies' in the Menai Straits on Saturday 17 July 1965. (*J&C McCutcheon Collection*)

St Trillo arriving at Llandudno Pier during the 1960s. (*J&C McCutcheon Collection*)

White Funnel Fleet

Every SUNDAY Evening

MAY 28th — SEPTEMBER 10th
Except June 4th and 18th and September 3rd

"MUSIC AT SEA"

aboard the St. Trillo

"The most cheerful way to spend Sunday evening"

Live Music
in the
Modern Manner

FULLY LICENSED BAR AND BUFFET ABOARD

Leave Llandudno Pier 7.30 p.m., back at 9.0 p.m.
FARE 6/- (children half-price)

(Tickets obtainable at the Company Office, Llandudno Pier Gates;
or on board the vessel)

CONDITIONS OF CARRIAGE. All tickets are issued and passengers carried subject to the Company's conditions of carriage as exhibited on Piers, at the Company's Offices, Agencies, and on the St. Trillo. Sailings are subject to weather and circumstances.

For further particulars and details of daily sailings please apply to any agent of the Company or

P. & A. CAMPBELL LTD., LLANDUDNO PIER GATES
Telephone 76837

(T. & W. G. 1620)

Handbill for Sunday evening 'Music at Sea' cruises by the *St Trillo*. It was billed as 'The most cheerful way to spend Sunday evening'!

St Trillo in the Swillies with Captain Williams on the Bridge in 1964. *St Trillo* had been sold in February 1963 for further service on the Bristol Channel and was to be managed by P&A Campbell. Captain Williams remained in command and some time later it was announced that the *St Trillo* would take up the Llandudno to Menai Bridge route. (*J&C McCutcheon Collection*)

Patrick Murrell and Mr Bailey aboard the *St Trillo* close to the Tubular Bridge in the Menai Straits on Saturday 8 August 1964. (*J&C McCutcheon Collection*)

Mr Eaton Williams and fellow passengers pose aboard the *St Trillo* at Caernarfon on Saturday 27 June 1964. (*J&C McCutcheon Collection*)

A deck view of *St Trillo* in the Swillies during the 1964 season. (*J&C McCutcheon Collection*)

St Trillo off of the Little Orme in 1964. It was reported that Liverpool to Llandudno services during 1964 were not terribly successful although the Llandudno to Douglas route fared better. (*J&C McCutcheon Collection*)

St Trillo arriving at Llandudno Pier in 1964. *St Trillo* was advertised for sale in mid-January 1963 soon after a group of Anglesey businessmen and the Llandudno Pier Company had tried to re-open a service between Llandudno and the Menai Straits. They stated that if the *St Trillo* couldn't be purchased, then a smaller vessel would be built for service in 1964. A shipbuilding company in Anglesey had already quoted for this. A retired businessman from Liverpool also tried to acquire the *St Trillo* for further service in the River Mersey as well as twice weekly trips to North Wales. Richard Thomas and William Thomas made their final bid of £17,500 (increased from £15,000) but this was exceeded by Townsend Ferries on behalf of P&A Campbell. *St Trillo* then went to Birkenhead for inspection and she gained the familiar Campbell livery. (*J&C McCutcheon Collection*)

St Trillo with the Little Orme in the distance in 1964. *St Trillo* entered the 1965 season after a winter overhaul and was promised to be much faster and 'minus her smoke screen'. She started her North Wales schedule on 6 May on charter as tender to the liner *Kungsholm* at Llandudno. A few days later, she was chartered by the Mersey Docks & Harbour Board before starting the main North Wales season from Llandudno on 24 May. (*J&C McCutcheon Collection*)

Poster advertising sailings by the *St Trillo* from Caernarfon in 1964. (*J&C McCutcheon Collection*)

St Trillo about to go under the Britannia Tubular Bridge on Saturday 25 July 1965. (*J&C McCutcheon Collection*)

A near empty deck scene in the Menai Straits around 1967. (*J&C McCutcheon Collection*)

RAIL and SEA

EXCURSIONS

in conjunction with P. & A. Campbell, Ltd.

WHITE FUNNEL FLEET

LLANDUDNO — MENAI BRIDGE SERVICE

Mondays to Fridays 17th June to 6th September 1963

FROM

Abergele	**Llanfairfechan**
Bangor	**Penmaenmawr**
Colwyn Bay	**Prestatyn**
Llandudno Junction	**Rhyl**

The vessel operating the services shown in this leaflet, "St. Trillo," is equipped for the service of light refreshments and is fully licensed. Both bars and buffets are open throughout the voyage. .

Children under three years of age, free; three years and under fourteen, half fares
Fractions of –/1d. reckoned as –/1d.)

LONDON
MIDLAND
REGION

TICKETS CAN BE OBTAINED IN ADVANCE AT
STATIONS AND OFFICIAL RAILWAY AGENTS

Further information will be supplied on application to Stations,
Official Railway Agents, or to W. BROWNLEE, District Manager,
Chester. Telephone Chester 24680 (Ext. 28).

P&A Campbell brought a new focus to advertising cruises in North Wales. Rail and steamer services were heavily promoted. Passengers travelling by the morning sailing on Mondays and Thursdays were able to take a walk to Llanfairpwllgwyngyl lgogerychwyrndrobwilliantysiliogogogoch – the longest destination in the UK! Here passengers were able to purchase the world's largest platform ticket for three pence.

A splendid shot of *St Trillo* at Liverpool. Weather is the main enemy of pleasure steamers and also the easiest way to explain a poor passenger season. Despite us thinking of summers of the past as always being bathed in bright summer sun, it appears that the summer of 1962 was described as being 'possibly the worst one in memory'. The 1963 season was stated to be even worse! It was difficult therefore for the already 'challenged' North Wales services to survive and prosper.

Regular passengers pose alongside *St Trillo* at Llandudno on 14 May 1966. Note the destination board for Llandudno placed on the side of the steamer. (*J&C McCutcheon Collection*)

On 6 May 1964 the Mersey ferry *Royal Daffodil* acted as a tender to the liner *Kungsholm*, anchored off of Llandudno. Captain Dop of the *St Tudno* was aboard. It was later announced that he had been appointed pier master at Llandudno. In this photograph, the famous Captain Dop can be seen handling the rope at Llandudno Pier at 2.00pm on Thursday 17 June 1965. (*J&C McCutcheon Collection*)

During the 1963 season the 'St Trillo Trio' provided 'music in the modern manner' for passengers aboard the *St Trillo* who wanted a pleasant one and a half hour Sunday evening cruise from Llandudno. The summer of 1963 witnessed horrendous weather and this greatly affected the profits of P&A Campbell. Despite losses, the Chairman stated that the foray into North Wales had been profitable for the company.

St Trillo alongside Caernarfon Pier on 27 July 1963. *St Trillo* inaugurated the P&A Campbell service from Llandudno on this day when she cruised to Caernarfon. This was the first time that this had been undertaken for many years. A fortnight later she made the first round Anglesey cruise since 1947.

A deckhand poses with his rope and looks towards the camera as *St Trillo* makes her approach to Caernarfon during one of her cruises around Anglesey. (*J&C McCutcheon Collection*)

1967 saw a fairly successful season for the *St Trillo* in North Wales. New ventures to New Brighton and Holyhead proved to be unsuccessful but the round Anglesey trips met with some success. Bad weather yet again affected cruising in North Wales during the summer of 1967 and many sailings were cancelled or curtailed because of this.

P&A Campbell were very good at advertising their services. They even had a Mini van made to advertise their services as well as being used to assist the steamers. The van is shown at Llandudno in May 1964. P&A Campbell were fortunate in that by the early to mid-1960s they were offering a wide selection of cruises and inclusive trips along with Crosville Motor Services and British Railways. This enabled them to gain maximum publicity for their cruises spread across the North West, North Wales and beyond. The publicity material produced by BR and Crosville supplemented the already good publicity produced by P&A Campbell.

Crew relaxing aboard the *St Trillo* in Douglas harbour on Saturday 6 May 1967.

St Trillo about to leave empty from Liverpool to Birkenhead in May 1966. (*J&C McCutcheon Collection*)

St Trillo tied up at Port Dinorwic on 14 March 1965. (*J&C McCutcheon Collection*)

St Trillo alongside Liverpool with the *Mona's Isle* alongside her on Saturday 14 May 1966. The previous season of 1965 season was pretty mixed for the Isle of Man Steam Packet Company on their North Wales services. The Llandudno to Douglas service had been very popular whereas passenger numbers on the Liverpool to Llandudno trips were pretty poor. (*J&C McCutcheon Collection*)

St Trillo close to the Mersey tunnel shaft in May 1966. The relative success of the *St Trillo* by P&A Campbell was, to a large extent, due to the company not having to cope with the heavy running costs of the *St Tudno* and *St Seiriol*. *St Trillo* was well suited to her North Wales role in the mid-1960s. (*J&C McCutcheon Collection*)

St Trillo at Liverpool with the Liver Building in the distance on Saturday 14 May 1966. (*J&C McCutcheon Collection*)

St Trillo at Port Dinorwic in 1966. Port Dinorwic and its marina are situated in the Menai Straits between Bangor and Caernarfon. Excellent winter lay-up and dry dock facilities were available at Port Dinorwic for the steamers. (*J&C McCutcheon Collection*)

St Trillo waiting ready to embark passengers on a cruise from Liverpool on 15 May 1966. By 1967, P&A Campbell were expanding coach services to connect with the St Trillo. Coaches travelled from locations such as Aberystwyth and Borth. The company also added limited new calls to destinations such as Holyhead and New Brighton. (*J&C McCutcheon Collection*)

St Trillo alongside Caernarfon on Wednesday 28 June 1967. The first call at Victoria Wharf, Caernarfon, was made on 27 July 1963. This was the first call since before the Second World War. (*J&C McCutcheon Collection*)

St Trillo waiting ready to embark passengers on a cruise from Liverpool on 15 May 1966. By 1967, P&A Campbell were expanding coach services to connect with the St Trillo. Coaches travelled from locations such as Aberystwyth and Borth. The company also added limited new calls to destinations such as Holyhead and New Brighton. (*J&C McCutcheon Collection*)

St Trillo at Port Dinorwic in 1966. You can appreciate the long deck saloon in this photograph. It extended to almost the full length of the steamer and provided excellent cover in poor weather. Equally good was the open top deck that was fabulous when weather was fine and sunny. (*J&C McCutcheon Collection*)

Poster advertising cruises to view the liner *Kungsholm* from Llandudno by the *St Trillo*. The 1960s saw the North Wales pleasure steamers act as a tender to the liner *Kungsholm* off Llandudno. Passengers were bought ashore and joined motor coaches for tours of places such as Bodnant, Conway and Llanberis. On 6 May 1968, *St Trillo* had one of her propellers fouled when a nylon rope from the *Kungsholm* wrapped itself round the screw. Over 400 elderly American tourists, many of whom were in poor health, spent a good many hours being tossed about in uncomfortable conditions. Initially, they were to be transferred across the bows to waiting lifeboats but the offer of a tow from the trawler *Kilravock* was accepted. The American passengers were put up for the night in Llandudno hotels and were transferred the following day to Liverpool to rejoin the *Kungsholm*. Their time on the *St Trillo* and at Llandudno must have been a memorable experience for them. At the time, *St Trillo* was commanded by Captain Owen Williams and Captain Power. (*J&C McCutcheon Collection*)

Queen of the Isles was chartered by P&A Campbell to take up North Wales services in late August and September 1967. *Queen of the Isles* is seen here arriving at the wide landing stage of Llandudno pier on 27 September 1967. (*J&C McCutcheon Collection*)

The bridge of the *Queen of the Isles* at Llandudno Pier on 27 September 1967. The expansion of services by P&A Campbell in North Wales during 1967, in the absence of the Isle of Man steamers, wasn't a great a success as was originally anticipated. *St Trillo* did, though, manage some good round-Anglesey cruises but the new ventures at New Brighton and Holyhead weren't popular with the public. *Queen of the Isles* had taken over North Wales service during most of September while the *St Trillo* was in service on the Bristol Channel. *St Trillo* later returned to North Wales to conclude services on 1 October. (*J&C McCutcheon Collection*)

Queen of the Isles during her first cruise round Anglesey on 8 September 1967. With the arrival of the *Queen of the Isles* in North Wales, 1960s bad luck hit yet again when some cruises had to be cancelled due to incredibly low water in the Menai Straits and the greater draught of the *Queen of the Isles*, which made navigation difficult or impossible. (*J&C McCutcheon Collection*)

Queen of the Isles alongside Llandudno Pier at 4.15 p.m. on 27 September 1967. Around a year after this photograph was taken, some £35,000 was spent (mainly by the Isle of Man Steam Packet Company) on the landing stage at Llandudno Pier. Even with this expenditure things didn't run well and instead of work being finished in May, ready for the season, work wasn't completed until September. (*J&C McCutcheon Collection*)

Queen of the Isles waits at a pier ready to embark her passengers. *Queen of the Isles* had a much smaller passenger capacity than the *St Trillo* and could only carry around 300 passengers. This obviously caused problems on busy sunny days when many passengers had to be turned away. (*J&C McCutcheon Collection*)

A view from the bow as the *Queen of the Isles* approaches the magnificent Llandudno Pier. The landing stage was constructed in 1891 and was further strengthened at the start of the twentieth century before further rebuilding in 1935. (*J&C McCutcheon Collection*)

Passengers aboard the *Queen of the Isles* enjoying their North Wales cruise. *Queen of the Isles* undertook cruises in North Wales during 1968. One of these was a direct run between Liverpool and Menai Bridge on 8 May. This marked the first such sailing since the cessation of services by the Liverpool & North Wales Steamship Company earlier in the decade. (*J&C McCutcheon Collection*)

Queen of the Isles alongside Llandudno Pier. You can appreciate the fine landing facilities at Llandudno from this photograph. (*J&C McCutcheon Collection*)

Queen of the Isles embarking her passengers at Llandudno Pier. The *Queen of the Isles* was chartered for North Wales service from 4 September 1967. This view shows the attractive deck of the vessel in fine weather. Her white hull was also an attractive feature. (*J&C McCutcheon Collection*)

A view from *Queen of the Isles* along the North Wales coast on 7 September 1967. *Queen of the Isles* was built by Charles Hill of Bristol. (*J&C McCutcheon Collection*)

P&A Campbell's *Queen of the Isles* in 1968. The cessation of sailings in North Wales followed poor financial results. The season had started late as Llandudno Pier hadn't been repaired on time. Sailings were therefore badly affected. Engine trouble on the *St Trillo* was the final nail in the coffin and she lost an incredible eighteen peak season days. Despite P&A Campbell providing a good and varied service, the disastrous loss of a pier and mechanical problems caused maximum disruption. (*J&C McCutcheon Collection*)

Queen of the Isles during her first cruise round Anglesey on 8 September 1967. Passengers were able to appreciate the scenic beauty of Anglesey in fine late summer weather. (*J&C McCutcheon Collection*)

Queen of the Isles at Douglas on the Isle of Man. *Queen of the Isles* was a great deal faster than the *St Trillo*. She was also a far better sea-going boat, making the trips between Llandudno and Douglas a great deal more comfortable for passengers.

WHITE FUNNEL FLEET

Sailings from

LIVERPOOL

(Princes Landing Stage)

by the Motor Vessel "QUEEN OF THE ISLES"

The Queen of the Isles is a vessel of 515 tons, is licensed by the Board of Trade to carry 300 passengers anywhere in the United Kingdom. The vessel has ample covered accommodation, and delightful open decks. Light refreshment can be obtained and the fully licensed bar remains open throughout the voyage.

Saturdays July 27th & August 10th & 31st

Grand Afternoon Cruise along the Coast, passing the Bar Lightship and across Liverpool Bay towards Blackpool.
Leave Liverpool at 3.15 p.m. back 5.0 p.m.

Fare 8/6d. Children 3—14 Half Price.

Single trip to Llandudno and Menai Bridge.
Leave Liverpool 5.15 p.m. due Llandudno 8.0 p.m. Menai Bridge 9.30 p.m.
Fares Llandudno 22/6 Menai Bridge 25/- (Children 3—14 half price).

Note: The Queen of the Isles leaves Menai Bridge 10.20 a.m. Llandudno 12 noon for Liverpool (due 2.45 p.m.).

FOR GENERAL INFORMATION, AND CONDITIONS OF CARRIAGE—PLEASE SEE OVERLEAF

Handbill for cruises by the *Queen of the Isles* from the Princes Landing Stage at Liverpool on Saturdays in July and August 1968. These short cruises took passengers towards Blackpool as well as providing links with Llandudno and Menai Bridge. The passenger facilities aboard the *Queen of the Isles* were somewhat limited. It did, though, have a buffet and a bar.

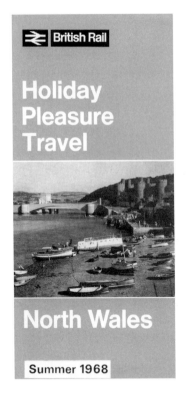

Brochure produced by British Rail advertising a wide range of attractive train and pleasure steamer services in North Wales during the 1968 season. As well as steamer services between Llandudno and Menai Bridge, other attractions could be linked in with a short break or day trip. These included trips on the Festiniog narrow guage railway and the Snowdon mountain railway.

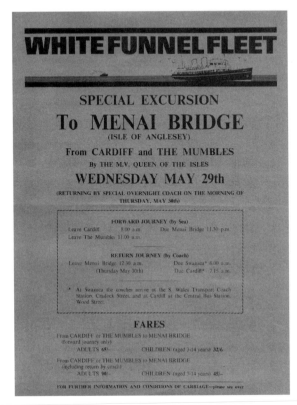

Handbill for the start of season cruise from Cardiff to Menai Bridge on Wednesday 29 May 1968. This attractive cruise departed from Cardiff by the Queen of the Isles. Passengers then cruised along the entire west coast of Wales to arrive at Menai Bridge some fifteen and a half hours later. Passengers then joined a coach straight away for the less exciting seven-hour trip back to South Wales. They arrived at Cardiff on the following morning. The fare was £4.50 for adults.

After leaving North Wales, *Queen of the Isles* saw further service in Tonga as *Olovaha*, as *Gulf Explorer* in New Zealand and as *Queen of the Isles* at the Great Barrier Reef before becoming *Western Queen* in the Solomon Islands. *Queen of the Isles* had a very exotic career after her time in North Wales!

A view in the Menai Straits in the mid-1960s. In 1965 the time of the sailing on Sundays between Liverpool and Llandudno moved to 11.15 a.m. from 10.45 a.m. This allowed passengers more time to get to the pier head on the day of the week when train and bus services were limited. During this year, the Isle of Man Steam Packet Company also introduced two sailings between Llandudno and Douglas on 1 and 8 August. It was announced that passenger figures had increased on this service during the two years previous to 1965. During the 1965 season, twenty-two sailings were scheduled between Llandudno and Douglas.

Queen of the Isles at Liverpool with the *Manx Maid* astern of her in early May 1968. The *Queen of the Isles* only operated from Liverpool and North Wales for a short time but she gained a good reputation for her sea-going capabilities. (*J&C McCutcheon Collection*)

A large crowd gather on Menai Bridge Pier to join a steamer. The P&A Campbell service in North Wales was finally closed in 1969 because of poor financial results. (*J&C McCutcheon Collection*)

Queen of the Isles alongside Llandudno Pier at 4.30 p.m. on 6 September 1967. During 1967 she had been chartered to the Mersey Docks & Harbour Board to take schoolchildren on cruises to view the facilities and workings of the docks.

St Trillo became the final survivor of the once-strong North Wales Steamship Company fleet. She took on a new lease of life during the 1960s after the two other large steamers were withdrawn. *St Trillo* spent her final season in North Wales in 1969. At the end of the season she was laid up at Barry. She finally arrived at the scrapyard in 1975. It was the end of an era for the Liverpool and North Wales steamers. (*J&C McCutcheon Collection*)

Snaefell alongside Llandudno Pier. *Snaefell* operated the first Isle of Man Steam Packet service to Llandudno on 17 May 1964 under Captain Craine. Sailings were operated on Sundays, Tuesday and Thursday throughout most of the season.

The Isle of Man Steam Packet continued to undertake sailings from Llandudno long after other services had ceased. With the withdrawal from service of the *St Trillo*, the Steam Packet Company offered two-hour coastal cruises in addition to the Liverpool to Llandudno service. By the mid-1970s, the Llandudno to Douglas service operated for around five days a week. These could carry up to 2,000 passengers. The North Wales coastal cruises were attracting up to 1,450 passengers at this time. The North Wales service was therefore profitable for the Steam Packet Company. By 1980, the *Mona's Isle* was withdrawn and this marked the end of the Liverpool to Llandudno service. The Douglas service did, though, soldier on with the *Manxman* until she was sold in 1982.

King Orry arriving at Llandudno Pier in July 1974. The Isle of Man Steam Packet Company dominated the Llandudno to Isle of Man service after 1962 and the first cruise operated from the pier was on 26 June, by the *Manxman*. It was later announced that a total of over 18,000 passengers had been conveyed by the Isle of Man Steam Packet Company during the first full season in 1963. By 1978, the Isle of Man Steam Packet Company was still operating cruises from Liverpool to Llandudno on three days of the week. To increase passenger usage they sold special books of vouchers that offered a reduced fare. After arrival at Llandudno, a special two-hour cruise was offered to Puffin Island, Red Wharf Bay and towards Point Lynas.

St Trillo about to load her passengers while alongside Caernarfon Pier in 1966. By the 1970s, regular steamer trips in North Wales were almost over. (*J&C McCutcheon Collection*)

Balmoral was to become a provider of pleasure steamer cruises in North Wales during the 1970s, when she operated as part of the 'White Funnel Fleet'. She came to the North Wales after over twenty years on the Solent operating a regular service for Red Funnel. During the 1970s, she often operated as a tender to the liner *Kungsholm*.

Deck views of the
Balmoral taken
during a cruise in
the Menai Straits
in 1971. (*J&C
McCutcheon
Collection*)

Deck views of the *Balmoral* taken during a cruise in the Menai Straits in 1971. *Balmoral* has changed quite a bit since this time due to the loss of her old car deck and the addition of new lifesaving apparatus. (*J&C McCutcheon Collection*)

The bow of the *Queen of the Isles* seen from the deck of the *Balmoral* at Douglas on the Isle of Man. (*J&C McCutcheon Collection*)

WHITE FUNNEL FLEET

Special Sailing from
Menai Bridge Pier

Sunday, May 16th, 1971

Grand Afternoon Cruise

through the Menai Strait passing
Puffin Island thence along the
Anglesey Coast through Red Wharf
Bay and towards Port Lynas.

Leave Menai Bridge 2.30 p.m. back about 5.45 p.m.

Fares 75p (children 40p)

For further information and Conditions of Carriage
please see over

Handbill for a cruise by *Balmoral* on
Sunday 16 May 1971, from Menai Bridge
through the Straits towards Port Lynas.
On the previous day, *Balmoral* was on
charter to the Coastal Cruising Association
for a short cruise from Menai Bridge.
Interestingly, dogs were carried at half the
adult fare.

Balmoral at Menai Bridge Pier during her White Funnel days. (*J&C McCutcheon Collection*)

A view of the deck of the *Balmoral*. She became a popular addition to the North Wales fleet. *Balmoral* was built for service between Southampton and Cowes and entered service in 1949. *Balmoral* is widely regarded as 'The UK's Widest Travelled Pleasure Steamer' and despite several changes in livery and owner, *Balmoral* has become a great survivor. Her greatest asset is her versatility and reliability as she is able to visit most harbours in the UK.

Balmoral at Liverpool during the 1970s. *Balmoral* became part of the White Funnel Fleet in 1969 and saw service in North Wales as well as the Bristol Channel. At this time, the old car deck at the stern was used as a sun deck along with deckchairs. It was a popular place for North Wales regulars.

Balmoral carried on the P&A Campbell tradition in North Wales and the Bristol Channel as the fleet and timetables contracted. (*J&C McCutcheon Collection*)

Balmoral departing from Llandudno pier during the final months of the White Funnel Fleet in the 1970s. (*J&C McCutcheon Collection*)

Menai Pier with *Balmoral* alongside it. Although *Balmoral* now only makes very rare visits to North Wales, she has one of the longest links of any pleasure steamer with North Wales. (*J&C McCutcheon Collection*)

Balmoral at Liverpool. The 1970s saw the end of regular pleasure steamer cruises along the North Wales coast from Liverpool. This was similar to the decline in other areas of the UK. By the late 1970s, things were to change as *Waverley* began to visit. These visits were, though, irregular and would never echo the regular service of the past. (*J&C McCutcheon Collection*)

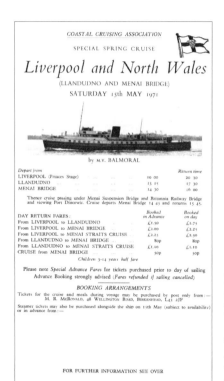

Handbill advertising the Coastal Cruising Association charter cruise of the *Balmoral* from Liverpool, Llandudno and Menai Bridge on Saturday 15 May 1971. This was the first time since 1962 that such a cruise took place. The cruise also went onwards from Menai Bridge. This gave passengers from Liverpool the first opportunity since 1947 to sail through the waters of the Menai Straits, past Menai Bridge.

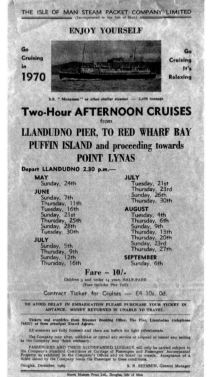

Handbill advertising afternoon cruises from Llandudno to Red Wharf Bay and Puffin Island during the 1970 season. By this time, the Isle of Man Steam Packet Company was becoming the main operators of services. One of the regular steamers from Llandudno was the well-loved *Manxman*, which was finally broken up in 2011.

A wonderful scene as *Waverley* arrives at Llandudno Pier on 1 May 1977. This was the 'Year of the Pier' and the sight of a traditional paddle steamer going alongside a traditional pier was a perfect image for that year! This image also must have shown many that operating *Waverley* away from the Firth of Clyde was a sensible and realistic idea – just look at those crowds ready to join the steamer! The idea to charter *Waverley* to celebrate the centenary of Llandudno Pier was a brilliant one. Twelve passengers joined the crew for the journey south from the Clyde. On Thursday 28 April, *Waverley* undertook a cruise between Campbeltown and Ayr before departing at midnight down Campbeltown Loch and passing Davaar. *Waverley* arrived at the Princes Landing Stage at Liverpool at 4.30 p.m. on 29 April 1977. The following day, *Waverley* departed from the Princes Landing Stage for a cruise along the North Wales coast. The finale of this cruise was her participation in the Llandudno Pier centenary celebrations. Over 3,500 people welcomed *Waverley* at Llandudno, with many of these dressed in fine and elaborate Victorian costumes. During the following week, a full range of cruises were operated on the Mersey. An estimated 8,000 people welcomed *Waverley* at the Lancashire fishing port of Fleetwood after she had cruised from Liverpool past Southport and Blackpool. Over 700 happy people joined *Waverley* for the cruise from Fleetwood to cruise in Morecambe Bay. The following day saw *Waverley* depart on the ten-and-a-half-hour trip back to Ayr.

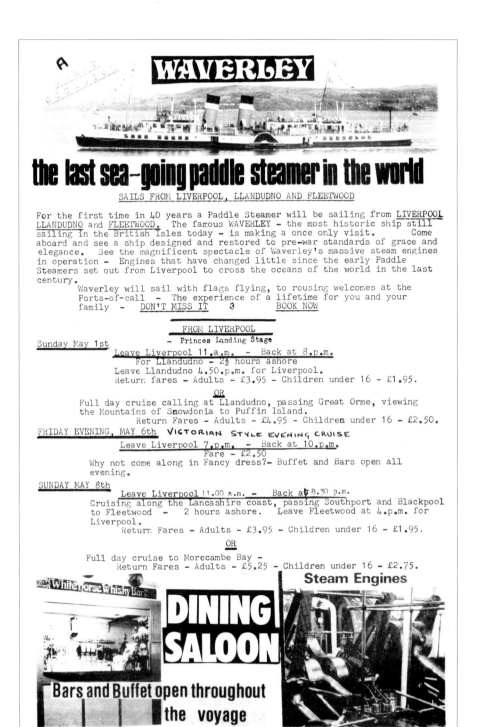

WAVERLEY

the last sea-going paddle steamer in the world

SAILS FROM LIVERPOOL, LLANDUDNO AND FLEETWOOD

For the first time in 40 years a Paddle Steamer will be sailing from LIVERPOOL LLANDUDNO and FLEETWOOD. The famous WAVERLEY - the most historic ship still sailing in the British Isles today - is making a once only visit.   Come aboard and see a ship designed and restored to pre-war standards of grace and elegance. See the magnificent spectacle of Waverley's massive steam engines in operation - Engines that have changed little since the early Paddle Steamers set out from Liverpool to cross the oceans of the world in the last century.

Waverley will sail with flags flying, to rousing welcomes at the Ports-of-call - The experience of a lifetime for you and your family - DON'T MISS IT   3   BOOK NOW

FROM LIVERPOOL
- Princes Landing Stage

Sunday May 1st
Leave Liverpool 11.a.m. - Back at 8.p.m.
For Llandudno - 2½ hours ashore
Leave Llandudno 4.50.p.m. for Liverpool.
Return fares - Adults - £3.95 - Children under 16 - £1.95.

OR

Full day cruise calling at Llandudno, passing Great Orme, viewing the Mountains of Snowdonia to Puffin Island.
Return Fares - Adults - £4.95 - Children under 16 - £2.50.

FRIDAY EVENING, MAY 6th VICTORIAN STYLE EVENING CRUISE
Leave Liverpool 7.p.m. - Back at 10.p.m.
Fare - £2.50
Why not come along in Fancy dress?- Buffet and Bars open all evening.

SUNDAY MAY 8th
Leave Liverpool 11.00 a.m. - Back at 8.30 p.m.
Cruising along the Lancashire coast, passing Southport and Blackpool to Fleetwood - 2 hours ashore. Leave Fleetwood at 4.p.m. for Liverpool.
Return Fares - Adults - £3.95 - Children under 16 - £1.95.

OR

Full day cruise to Morecambe Bay -
Return Fares - Adults - £5.25 - Children under 16 - £2.75.

White horse Whisky Bar

DINING SALOON

Bars and Buffet open throughout the voyage

Steam Engines

Handbill advertising cruises by *Waverley* on her first visit to Liverpool and Llandudno in May 1977. *Waverley* offered a fine programme of cruises that offered the perfect mix of a sea cruise with a short time ashore. Passengers were even encouraged to join the steamer in Victorian dress to make the cruise even more special. School cruises were also heavily promoted to ensure that the steamer was full each day.

POSTED ON BOARD THE
PADDLE STEAMER
"WAVERLEY"

Llandudno
YEAR
OF THE
PIER

1877 - 1977

N. E. BLADON
24 BRYN LUPUS DRIVE,
LLANRHOS,
LLANDUDNO,

Llandudno and its pier is a catalyst in the story of the paddle steamer *Waverley*. The rather limited season and revenue-earning potential of the Firth of Clyde meant that by the late 1970s a radical re-think of *Waverley*'s cruising programme was required. After an approach for *Waverley* to attend celebrations at Llandudno in the 'Year of the Pier', *Waverley*'s operators decided to boldly take up the offer. The rest as they say is history! This first day cover commemorates *Waverley*'s visit and was posted aboard the steamer.

Waverley departing the Lancashire port of Fleetwood on 8 May 1977 with Knott End in the distance. *Waverley*'s need to be at Llandudno enabled her to carry out a limited programme of cruises in adjacent areas. Fleetwood, with its former Furness Railway connection, provided an ideal base from which the first paddle steamer cruises for several generations were carried out. It seemed as though the whole town turned out to see *Waverley* arrive and depart.

A pipe band joins *Waverley* to entertain her passengers during her first historic cruise on 30 April 1977. *Waverley* was open to the public that day and a huge numbers of Liverpool people went aboard to view this unusual visitor. On that evening, a reception was held on the steamer at which the Lord Mayor of Liverpool welcomed *Waverley*. (*J&C McCutcheon Collection*)

Passengers pose
aboard *Waverley*
on her first visit to
Liverpool in May
1977. Huge crowds
gathered to see and
enjoy *Waverley*
wherever she went.
(*J&C McCutcheon
Collection*)

A Liver Bird looks down on *Waverley* framed against the 'Three Graces' at Liverpool. The Liver
Building, Port of Liverpool Building and Cunard Building are shown with *Waverley* on 6 May
1977. A paddle steamer had finally returned to the River Mersey.

Waverley arriving in the River Mersey for the first time on 29 April 1977. The venture to Liverpool, North Wales and Lancashire was a massive success from a marketing point of view, although financially it was mixed. It opened eyes to the fact that there was a huge market eager to see and use *Waverley* away from the Firth of Clyde. The cynics were silenced and seeds had been planted that would see *Waverley* visit here, as well as the rest of the UK, in the years ahead.

Waverley on a cruise from Liverpool to Fleetwood in May 1977. The cruise that day left Liverpool and passengers passed Southport and Blackpool before arriving at Fleetwood for two hours ashore. The fare cost £3.95 for the nine-and-a-half-hour excursion. Passengers not wanting to go ashore at Fleetwood could continue their cruise in Morecambe Bay.

Waverley steaming in the River Mersey on 19 April 1980. *Waverley* has recreated some of the most famous and well-loved cruises of North Wales. As always, keeping this tradition alive is a struggle when confronted by deteriorating piers, increasing car usage, rising fuel and other costs.

Waverley entering the docks at Liverpool on 19 April 1980. *Waverley* made frequent visits to Liverpool and North Wales during her first visits south from the Firth of Clyde. It must have seemed unreal when a paddle steamer once again plied the North Wales coast after such a long time.

Balmoral arriving at Menai Bridge in 1986. *Balmoral* was familiar to North Wales enthusiasts as she had undertaken many cruises in the area when owned by P&A Campbell. She has returned every year since 1986 as part of her yearly schedule as 'Britain's widest travelled Pleasure Steamer'.

Balmoral has just passed under the Menai Suspension Bridge. *Balmoral* spends a great deal of her season each year on the Bristol Channel as well as visiting other areas such as the River Thames and South Coast.

The narrowness of the Menai Straits can be appreciated in this photograph taken from *Balmoral*. The only real opportunity of viewing this special scenery is aboard the *Balmoral* when she visits each year.

Balmoral is shown alongside Llandudno Pier ready to embark more passengers from the famous Welsh resort. Unfortunately, the landing facilities at Llandudno have made calls at this important calling place infrequent in recent years. This shows the heavy reliance on well-maintained piers for pleasure steamers.

Passengers enjoying *Balmoral* in bright sunshine along the North Wales coast. *Balmoral* has now spent a significant part of her career cruising around the UK's coastline. Her preservation career started in 1986, when she was purchased and refitted as consort to the famous *Waverley*.

The strong and functional design of the Tubular Bridge can be appreciated in this view on one of *Balmoral*'s cruises. *Balmoral* usually undertakes her Menai Straits cruises from Llandudno or Menai Straits Pier.

Passengers enjoying one of *Balmoral*'s cruises in North Wales. In the early 1990s, *Balmoral* was able to recreate cruises from popular seaside resorts such as Blackpool to Morecambe. Unfortunately, storms later in the decade heavily damaged Blackpool North Pier's landing arm and these popular cruises had to be abandoned when the facilities were demolished.

Balmoral is now the last regular provider of pleasure cruises in North Wales. She has provided cruises in the area for over more than forty years in both her career for P&A Campbell and as a consort for the *Waverley*. Her visits may have become more infrequent as piers have become unusable, but she alone carries on the great tradition of North Wales coastal cruising and allows passengers to remember with great fondness the heyday of the *St Trillo*, *St Seiriol* and *St Tudno*.